The Blockchain and the New Architecture of Trust

Information Policy Series

Edited by Sandra Braman

The Information Policy Series publishes research on and analysis of significant problems in the field of information policy, including decisions and practices that enable or constrain information, communication, and culture irrespective of the legal siloes in which they have traditionally been located, as well as state-law-society interactions. Defining information policy as all laws, regulations, and decision-making principles that affect any form of information creation, processing, flows, and use, the series includes attention to the formal decisions, decision-making processes, and entities of government; the formal and informal decisions, decision-making processes, and entities of private- and public-sector agents capable of constitutive effects on the nature of society; and the cultural habits and predispositions of governmentality that support and sustain government and governance. The parametric functions of information policy at the boundaries of social, informational, and technological systems are of global importance because they provide the context for all communications, interactions, and social processes.

The Blockchain and the New Architecture of Trust

Kevin Werbach

The MIT Press
Cambridge, Massachusetts
London, England

This book was set in Stone Serif by Westchester Publishing Services. Printed and bound in the United States of America.

Library of Congress Cataloging-in-Publication Data

Names: Werbach, Kevin, author.
Title: The blockchain and the new architecture of trust / Kevin Werbach.
Description: Cambridge, MA : MIT Press, [2018] | Series: Information policy
    series | Includes bibliographical references and index.
Identifiers: LCCN 2018011211 | ISBN 9780262038935 (hardcover : alk. paper)
Subjects: LCSH: Electronic funds transfers. | Blockchains (Databases) |
    Bitcoin. | Trust. | Finance--Technological innovations.
Classification: LCC HG1710 .W47 2018 | DDC 332.1/78--dc23
    LC record available at https://lccn.loc.gov/2018011211

10 9 8 7 6 5 4 3

Contents

Series Editor's Introduction

Sandra Braman

Some believe that the blockchain, the technology that underlies crypto-currencies such as Bitcoin and can do so much more, makes it possible for people to create their own custom legal systems. Others go even further, arguing it will replace the nation-state altogether. But as Kevin Werbach, in *The Blockchain and the New Architecture of Trust*, points out, we have heard this before, with the Internet, and as before, he argues, not only will governments find a way to regulate blockchains—and *with* blockchains—but doing so is what will allow us to make the best uses of this clearly disruptive and, indeed, transformative innovation.

We are already seeing the potential. Walmart has found that using a blockchain for supply chain information allows it to identify items associated with food-borne disease that need to be removed from shelves in seconds rather than weeks. Where political and economic turbulence have left property records uncertain, the blockchain can keep land titles straight. The UN World Food Programme's efforts to use the blockchain in its efforts to support refugees have been successful. The Delaware Blockchain Initiative is using it to record stock ownership in a manner that increases the efficiency and transparency of the stock market. A myriad other uses of the blockchain have been conceived, are under experimentation, or are already in use.

The blockchain looks purely technical but, again like the Internet, it is sociotechnical in nature. Humans are essential to its performance: proof of work systems that support major platforms depend on miners, decisions about investing in blockchain hardware and software are made by humans, people are critical to blockchain operations in a variety of contractor and curator roles, and it is on the basis of human subjectivity that blockchains rise and fall. For cryptocurrencies, it is where the blockchain interfaces with the world of "fiat," or government-backed currencies, that legal interventions can be particularly valuable for many of the same reasons that, as Josephine Wolff points out in *You'll See This Message When It Is Too Late*, those are especially effective points for defending against and mitigating the costs of cybersecurity attacks. Of the many possible relationships between the law and the blockchain as modes of governance, Werbach argues that the most successful and effective will also be sociotechnical, combining "dry code" and human "wet code."

Acknowledging the structurational (and thus constitutive) effects of network architecture and technology—particularly software—design is now a commonplace, but just *how* the blockchain and law govern differs in several ways. The law works because we trust the individuals and entities through which its processes unfold; the blockchain does so because the system in its entirety is trusted although there are neither individuals to whom nor institutions to which we can point as responsible. The legal ideal is that each element of every process has integrity, while with the blockchain the output of the system as a whole can be trusted even if some of its components cannot. Legal systems attempt to constrain self-interest on behalf of society as a whole; the blockchain takes advantage of self-interest because it improves the security of the network for all. Traditional contracts assume the arrangements established take place within the context of ongoing relationships; for smart contracts, each transaction is treated in isolation. The law can manage possibilities not foreseen when regulations or contracts were written by allowing for additional steps to be taken before a commitment is executed or turning to courts, if necessary, after the fact; blockchains can do none of these things although it is known, by now, that their execution can lead to outcomes that none of the participants in a system foresaw or may find acceptable. The law is, *de facto* and in many ways by intent, slow-moving as it takes all of these matters into account and adds friction of various types that help prevent abuses of the system; the blockchain is remarkable and desirable for its efficiencies even though as blockchain systems scale and persevere over time efficiency issues will remain of premiere concern.

Werbach's approach to governance and the blockchain builds upon Nobel Prize–winner Elinor Ostrom's insights into the polycentric nature of governance, driven by complex motivational structures operating across multiple scales and involving a wide range of types of public, private, and community-based arrangements. He argues that there are times when it may be best to use the blockchain to govern and other circumstances in which the law should remain supreme, but for many purposes the optimal approach may be to use wet (human) code and dry (technological) code in combination. The blockchain can supplement legal approaches to ensuring compliance with obligations by offering new means of achieving legal objectives, as when its use to record stock ownership could be integrated into the established securities system without changing or displacing any existing legal relationships. Blockchains can be used as policy tools by geopolitically recognized governments—and by those who would oppose authoritarian tendencies of such governments via, for example, its censorship resistance. The technology can be used to make legal compliance workable in situations in which existing mechanisms cannot handle the volume of activity, knowledge of what is being regulated is inadequate, or technological or social innovations have so changed the alignment of incentives that the legal system falls behind; a shared registry for orphan works would be such an instance. And the blockchain can be used as a substitute for legal systems when such is needed, in conflict zones or parts of the developing world.

The book's recommendations for how the two forms of governance might work together go in both directions—making the law more code-like, and code more law-like. Law can become more code-like through uses of regulatory sandboxes, like safe harbors but more limited in time or scale; by pushing the use of boilerplate in the contracts of private law to its modular extremes; and by treating institutions involved as information fiduciaries. Code can become more law-like by literally linking smart and legal contracts via incorporating the code of each within the other; experimentation with this is already underway. Traditional legal enforcement mechanisms can be incorporated into smart contracts, and law-like governance processes can be built into blockchain platforms for "on-chain governance." Rule of law itself might come to be treated as a service.

Thinking about the blockchain stimulates us to reconsider long-standing concepts. It adds dimensions to how we understand the social construction of reality by introducing the possibility of genuinely shared truths via the ledger. Our understanding of the commons must now take into account key distinctions among shared data, shared control, and a shared system state. Seminal insights into the macro- and microeconomics of information such as Frank Knight's 1921 distinction between risk and uncertainty and Cristiano Antonelli's 1992 understanding of the ways in which coordination and collaboration are as important as competition in the network economy—facilitating the development of new types of organizational forms—are taken several steps further.

There are dangers. Governments can use blockchain technologies for authoritarian purposes. As Werbach puts it, public blockchain networks are often described as censorship resistant, but one person's censorship may be another person's rule of law. An entity, whether nongovernmental or governmental, that achieves 51 percent of available processing power could become a tyrant. (Russia has already announced that the blockchain will "belong" to Russia as the Internet "belonged" to the U.S., sending a team lead by an individual who previously worked for the FSB, the Russian intelligence agency that is the successor to the KGB, to the International Standards Organization committee working to establish technical standards to be adhered to globally by those using blockchains.) A new class system based on blockchain identity—whether one is verified for blockchain purposes, or not—might emerge, with consequences for those who are not verified that may look like those that have historically arisen from identity differences based on such factors as race, or ethnicity, or socioeconomic class. Those who fear that digital entities that are smart, learning, and—as some types of software have now been for a while—autonomously evolving, may decide to shape a world that preferentially serves computers rather than humans, and may be putting the following pieces together: Blockchain contracts are self-executing. So far limits to possible uses of the blockchain are not evident. And what the blockchain depends upon, where its values and functions come from, is in essence computing for computing's sake.

Approaching the blockchain from the perspective of governance takes us back to the most basic of questions: Where does government come from? We can thus read this book on two levels. *The Blockchain and the New Architecture of Trust* is essential reading about the opportunities and dangers raised by the blockchain technology and about the range of possible relationships between the blockchain and the law. As Kevin Werbach thinks his way through these questions, though, he is also addressing another. Historians of the law describe the current era as one in which law-state-society relations are undergoing transformations as fundamental as those that took place hundreds of years ago when the secular international system of states was first formed. Werbach explains to us just how that is happening as he examines the new approach the blockchain brings to building an architecture of the trust that is necessary for effective governance of any kind. And he tells us how we can engage with the process in ways that allow us to protect the human rights and civil liberties values we have fought so hard to protect, as well as the efficiencies and confidence through which the economy and all of our other human activities flourish.

Acknowledgments

I blame Owen Davis. Four or five years ago, my serial-entrepreneur friend demanded to know why I wasn't focusing more attention on Bitcoin. I was taken aback. Sure, I'd read about the cryptocurrency phenom du jour, but it didn't excite me. I wrote a report on digital cash way back in 1999. Owen insisted this was something bigger. I took a closer look ... and fell down the blockchain rabbit hole.

More people than I could list contributed to my understanding in the years that followed, intentionally or otherwise. As a legal scholar, I have the great fortune to work in an environment at the Wharton School that allows and encourages exploration of new research areas. Still, if Sandra Braman had not reached out to me, a draft law review article would have never been the foundation for this larger and broader work. I am glad she did. Thanks also to Gita Devi Manaktala and the staff at MIT Press for shepherding the process. Natalie Houston helped me stay focused on the task, and I am grateful to Adel Boyarsky and Lena Sutanovac for excellent research assistance. Portions of this book were developed for articles subsequently published in the *Duke Law Journal* (with my co-author Nico Cornell) and the *Berkeley Technology Law Journal*.

I am indebted to Ifeoma Ajunwa, Brian Berkey, Vince Buccola, Robin Chase, Julie Cohen, David Crosbie, Deven Desai, Dan Hunter, Julian Jonker, Joey Krug, Sarah Light, Richard Shell, Tim Swanson, Christian Terwiesch, Karl Ulrich, Adam Werbach, David Zaring, and anonymous reviewers for feedback on sections of the manuscript. As I developed the book, Jeremy Allaire, Amber Baldet, Brian Behlendorf, Arthur Breitman, Kathleen Breitman, Matt Corva, Chris Dixon, Brian Forde, Simon Johnson, Aaron Krellenstein, Caitlin Long, Luka Müller-Studer, Patrick Murck, Abe Othman, Neepa

Patel, Bruce Pon, Houman Shadab, Elizabeth Stark, Joel Telpner, Stefan Thomas, Andrea Tinianow, Steve Waldron, Albert Wenger, Aaron Wright, and Kaliya Young graciously participated in interviews or other conversations that helped enhance my understanding of the unfolding blockchain phenomenon.

I cannot possibly express sufficient appreciation to my wife, Johanna, and my children, Eli and Esther, for what they mean to my life.

And Satoshi, if you're out there, thanks.

Introduction: The Parable of the Tree

Buttonwood to Blockchain

On May 17, 1792, twenty-four men stood beneath a buttonwood tree and affixed their names to a document that transformed the world.[1] They were all acquaintances who lived within a few blocks of one another in Manhattan; later they would choose to do business in a local coffeehouse. These traders assembled each day on Wall Street to buy and sell government bonds and corporate stocks. Their agreement's modest goal was to squeeze out the local auctioneers who commonly rigged prices. How little they knew.

Fast-forward two-and-a-half centuries in time, but just three blocks away in space. The Depository Trust & Clearing Corporation (DTCC), a company descended from the Buttonwood Agreement, today processes $1.5 quadrillion of transactions annually.[2] That is $3 billion per minute, or the annual output of the entire world economy every month.[3] The financial flows that it and its sister entities track are the lifeblood of our civilization.

The story of how we got from the eighteenth-century foundations of the New York Stock Exchange (NYSE) to the contemporary global financial system can be told in many ways. I use it here to illustrate an even larger story. What brought together those early stockbrokers was the same force that led the DTCC to own virtually every share of stock traded in the United States. (If you find that last bit unbelievable, read on.) It is a critical factor often underappreciated in the fate of nations, and of human relationships. It is both the objective of the legal system and what takes over where the law ends. It is trust.

Trust is the buttonwood tree of society: Its roots run deep and its branches extend everywhere. It is invisible and difficult to pin down. Yet the dynamics of trust—its architectures—influence virtually every aspect of the world that we see around us. The differences between the traders under the

Figure 0.1
Traders signing the Buttonwood Agreement.

buttonwood tree and modern Wall Street are not just matters of size and speed; they are rooted in mechanisms of trust.

When a new form of trust comes along, it is a bit like a new theory of physics. The revolution never completely displaces what came before. Albert Einstein's theory of relativity changed everything. Yet students a hundred years later still learn Isaac Newton's mechanics from the seventeenth century, which more comfortably capture our day-to-day world. And classical relativity itself now survives in unsettling tension with quantum mechanics. Both theories seem correct, despite their inconsistency. The task for experts is to reconcile the models with each other and with our experience of reality. The same goes for models of trust.

On January 3, 2009, a new trust architecture entered the world with the launch of Bitcoin.[4] Its manifesto was posted under a pseudonym on the modern equivalent of the cathedral door where Martin Luther nailed his theses: an Internet discussion list. Its author consciously stood on the shoulders of giants and quickly disappeared. Yet a seed was planted. In the years since, others took the ideas far beyond the original paper. Fortunes have been made; billions have been invested; thousands of companies have been founded; new industries have emerged; and the world's most influential corporations and governments have taken notice. There have also been thefts, controversies, scams, fractures, lifetime prison sentences, and speculative bubbles. And this is just the beginning.

The great innovation is most commonly called the "blockchain." Even seasoned technology experts often find it difficult to grasp.[5] It can be implemented in a variety of ways, in a diverse array of contexts. At the core, though, it represents a simple idea: Trust a system without necessarily trusting any of its components. More specifically, a blockchain network allows participants to trust the information recorded on a shared ledger without trusting anyone to validate it. And no one—not an owner, not an exchange, not even the government—has unbridled power to stop or alter transactions on the network.

To some, the blockchain represents freedom from corporate power, government power, and the legal system that reinforces both. To others, it is a way to empower criminals and a new group of shady insiders. Alternatively, perhaps it is just the way that all organizations eventually will do what they do more efficiently. It is money, or all about money, yet it is not about money at all. It is a creature of pure mathematics, or of economics, or of psychology, or of governance. It is the subject of boundless enthusiasm, much of it wildly uninformed. The communities and systems around it are developing at a breakneck pace. It could change the world ... but crucially, how and when remain uncertain.

One aspect is already clear: The blockchain does not eliminate the need for trust. It represents, rather, the reemergence of trust in a new form. Those early stockbrokers under the buttonwood tree came together based on their personal relationships and granted power to an intermediary, the exchange. Blockchain network participants trust despite the absence of any central authority or interpersonal connections. This new approach has a plethora of valuable real-world applications, but also faces significant challenges. Its potential, and its limitations, track the contours of the trust it enables.

Many are skeptical. Legendary investor Warren Buffett called Bitcoin a "mirage."[6] Nobel Prize–winning economist and commentator Paul Krugman described it as "evil."[7] And JPMorgan Chase CEO Jamie Dimon, one of the world's most respected bankers, labeled Bitcoin "a fraud," later declaring that "it is creating something out of nothing that to me is worth nothing."[8] Yet even as Dimon made these statements, his firm was investing in blockchain-based technology and hosting conferences on the "cryptocurrencies " it enabled.

Dimon may well be right that things will "end badly" for the growing numbers of speculative cryptocurrency investors. This book will not offer advice on whether bitcoin or other cryptocurrency tokens are worth buying, any more than a work on modern portfolio theory would tell you which stocks to pick. Short-run volatility today makes cryptocurrency investing a trader's game rather than a reflection of long-term value. And the investment potential of cryptocurrencies is just the tip of the iceberg. Over the long run, the important questions are whether the approach to trust that the Bitcoin network introduced is fundamentally sound, and if so, what factors might lead to the success or failure of systems employing it.

Cryptocurrencies present one thing on the surface (money from nothing) and something considerably deeper underneath (a new pattern for generating trust). That helps to explain why they are today both overhyped and underappreciated. In the words of venture capitalist Naval Ravikant, "Bitcoin is a tool for freeing humanity from oligarchs and tyrants, dressed up as a get-rich-quick scheme."[9]

What makes an innovation transformative is only partly the technology itself. The most sophisticated advances may not address real-world problems. And the winning solutions need the right combination of development talent, entrepreneurial vision, financial wherewithal, and a healthy dose of luck. The process by which innovations take hold, known as "diffusion," depends on factors such as communication patterns among market participants and compatibility with current consumption patterns, as the innovation migrates from early adopters to successively more risk-averse user categories.[10] The same factors will shape adoption of the blockchain. Its success is as much a function of the environment as of its technical virtuosity.

The soil in which the blockchain took hold was the crumbling of trust in governments and corporations amid the financial crisis of 2008. Although the global economy largely recovered from that shock, the erosion of trust endured. In the U.S. and many other countries, indicia of both interpersonal and institutional trust have been dropping for decades. Measures of the credibility of the government and media have never been lower. Our news and information ecosystems are fragmented and unreliable. Concerns about privacy, security, and surveillance dominate both popular and academic discourse about technology. The great information platforms that arose with the Internet are increasingly seen not as disruptors of entrenched incumbents, but as new monopolies exercising arbitrary power through their control over data.

The blockchain offers a new approach to some of these challenges that, paradoxically, seems to establish collective trust on a foundation of mutual distrust. It is built on open-source software and decentralized foundations that allow anyone to participate. And the trust it offers has unusually broad applicability. Initially championed by radical technolibertarians, block-chain-related technologies now count major corporations, entrepreneurs in many sectors, and even governments as their advocates.

Enthusiasm for the blockchain has been remarkable for such a novel technology. Venture capitalists poured over $1 billion into blockchain-based start-ups between 2013 and 2016.[11] The value of cryptocurrencies collectively spiked to hundreds of billions of dollars in 2017. Technology giants such as IBM, Microsoft, and Intel are making major blockchain commitments. Individuals around the world who never invested in anything more exotic than a mutual fund are rushing to buy cryptocurrencies, or application tokens issued by early-stage start-ups. Even well-established observers such as Goldman Sachs see tens of billions of dollars in annual benefits just from "low-hanging fruit" opportunities.[12] By July 2017, according to a survey from U.K.-based Juniper Research, a majority of major companies (i.e., those with more than twenty thousand employees) surveyed were either considering or deploying distributed ledger technology.[13]

The potential is great. The blockchain could help financial institutions to clear stock transactions, global supply chains to ensure food safety; localities to keep track of who owns what rights in real property, publishers to deliver online advertisements to users, utilities to track dispersed energy sensors and buy power from microgrid operators, immigrants to send money back to their relatives in the developing world, health-care providers to access medical records, and aid organizations to track distributions. These and many other examples will be discussed throughout this book. The diversity of potential blockchain applications is as breathtaking as their scale.

All this is true. Yet it is only half the story. Much of the investment activity around cryptocurrencies is pure speculation, and some involves fraud or price manipulation. Viewed from every angle, the level of blockchain adoption is still rather small. There are far more prototypes than production systems. Sustainable business models remain largely unproved. And just because a firm can use a distributed ledger approach does not mean it should. The advantages in practice are not always as great as promised, and the implementation challenges often have little to do with the technology itself.

As a result, use cases for blockchain-based systems are not certain, and most are likely to take longer than expected.[14] Bitcoin, the first and most significant blockchain implementation, might never see widespread adoption for retail payments, its original intended purpose. Almost a decade in, some fundamental technical questions are not yet resolved. Even the premise that the blockchain will promote decentralization rather than concentrations of power is debatable. Meanwhile, governments will be neither ignorant nor impotent in the face of significant consumer harm or illicit activity. The two critiques that have dogged the field since its inception remain insufficiently refuted: that the blockchain is a better tool for criminals than for legitimate users, and that committing resources while trusting no one is a dangerous proposition.

These problems are not surprising. As the economic historian Carlota Perez has documented in her book *Technological Revolutions and Financial Capital*, speculative bubbles are a common feature of what in hindsight were major technology-fed business revolutions.[15] Excessive enthusiasm attracts fraud and get-rich-quick schemes as much as serious investment. Moreover, as fast as technology moves, people and systems take time to change. Robust infrastructure and standards do not appear overnight. The Internet, the technological wave to which the blockchain is often compared, spent two decades as a research network; and even once commercial adoption began to take off, maturation took a further decade or more. And most critically, if solutions built on blockchains and related distributed ledgers are to be both trusted and trustworthy, they must confront the hard problems of governance.

Even if the math works perfectly, blockchains are systems designed, implemented, and used by humans. Subjective intent remains relevant even when expressed through objective code. The businesses and services built around blockchains are vulnerable to selfish behavior, attacks, and manipulation, even if the networks themselves are secure. Incentives for different participating communities cannot always be aligned. And when something goes wrong—which it will—those who lose out will not be content to accept their fate meekly.

If trust means nothing more than confidence in outcomes, one can have it without needing to deal with human complexities. But that is not what trust is. Philosophers, psychologists, sociologists, and management scholars who have studied trust may not agree on a single definition, but they generally conclude that trust implies some degree of uncertainty or vulnerability. That is why former President Ronald Reagan's favorite Russian proverb, "Trust, but verify," is often criticized as meaningless. In the words of

Washington Post columnist Barton Swaim, "If you trust, you will not insist on verifying, whereas if you insist on verifying, clearly you do not trust."[16] The blockchain is an ingenious solution for verification, but that alone is insufficient. What it takes to promote robust trust through blockchain-based systems is the subject of this book.

Logically Centralized, Organizationally Decentralized

The basic function of blockchains is to reliably share information among parties who may not trust one another. In other words, everyone can have his or her own copy of a ledger and trust that all those copies remain the same, even without a central administrator or master version. The technical term for this process is "consensus." Venture capitalist Albert Wenger of Union Square Ventures calls blockchains logically centralized (there is only one ledger), but organizationally decentralized (many unrelated entities can maintain copies of that ledger).[17]

In a blockchain system, the very act of committing the transactions to the ledger in one location does so everywhere. Think of the dual-pen tool called a "polygraph" (no connection to the lie detector) that Thomas Jefferson used to make copies of his correspondence, as shown in figure 0.2. With a polygraph, the copy is created in parallel with the original. There is no need for a third party to transcribe the author's words. The blockchain and related approaches extend that model to many copies distributed physically and operationally.

Nodes in a blockchain network are in constant communication in order to remain synchronized. Maintaining that consensus without trusting a master copy is the hard part. If successful, this approach addresses significant limitations of centralized ledgers. If one node keeps a master record, it becomes a single point of failure for the system. Users cannot be certain that the information they see is accurate because it is outside their control. The central control point or intermediary can become extremely powerful—and can misuse that power. If, on the other hand, each organization keeps its own ledger (as with most corporate financial records), every transaction is recorded independently at least twice. Whenever, for example, a company pays a vendor or a bank cashes a check from another bank's customer, their ledgers must be synchronized after the fact. This introduces complexity, delay, and possibilities for error.

Figure 0.2
Thomas Jefferson's polygraph.

From a seemingly mundane change in tracking methods, a wealth of opportunities arise. Money, for example, depends on people trusting that their coins are valid, counterfeiting is limited, and bank balances are accurate. According to the economic anthropologist David Graeber, "the value of a unit of currency is not the measure of the value of an object, but the measure of one's trust in other human beings." In the modern world, that trust means having faith in financial services firms, central banks, law enforcement, and computerized processes, which becomes increasingly difficult with more parties and transactions that cross borders. The first blockchain application sought to replace all that with a form of private, distributed money: bitcoin.

The most extraordinary fact about the Bitcoin system is that, a decade after its launch, with the exception of a few early bugs that were fixed before there was much at stake, it has remained intact. The Bitcoin ledger is a transparent bank vault that contains currency worth many billions of dollars. Despite the novelty of the technology, the unruliness of its community, and the massive temptation for criminals to attack a system that literally prints money, the integrity of the Bitcoin consensus network has never been breached.

This does not mean that no one has been cheated.[18] Thieves have made off with several billion dollars' worth of bitcoin and other cryptocurrencies by exploiting weak points after the tokens are in users' or service providers' hands. The very success of cryptocurrencies creates new problems that call for new solutions.

A digital coin is a bearer instrument, meaning that, like ordinary cash, it is valuable in itself. The same approach can be applied to any valuable right, such as ownership in scarce goods, storage or computing power on a network, or access to use an application. And even without exchange of value through such digital tokens, having one shared ledger can add value to a universe of multi-organizational record-keeping activities.

The potential impacts are stunning. The distributed model of the block-chain could, in time, power a new economy of decentralized applications and services. Some of these might compete with existing platforms such as social networks and e-commerce marketplaces; others involve novel solutions such as prediction markets.

"Money is useful for organizing institutions and people in the real world," says venture capitalist Chris Dixon of the influential firm Andrees-sen Horowitz. "Now we have a native source of money on the Internet. We're just now discovering all the ways it could be useful."[19]

The overall trajectory of any great technological innovation can be observed only in hindsight. Market vicissitudes that seem decisive at the time may turn out to be insignificant or misleading. Over the long run, though, technologies succeed when they solve real problems and create real value. Sooner or later, they find fertile conditions. The blockchain's ultimate impacts on business and society will depend on its effectiveness as a new architecture of trust.

Law and Quantum Thought

There is another factor that is often missing from business accounts of tech-nological innovation: law. Law's relationship to the blockchain is widely misunderstood by both its advocates and its critics. The blockchain is not a technology of radical lawlessness, any more than of radical trustlessness. Nor does it represent a full-blown alternative that will decisively shrink law's application in the world. Whether and how blockchain-based systems will be regulated are important challenges to resolve, but even more important is the question of how blockchains regulate. These systems operate as mechanisms of law and governance, which will interact with established ones. There will be no universal answer. And in most cases, blockchain technology is likely to supplement or complement conventional legal regimes, not replace them.

"Quantum thought" is Nick Szabo's term for simultaneously considering two mutually contradictory ideas, analogous to the odd finding in quantum mechanics that light exists simultaneously as a particle and a wave.[20] Szabo is a computer scientist who conceptualized smart contracts, an important element of blockchain-related systems. He argues that this mental approach is important when operating at the edges of existing fields to create new concepts.[21] Blockchain technology draws upon cryptography, computer science, economics, and political theory, among other bodies of knowledge. Those who fixate on one dimension, whether as advocate or critic, tend to miss out on other factors of critical importance.

Lawyers are also very familiar with arguments in the alternative: "Your Honor, my client was miles away from the scene of the crime. But if he was there, he did not fire the gun. And if he did fire the gun, it was in self-defense." This much-mocked mode of reasoning is a valuable intellectual stance in the face of uncertainty. The judge or jury will resolve the outcome, but until that happens, the failure to fully evaluate any possibility is a mistake. Sometimes the unexpected happens. Sometimes it happens as a *consequence* of decisions based on other assumptions. Technologists inhabit the worlds of deterministic logic and computable probabilities, but lawyers are at home amid unpredictability, noncompliance, and even the possibility of catastrophe.

Law has much to contribute to the blockchain community. Concerns about money laundering, consumer protection, and financial stability do not disappear even when the cryptography works as promised. Taxation does not become unnecessary when there is a new mechanism for moving money secretly. Disputes do not go away because a computer can execute a transaction without human intervention. Bad actors will act badly. All these scenarios will give rise to calls for legal or regulatory action. Some will be justified. If the community flatly rejects every effort to ensure compliance with legal obligations, the blockchain will be an outlaw technology, active in the dark spaces online but largely irrelevant to the mainstream economy. That would be a tragic waste of potential.

At the same time, the blockchain offers important lessons for the legal community. Bitcoin demonstrates that a distributed network with no one in charge can govern itself well enough to avoid collapse and scale in value over an extended period. Trust, which previously required either the delegation of power or tight-knit relationships, can arise from a collection of independent actors running open-source software. The most important contribution that law can make here is not any particular set of rules, but the jurisprudential discipline of rule-making and rule enforcement, or what is often called "governance." The communities building blockchain technologies and systems can in many ways govern themselves, but only if they take this challenge seriously. Regulators can also improve their effectiveness by leveraging the technology. Alternatively, ill-considered regulatory actions could push blockchain activity to other countries, send it underground, and stop valuable innovation in its tracks.

In fast-changing environments, there is a danger both of regulating too early and of regulating too late. The best approach is to use quantum thinking to assess the risks of each. Law and the blockchain are bound to engage in a shifting dance. This begs the question of what values should shape their relationship. Technology implemented in the world is never neutral. Transformative innovations can have various impacts based on their technical architectures, as well as the legal regimes under which they operate. Decisions made early on have an outsized impact. Once architectures and legal environments are put in place, they often become increasingly difficult to change.

The Path Ahead

This book is divided into three parts. Part I explains where the blockchain came from, how it works, and what it makes possible. One dimension of the story is technical. The blockchain realized the long-sought dream of digital cash through Satoshi Nakamoto's clever design, and extensions such as permissioned ledgers and smart contracts took it even further. A second dimension is what it means to talk of the blockchain as a new architecture of trust. Trust is a deeply powerful phenomenon. Its subtleties are often missed despite a centuries-long history of intellectual discourse over the concept. The blockchain purports to create trust without trusting. The truth is more complicated (but no less interesting). A third dimension of the story concerns the business implications of the blockchain phenomenon. Despite an excess of hype and a speculative frenzy, there are significant, real value propositions for distributed ledger technology. Yet the scope of the blockchain opportunity reveals the gaps that the technology alone cannot overcome. There have already been several incidents where the promise of distributed trust broke down.

Part II locates the solution to these challenges in the very things that the blockchain was supposedly designed to circumvent: governance, law, and regulation. Here, too, what seem like novel issues reflecting the exotic nature of blockchain technology repeat historical patterns. When the Internet first became a mass medium in the 1990s, it raised strikingly similar questions about the relationship of law to decentralized online communities. Legal scholars offered strikingly similar responses to participants in today's blockchain debates. Then as now, the best answer is neither celebration of technology's primacy nor dismissal of its power. Distributed ledgers are, at their core, legal technologies: they are mechanisms to coordinate and enforce rules governing behavior. Their strengths and weaknesses should be evaluated in comparison to other mechanisms for achieving the same goals.

Part III looks forward. It identifies concrete steps to bridge the gaps between law and distributed ledgers, from both directions. Some are already under development; others will require collective action to address potential problems before they become endemic. The final chapter of the book considers how, if it succeeds as the foundation for a new trust architecture, the blockchain might reinvigorate the Internet itself. The Internet as it developed became part of the problem rather than the solution to the spreading trust crisis in society. Although it will not close the yawning trust gap by itself, the blockchain offers a new hope. Realizing that hope will require both technology innovators and governments to make good decisions. That can happen only with a solid understanding of how the blockchain relates to law, as well as to trust, which this book seeks to provide.

This story will take us around the world, from frantic efforts on three continents to respond to a catastrophic cybertheft, to Chinese farms supplying multinational retailers, to a brilliant but conflicted British engineer working at Google's Zurich office, and many places in between. Developments are so fast-moving that some examples will likely be outdated by the time you read this book. The start-ups prominent today may not be the long-term survivors. Yet there are also timeless themes in play. Viewing the blockchain story as a tale of trust, not just technology, helps to separate the enduring aspects from the ephemeral.

The blockchain can seem like an alien technology or an artifact from the future that inexplicably surfaced in the present. Situating it as an engine of law and trust helps anchor the phenomenon. How well systems based on blockchain-related technology realize its vast potential will depend on how well they address deep, familiar challenges.

Two weeks after the surrender of the last Confederate army marked the end of the Civil War, the buttonwood tree of Wall Street fell down during a storm. By then, it was a well-known landmark and a symbol of the rise of the U.S. as a global financial power. Much had changed in the four score minus seven years since those stockbrokers signed their agreement. A nation then not far removed from its founding was now emerging from its most harrowing conflict. Much more would change in the subsequent century and a half. The trust that was useful when the whole Wall Street community fit into a coffeehouse is quite different than what is needed today.

The buttonwood tree has been gone since 1865, but its echo survives in the code defining the newest architecture of trust. Blockchains are organized using a mathematical structure of branching nodes. It is called a "hash tree" or "Merkle tree," as shown in figure 0.3.

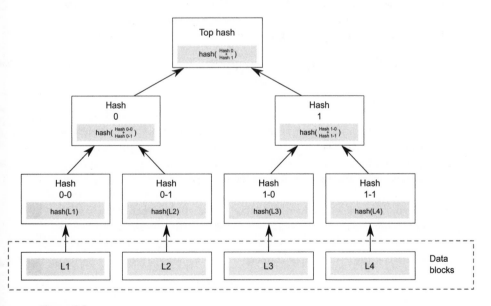

Figure 0.3
The Merkle tree structure of a blockchain.

Merkle trees allow efficient verification of the integrity of large data structures. The cryptographer Ralph Merkle filed a patent on the concept in 1979. The expiration of the patent in 2002 allowed developers to incorporate the concept freely into open-source software. Six years later, this was one of the preexisting technologies that Satoshi Nakamoto assembled to create Bitcoin. Where the original tree served to mark a convenient meeting spot, this one stitches together a reliable digital record from a cacophony of independent voices. Whether its significance matches that of its predecessor remains to be seen.

The story of the blockchain, law, and trust is still unfolding. It just might be one of the most important stories of our time.

A Comment on Terminology

Blockchain technology is a fast-developing area. Words are often used inconsistently.[22] I have tried to employ technically accurate terms, while keeping the account accessible to a nonspecialist audience.

A "blockchain" (sometimes rendered as "block chain") is a data storage system using linked sequential chunks of information. It is literally a chain of blocks designed to create an immutable ledger of transactions. What I call a "blockchain network" or "blockchain system" is the collection of computers running software that maintains a blockchain in a consistent state called "consensus." "Distributed ledger" is a more general term for blockchains and similar consensus-based systems. "The blockchain" is something of a misnomer. However, it is used in a generic sense, like "the Internet," to describe the universe of distributed ledger networks.

"Cryptocurrency" is a currency based on cryptography rather than central-bank control of the money supply. Some regulators prefer to call systems like Bitcoin "virtual currencies," arguing that a "digital currency" must be denominated in a traditional government-issued "fiat" currency.[23] Virtual currency, however, includes many pre-Bitcoin systems with only limited connection to money, such as frequent-flyer miles and reward points for video games. Cryptocurrencies have the essential features of fiat currency but operate without government involvement. Therefore, I prefer the approach of the Bank for International Settlements, which recognized "digital currency" as the prevailing term.[24] Finally, Bitcoin is capitalized when describing the network, but not when referring to the unit of currency, as with dollars or yuan.

1   A Revolution in Nine Pages

1   The Trust Challenge

Without Relying on Trust

"We have proposed a system for electronic transactions without relying on trust." Thus begins the concluding section of a nine-page document posted to the Cryptography online mailing list on Halloween 2008. Titled "Bitcoin: A Peer-to-Peer Electronic Cash System," the paper listed Satoshi Nakamoto (a pseudonym) as its author.[1] Despite significant effort, the identity of Bitcoin's creator has never been conclusively determined.[2] He was last heard from in 2011. Ironically for a prophet of decentralization, the surname "Nakamoto" in Japanese means "of central origin."

Whoever Satoshi was, one thing is clear: He, or she, or they, were dead wrong.[3] Trust is central to Bitcoin, as well as to the wave of blockchain and distributed ledger solutions following its approach—and not just because the words "trust" or "trusted" appear thirteen times in the short paper. Bitcoin would be useless if it were not trusted. The astonishing rise in the value of cryptocurrencies since Bitcoin is based entirely on people's willingness to trust that entries on privately operated, distributed digital ledgers are as real as money. The hundreds of nonfinancial, blockchain-based start-ups and enterprise blockchain projects rest on a similar belief. Distributed ledger networks bring together communities that otherwise would not trust each other sufficiently. They are, according to the title of a cover story in *The Economist*, "trust machines."[4] Bitcoin's blockchain mechanism just might have launched a revolution in trust—and not a moment too soon.

A Crisis of Trust

For fifteen years, the public relations firm Edelman has conducted global surveys of trust in government, business, and the media. Its yearly report, released at the World Economic Forum annual meeting in Davos, offers a detailed snapshot of societal trust patterns. The picture is not encouraging. Most of the trust indexes have been on a downward trend for some time. Recently, the erosion of trust has accelerated. The 2017 Edelman Trust Barometer report was entitled *An Implosion of Trust.*[5] Only 15 percent of the general population believes "the system" is working. The "profound crisis of trust" revealed in the survey is both deep and wide. It extends across all categories of institutions—including government, the media, corporations, and nongovernmental organizations (NGOs)—and is shared by both the informed public and the mass population.

Other recent surveys offer similar findings, especially in the United States.[6] Only one in five Americans in a Pew Research Center poll said they trusted the government in 2015, a year before a wrenching presidential election that brought that skepticism to new heights.[7] And Americans, it seems, do not trust each other much more. As early as 2013, only one-third of Americans said in an Associated Press poll that most people can be trusted, compared to half in 1972, when the General Social Survey first asked the question.[8] Nearly two-thirds—a record high—said that "you cannot be too careful" when dealing with people. No one who follows current events would be surprised at these statistics.

The contemporary trust crisis is the culmination of patterns that have been developing for many years. Two influential, best-selling books published around the turn of the millennium, Robert Putnam's *Bowling Alone* and Francis Fukuyama's *Trust*, warned of the fraying of societal trust. Using a blizzard of surveys and other research, Putnam highlighted the erosion of local trust networks in America, epitomized by the decline in bowling leagues relative to individual bowling.[9] He viewed this as a pernicious development that explained the growth of social pathologies. Five years earlier, Fukuyama similarly had sounded the alarm about a crisis of trust globally, and particularly in contemporary America.[10] Despite its reputation for rugged individualism, he pointed out, America actually benefited from high levels of interdependence. But that appears to be changing. The trust crisis that writers such as Fukuyama and Putnam warned of two decades ago is now a reality. The consequences may be dire.

We all make decisions based on trust every day. Should I get into the back seat of this car? Does the package of tuna that I want to purchase harbor a deadly virus? Do I go on a date with this person? Should I type my credit card number into this box on my computer screen? There are few human interactions, and fewer still business transactions, that do not depend in large part on the qualities of trust involved.[11] According to the sociologist Niklas Luhmann, trust makes human society itself possible.[12] Without trust, we would need to verify and secure the reliability of everyone we encountered. That would be an impossible task. Trust is the oil that lubricates social and business interactions and the factor that renders the boundless complexity of the modern world tractable.

Trust, however, is more than a gateway. It has consequences. Trust shapes interactions, potentially in very significant ways. Those who are trusted are powerful. Those who are not must work harder at every turn to gain the confidence of others, putting them at a great disadvantage. Systems that alter the scope of trust, therefore, change societies. Trust shapes both the macrostructures of national economic performance and the microstructures of individual and firm interactions. Around the world, high-trust societies outperform low-trust ones.[13] Business scholars similarly find empirically that companies where trust is high perform better.[14]

Trust functions as social capital. It creates reserves of goodwill that facilitate social interactions and business transactions. The wealth of society is thereby increased.[15]

Trust originated in the narrow confines of families and small local communities. In the modern world, though, it is simply impossible to limit interactions to those circles. High-trust societies have developed cultures, social norms, and legal systems that give their citizens the confidence to extend trust to strangers. In a high-trust environment, there is less need for intrusive regulations and coercive enforcement because people are willing to act without them. Most people are trustworthy most of the time. And when they are not, the combination of legal sanctions and social pressure can address misconduct.

In economic terms, trust reduces transaction costs. It frees parties from the expenses of acquiring information and monitoring the behavior of those they transact with.[16] Trust relationships tend to be more flexible than untrusted ones because the parties do not need to specify in detail what constitutes allowable conduct. That, in turn, improves performance.

Nobel Prize–winning economist Ronald Coase's influential "theory of the firm" can be understood as a response to the limitations of trust.[17] Firms impose hierarchical management and control structures because otherwise they cannot trust their employees or partners to behave reliably. If there were more trust, that would allow valuable new business arrangements to flourish. The sharing economy theorist Rachel Botsman believes that is exactly what is happening today: "We are inventing a type of trust that can grease the wheels of business and facilitate person-to-person relationships in the age of distributed networks and collaborative marketplaces."[18]

Trust seems like an unalloyed good. Why, then, does Oliver Williamson, Coase's fellow economics Nobel laureate, declare it a "diffuse and disappointing concept" that produces "no obvious value added"?[19] Why would the progenitor of the blockchain approach write, shortly after the launch of his great invention, "The root problem with conventional currency is all the trust that is required to make it work"?[20] And why would Ray Dillinger, the cryptographer who reviewed the original Bitcoin software code, call trust "almost an obscenity"?[21]

Trust is more complex than it seems. If we wish to understand the potential and dangers of the blockchain, we must start by examining the concept of trust and its manifestations in the contemporary world.

Trust is one of those "I know it when I see it" concepts that, upon closer examination, become maddeningly difficult to pin down. As the business ethics scholar Larue Tone Hosmer wryly observes, "There appears to be widespread agreement on the importance of trust in human conduct, but ... an equally widespread lack of agreement on a suitable definition of the construct."[22] Over the past few decades, scholars in management, psychology, philosophy, and other fields have developed substantial bodies of literature on the meaning of trust.[23] This scholarship sheds light on both the significance of trust and its essential components.

Trust is not binary. It is a rare situation where trust is wholly absent. If we could not take anything for granted without verifying it first, we would be hard-pressed to make it through a day. Instead, there are different degrees of trust. Putnam distinguishes "thick" trust, arising from close-knit social relationships, from "thin" trust, among a society in general.[24] Fukuyama differentiates high-trust and low-trust societies.[25] Management scholars Jay Barney and Mark Hansen differentiate "strong" trust (not backed by guarantees of performance), "semi-strong" trust (where the parties create enforcement mechanisms, but they are subject to potential failure), and "weak" trust (where law or some other mechanism guarantees performance).[26] Fernando Flores and Robert Solomon differentiate "naïve" trust, based on pure faith, from "authentic" trust, grounded in relationships.[27] Trust can be viewed on a spectrum along multiple dimensions.

Defining Trust

The simplistic definition of trust is cognitive risk assessment: Am I justified in relying on this person or organization?[28] I trust the pilot to fly my plane safely to its destination because I know that accidents are quite rare. I give my credit card to a server in a restaurant because I reasonably assume that she will not use it to run up unauthorized charges (and if she does, my credit card company will reverse them). Oliver Williamson, the economist, calls this phenomenon "calculativeness" because it is subject to rational calculation.[29] If I give my car keys to a valet, the potential loss if he or she steals my car may be great, but the probability is low, monitoring is easy, and redress—through law enforcement or insurance—will likely make me whole. On the other hand, if I am asked to wire my life savings to a Nigerian prince I met by email, I had better be pretty confident about the forthcoming reward.

While the cognitive dimension is important, it cannot represent the entirety of trust.[30] Otherwise, trust would be nothing more than rational reliance. This is the line between trust and verification. A lender insisting that a borrower provide detailed, audited financial statements and extensive collateral may be confident of repayment, but no one would call that a relationship of trust. If the lender approves a loan to a longstanding customer without documentation, it may well be because her information about the customer and experience from prior encounters make it a rational, self-interested decision, not truly one of trust. This was Williamson's reason for distinguishing trust from calculativeness.

Yet sometimes we act in ways that cognitive risk assessment cannot explain. Some people do respond to Nigerian email scams or lend money to friends who they know are unlikely to repay it. And as Fukuyama highlighted, rates of trust vary among societies, suggesting deeper cultural and other factors at work. In some countries, trams and buses operate on the honor system. Riders are expected to deposit money or swipe a card to pay, but there is no conductor checking that they do so. Almost everyone pays anyway. In other countries, such a system would lead to rampant nonpayment. The level of enforcement alone does not explain the variance.

Through a variety of "prisoner's dilemma" experiments, behavioral economists have shown that people are often inclined to trust one another even when doing so is not the rational strategy.[31] Field studies also highlight many real-world examples in which trust overcomes conflicts that appear intractable from a rational-actor perspective.[32] We have an innate bias to trust because civilization likely would not function otherwise. Fukuyama believes that 20 percent of all economic activity cannot be explained in rational terms and is rooted in things like reciprocity, moral obligation, and duty to community, even in the modern world.[33]

There is, moreover, something hollow and unsatisfying in a conception of trust limited to rational calculation. As Botsman writes, "[I]t makes trust sound rational and predictable, and it does not really get to the human essence of what it enables us to do and how it empowers us to connect with other people."[34] Surely the fact that Uber, Lyft, and Airbnb provide reputation scores encourages people to enter a stranger's car or apartment. But that risky act still requires some degree of faith in human goodness. This willingness to trust even when the risks are uncertain—or even rationally unjustified—produces the spillover benefits that make trust so powerful. If you trust me beyond rational risk assessment, I am more likely to do the same for you.[35] And if we can dispense with monitoring or enforcement mechanisms, costs go down and transactions go up.

Philosophers call this nonrational component the "affective dimension" of trust.[36] It is the optimistic disposition toward others that operates outside strategic motivation. It is an expectation of goodwill on the part of an agent.[37] Compared to cognitive trust, this form of trust is, in the words of three management scholars, "a more complex psychological state"[38] that incorporates social and emotional factors. It is the aspect of trust concerned with motives, not just actions.[39] This dimension of trust becomes important when, as is often the case, the parties cannot precisely estimate costs and benefits. In the words of David Lewis and Andrew Weigert, "Trust begins where prediction ends."[40]

There are also moral aspects to affective trust.[41] It is trust as an expression of our goodness, not simply our self-interest. Putnam says that those who are trusting are "all-round good citizens."[42] And Fukuyama describes trust as "a set of ethical habits and reciprocal moral obligations internalized by members of a community."[43] A willingness to trust others beyond rational calculation shows that principles matter to you more than the bottom line. Even in a business context, we think well of the bank that gives a delinquent but sympathetic borrower another chance, rather than foreclosing when it has the right to do so.

There is a catch to all this. One of Herman Melville's characters captures the appeal of affective trust by critiquing the alternative of cognitive risk assessment: "[T]o doubt, to suspect, to prove—to have all this wearing work to be doing continually ... It is evil!"[44] The speaker is the title character of Melville's final novel, *The Confidence-Man*. Through his various swindles on a Mississippi steamboat, he illustrates how trust can be exploited by the untrustworthy. Trust is not an ironclad guarantee of performance. To trust is to be vulnerable to the one trusted.[45]

To engineers, vulnerabilities are security flaws to be prevented. Here, I use the term in the more precise sense, meaning exposure to the possibility of harm. Vulnerability is to injury as comparative advantage is to success: correlated, but not identical. And the outcome represents only one side of the ledger. Driving a car leaves you vulnerable to accidents, but most people consider the trade-off worth it. Giving the keys to your sixteen-year-old child may not be a sound decision—most car rental firms refuse anyone under twenty five—but parents generally have enough faith to accept the vulnerability. The externalities of the trust relationship extend beyond the actuarial consideration of insurance costs. In game-theoretic terms, your vulnerability signals to the other party that it might successfully employ a similar trusting strategy, producing the best possible outcome in a prisoner's dilemma situation.

Even if the decision to trust is a rational one, there is some risk that it will prove to be a bad bet. According to ethicist Annette Baier, trust is "letting other persons (natural or artificial, such as firms, nations, etc.) take care of something the trustor cares about, where such 'caring for' involves some exercise of discretionary powers."[46] And that discretion implies that the trustee may turn out to be untrustworthy, despite efforts at verification. As business scholars Jeremy Yip and Maurice Schweitzer observe, "Some of the most egregious unethical behaviors occur because individuals exploit trust."[47] Trust is distinct from trustworthiness.[48] Yet we trust anyway. As the eighteenth-century critic and dictionary author Samuel Johnson observed, it is "happier sometimes to be cheated than not to trust."[49]

Trust can fail in three ways: direct violations, opportunistic behavior, and systemic collapse. Each will appear in the blockchain context.

Violations of trust are the clearest examples. The mechanic who charges for unnecessary work, the friend that you ask to hold your candy bar but who eats it instead, the teacher who sexually abuses a student—each takes advantage of the trustor's vulnerability to cause harm. Some trust violations have serious legal and ethical consequences, but in other cases, the loss of trust is itself the major consequence. According to experimental research by Maurice Schweitzer and two Wharton School colleagues, trust can be repaired if those who engage in untrustworthy actions apologize and behave in a trustworthy way going forward.[50] However, they found that trust is difficult to restore when the untrustworthy behavior involves deception.[51] That is the foundation for the second category of trust breakdown: opportunism.

"Opportunism" means violating the spirit, but not necessarily the letter, of an agreement by taking advantage of asymmetric information.[52] The opportunist is untrustworthy because he or she takes advantage of the trustor rather than exercising the necessary benevolence. Courts have used several legal doctrines to address opportunism in contractual transactions, with mixed success.[53] And policing opportunistic behavior is a central goal of corporate law under the contemporary mainstream theory of the firm. According to this theory, corporate governance responds to the potential for opportunism in the principal/agent relationship between shareholders and managers.[54] Those managers in turn must monitor employees, imposing transaction costs.[55]

Finally, trust sometimes fails, not because the parties to an arrangement are necessarily untrustworthy, but because the environment is inimical to trust. There is a systemic failure that makes it unwise for anyone to be trusting. Tom Tyler has detailed how unfair administration of the criminal justice system undermines trust, and therefore law-abidingness.[56] The problem is worse in countries without a robust rule of law or property rights. According to the Peruvian economist Hernando de Soto, the absence of enforceable property rights for the poor prevents the establishment of functioning market economies in the developing world.[57]

Systemic trust collapses may also occur when relationships cross too many boundaries, whether organizational or political. Without a common legal environment or business structure, the transaction costs of establishing baselines for trust may be too great. And trust breaks down when a trust platform itself is undermined. When the credit bureau Equifax admitted in September 2017 that personal information on over 140 million Americans had been accessed from its servers, it lowered the level of trust in credit and identity services generally.[58] Even before that, a study by the U.S. Department of Commerce in 2016 had found that almost half of Americans were deterred from using e-commerce services thanks to security or privacy concerns.[59]

Trust, therefore, is a two-sided coin. On one side is a belief rooted in some combination of rational and emotional factors; on the other is acceptance of uncontrolled risk. The organizational behavior scholar Roger Mayer and his coauthors, in a much-cited article, surveyed conceptions of trust in several disciplines and proposed an integrative definition: "[Trust is] the willingness of a party to be vulnerable to the actions of another party based on the expectation that the other will perform a particular action important to the trustor, irrespective of the ability to monitor or control that other part."[60]

In short, trust is confident vulnerability.[61] The benefits of trust arise from its ability to stimulate what Botsman describes as a "confident relationship to the unknown."[62] That also generates costs. This Janus-faced aspect of trust—a source of strength as well as danger—explains why the author of the Bitcoin whitepaper found it so distasteful. There is no trust without vulnerability. And vulnerability traditionally means giving up power to others. You trust the bank by giving it the power to control your money. You do exactly the same with the con man.

Trust Architectures: Peer-to-Peer, Leviathan, Intermediary

The constellation of design decisions that shape a system is known as its "architecture." Architecture is power because it defines the limits of human interactions. Just as the physical architecture of neighborhoods determines the character of communities, the digital architecture of communications networks and information systems shapes opportunities for innovation, creativity, and free expression online.[63] For technologies, architecture describes the ways the components of a system interact with one another.[64]

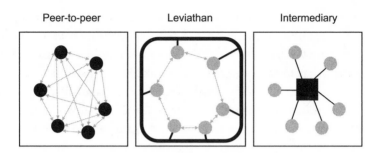

Figure 1.1
Symbolic representations of the three established trust architectures. The black
elements of each are the trusted components.

Trust also has architectures. Just as people are predisposed to trust in different ways, there are multiple ways trust is formed. These architectures describe
the institutional structures for manifesting trust.[65] As digital economy expert
Arun Sundarajaran of New York University observes, "If you look back at history, every time there was a big expansion in the world's economic activity, it
was generally induced by the creation of a new form of trust."[66]

As figure 1.1 illustrates, over time, three main architectures of trust have
developed: peer-to-peer (P2P), Leviathan, and intermediary.[67]

The first architecture, P2P trust, is based on relationships and shared
ethical norms: I trust you because I trust *you*. It was the earliest human
trust structure to develop. Interpersonal trust among families and clans long
predated the rise of the state. Yet P2P trust architectures endure even today.
They can develop in communities with shared social norms, so long as they
adopt effective governance mechanisms. This is the domain of "commons
regimes" explored by Nobel Prize–winner Elinor Ostrom and others, where
order is achievable without formal legal rules.[68] Adherence to a set of principles for self-governance, as well as the flexibility of individuals and communities to adjust in order to solve problems, can be enough.

P2P trust tends to be thick because it rests on mutual commitments and
personal relationships rather than momentary convenience. However, it has
a relatively small radius. You might trust a stranger peer-to-peer, but only for
an unimportant transaction (such as a purchase at the convenience store). For
example, the design rules for, in Ostrom's words, "governing the commons"
require clear group boundaries and the opportunity for those affected by
rules to participate in modifying them.

More recently, Internet law scholars such as Yochai Benkler and Brett Frischmann have shown how commons management operates online for systems such as Wikipedia, open-source software communities, user-moderated content sites such as Reddit, and WiFi unlicensed wireless technology.[69] These models expand the scope of peer-to-peer trust. However, they still depend on a combination of formal rules and communal standards that are rarely present in complex, impersonal marketplaces.

The second major trust architecture borrows its name, "Leviathan," from the seventeenth-century philosopher Thomas Hobbes. He situated trust as the foundational force in the establishment of civilization, although he rarely used the term expressly. In the state of nature, he famously argued, life is "solitary, poor, nasty, brutish, and short."[70] No one can benefit from transactions or personal investments of effort because all people must worry that others will cheat on or steal from them.

To avoid this "war of all against all," Hobbes imagined that civilized societies make a onetime deal: They grant a monopoly on the legitimate use of violence to the state. Once this takes place, the state—Hobbes's mythical, all-powerful Leviathan—can enforce private contracts and property rights. Knowing that there are penalties for breach not based on their own power for self-help, individuals and organizations feel comfortable taking the risks inherent in trusting relationships.

With Leviathan trust, the state or some other powerful central authority operates largely in the background to prevent others from imposing their will through force or trickery. Only rarely does it exercise its power directly, and when it does, it is primarily via law enforcement or military activities for the purpose of maintaining a baseline level of trust in social stability.

The main elements of the Leviathan trust architecture that people see are bureaucratic rules for participation and dispute resolution. The legal system, with its thicket of doctrine, defines constraints on arbitrary state power. When that fails, so does trust. The social psychologist Tom Tyler surveyed members of different ethnic groups about their interactions with the criminal justice system. He discovered that people tend to obey the law only when they perceive that it operates on the basis of procedural fairness.[71]

The final major way that trust is traditionally structured is through intermediaries. In this arrangement, the local rules and the reputation of the intermediaries take the place of social norms and government-issued laws to structure transactions.[72] Intermediaries provide valuable services that induce individuals to hand over power or control. Credit bureaus such as Experian and Equifax, for example, wield great authority because they enable transactions such as loans. Individual lenders, at least historically, had a much harder time accumulating the data necessary to assess individual creditworthiness.

What makes activity happen in this arrangement is the intermediaries' ability to aggregate activity on both sides. Financial services relationships are a good example of intermediary trust.[73] Commercial banks sit in the middle of the transaction flow between depositors and borrowers, generating and paying interest along the way. Investment banks structure and intermediate financial transactions in capital markets. Financial services now generate roughly 30 percent of all corporate profits in the United States, all based on the power of such intermediation.[74]

Intermediary trust is particularly significant online.[75] Advertisers trust Google because it shows them transparent pricing and performance metrics for their ads, while users trust it because it returns high-quality search results surrounded by ads they find relevant. Amazon and eBay create trusted environments for transactions. Uber and Airbnb make markets around transportation and lodging, through which users interact with strangers in ways they never would otherwise. They are often described as peer-to-peer, but users are actually trusting the platform, not personal relationships or community-defined governance regimes.

All these architectures give rise to a trust trade-off, in which users give up some freedom to gain the benefits of trust. In peer-to-peer trust, they must heed the norms of the community; in Leviathan trust, they are subservient to the state; and in intermediary trust, they lock themselves into walled gardens by ceding control over personal data. Recent debates about the power of online platforms such as Google and Facebook reflect this concern.[76] These platforms control how users see the world by shaping their information diets, and they control markets through the power of intermediation. Network effects make it difficult for competitors to undermine their dominance. This challenge will be explored in greater depth in chapter 11.

Trustless Trust

The blockchain creates a new kind of trust that none of the established models encompasses. Prominent venture capitalist and LinkedIn founder Reid Hoffman describes it as "trustless trust."[77] The phrase has caught on.[78]

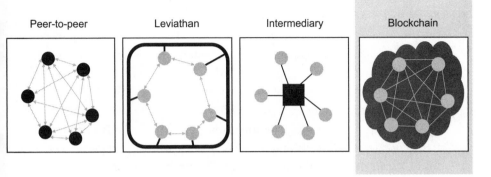

Figure 1.2
The blockchain's "trustless" trust architecture, promoting trust in the network without trusting any individual actor, compared to alternatives.

Although it sounds self-contradictory, both sides are important. If cryptocurrencies and distributed ledgers did not inspire trust, they would fail. Yet if they achieved trust by proxy through governments or strong intermediaries, they would not significantly differ from the status quo.

On a blockchain network, nothing is assumed to be trustworthy ... except the output of the network itself. This distinctive arrangement defines the landscape for the blockchain's interactions with law, regulation, and governance.

In any transaction, there are three elements that may be trusted: the counterparty, the intermediary, and the dispute resolution mechanism.[79] The blockchain tries to replace all three with software code. People are represented through arbitrary digital keys, which eliminate the contextual factors that humans use to evaluate trustworthiness. The transaction platform is a distributed machine operated by unknown participants who are in it purely for the money. And dispute resolution occurs through "smart contracts" executing predefined algorithms. What makes a transaction valid are cryptographic proofs that the other party can verify mathematically. Hence the common saying, "in proof we trust," among bitcoin aficionados, in contrast to the legend "In God We Trust" on U.S. bank notes.

Online transactions already rely on encryption and algorithmic reputation systems. Every time you buy something from Amazon.com or use Facebook to keep up with your friends, you are trusting a largely automated, software-based system. Even when you stick your debit card into an ATM and receive cash out of a slot, you are trusting a machine to do what was quintessentially human work.

The important point is what we trust the machines *for.* We have confidence that a computer will not be stupid, or slow, or forgetful, or biased in the way that a human record-keeper might be. That is what computers do well: They rapidly and consistently execute programs. But there are things that machines traditionally do not do, or cannot do. Blockchains do more than inspire confidence in the reliability of their ledger entries. They generate a particular kind of trust that should be examined on its own terms.

Blockchain trust is intangible. You cannot see a bitcoin; it is just a set of transaction records on a distributed ledger. Yet that is hardly unique in today's world. We accept that our bank accounts represent actual money and our stock purchases represent real equity, even though we view them electronically. Intellectual property rights such as copyrights, trademarks, and patents are valuable sources of competitive advantage and alienable assets in themselves. Furthermore, intangibility is a standard issue with all online interactions.[80]

The more significant aspect of blockchain trust is that it severs the connection between institutional actors and the trustworthy system. To accept a cryptocurrency transaction as valid is to trust the network it is based on, without necessarily trusting any individual participant or higher authority.[81] One can accept the consensus of a distributed collection of independent computers as the true state of the ledger. In its simplest form, this is the trust revolution of the blockchain and distributed ledger technology. It imbues trust in collectives of machines, while draining it from those machines' human masters.

There have always been those who desire a world free from corporate and governmental control. Leading figures in the personal computer revolution were influenced by the counterculture values of the 1960s. A generation later, many of those who promoted the rise of the Internet saw it as a way to connect people around the world directly, without the interference of nation-states. The small but sophisticated Cypherpunk movement sought technical solutions to implement this vision.[82] It saw the Internet as proof that even the heavy hand of the state had to give way to the laws of mathematics underlying cryptography and the software engineering underlying packet-switched data networks. The early Sun Microsystems engineer John Gilmore famously declared that "the Net interprets censorship as damage and routes around it."[83]

The current era is one in which trust in corporations and governments is deeply shaken, while faith in technology as a force for change remains intact. It is the perfect environment for an approach that seemingly uses the latter to make the former obsolete. As Brian Behlendorf, executive director of the Hyperledger open-source distributed ledger consortium puts it, "Blockchain technology can allow us to do business in an environment of declining trust."[84] It is the appropriate trust architecture for the current historical moment.

Yet contrary to Reid Hoffman's elegant turn of phrase, the blockchain is not entirely trustless. It may promote justified confidence, but not without vulnerability. What Satoshi Nakamoto and those who followed him created was actually a new kind of trustworthiness, powerful yet imperfect.

Blockchain trust is not an oxymoron. It is a distinctive phenomenon that deserves to be examined on its own terms. Doing so is the key to understanding not just how blockchain technology operates, but why it will succeed and where it will fail.

2 Satoshi's Solution

Too Trusted to Fail?

There is a well-known logic puzzle involving two guards, each of whom stands before a doorway. One door leads to riches, the other to death. You must question the guards to select the right door. One guard always answers truthfully; the other always lies. The catch: You do not know which is which. The puzzle at first seems impossible. You will never know whether an answer you receive is truthful. Yet there is an elegant solution: Ask one guard which door the *other* would recommend—whatever answer you get, go through the opposite door. The truthful guard will point you to the door of death because that is what the liar would do. The liar knows that the truthful one would direct you to the door of riches, so he also points you to the door of death. Choose the other one.

Satoshi Nakamoto solved the puzzle of digital cash—and in so doing, developed a new trust architecture—using a similar approach: inverting the problem. The mechanism for people to make payments confidently with a decentralized digital currency is to pay people with it. Rather than treat money as purely the output of the system, Bitcoin uses it as an input.

When Satoshi posted his ideas online in 2008, only a few initial commenters reacted with immediate excitement. The Bitcoin whitepaper made clear that it was in many ways derivative of earlier work, and its goal—a digital currency whose value could be trusted without government oversight—was a familiar objective in the community. Today, the whitepaper is held in awe as the founding document for a worldwide technology revolution. Waves of blockchain, cryptocurrency, smart-contract, and permissioned-ledger development followed. To understand the potential and challenges of this burgeoning movement, one must first appreciate Bitcoin and how it came to be.

The blockchain is much more than a technology of finance. However, that is where it started. And for all intents and purposes, a transformative innovation in finance becomes a transformation in every other sector. Money, the foundation for the quantified exchange of value, makes the world go around. In the words of the historian Yuval Noah Harari, "money is the most universal and most efficient system of mutual trust ever created."[1] This is because, as the German economist Georg Friedrich Knapp explained a century ago in *The State Theory of Money*, what makes currency valuable is not the inherent worth of a physical asset, such as the precious metals in coins.[2] It is the willingness of others to accept it. Money is, at bottom, a formalization of pure trust.

Skeptics who claim that cryptocurrencies such as bitcoin are necessarily valueless because they rest on nothing mistake currencies for the assets they denominate. No major currency in the world today is based on anything tangible. True, the United States stockpiles a great deal of gold in Fort Knox. If a real-life Auric Goldfinger of James Bond fame stole it all, however, automated teller machines and grocery store clerks would not stop accepting dollar bills. If most of the world can trust pieces of paper and their even-more-abstract digital representations as currency, there is no principled reason they cannot do the same for cryptographically defined money such as bitcoin. It all comes down to whether the relevant monetary system inspires the requisite confidence. Any particular cryptocurrency may crash in price and even go to zero, but that is different than saying cryptocurrency is inherently worth nothing at all.

The fact that money represents an abstraction of value paved the way for bitcoin and the blockchain in a second sense. Modern finance can take the most stolid of assets—a home, say—and transform it into exotic collateralized mortgage obligations whizzing across the screens of worldwide derivatives traders with their algorithmic trading engines. As such arrangements become more and more complex, the relationship between the real assets and the financial instruments becomes increasingly attenuated. This is the great promise of what financiers call "securitization."

That process unraveled in the financial crisis of 2008. What seemed to the world's brightest investors, bankers, and regulators like foolproof schemes crashed almost overnight. There were certainly abuses, and companies that should have been punished more severely for their role in those abuses.

Ultimately, though, greed is not an unusual condition in the financial sector. It the normal state of things. Systemic risk was what made the crisis so scary. Instruments that seemed to be diversified and disconnected, like bundles of thousands of individual mortgages, suddenly proved highly correlated. It was not just that some banks and bankers were untrustworthy—that came as little surprise—but that the very essence of modern finance could no longer be trusted. The financial world was not as decentralized as it seemed. And if money could not be trusted, what could?

The system in 2008 was so fragile because trading activity was decoupled from the real assets underlying those trades. Derivative financial instruments, such as futures and options, have a long history, but both trading volumes and complexity exploded in recent decades. That is largely the consequence of how an earlier crisis within the financial sector was solved. That one made far fewer headlines and seemed to have a neat resolution. Yet it laid the groundwork for the later disaster. And once again, the central theme was trust.

The Buttonwood Agreement of 1792 was a manifestation of peer-to-peer (P2P) trust. The stockbrokers assembled under a buttonwood tree not because it had any special status, but because it was what modern game theorists would call a "Schelling point": a logical place that any of them would expect the others to pick for a meeting.[3] They agreed not to do business with any other traders, and to charge each other uniform commissions, because they were not strangers. They all knew each other and were confident in the cohesion of the community. Any of them might have profited, at least in the short run, by defecting from the agreement and trading through independent auctioneers. In the long run, though, they knew they would be better off controlling the terms of the exchange collectively. They trusted their rivals to stick to the deal because they were also their friends and neighbors.

The institution based on the Buttonwood Agreement—the New York Stock Exchange (NYSE)—would grow to become the world's most powerful financial marketplace. Nowadays, seeing that a company is listed on the NYSE is evidence enough to respect its legitimacy. You do not need to know anything about the member organizations of the exchange or its governance mechanisms to feel confident enough to purchase a stock listed on it. The NYSE today is a powerful manifestation of intermediary trust.

On its surface, Wall Street is one of the most scalable transaction markets in the world. The volume of equities trading has grown to levels that would have been unheard of a few decades ago. Both the exchanges that process transactions and the trading firms that enter into them were computerized long ago, and those computer networks are frequently updated with more capacity and new technology. Yet dig deeper, and the system looks considerably less advanced.

At the very heart of Wall Street is the process of issuing and tracking shares of corporate stock. How many shares has a company issued, and who owns them at any given moment? Until the 1970s, stock ownership was tracked through paper certificates. It was the physical equivalent of P2P trust. Every transaction had to be based on a direct relationship represented in the transfer of the certificate.

As trading volumes increased, that structure became increasingly unsustainable. At one point, messengers would crisscross lower Manhattan with wheelbarrows full of stock certificates, moving them between brokerage houses to settle a trade.[4] The transaction could be made in an instant over the phone or on a computerized system, but the actual thing of value—the stock certificate—moved in the same way that it did in the days of the Buttonwood Agreement. Delays and errors got so bad that the NYSE ground to a virtual halt.

The solution to what became known as the "paperwork crisis" was to allow brokerage firms to "net" transactions.[5] If Morgan Stanley customers bought 1,000 shares in a day from Merrill Lynch customers, and Merrill Lynch customers bought 1,000 shares of the same stock from Morgan Stanley customers, there was no need to send 2,000 shares between the two companies. The transactions simply offset. Each company kept its own records of its customers' holdings, but the system required a central depository that kept all the stock certificates. This organization is the Depository Trust & Clearing Corporation (DTCC), mentioned in the introduction to this book. The DTCC and its subsidiary, Cede & Company, are technically the record owners of virtually every share of stock traded in the U.S. When investors buy shares, they are actually buying claims on stock held at the DTCC. There are similar central securities depositories (CSDs) in other major financial centers.

The move to CSDs was a critical step in the dematerialization of finance. The U.S. decision in 1971 to go off the gold standard meant that there was officially nothing backing the purchasing power of the dollar, other than the full faith and credit of the government. Although in practical terms, the dollar had not been a proxy for precious metals for some time, this step formally established it as nothing more than a token representing an abstract value. The DTCC did the same for stocks, decoupling the abstract rights of share ownership from the physical instantiation of certificates. From there, it was a slow but fairly straight line to the idea that any asset could be securitized: represented as a collection of financial rights and obligations to be traded and rearranged in ever more complex ways.

The high point of securitization was the emergence, at the turn of the twenty-first century, of instruments such as credit default swaps and collateralized mortgage obligations. These exotic arrangements created markets with notional values in the trillions of dollars by slicing and dicing and recombining bets about bets about payments around ordinary assets such as homes.[6] Financial wizards pushed the envelope of such innovations to generate monumental levels of paper wealth—until the music stopped and the financial system nearly fell apart.

The global financial crisis of 2008 was both sudden and devastating. A booming economy in the U.S. and other major developed countries turned into a deep and painful recession almost overnight. Mortgage defaults skyrocketed and liquidity in the financial system seized up. Stock markets throughout the world plunged. Pillars of Wall Street such as Lehman Brothers and Bear Stearns collapsed, and others were saved only through extraordinary government intervention. The contagion spread to what seemed like some of the most trustworthy institutions in the economy, including AIG, the world's largest insurer, and Fannie Mae, the government-backed purchaser of mortgages. The recovery took many years.

The immediate causes of the crisis were factors such as an unsustainable rise in housing prices, excessive leverage and speculation by financial services firms, and securitization of mortgages into complex instruments whose systemic risks were underappreciated. However, these explanations fail to account for the extent of the damage. The economists Paola Sapienza and Luigi Zingales, in seeking to explain the speed and depth of the crisis, came up with the following striking thesis:

> Something important was destroyed in the last few months of 2008. It is an asset crucial to production, even if it is not made of bricks and mortar. While this asset does not enter standard national account statistics or standard economic models, it is so crucial to development that its absence—according to Nobel laureate Kenneth Arrow—is the cause of much of the economic backwardness in the world. This asset is trust.[7]

Based on survey research, Sapienza and Zingales found that investors' trust in the stock market dropped significantly as the crisis unfolded. Even more significantly, investors did not fully trust the government response after the fall of Lehman Brothers set off a potential cascade across the financial system. A massive government bailout saved banks and related firms deemed "too big to fail," while homeowners defaulting on mortgages that they should never have taken out received only limited assistance. The U.S. Treasury Secretary at the time, Hank Paulson, was formerly the head of investment bank Goldman Sachs. In the research by Sapienza and Zingales, survey respondents criticized Paulson and his government colleagues for serving the interests of their erstwhile Wall Street colleagues rather than the public.

The loss of trust in the financial sector during this period was pervasive, but the perceived failure of government before and during the crisis was particularly devastating. Failures alone do not necessarily undermine trust. No one was surprised that stock markets that go up can also go down. And the nature of capitalism is that firms that take risks in order to profit may find themselves insolvent in some cases. At some point, however, when the invisible hand of the markets falters too severely, the visible hand of the government must reach in. The institutions of central banking and regulation that came out of the Great Depression in the 1930s were designed for this backstop role. In 2008, however, they failed to prevent the crisis, and in some ways they even made it worse.

In propping up banks that caused the crisis, and not the homeowners and others who suffered its consequences, regulators created a condition of moral hazard: Bankers enjoyed all the gains from risky behavior yet experienced only some of the losses. That increased the likelihood that they would take the same course again. In economic terms, there was a failure of mechanism design, the branch of game theory that takes as its starting point certain attributes—such as financial stability—and constructs incentive structures to make it the dominant strategy.

One lesson from the painful experience of the crisis was that the system was broken and had to be fixed. This was generally the conclusion of the investment and political communities. Reforms such as the Dodd-Frank Act in the U.S. and new systemic risk controls were instituted to prevent a reoccurrence of the cascading failures of 2008.[8]

A darker interpretation is also possible, however. Perhaps the system cannot be fixed. Perhaps bankers motivated to maximize their returns in the short term cannot be trusted to act in the long-term interests of society. Perhaps, given the importance of financial services to the economy, some degree of risk will always be socialized to the citizens as a whole, even as the gains from risk-taking accrue to the financiers alone. And perhaps government is at some point neither able to nor interested in serving as a truly honest broker. If this is the case, it means the system itself cannot be trusted. It relies, at bottom, on humans. The decision-makers who generate trust are fallible, inefficient, and potentially biased. The only alternative is to remove them.

The financial crisis thus showed the limits of all the established trust architectures. P2P relationships could not scale to meet modern demands. Intermediaries allowed for dematerialization but eventually created financial services organizations that were too big to fail and incentivized to take risks that they didn't fully appreciate. And the Leviathan standing behind private interactions proved alternately powerless and part of the problem. The stage was set for a new approach.

In the Beginning, There Was Bitcoin

Even a worthwhile innovation will only take off in a receptive environment. There must be networks of people and financial support to take the basic insights and grow them. And there must be latent demand, which the innovation unlocks. Timing is crucial and largely a matter of good fortune. Start-ups with big dreams to transform commerce and media were swept aside in the dotcom bust of 2001, but today many of the same concepts form the foundations for multibillion-dollar companies.

The fall of 2008, six weeks after the collapse of Lehman Brothers, turned out to be a perfect time for the Bitcoin whitepaper to appear. To be sure, Satoshi Nakamoto was developing the concept for some time before. The introduction to the paper says nothing about macroeconomic risks. Instead, it begins with the microlevel problem of trust in electronic payments:

> Commerce on the Internet has come to rely almost exclusively on financial institutions serving as trusted third parties to process electronic payments. While the system works well enough for most transactions, it still suffers from the inherent weaknesses of the trust based model.[9]

This sounds somewhat dull and abstract as the rationale for such a powerful innovation. But it is actually the same issue that brought down the global economy in 2008. Parties transacting are necessarily beholden to intermediaries. If trust in those intermediaries proves misguided, the parties themselves have little or no recourse. Laws and regulations are designed to ensure that private intermediaries are trustworthy. The same applies to governments, which are just another kind of institution, subject to the same basic limitations. The system works well, most of the time—until it does not, in cases of censorship, corruption, monopoly, or fraud.

Hence the motivation behind Bitcoin: a currency that allows trusted electronic payments without the involvement of financial intermediaries or governments. Whatever was in Satoshi Nakamoto's mind when he developed Bitcoin, readers surely experienced his paper through the lens of current events. A growing community saw the potential of this operational system. It seemed like the last, best hope for trust in an untrustworthy financial world.

The technical challenges that Bitcoin addressed were familiar in academic computer science research. Virtually every component of Satoshi Nakamoto's solution was adapted from prior work. As the computer scientists Arvind Narayanan and Jeremy Clark explain, "Nakamoto's genius, then, wasn't any of the individual components of bitcoin, but rather the intricate way in which they fit together to breathe life into the system."[10] At a general level, Bitcoin rests on three established foundations: cryptography, digital cash, and distributed systems.

Cryptography is the science of secure communications.[11] It goes back thousands of years but has flowered during the computer age. The power of cryptography is that it is a form of applied mathematics. Its claims can be proven formally and its algorithms implemented through computers whose power increases every year. Every online purchase depends for security on cryptographic digital signatures, which verify that credit card information is transmitted securely to merchants. One dimension of cryptography is encryption, which makes secret information difficult for an attacker to obtain without a key. Bitcoin actually uses no encryption to keep information secret. It was designed not to hide transactions, but to make them secure and trustworthy. To that end, it uses cryptography systematically.

Bitcoin holders are identified through cryptographic private keys, which are secret strings allowing access only to the possessor.[12] As a result, the system operates on a semi-anonymous basis.[13] Every Bitcoin transaction is digitally signed with private keys, so anyone can verify that it was made by the appropriate party. There are no actual coins on the Bitcoin ledger. What we call a "coin" is formally a chain of digital signatures representing verified transactions. One's bitcoin stash is the unspent output of those prior transactions.

Secure exchange of value, or money, is a familiar application for cryptography. The cryptographer David Chaum is credited with describing the first secure digital currency system in a paper published in 1982.[14] That was a quarter-century before Bitcoin, and more than a decade before the Internet was widely available for commercial activity. In the intervening years, there were numerous other systems proposed, with serious attempts to implement several of them. Chaum launched a company called Digicash in the late 1990s to implement his ideas, and a variety of other schemes used different approaches, including E-Gold and Liberty Reserve.[15] None succeeded on any scale. And regulators took a dim view of private, anonymous currencies that could be used to fund illegal activities such as terrorism, especially after the 9/11 attacks in 2001.

Nonetheless, an active global community continued to work on the problem. The International Financial Cryptography Association began hosting Financial Cryptography conferences in Caribbean tax-haven locales in 1997.[16] There and elsewhere, cryptographers gathered with sympathetic bankers and entrepreneurs to devise technical mechanisms that could replace the centralized trust in institutions or governments with decentralized, cryptographic approaches. Many of the techniques that these pioneers developed made their way into Bitcoin.

Bitcoin was decentralized in a way that the major earlier digital cash systems were not. They relied on central servers to manage the flow of currency. Even if those servers were secure and trustworthy, they presented an attack surface both for regulators interested in shutting the system down and for thieves interested in exploiting it. Bitcoin instead used a P2P network of validation nodes, which communicate on a decentralized basis.

The counterintuitive idea that a computer network could operate consistently with no master controller might have sounded suspect in 1982. By 2008, however, not only was the Internet well established, so was the idea of distributed systems. Napster and similar P2P file-sharing services briefly threatened the music industry in the late 1990s before being sued out of existence for contributing to copyright infringement.[17] Others applied the same techniques to file storage, real-time communication, and a variety of other contexts. Many key elements of the blockchain approach, such as a shared transaction ledger and a secure, collective voting system for validation, were based on earlier distributed systems research.[18]

In the Bitcoin whitepaper, Satoshi Nakamoto put together cryptographically secured digital cash with a P2P validation network for a shared ledger,
adding a few elegant tweaks along the way. Over the subsequent months, he
engaged in online dialogues with digital cash aficionados. They quickly produced software code that could implement the concepts described in the
paper. On January 3, 2009, the first block of Bitcoin records was validated.
(The first actual transaction occurred nine days later.) Satoshi embedded
in that "genesis block" the phrase, "The Times 03/Jan/2009 Chancellor on
brink of second bailout for banks," a reference to a news item on the ongoing efforts to contain the then-current financial crisis. The implication was
clear: Bitcoin was to be the new, sound form of money. The world's banks
and governments had failed, but computer science could do better.

Bitcoin made digital cash a reality. Its supporters began operating mining nodes to validate transactions. Dozens, and then hundreds, and then
thousands of developers started building software, services, and even specialized hardware around the core platform that Satoshi described. The software code was extended and improved, eliminating bugs and improving its
performance. A few companies began to accept bitcoin in lieu of traditional
currency. Others created exchanges to trade back and forth.

The price of bitcoin is set by the market. It is worth what buyers are willing to trade for it in other currencies. Bitcoin's value has fluctuated, and even
crashed at times. Over time, however, people have consistently proved themselves willing to buy it. That fact is more significant than the rapid price
appreciation during speculative periods in 2013 and 2017. To be sure, even
at its peak, bitcoin's asset value[19] is a far cry from the $3 trillion U.S. dollar
money supply, and its trajectory remains uncertain. But its success to date is a
remarkable accomplishment. There have been many privately issued currencies before—everything from S&H Green Stamps to cigarettes traded among
prisoners falls into that category—but never one like bitcoin, so widely
adopted, completely decentralized, and secured through cryptography.

Nakamoto Consensus

To cryptographers, Satoshi Nakamoto offered a new solution to the "Byzantine Generals Problem."[20] The metaphor (illustrated in figure 2.1) is that
a group of generals needs to coordinate an attack on a city. However, its
members cannot be sure that one or more of their number are not traitors,

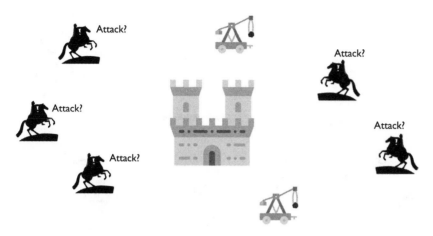

Figure 2.1
The Byzantine Generals Problem, in which generals must coordinate an attack without a trusted means of communication.

or that the messages that they exchange are faithfully relayed. What is the highest percentage of dishonest messages the generals can tolerate and still accurately plan their attack? If most of the network is untrustworthy, the situation is hopeless. The generals need a way to settle on a strategy that reflects, ideally, the majority view. But they can rely only on messages they see, not any trusted central authority.

The Byzantine generals' conundrum is analogous to Bitcoin network participants seeking confidence that the transaction ledger they see represents the majority view of the network. The solutions to this challenge are known as "Byzantine Fault-Tolerant (BFT) algorithms" because they allow the Byzantine generals to trust their view of the consensus even though some of the information they receive may be faulty. A number of BFT algorithms were developed in the research literature before Bitcoin. These generally involved some sort of secure voting mechanism among network participants. However, academic interest had waned, and there were few commercial applications of these ideas.

Bitcoin's solution is Nakamoto Consensus.[21] Without a robust means of ensuring consensus, for example, any Bitcoin participant could spend the same bitcoin multiple times (known as the "double-spend problem"), or claim that it had more currency than it really did. The trouble with most approaches to consensus on digital systems is that it is easy to create a

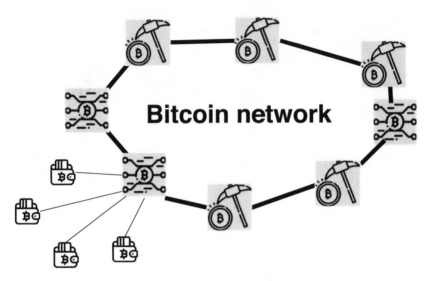

Figure 2.2
Full nodes on the Bitcoin network maintain a complete copy of the blockchain. Some are miners, who compete to validate new blocks every ten minutes. Most end users use wallets (often provided by exchanges) that are maintained through a full node.

nearly infinite number of fake network nodes. If every node gets one vote, dishonest actors will vote many times because there is no central registry to verify their identity. This is known as a "Sybil attack," for a 1970s-era book and movie about a woman with multiple personality disorder who assumed a dizzying array of identities.[22] Even if most real users are honest, an attacker can create enough nodes to dominate the network and impose its own false consensus on the system.

Satoshi's solution combined cryptographic techniques with insights from game theory.[23] As with other BFT protocols, consensus in Bitcoin is determined by a network of actors (shown in figure 2.2), who express themselves by voting to update the ledger.[24] In Satoshi's version, these actors engage in a process known as "mining," in which they compete for the right to verify a chunk of Bitcoin transactions.[25] Mining is a kind of repetitive lottery, in which the winner of each lottery gets to validate the next block. Who wins each time is random, though, so a bad actor cannot guarantee that it will define the consensus. All the other full nodes independently check the ledger to verify that the new block is legitimate.

The major limitation of such a protocol is the possibility of Sybil attacks: if it is easy and rewarding to be untrustworthy, someone probably will be. Cheaters will create millions of artificial nodes and greatly increase their chance of winning the lottery. Hence, the next core technique in Bitcoin, proof of work, follows.[26] Proof of work makes voting costly. Bitcoin's proof-of-work system requires miners to solve arbitrary cryptographic puzzles involving one-way functions known as "hashes."[27] Converting a file into a hash is easy, but going from the hash back to the original file is virtually impossible except through massive trial and error. Satoshi Nakamoto borrowed the idea of hashing puzzles from HashCash, a proposed solution to email spam published several years earlier.[28]

In the proof-of-work system, any miner's chance of winning the lottery is proportional to the amount of processing that it dedicates to the problem. Given the level of competition, each vote requires massive and growing computing power, which is sufficiently expensive to deter Sybil attacks.[29] This is the only way to increase the chances of winning the right to validate the next block. The benefits of cheating are less than the costs. The system periodically adjusts the difficulty of the hashing problems, so a valid solution is generated roughly once every ten minutes.[30] As a result, improvements in computing technology or significant increases in mining hardware investment do not break the system.

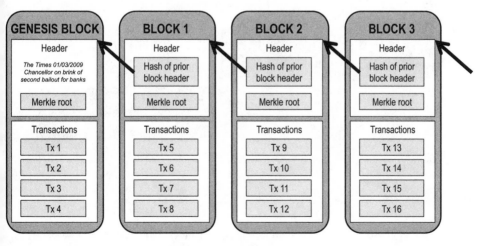

Figure 2.3
A simplified structure of a Bitcoin blockchain.

Nakamoto Consensus affirms the integrity of both each individual transaction and the ledger as a whole. It does so by aggregating transactions into blocks, which are organized using the Merkle tree structure illustrated in figure 0.3 in the Introduction of this book.[31] Each validated block is cryptographically signed with the hash of the prior block, and this creates a secure chain of sequential blocks, which every node checks independently when a new one is added.

Sometimes two nodes propose different chains, either because they solve hashing problems almost simultaneously or because someone is attempting to cheat. In that situation, the longest chain represents the consensus state of the system.[32] Assuming all goes as designed, only an attacker with a majority of total computing power in the entire network (known as a "51-percent attack") can "fork" the longest chain with a fraudulent block (see figure 2.4).[33] Because nodes revalidate the blockchain each time, changing a prior block becomes increasingly difficult as new blocks are added after it.

A public blockchain such as that of Bitcoin broadcasts all transactions across the network and is totally transparent.[34] Every full node on the

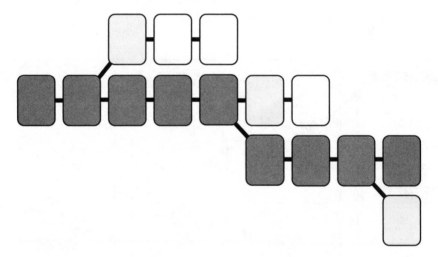

Figure 2.4
A stylized illustration of blockchain forks. The dark blocks represent the consensus blockchain; the lighter blocks are potential forks rejected by the consensus.

network maintains a copy of the entire transaction history all the way back to the genesis block, now over 100 gigabytes in size.[35] Today, individual users generally do not serve as miners because industrial-strength processing power is required. Individuals generally connect through wallet services or light clients rather than operating a full node, which requires some technical sophistication.[36]

Not only are the contents of the Bitcoin blockchain available to all, but the software involved is open source and freely available.[37] Bitcoin is designed to be resistant to both censorship and tampering. There is no central control point that a government could manipulate or block, and once a transaction is recorded, it cannot be changed easily. User A could send some bitcoin to user B, and then user B could send some or all of it back, but there is no easy way for user A, the miners, or anyone else to reverse the initial transfer.[38] Attempted tampering with the ledger is easy to identify by looking at the public blockchain record.

The final key piece of Nakamoto Consensus is the game-theoretic or psychological dimension: Why will miners bother? Proof of work is expensive, literally: It requires expensive computing hardware, and even more expensive electricity at scale. Altruism will not be enough to incentivize miners to perform validation of blocks.

Here was Satoshi Nakamoto's brilliant inversion. The miner that successfully validates a block receives a reward in a valuable currency: bitcoin. That is, in fact, the only way that more bitcoin is created. This solves several problems, including how currency can enter the money supply without a central bank. New bitcoin enters the world through the block reward mechanism, at a rate that declines over time.[39] Since mid-2016, the reward has been 12.5 bitcoin; it will be cut in half automatically again around 2020. Miners thus act purely out of self-interest, but in doing so, they fulfill a socially beneficial role. In Satoshi's design, as the block reward decreases automatically over time, voluntary fees from those sending transactions gradually replace it.

Because bitcoin is both the output and input of the system, one could equally well describe the Bitcoin network as a trust infrastructure designed to support a digital currency and as a digital currency designed to support a trust infrastructure. Mining secures the network. The more money that miners spend to win block rewards and transaction fees, the more costly it would be for a malicious agent to overwhelm them and break the network. The term "cryptoeconomics" describes this novel enforcement mechanism, which combines cryptographic security and economic incentives.[40]

The Significance of Cryptocurrency

What we consider to be money says a great deal about the construction of our society. As the British economist Herbert Frankel wrote in his book *Two Philosophies of Money*:

> The trust in money—i.e., in who does the defining—therefore implies trust in the maintenance of the monetary order. This is not a question merely of how particular individual rights, debts, or obligations are dealt with. What is at issue here is a much more basic question: How can a trustworthy society, with stability of character be maintained and continue to be relied upon?[41]

The initial interest in Bitcoin focused on its status as a global, private, digital currency. Currency transactions are heavily regulated.[42] Bitcoin raised the tantalizing prospect (for some) of money neither issued nor controlled by any government. It could allow more efficient cross-border payments and financial assets that corrupt governments could not seize. It might even be a means to democratize and improve efficiency of the global financial system. There is, in theory, no need for the thicket of financial intermediaries when transacting in bitcoin. All transactions are reflected in the consensus state of the system.

On the other hand, a currency not issued or regulated by governments could be a haven for lawlessness, consumer abuse, and financial speculation.[43] For some time, Bitcoin had a somewhat unsavory reputation. As noted earlier in this chapter, one obvious use for a global currency outside the control of governments and the banking system is illicit activity. In addition, because the Bitcoin network is based around private cryptographic keys that do not require any proof of real-world identity, it can evade anti–money laundering (AML) controls and Know Your Customer (KYC) regulations designed to prevent terrorism financing and enforce sanctions.

The bitcoin-based marketplace Silk Road, used primarily for transactions involving drugs and other contraband, was the most spectacular example.[44] It was eventually shut down by the Federal Bureau of Investigation (FBI), and its creator, Ross Ulbricht, was sentenced to life in prison (he is currently in a federal prison in Colorado). However, during its three years of operation,

Silk Road processed sales worth 9.5 million bitcoin.[45] To get an idea of how big that number is, there were less than 12 million total bitcoin in circulation at the time. Another service, Satoshi Dice, processed 1.8 million bitcoin in 2012 for an online gambling game that was illegal in many jurisdictions.[46] For the first few years, therefore, the taint of illegality around Bitcoin was not unjustified.

Just because a decentralized currency may empower bad actors, however, does not mean that it will. Despite significant price fluctuations, users continue to show faith in bitcoin as a currency, and it is accepted at legitimate businesses such as Overstock.com and Expedia. Trading activity around bitcoin and its derivatives is even more active. Regulators are developing rules to ensure that Bitcoin service providers take responsibility for their users. Developers are creating identity layers that can operate on top of Bitcoin and other blockchain-based systems for regulatory compliance.[47] In fact, they may actually prove to be an important mechanism to combat money laundering. A May 2016 Goldman Sachs report suggests that storing account and payment information on a blockchain could improve data quality and reduce compliance costs, saving $3 billion to $5 billion annually in AML expenses.[48]

Cryptocurrency enthusiasts envision digital tokens as being widely accepted for all sorts of financial payments by people around the world, as credit cards are. Others envision bitcoin dethroning gold as the preferred hedge against the uncertainties of government-issued currencies. One or both of those might still happen, but such possibilities are years away. There are very significant technical, operational, and regulatory barriers to any cryptocurrency achieving the status of traditional money or precious metals. Although a variety of businesses accept it, bitcoin has shown no sign of becoming the popular currency for consumer payments that many of its enthusiasts predicted.

Some find a currency that no government can censor or tamper with a world-changing innovation in itself. On discussion boards, boosters talk of "hyperbitcoinization," when the failure of a national currency leads to a rapid changeover to bitcoin as the primary medium of exchange in the global economy.[49] Most people, it is fair to say, are skeptical of such a scenario. For the foreseeable future, the value of cryptocurrencies will be pegged to fiat currencies.[50]

There are some edge cases today where a cryptocurrency would seem more appealing than government-issued money. For instance, Zimbabwe switched to the U.S. dollar in 2008 following hyperinflation of its currency, but with dollars scarce, a growing number of citizens and businesses are turning to bitcoin.[51] Latin American countries facing hyperinflation, such as Argentina and Venezuela, have seen some of the most active adoption of bitcoin for payments.[52] The left-wing Syriza coalition in Greece, under pressure to adopt severe austerity measures in 2015, seriously considered abandoning the euro as its currency and switching to bitcoin.[53] In such countries, though, the very chaos and corruption that undermines the traditional currency make it difficult to coordinate widespread popular adoption of a decentralized cryptocurrency alternative.

Countries with well-functioning central banks are looking at tokenizing their currencies to improve liquidity and visibility.[54] Singapore has already experimented with a shadow version of the Singapore dollar, creating a prototype for recording payment transactions between banks on a distributed ledger.[55] Christine Lagarde, managing director of the International Monetary Fund (IMF), acknowledges that:

> [C]itizens may one day prefer virtual currencies, since they potentially offer the same cost and convenience as cash—no settlement risks, no clearing delays, no central registration, no intermediary to check accounts and identities. If privately issued virtual currencies remain risky and unstable, citizens may even call on central banks to provide digital forms of legal tender.[56]

Tokenization could be an important development, in some ways similar to the great shift from the gold standard in the last century. It would have far-reaching consequences, both positive and negative. The Bank of England, for example, has expressed concern that a central bank digital currency would quickly shift deposits from commercial banks, depriving them of capital and potentially paralyzing the financial system.[57]

These efforts primarily involve governments issuing their own cryptocurrencies with mechanisms for identity verification, not using a decentralized, private, semi-anonymous system such as Bitcoin. Ironically, the countries moving fastest to develop central bank digital currencies are more authoritarian ones, which see benefits in having universal surveillance over a common ledger.[58] A traceable cryptocurrency replacing cash would actually be a step backward in terms of anonymity of financial transactions.

Whether one views Bitcoin as an irrevocable move toward the elimination of fiat currencies, the early days of an alternative private global financial system, an interesting but essentially failed digital cash effort, a dangerous threat, a fraud, or something else depends largely on prior convictions. Bitcoin is real, but its ultimate impact remains quite uncertain. Nonetheless, the domain of money is so vast that Bitcoin need not occupy a large portion of the field to have significant global implications. And Bitcoin's impact pales in comparison to the larger revolution that Satoshi Nakamoto's paper unleashed. If money issued by a decentralized network can be trustworthy, so can anything else that such a network might manage. The next chapter explores this potential.

3   More than Money

It All Started When They Nerfed the Siphon Life Spell

World of Warcraft is among the most successful video games of all time, with over 12 million paying players at its peak. In 2010, as part of its regular fine-tuning of the game, the developer weakened a popular attack for the warlock class. It proved to be a fateful decision. Vitalik Buterin, a brilliant Canadian high school student, was among the hardcore players disgusted by the move. Viewing it as an example of the "horrors centralized services can bring,"[1] he quit the game and cast about for something else to spend his time on. He found Bitcoin. Although he was quickly hooked, Buterin thought digital currency was too limiting. As he recalled, "I went around the world, explored many crypto projects, and finally realized that they were all too concerned about specific applications and not being sufficiently general."[2] So at age 19, he resolved to finish the revolution that Satoshi Nakamoto began.

Buterin may well have succeeded. Ethereum, the project he initiated, became the most prominent manifestation of the blockchain's second act. This new stage would put the strange, outsider technology on the front pages of major newspapers and make it a prominent topic for captains of industry, titans of finance, and leaders of government. It would raise the stakes considerably, in both positive and negative ways. A cryptocurrency that can be used to buy a pizza, as bitcoin was in 2010, is an impressive achievement, but distributed ledgers that support multibillion dollar (or perhaps someday multitrillion dollar) global business ecosystems are something else entirely.

Bitcoin kicked off the blockchain era as a historical matter. However, it represents just one corner of the relevant conceptual space. The common term encompassing the larger family of approaches is "distributed ledger."[3]

Bitcoin can be understood as the first widely adopted distributed ledger system. You may believe that you sent me five bitcoin out of the twenty you originally held, but how do I keep track? And how do I know that is really bitcoin, and that you obtained it from a legitimate transaction? Transferring valuable assets requires an agreed-upon recording mechanism. Viewing Bitcoin and its progeny in this way helps to clarify why their potential is so much greater than digital cash.

A ledger is a record of accounts. Perhaps the most familiar ledgers are those used for double-entry bookkeeping, the foundation of accounting. However, ledgers are not limited to recording debits and credits for corporate balance sheets. Real estate markets could not exist without land title registries. Democracy requires ledgers for tallying votes. Copyright depends on both public and private records tracking the registration and assignment of rights. The modern firm depends on ledgers not just for its financials, but for the relationships among its internal agents and external partners, as well as its supply-chain, back-office, and customer-facing activities. Influential sociologists such as Max Weber and Werner Sombart argued that double-entry bookkeeping was the foundation of modern capitalism. In Weber's words, "the most general presupposition for the existence of this present-day capitalism is that of rational capital accounting. ..."[4]

Ledgers comprise the foundational infrastructure for keeping track of things. By establishing a reliable record of ownership and asset flows, they strengthen property rights. They also allow such rights to be subdivided and transacted around, through increasingly complex contractual agreements. Standards such as Generally Accepted Accounting Principles (GAAP) can be adopted on top of the ledgers, and then auditing/reporting requirements, internal controls, and more can be further layered on top. As record-keeping migrated from paper records to stand-alone computers to digital networks, the scope of ledgers increased. In the modern world, with massive numbers of financial transactions and equally massive movement of other assets around the world, ledgers are more important than ever.

Blockchain systems are networks of ledgers. The start-up Ripple was apparently the first to use "Internet of Value" for this larger phenomenon.[5] It captures the idea that just as the Internet linked networks for the exchange of information, blockchain will exchange valuable assets. Money is just the first such asset. A diamond necklace, shares of stock, a trademark, and tickets to a concert are assets with value. And in today's world, data has value as well.

Google built one of the world's most profitable companies on its ability to collect, analyze, and leverage data into valuable services. Distributed ledgers hold out the possibility of similarly powerful data aggregation, but without the downsides of centralized control.

Bitcoin, at least initially, was limited to a single function: cryptocurrency payment transactions. Ethereum represented a leap to dynamic ledgers that can, in theory, support any application that can be coded in software. In such an environment, moreover, platforms can be separate from applications. A spreadsheet is both a ledger and the software application implementing that ledger. A cloud computing platform such as Amazon Web Services, however, is distinct from applications and services that operate on top of it. In the same way, the Bitcoin network platform was originally indistinguishable from the bitcoin payment currency, but public blockchain networks are foundations for a range of decentralized applications (Dapps).

As far back as 2010, Satoshi Nakamoto and other Bitcoin developers speculated in online discussions about using blockchain technology in areas beyond digital cash.[6] Namecoin, the initial system based on those conversations, makes Internet domain name registration censorship resistant in the same way that Bitcoin does for payments. It launched in 2011 as the first fork of the Bitcoin codebase.[7] There are also ways to create new cryptocurrencies or more dynamic functionality while continuing to record information on the Bitcoin ledger. Bitcoin allows subdivisions down to one hundred-millionth of a coin (called a "Satoshi"). A worthless sliver of a coin can be tagged or "colored" to represent some other asset, even a full-fledged alternative coin.[8] There are also processes called "merge mining" and "pegged sidechains," under which a cryptocurrency network can piggyback onto Bitcoin's proof of work to validate its transactions.[9] All of these approaches, in effect, borrow the trust that Bitcoin's consensus network generates for new purposes.

As some teams sought to build on top of the Bitcoin ledger, others envisioned new cryptocurrency systems created from scratch. These "Bitcoin 2.0" networks generally diverged from Bitcoin's two design goals: They addressed something other than payments, they relaxed the requirement that no third parties be trusted, or both. Ripple launched in 2012. It kept Bitcoin's focus on payments, but it incorporated a limited number of trusted validation nodes to serve regulated banks interested in more efficiently moving money across borders. The general-purpose Ethereum network became operational in 2015.[10] Other cryptocurrency platforms are pushing on different dimensions. For example, Monero, Dash, and ZCash offer cryptocurrencies with stronger anonymity protection than Bitcoin. And both NEO and Qtum are positioning themselves as the "blockchain of Asia," taking advantage of the strong interest in cryptocurrencies in that part of the world.

Today, there are a few dozen other public blockchain networks in operation. And that is just the tip of the iceberg. As of late 2017, there were more than 80,000 blockchain-oriented projects on the open-source software repository Github.[11] One site listed more than 1,500 cryptocurrency tokens available as of April 2018, mostly running on top of Ethereum or other foundational consensus platforms.[12] These tokens serve a wide variety of functions. For example, the Basic Attention Token (BAT) issued by the start-up Brave is used to compensate users for viewing targeted advertisements. The Filecoin token associated with Inter Planetary File System (IPFS) compensates those who share hard drive space for distributed cloud storage. Numerai compensates data scientists who propose successful algorithms that it can put to work through its hedge fund. Earn.com is a social network that pays users in tokens for completing tasks such as responding to emails or filling out surveys.[13]

So-called Bitcoin maximalists argue that Bitcoin's strong security—due to its extended history and greater processing power devoted to mining—will make it the best platform for all cryptocurrency-based activities. They see investment in other platforms as a distraction. An opposing faction views Bitcoin as the proof of concept for cryptocurrencies or distributed ledger technologies, which will soon be left behind as other platforms surpass its functionality.

One of the key issues is scalability. As activity has increased, throughput on the Bitcoin network has slowed. Those wishing to put through transactions have been forced to attach substantial fees to incentivize miners to process them quickly. In Satoshi Nakamoto's original design, transaction fees would ramp up only once the Bitcoin block reward dwindled, and yet in 2017, they often spiked to $10 or more per transaction. This made small-value payments uneconomical, killing the original core use for the currency. There are a number of scaling proposals for Bitcoin, including solutions to handle most transactions off the blockchain while continuing to rely on the consensus process for security. The open question is whether retrofitting Bitcoin makes more sense than switching to a network with better scalability designed into it from the beginning.

There is also the matter of Bitcoin's proof-of-work system. All that processing power is costly and deliberately wasteful. As the price of bitcoin increases, miners are willing to spend more and more to chase the block rewards. The immense power requirements make Bitcoin a growing contributor to energy demand, and thus carbon emissions. As the price of bitcoin spiked in 2017, it was estimated that each transaction burned enough energy to power an American home for a week.[14] One analyst suggested that by 2020, the Bitcoin network could consume as much electricity as the nation of Denmark.[15] In an era of climate change, this is a serious issue. And, as will be discussed in chapter 6, mining has largely consolidated into a small number of powerful pools, creating a variety of concerns.

The leading contender as an alternative consensus approach for public blockchain networks is proof of stake (POS). Instead of mining, holders of a POS cryptocurrency compete to validate transactions by staking some of their holdings. If the majority of the network rejects their block, the staked currency is "slashed" and destroyed. If the block validation succeeds, the validator earns a reward. POS mimics the cost/benefit trade-off of mining, without all the processing. Instead of proving their commitment by dedicating expensive computing power, those who wish to validate blocks put resources at risk of slashing. POS thus relies on game-theoretic incentives to promote compliant behavior.

Some blockchain networks already operate on POS. Most notably, Ethereum has committed to shift over time to a POS solution called Casper. Other blockchain systems such as Steem.it and EOS use a variant called delegated proof of stake, in which token holders vote for representatives who validate blocks. POS does not yet have proof of work's track record of operating securely at scale. And there are worries that it will advantage large holders of the cryptocurrencies, furthering consolidation of power and concerns that the system can be gamed. As with any economic system, behavior in the real world with many participants and significant sums involved will likely be different than on paper.

With the upsurge of interest in blockchain technology and cryptocurrencies, developers are exploring a number of other consensus approaches. Dfinity and Algorand, for example, use novel cryptography to select groups of validators randomly for each block, without Bitcoin's cumbersome mining process or risky staking. Hashgraph is based on a "gossip" protocol where transaction information, and votes about its accuracy, propagate across nodes in the network. Chia replaces proof of work's expensive computation with proof of available hard drive space. IOTA, a distributed Internet of Things (IoT) system for controlling network-connected devices, does away with the blockchain data structure entirely in favor of what it calls a "tangle," which arguably works better for a huge number of nodes with limited computing power.[16]

These and other techniques promise greatly improved performance and security compared to more-established solutions. Several have impressive technical backing, such as Algorand's Silvio Micali, a prominent MIT cryptographer, and Chia's Bram Cohen, who created the widely-used BitTorrent file-sharing protocol. Despite their variety, all these approaches are recognizable descendants of Bitcoin. They produce a trustworthy common truth in a network with no central control or intermediation.

None of the newer systems yet has the real-world validation and developer traction of Bitcoin and Ethereum. However, it is too early to reach definitive conclusions about which approaches will prevail. Periods of intensive experimentation inevitably produce wrong turns and dead ends along with breakthrough innovations. The most notable fact is the sophistication and diversity of innovation around blockchain-related consensus technologies. Even more striking, this burst of activity is not limited to start-ups. It has grown to include some of the world's most powerful companies.

Permissioned Ledgers

In theory, anyone can operate a full node on the Bitcoin network, mine cryptocurrency, and verify transactions. There is no way to tell on the network itself if a participant is a Fortune 500 company or a wanted international criminal.[17] No government can censor the contents of the Bitcoin blockchain because it is distributed among many computers around the world running open-source software. It would keep running even if most of them were taken offline. No private actor can force the network to move in a certain direction except in the unlikely event that it controls a majority of mining power. Everyone has the same access to the network and the same full visibility into prior transactions.

This decentralization comes at a cost. One type of cost relates to performance. Broadcasting all transactions to all network nodes creates a huge amount of overhead compared to traditional databases. Another relates to usage. For certain applications and participants, completely open access and full visibility are nonstarters. In regulated industries, for example, there may be legal requirements to know the identity of counterparties. There may also be regulatory or contractual requirements to keep the details of certain transactions confidential. And in Europe, the General Data Protection Regulation (GDPR) mandates a right to be forgotten for personal data, which obligates data processors to erase certain information upon request.[18] This, as well as the whole GDPR framework of information rights, will be difficult to square with the irreversible transaction ledgers of public blockchain networks.[19]

These costs might be worth it to achieve strong censorship resistance and cryptoeconomic security, at least for some use cases. And they are likely to drop over time with the appearance of new technologies to improve the performance of blockchain networks. Large classes of potential distributed ledger users, however, are more than willing to trade a limited degree of decentralization for efficiency.

Bitcoin rekindled interest in Byzantine Fault-Tolerant (BFT) algorithms other than proof of work. This led to the development of a new class of distributed ledgers. They are still decentralized, in that no entity controls the network. However, only those verified actors with permission from a coordinating body can validate transactions, propose new ones, or in some cases even view the ledger. Hyperledger executive director Brian Behlendorf calls this concept "minimum viable centralization."[20] The primary adopters of this approach to blockchain are major corporations around the world. The major software and services firms for those enterprises, such as IBM, Microsoft, PWC, Oracle, and HPE, have also jumped on the bandwagon.

Many of the things that enterprises would like to do with distributed ledger systems involve relatively small networks of identified players. A group of advertisers and publishers seeking to reduce online advertising fraud, for example, probably does not need a way for completely anonymous parties to participate. In such consortium settings, many of the benefits of blockchain-based systems can be achieved through other distributed ledger structures that allow only those with permission to access the network.[21] These are referred to as "permissioned," "private," or "consortium" ledgers.

The leading two organizations pushing the development of permissioned networks are Hyperledger and R3.[22] Hyperledger manages a suite of distributed ledger packages offering different functionalities, most notably Hyperledger Fabric, based on initial work by IBM. Its solutions are designed to be modular. A permissioned network could plug in Hyperledger Burrow's smart-contract execution engine or Hyperledger Indy's user-controlled identity module, or use some other solution. They can also swap out different consensus mechanisms depending on their needs.

Hyperledger is a project of the nonprofit Linux Foundation, which works to standardize open-source technologies and create connections between enterprises and developers. Behlendorf, its leader, is a noted Internet and open-source technologist who created Apache, the leading web server software, before working with the Obama White House, the World Economic Forum, and Paypal cofounder Peter Thiel's venture capital firm.

R3 is a for-profit firm that operates a consortium of more than eighty major enterprises, including many prominent financial services companies.[23] R3's Corda platform uses distributed ledger technology to manage agreements between financial institutions, involving cash, securities, or derivatives. As R3's Richard Gendal Brown explained in a blog post:

> The financial industry is pretty much defined by the agreements that exist between its firms and these firms share a common problem: the agreement is typically recorded by both parties, in different systems, and very large amounts of cost are caused by the need to fix things when these different systems end up believing different things.[24]

Corda employs a distributed ledger to maintain a shared record of the web of financial agreements among banks. Because it is designed to supplement the current legal structure, only identified institutions can participate in the network. The data structure for recording transactions is a standard relational database rather than a blockchain, and the consensus system is based on a more conventional BFT algorithm. The system can explicitly invite regulators, who can operate what Corda terms "supervisory observer nodes" with access to real-time information about transactions, into the process.

Permissioned networks such as Corda and Hyperledger Fabric generally do not need proof of work because they maintain a residual level of trust in the identity of network participants. This allows them to avoid the costly and capacity-limiting mining process. How much of a benefit this is depends on whether the permissioned ledgers can maintain sufficient security and censorship resistance, and whether the difficulties associated with proof of work are alleviated over time through technical advances. These projects also do not require a dedicated cryptocurrency token because their purpose is purely to support distributed ledger applications. Ripple combines a permissioned network with a currency, XRP, that can be traded but is not created through public mining.

There is something of a religious war between proponents of public and permissioned ledgers. Advocates of public networks such as Bitcoin and Ethereum argue that permissioned networks are essentially just databases. So long as someone must be trusted, argues Union Square Ventures partner Albert Wenger, you are basically part of the status quo.[25] A distributed ledger might offer some incremental performance improvements, but it will not change the structure of industries or open the door for dramatic innovation. In fact, the argument goes that because the consortium controls access, permissioned ledgers could actually reinforce the power of incumbents. Some on the public network side of the argument say that permissioned networks should not even be part of the same conversation. At a minimum, they should not be lazily labeled blockchains when, as in the case of R3, they do not even store data in sequential chains of blocks.

On the other side, permissioned network advocates say that there is a world of difference between traditional database technology and distributed ledgers. Databases generally assume that all nodes will be run by a trusted actor—usually within the same company. Normal databases can be distributed and synchronized across multiple machines. However, those synchronization algorithms are designed to guard against machines crashing, not machines going rogue and trying to undermine the network.[26]

Distributed ledgers, by contrast, assume that nodes are operated by independent parties who do not trust one another and could be actively hostile adversaries. Antony Lewis, the Singapore-based director of research at R3, describes this as the difference between shared data and shared control.[27] Traditional databases share data. Once that happens, however, those that share lose control to whatever organization operates the database. The operator always has the technical ability to access or change information. Distributed ledgers, on the other hand, share control. Each party maintains control over its own data, even if others can see and use it under specified terms. There is no other entity who can override that control.

It is not so much that theoretically, no traditional database could store the information residing on permissioned ledgers. No actual database ever would. Bruce Pon, chief executive officer (CEO) of the blockchain-oriented database start-up BigChainDB, describes an example application from the automotive industry.[28] A major supplier such as Bosch has a database of all the parts it offers. It will not cede control of that data. If car manufacturers, distributors, and others want access, they must build to Bosch's application programming interfaces and pull data into their own databases. Each of them must repeat the process for every supplier. If there are inconsistencies in the data between systems, they must be resolved.

With a distributed ledger, on the other hand, everyone in the network could share one immutable set of records. Changes are manifested simultaneously everywhere. Yet participants still control their own data. So if Bosch wished to update information about some of its parts on a distributed ledger, it could do so directly. It would not have to rely on the performance of a third-party operator, or accept a manufacturer's inventory records as correct.

Permissioned-ledger solutions such as R3 and Hyperledger Fabric are designed to support shared ledgers across organizations, even when those organizations are competitors. They generally provide granular controls on who can see and manage information on the ledger, which has a side benefit of improving performance by eliminating the need to broadcast everything to all nodes. And, in most cases, they are built on BFT algorithms based on years of academic research. The permissioned-ledger community argues that its solutions are as secure as those that a public proof-of-work network offers, if not more so.

The choice between public and permissioned ledgers largely comes down to the problem that one is trying to solve, as well as the constraints on the solution. Adam Ludwin, the CEO of Chain, which makes blockchain technology solutions for financial service providers, says that the value of a fully distributed solution, which generally means a public network, depends on "how much a given user group NEEDS censorship resistance in a given market."[29] Bitcoin needed it because freedom from government limitations on money is its reason for existence. In other contexts, there may be different reasons why a distributed approach is needed or desirable.

Permissioned networks were a big factor in the rise of enterprise and government engagement with distributed ledger technology during 2016 and 2017. That helped to validate the legitimacy of the blockchain concept, which no doubt played a role in the huge run-up in public cryptocurrency prices. And the two approaches may be converging. JPMorgan's Quorum system, for example, is a fork of the Ethereum software with privacy and permissioned access added on.[30] Bitfury's Exonum is a permissioned blockchain that periodically anchors transactions to the public Bitcoin ledger.

The Enterprise Ethereum Alliance is working to making Ethereum suitable for enterprise use cases. Coming from the other direction, Hyperledger Fabric can plug in different consensus mechanisms, so it could operate on top of a public blockchain network in the future.

"Over time the public network wins. Cloud computing is the proof of that," predicts serial technology entrepreneur and Circle Internet Financial CEO Jeremy Allaire.[31] Allaire's first company created Cold Fusion, the application server technology that powered the original wave of dynamic applications on the web. He sees distributed ledger technology following a similar evolutionary path as the Internet. Major corporations and governments initially stuck to private intranets and local data storage until the security on public networks improved sufficiently. He continues: "The benefit of public blockchains is the security, because there is an underlying incentive system. Fiduciary trust applications will gravitate to the most secure infrastructure. And the most secure infrastructure will be public blockchains."

Many thoughtful observers see a similar convergence. When the price of bitcoin fell in 2014–2016, interest shifted away from cryptocurrencies and toward permissioned networks. The subsequent spike in cryptocurrency prices and high-profile, innovative, network-centric applications based on cryptocurrency tokens swung the pendulum the other way. It will not be the last shift. As the separate communities mature, they will learn from each other, and users will drive them to find the best of both worlds. However, this transition will take time. The development of governance systems, discussed in chapter 7, will be an important factor.

Smart Contracts

For the next piece of the story, we return to the former World of Warcraft player described at the beginning of this chapter. In 2013, Vitalik Buterin dropped out of college. Armed with a $100,000 Thiel Fellowship, he set about to create what became the Ethereum project. Ethereum, and other systems like it, opened up the full scope of the blockchain opportunity. They did so by further developing a mechanism known as a "smart contract."

Distributed ledgers are active, not passive. In other words, the ledgers do not simply record information passed to them. They are part of a consensus system, so they must ensure that recorded transactions are actually completed to match the consensus.[32] For Bitcoin, that means that the system self-enforces financial transfers.[33] I cannot initiate a transaction promising to send you bitcoin and then renege; the synchronization that reconciles and completes the transfer is part of the process. This is the smart-contract functionality. Both the specification of rights and obligations and the execution of that contractual agreement occur through the platform. That is very different from traditional financial transactions, where clearing and settlement are distinct processes from the agreement itself, and disputes go through the court system.

Smart contracts turn a distributed ledger into a distributed computer. One way to understand Satoshi Nakamoto's innovation was that he solved the problem of decentralized time-stamping. To trust that a coin was not spent twice, there must be a reliable way to track exactly when each transaction happened. On a decentralized network, however, there is no master clock to which every machine can synchronize. That would be a trusted third party![34] And even without one, nodes would need to trust the time stamps that other nodes reported.

The proof-of-work system imposes consensus on the precise order of transactions. Nodes are agreeing not just on what happened, but in what sequence it happened. The same consensus algorithms that allow each node to have an identical copy of the ledger, therefore, allow it to perform identical computations, in the same order. That provides what computer scientists call "shared state": a picture of the status of the system at any moment.

According to Adam Krellenstein, cofounder of the smart-contract startups Symbiont and Counterparty, blockchain networks are the first real-world systems to achieve shared state without any trusted central authority.[35] That opens up a world of possibilities. Now distributed ledgers are a way to do virtually anything that computers can do, but in a decentralized manner. Smart contracts function as software programs that execute on a blockchain.[36]

Nick Szabo developed the idea of smart contracts in the 1990s, well before Bitcoin existed.[37] His illustration was the humble vending machine. A vending machine fully executes a contractual agreement by taking in money and dispensing products. It also provides sufficient security to make breaching the contract—breaking into the machine—unprofitable. For all practical purposes, the machine is the entirety of the contractual environment. It needs no human intervention, either to perform the contract or to resolve disputes in court.

Until Bitcoin, there were few practical applications of these ideas. Vending machines work as proto-smart contracts because they sell items of low value, operate face to face, and take cash[38] (a bearer instrument). Distributed ledgers made it possible to implement similar arrangements digitally, across networks, for any kind of asset or agreement, without any trusted actor. For example, insurance agreements, mortgages, wills, and software licenses are all transactions that today require human intermediation, but could conceivably be automated through smart contracts. Even after Bitcoin gained strength, though, it took several years for robust smart-contract platforms to be introduced.

The Bitcoin protocol was designed explicitly for a currency, so it only needed the functionality necessary to support financial transactions. Adding richer programming capabilities to blockchain transactions adds security risks and various other complexities. The more you can do with a software-based system, the more opportunities for bugs, exploits, and hacks. Bitcoin also lacks a representation of shared state in the form of accounts, which specify cryptocurrency holdings at any moment. Instead, it uses a format called "unspent transaction output (UTXO)." The bitcoin associated with a private key need to be totaled up each time from previous sending and receiving transactions. UTXO is technically simpler for digital cash, but it makes it harder to operate general-purpose smart contracts.

Overcoming these limitations was the goal of Ethereum, the most prominent smart-contract platform.[39] Ethereum offers a Turing-complete programming language, meaning that in theory, any application that runs on a conventional computer can be executed on the distributed ledger through its consensus network.[40] Ethereum is designed as a complete smart-contract platform, including development tools. It makes it relatively easy to code new kinds of applications on top, just as the web and various software tools such as application servers were the foundation for Google, Amazon, and eBay.

How exactly smart contract technology will be adopted is an open question. Szabo's 1997 paper, for example, envisioned a smart car lease. If the driver failed to make monthly payments, the car would automatically be rendered inoperable and control of the keys reverted to the bank. The same thing would occur at the end of the lease term, unless the agreement was a lease to purchase, in which case the bank's access would shut off upon full payment. Such a system would be designed to smooth enforcement of a familiar category of agreement. As will be discussed in chapter 6, though, it might also cause new problems when the automated enforcement goes too far.

Smart contracts can also enable entirely new kinds of arrangements. Perhaps the most successful early example of an application built on Ethereum is CryptoKitties, a game that launched in late 2017 and quickly became one of the biggest sources of traffic on the network.[41] The application generates unique digital collectibles in the form of cartoon kittens. The kittens, each of which is actually a cryptocurrency token executing smart contracts, can be bred with each other to randomly create novel offspring. Some of these are quite rare. At least one sold to a collector for over $100,000 in cryptocurrency. Although CryptoKitties is likely a short-lived fad, it suggests the diversity of uses for smart contracts. Digital assets that cannot be duplicated but can be sold and transformed could have serious applications in finance and other business domains.

Buterin's idea of a general-purpose computing platform on the same foundations as Bitcoin attracted significant excitement almost immediately after the Ethereum whitepaper was released in late 2013. Development began in 2014 and was eventually formalized under a Swiss foundation. Ethereum used the then-novel approach, now known as an initial coin offering, of selling pre-operational tokens to raise funding.

Today, there are networks of Ethereum developers around the world. Consensys, a Brooklyn, New York–based software development studio led by Ethereum cofounder Joe Lubin, is incubating dozens of Ethereum-based projects, several of which have already spun out as independent companies. And more than two hundred organizations, including Microsoft, JPMorgan, the government of India, Intel, Cisco, and Mastercard, are members of the Enterprise Ethereum Alliance, a group formed to promote Ethereum adoption among established businesses.[42]

Ethereum has its own native cryptocurrency, called "ether." It is now the second most valuable, after bitcoin. However, ether's primary purpose is not to serve as an investment vehicle or payment mechanism. It is the only way to purchase an internal, nontradable resource in the Ethereum system, called "gas." Gas buys processing cycles on the Ethereum network. A more complicated smart contract, requiring more computation, costs more gas. And there is a hard limit on the amount of gas that any Ethereum smart contract can expend.

Ethereum took this approach for two reasons. First, computation is costly. In the Ethereum network, as a public blockchain system, every verification node processes each smart contract.[43] The system is difficult to scale, especially if smart-contract developers are not parsimonious in their use of computation. It would quickly clog up if anyone could launch thousands of smart contracts with no cost. Second, smart contracts are programs.

They may have bugs or inefficiencies that eat up more computation than expected. Programmers can easily create infinite loops. A fundamental limit of a Turing-complete system such as Ethereum is something known as the "halting problem": It is formally impossible to determine ahead of time whether an arbitrary program will ever complete or run indefinitely. Without a gas charge and a gas limit, a smart-contract system such as Ethereum would quickly be overwhelmed.

Other smart-contract systems have similar mechanisms to prevent runaway programs, even if they do not sell gas for a native token. Although smart contracts are most prominently associated with Ethereum, they are a feature of most major blockchain networks under development, including the permissioned-ledger systems. There is also a project called Rootstock to jerry-rig full-fledged smart-contract functionality onto the Bitcoin network.[44]

Smart contracts are the engines that allow blockchain-based systems to support more than digital cash. They also reveal the full significance of the blockchain as an architecture of trust, for good or ill. If this were not obvious before, it became clear during what one account described as "arguably the most philosophically interesting event to take place in your lifetime or mine."[45]

The DAO Saga

Over the course of a few weeks in mid-2016, some 11,000 individuals worldwide committed cryptocurrency worth roughly $150 million to a virtual company with no employees, no management, and no legal existence. It was hailed as, "[a] new paradigm of economic cooperation ... a digital democratization of business."[46] Smart contracts, running on a blockchain platform, took the place of law, intermediaries, and personal relationships as the foundation for trust.

And then all hell broke loose.

By the time the scary saga reached its conclusion, the Ethereum network was forced to break immutability—one of the central elements of blockchain trust—in order to recover tens of millions of dollars from a thief, and potentially to save its own reputation. The implications are still being debated.

It all started when a group of Ethereum developers from a German startup, Slock.it, created a distributed crowdfunding system called The DAO.[47] It was designed to implement the concept of a decentralized autonomous organization (what the acronym DAO stands for), in which corporate governance and operations were conducted automatically through smart contracts. Users pledged ether in return for tokens that gave them the authority to vote on projects to be funded. Organizations seeking funding would sign up through another interface and receive ether if they received sufficient votes. Despite the novelty of the arrangement, users quickly pledged roughly 15 percent of the total supply of ether to the project.[48]

Amid the excitement, something went horribly wrong. Within weeks of the launch, a hacker took advantage of a bug in The DAO's code to siphon off more than a third of the ether.[49] Although clearly an attempt at theft, the hack was executed through a series of smart contracts that were formally valid within the system's rules. From the perspective of the smart-contracting system, the transactions were perfectly legitimate. Thus, even though the stolen funds were temporarily quarantined in an account, not immediately disbursed, there was no legal or technical way to recover them without undermining the entire system. Even if a court ordered the funds returned, there was no one to carry out that order.

There was a period of chaos as the Ethereum community struggled to respond, with several false starts. Ultimately, Buterin and the leaders of the Ethereum project had to convince a majority of nodes to implement a hard fork, which split the entire Ethereum blockchain. Only through this dramatic step, which effectively destroyed The DAO and weakened confidence in the Ethereum platform, could the stolen funds be returned.[50]

A hard fork creates two incompatible chains.[51] The Ethereum Foundation, which maintains the open-source code for the platform, provided a software update to miners. For those running the new software, the DAO hack never happened; their blockchains did not recognize the currency transfers. In all other respects, however, the blockchains were identical at the time of the fork. Other than the ether in question, the two blockchains showed the same users, with the same accounts.

Although most miners adopted the new software without incident, the move was not without controversy.[52] It meant that Ethereum transactions were not truly immune from centralized interference. It also raised concerns about what might happen when governments or other central authorities became concerned about records stored on distributed ledgers.[53] While the Bitcoin blockchain had executed hard forks in the past, those were technical fixes to double-spending bugs that undermined the integrity of the distributed ledger. The Ethereum hard fork retroactively invalidated otherwise valid transactions.

The assumption was that the prefork blockchain would wither away as miners abandoned it and ceased to engage in proof of work. That did not happen. A small group of miners kept running the old software, evidently dissatisfied with the Ethereum Foundation's willingness to break the ledger. A group of developers announced its intent to manage the software going forward, under the name "Ethereum Classic (ETC)."[54] And cryptocurrency exchanges began accepting ETC alongside the new post-DAO ether (ETH).

This odd situation created new security and double-spending risks. It also provoked reassessment of Ethereum's potential as the dominant blockchain-based application platform. And it left the Ethereum community wondering whether hard forks would be a recurring event when future glitches imperiled significant sums of cryptocurrency. Ethereum core developer Peter Szilagyi summarized the experience with profound understatement: "The DAO has shown us that it takes much more effort to write smart contracts than we originally anticipated. ..."[55]

It showed more than that. The DAO incident revealed quite starkly that a blockchain does not eliminate the need for trust. It can remove some of the trust dependencies of analogous systems, but when the going gets tough, something else must take their place. As explained in chapter 1, trust is confident vulnerability. A rational belief in the integrity of the network is just a part of that confidence.

The Ethereum community overcame the crisis with The DAO because Buterin and the Ethereum Foundation were able to marshal sufficient support for the hard fork. Most developers and miners, after a period of debate, agreed to go along. Other members of the community engaged in "white hat" (friendly hacking) operations to shield further funds from the attacker. Neither the network's software code nor the rational calculus of miner self-interest explains how Ethereum survived. It needed trust.

The benefits of distributed ledgers are real. Yet so are the dangers. More important, there is no shortcut that allows one to avoid those dangers. Trusted and trustworthy blockchains depend on messy efforts by communities of human beings, just like anything else of similar importance in society. The biggest mistake that one can make is not to dismiss blockchain technology as a fantasy or a fraud; rather, it is to embrace it too credulously. The triumph of the blockchain will require hard work to match potential with reality.

4   Why Blockchain?

Beyond the Whoppercoin

A fast food chain might be the last company one would envision as a leader in the emerging blockchain economy. It certainly was not what Satoshi Nakamoto had in mind when he created Bitcoin. Yet there was Burger King in the summer of 2017, announcing the launch of a cryptocurrency for its stores in Russia. Major media outlets such as the BBC, *Fortune,* and CNBC rushed to cover the news.[1] Customers could now earn virtual tokens, redeemable for food, with every hamburger they purchased. Ivan Shestov, head of external communications at Burger King Russia, described the so-called Whoppercoin in glowing terms: "Now [the] Whopper is not only [a] burger that people in 90 different countries love—it's an investment tool as well. According to the forecasts, cryptocurrency will increase exponentially in value. Eating Whoppers now is a strategy for financial prosperity tomorrow."[2]

The reality is less exciting. The Whoppercoin will not turn fast food consumption into the world's greatest investment opportunity, nor will it transform restaurants into virtual asset factories. Whoppercoin is just a loyalty program, of the sort companies like Burger King run all the time. There is little difference between Whoppercoins and the Monopoly Game cards annually offered at McDonalds, or airline frequent-flyer miles. The cryptocurrency angle is merely window dressing, to gain attention.

While the image of Whoppercoins increasing exponentially in value may be amusing and harmless, the blockchain hype that it epitomizes is not. If Whoppercoins, which provide no real differentiated value to customers or Burger King relative to conventional loyalty points, actually did appreciate substantially, it would be a dangerous sign of a speculative bubble.[3] Markets can decouple from economic reality for a time, but they always return to earth. And if helping people get rich eating burgers is a good application of the blockchain, is it really the world-transforming innovation that so many have predicted?

One can easily get caught up in the excitement about how the blockchain could "transform business, government, and society"[4] and is "pulling us into a new era of openness, decentralization, and global inclusion."[5] There are so many use-cases under development, from so many high-flying start-ups and major incumbent firms. The opportunities that the blockchain presents seem so powerful—and so disruptive. A torrent of popular press articles, whitepapers, and industry pronouncements assert that the blockchain is on the cusp of changing the way that companies and the global economy operate.

And perhaps it is. The potential of distributed-ledger technologies is almost too vast to contemplate. The blockchain appears to be what innovation scholars call a general-purpose technology (GPT), capable of influencing many sectors of the economy simultaneously.[6] Like earlier GPTs such as the steam engine, electricity, railroads, and the Internet, it may have many spillover effects beyond its direct applications.

Yet just because a technology could be revolutionary and has strong backing does not mean it will develop as promised. What seems just around the corner to early adopters may actually be a decade or two from maturity. In the words of the renowned futurist Paul Saffo, "never mistake a clear view for a short distance."[7] History is filled with hyped technological trends that never reached the promised level of adoption or fizzled into modest evolutionary improvements. For example, remember 3D television? Computer scientists in the 1960s were confident that general-purpose artificial intelligence was just a decade away, and David Chaum's Digicash promised ubiquitous digital micropayments in the early 1990s. There has been rapid development recently in both areas, but much later and in different ways than anticipated.

Whenever a hot new trend appears on the technology horizon—a surprisingly frequent phenomenon—companies flock to it, basking in the reflected glow. They generate press releases and Microsoft PowerPoint decks associating themselves with the meme du jour. It is a great way to get attention, look smart, and attract funding. Sometimes the new development really turns out to be transformative. Other times, it is just a fad. And often the trend is meaningful, but the companies' connection to it is weaker than it appears. There is already a term, "chainwashing," that refers to companies artificially associating themselves with the blockchain.[8]

With token-creation platforms such as Ethereum's ERC20 standard and Waves, Burger King's partner in the Whoppercoin venture, it is relatively simple for any company to issue a cryptocurrency. It is even easier to create a consortium, initiate a proof-of-concept project, or announce a start-up, none of which requires written software or significant financial commitments. Only a fraction of such initiatives will become real, thriving business ventures. The larger the firm involved, the more experiments it can launch with no real commitment to their success. It is critical not to confuse blockchain press releases with blockchain success stories.

The examples highlighted in this book are no exception. Five years from now, most of them may have ended or failed. For an entrepreneur or investor, of course, picking the winners matters a great deal. However, for those seeking to understand the market dynamics that will affect their own organization or influence public policy, what matters is the big picture. AltaVista, Friendster, and Pets.com failed, but searching, social networking, and e-commerce presented massive opportunities in the Internet economy.

Innovation is not just a synonym for new technology. As Wharton School professors Christian Terwiesch and Karl Ulrich explain, an innovation is a novel match between a need and a solution.[9] It requires both the push of new capabilities and the pull of market demand; either alone is insufficient. The discussion up to now has focused primarily on what the blockchain does. This chapter concentrates on what problems it solves. If distributed ledgers can address real and substantial needs in a superior way, they will eventually enjoy widespread adoption. If not, no amount of hype will mask the essential emptiness of the approach.

A blockchain is, in important ways, just an information-storage mechanism. Relational-database technology, the primary form of computer-based information storage and access, has been around since the 1970s. Techniques for distributing databases across many computers are also decades old, as are practical implementations of digital cash.

So, what needs does the blockchain address, either for the first time or in new ways? Anyone looking to adopt or invest in distributed ledger-based solutions needs to ask that question. The benefits of these systems come with significant costs, not least of which are their novelty and immaturity. If an existing technology can do the same thing, it is likely to be the better approach. Satoshi Nakamoto did not overcome the fundamental limits of computer science, nor of human nature. Curiosity and enthusiasm may be sufficient in the short term, but over the long run, distinctive advantages are what matter.

The Enduring Value of Intermediaries

The Cambrian Explosion of activity in the decade after Satoshi Nakamoto's whitepaper makes it difficult to separate hype from sustainable value creation. In particular, like the Internet, the blockchain is mistakenly viewed as the final answer to the problem of intermediation. Online services did undermine travel agents, newspapers, and other traditional informational intermediaries, but they also transformed them and interposed new platforms such as Google, Facebook, and Amazon. The blockchain's relationship to intermediaries is similarly more complex than it appears.

Many business plans for blockchain-based applications trumpet the elimination of intermediaries as their core advantage. Just as the insurance company Geico realized that it could cut prices by 15 percent by eliminating independent agents' commissions and selling policies directly, blockchain-based firms promise to cut out the middlemen and the deadweight costs they add. They display diagrams replacing layers of legacy intermediaries with direct transactions between parties through a blockchain ledger.

While excising unnecessary intermediaries can be a significant benefit of the blockchain architecture, that does not always occur. Some intermediaries perform functions that new blockchain-based platforms cannot, such as connecting to essential legacy systems. A world beginning with a clean sheet of paper may be familiar for start-ups, but any time existing firms need to be part of the network, some integration will be required. And any time a cryptocurrency application depends on a native currency that must be converted at the end points back and forth from fiat, the application itself adds a new layer of intermediation. If users are willing to employ bitcoin, ether, or another cryptocurrency end to end, that may not be necessary, but today, that is only rarely the case. If people did not care about fiat currencies, they would not be so excited about bitcoin's price appreciation demarcated in dollars.

The remittance market shows how the blockchain's disintermediation and cost reduction may not be as dramatic or fast as some speculate. Immigrants and temporary workers in developed countries send nearly $500 billion annually back to relatives in the developing world, generating roughly $30 billion in fees.[10] This scenario is frequently cited as a great example of potential blockchain disruption because remittances involve middlemen taking huge commissions for currency exchanges that cryptocurrencies make unnecessary.[11] But if one actually looks at these markets, the advantages are not so clear. When someone in the U.S. sends money to relatives in the Philippines through a blockchain-based remittance service using bitcoin, there are still transaction fees for going into and out of the system in the middle. And because of bitcoin's volatility, spreads may be higher than for the direct currency-to currency conversion that traditional operators such as Western Union employ.[12]

SaveOnSend, a comparison-shopping engine for money-transfer services, argues, "There is virtually no advantage between receiving money into a bank account [as with blockchain-based services] vs. picking them up from a cash agent [as with Western Union]—in most cases, a provider's margins are the same for either method."[13] Many remittance receivers in the developing world choose to pay high fees to local agents even when cheaper alternatives are available, most likely to circumvent paying taxes.[14] And most of the costs of international money transfers turn out to involve the physical arrangements at the receiving end, not the international conversion of funds.[15] Blockchain-based money-transfer firms may turn out to be very successful, but it is dangerous to assume that their success is guaranteed by the structure of the market. Most are already pivoting to focus on payment services other than remittances.

As the remittance example illustrates, innovation can take several forms. An incremental improvement in one component of a system or process will enhance performance, but it is unlikely to create new business opportunities. On the other hand, what technology strategy scholars Rebecca Henderson and Kim Clark call an architectural innovation—"the reconfiguration of an established system to link together existing components in a new way"—has the significant potential to disrupt industry structures.[16]

Blockchain technology constitutes an architectural innovation with tremendous promise because it functions as a new architecture of trust. It addresses needs that arise from the breakdown of conventional trust structures. Specifically, the blockchain offers four core value propositions:

- Decentralized control
- A shared view of the truth
- Collaboration across organizational boundaries
- The direct exchange of value through tokens

Decentralization

Decentralization allows blockchain networks to offer many of the benefits of centralized trust—scale, clarity, and support for complex transactions—without ceding power to either government authorities or intermediaries. Decentralization, however (like consensus), is difficult to define. Does it mean more than one center or a pure mesh with no centers at all?[17] How much decentralization is sufficient? And what actually gets decentralized in a decentralized system?[18]

There are many ways to decentralize, but they all share a common feature: No single entity is essential for the system to function. Often, the reason to decentralize is less a desire to prevent government censorship than the practical limitations of current systems.[19] Chris Ballinger is director of mobility services at Toyota Research Institute (TRI) in Los Angeles, the automaker's in-house think tank. Coming from a background as a chief financial officer, he would seem an unlikely champion for decentralized blockchain technology.[20] Yet it was in financial services—the complex and fragmented loan processes around cars—that he first recognized the potential of a shared distributed ledger. Now, at TRI, he is looking at how it might address some of the challenges of building safe autonomous (driverless) vehicles.

Autonomous cars use machine-learning technology to identify obstacles on the road and determine how to respond. The more data fed into the systems from various driving situations, the more accurate the machine-learning results. The way to acquire that data is to send test cars into the field with human backup operators. Experts estimate that reliable autonomous cars that regulators will accept on the road will require 1 trillion miles of driving data to train the machine-learning engines. That is about one-third of all the miles driven in the United States in 2016.[21]

The problem with collecting that much data is the lack of a central actor. The ones who want the data—autonomous car manufacturers—are not the ones who have the data. The ones who have the data—individual drivers and fleet operators—are extremely fragmented. And there is no marketplace for this latter group to use to sell their anonymized driving data if they wanted to. No one is in a position to create such a marketplace because neither drivers nor manufacturers would trust any one entity with their data.

The blockchain's decentralized structure offers a solution. Ballinger believes that a decentralized marketplace could establish property rights around user-driving data, secured through cryptocurrency tokens. Drivers would receive compensation for sharing their anonymized driving data with the marketplace, and car manufacturers would pay to access data from the same exchange.[22] The net result would replace the current system, where a central actor such as Google puts a swarm of research vehicles on the streets or buys data from fleets, with a decentralized market arrangement. For Toyota and other car manufacturers, this requires no great conceptual leap of faith. It is the same way that they buy other inputs to their vehicles such as steel. In economic terms, the distributed ledger aligns incentives between the erstwhile buyers and sellers of driving data. Toyota recently launched a consortium to advance the idea.[23]

In general terms, the problem of central control that blockchain-type systems address is related to trust. Trusting involves risk. There is always the danger that someone you trust turns out to be untrustworthy. Investors in Bernie Madoff's Ponzi scheme, for instance, lost their money because they trusted the wrong investment manager.[24] Law, regulation, and insurance are all mechanisms to limit such risks.

The Madoff scenario is the exception rather than the rule, at least in the United States. For those at the mercy of loan sharks, payday lenders, or extortionate money-transfer agents, however, the blockchain offers an appealing alternative. In countries without a strong adherence to the rule of law, the government itself may not be trustworthy. In such cases, the availability of a financial infrastructure that does not rely at its roots on sovereign authority is a powerful opportunity. And the unbanked may not have access to trusted financial institutions at all. The blockchain as a trust platform requires only an Internet connection and a computer, so it can go all sorts of places where the current financial system does not.

Centralized trust also creates vulnerabilities. A central point of control is a central point of failure. It is where malicious actors will target their efforts. There has been a parade of security breaches in recent years involving major central data repositories such as Yahoo!, the U.S. Office of Personnel Management, and Equifax. Organizations should adopt better information security practices, but this will never be enough.[25] So long as there are central points of control, vulnerabilities will be part of the "new normal" of our connected world.

The DigiNotar case is a striking example. Access to websites is secured through cryptographic certificates verifying that the user is connected to the correct site, with no interference in the middle. Every time you visit a secure site, such as for an electronic commerce transaction, your browser exchanges cryptographic keys. The sites obtain their secure certificates from central certificate authorities, a system known as "public key infrastructure (PKI)."

In 2011, DigiNotar, a Dutch certificate authority, was hacked.[26] Fraudulent certificates were issued, which allowed attackers to intercept and redirect traffic between users and Google's Gmail service. (The hack appeared to involve the government of Iran or its agents seeking to access email of Iranian Internet users.) The damage was limited because Google and browser vendors acted quickly to invalidate the fraudulent certificates. DigiNotar, until then considered a high-quality certificate authority, was forced into bankruptcy due to the incident, and others enhanced their security procedures.[27] So long as browsers must trust certificate authorities, however, some danger of centralized control remains.

Finally, centralized trust creates negative externalities even when those at the center remain trustworthy. This is the danger of intermediary trust. Intermediaries create value by pulling together networks. Stock exchanges are a prime example. A few traders can negotiate with one another directly to consummate trades, but as the market expands, a purely person-to-person approach breaks down. Exchanges emerged as central aggregation points for trading, greatly increasing the liquidity of the market. Often, markets have multiple layers of intermediation, as new activity creates new service opportunities. The online advertising ecosystem is a good example. There is a complex assortment of advertising networks, tracking systems, retargeting services, aggregators, analytics providers, and other services. Each of these addresses an opportunity or pain point, often one that only developed thanks to a previous round of intermediation.

Intermediaries serve many valuable roles.[28] They can match buyers and sellers, aggregate demand to produce economies of scale, reduce bargaining asymmetries, protect against opportunistic behavior by other market participants, and reduce transaction costs by facilitating and standardizing information flows. When the intermediary itself creates a foundational business opportunity between two or more communities, it becomes a platform, like Facebook or Uber.

The problem is that intermediaries also impose costs. When an intermediary is a private company, it expects to generate revenue in return for the value it provides. Google charges advertisers for exposing them to a large number of users, and for targeting advertisements precisely. Google's advertising revenues, now in the tens of billions of dollars annually, represent a cost of intermediation. The benefit is that until Google came along, there was no way to bring the two sides of the market together effectively. But if the search engine advertising marketplace could exist without Google at the center, it would not have to bear those costs. And as the number of intermediaries multiplies, so does the overhead. Search engine optimization firms, for example, are intermediaries that piggyback on Google. Those providers charge for their services, and Google has to expend resources to prevent excessive gaming of its search results.

Once intermediated markets are established, they can be difficult to overthrow. Network effects create strong barriers to entry. The much-ballyhooed peer-to-peer (P2P) social networking service Diaspora never seriously got off the ground as a Facebook rival. Even Google could barely dent Facebook's dominance after spending hundreds of millions of dollars on its Google+ alternative.

A blockchain-based network has a different value proposition than one built around traditional intermediaries. The intermediation resides in the ledger, not the ledger creator. There may still be an organization that generates revenue for establishing the network, or operates hardware nodes on which transactions are validated. However, this gives it no special power over the data involved. The participants in the network retain control themselves.

Shared Truth

The next appealing aspect of the blockchain's trust model is its potential for speed and efficiency. At first glance, this sounds odd. Bitcoin validates a block roughly every ten minutes, and it currently has a nominal limit of seven transactions per second. This is quite a small number: The Visa credit card network handles up to 10,000 transactions in the same period.[29] The overhead of synchronizing the distributed ledger is so great that, according to one estimate by Nick Szabo, the process operates 10,000 times slower than a conventional computer.[30] Other distributed-ledger systems achieve better performance by trading off some degree of decentralization or security, but even they cannot keep up with state-of-the-art, highly tuned enterprise databases.

Yet there is a hidden advantage to removing the need to trust actors you interact with. Trust is not transitive. I may trust you, and you may trust your bank. But that does not mean I trust your bank. For me to cash your check, our banks must enter their own trust relationship. With many thousands of financial institutions processing billions of transactions across hundreds of jurisdictions, this pairwise structure quickly bogs down—or, more accurately, it works only with huge inefficiencies and transaction costs.

A distributed ledger replaces those redundant processes with a single record that everyone trusts. "Seeing things together in real time is powerful," says Amber Baldet, blockchain program lead at JPMorgan.[31] "We spend millions on reconciling information between parties because they don't trust each other." In intermediary trust networks, those same reconciliation costs create lock-in and value-extraction opportunities for the intermediaries.

Shared truth seems like the opposite of decentralization. The one canonical ledger looks suspiciously like a new central authority. In actuality, the two concepts are complementary. "Decentralization" means that parties need not cede power to a third party. "Shared truth" means that the parties themselves cannot exercise exclusive authority. Everyone can have a copy of the master ledger, but no participant can claim its own ledger is the final word. Authority resides in the consensus. That consensus, however, is not seated in any one entity. It is an emergent property of the network as a whole.

The complexity of reconciling transactions between many interconnected trusted parties adds delay to the process. Stock trades, for example, typically settle after two days (a standard known as "T+2").[32] Faster settlement frees up capital that traders and multinational firms can put to work in other ways. There are limits on how low the number can go. Delayed settlement gives firms time to come up with collateral to settle trades, which is important in derivatives and other markets. The move to distributed ledgers will allow the actual settlement rate to converge with the greatest efficiency for market participants.

In essence, the traditional trust model of the financial system and the blockchain model both create decentralized ledgers. In the traditional system, every node is individually responsible for keeping its ledger in sync with the virtual consensus, but it only has visibility (and limited at that) into its direct partners. With the blockchain, every block added reconciles its transactions across the entire system. It effectively parallelizes what is otherwise a collection of serial processes. Each individual transaction takes longer to be recorded, but the global state of the system is updated more rapidly.

And because this occurs through one synchronized process, rather than a potentially large number of separate transactions, costs may be significantly lower. Goldman Sachs estimates that the blockchain could save $11 billion to $12 billion annually in settlement and reconciliation costs for securities transactions alone.[33]

Beyond financial services, any time that multiple parties record the same transaction, there is the possibility that their records will not align. There could be a trusted intermediary creating the marketplace, but everyone would still have to connect to a common interface that it establishes. Every company may have its own data formats, which it needs to convert to the common standard. And if there is ever an inconsistency in the data, that creates a need for manual intervention and exception handling in order to decide which version should control.

Opportunities for mistakes and disputes abound. Global firms spend many billions of dollars annually orchestrating networks of independent providers in supply chains. According to IBM, in just the shipping segment, 5 percent of total costs—about $10 billion annually—involve dispute resolution, when what arrives is not what was expected.[34] The shared truth of a blockchain ledger could reduce these losses by 20 percent, in IBM's estimation, through better tracking on a common ledger.

In addition to avoiding disputes before they happen, a universal view of truth fosters auditability after the fact. If all the information is recorded on a single distributed ledger and any changes to that ledger are automatically and immutably recorded, auditing transactions becomes much easier. It no longer requires a forensic reconstruction of activity. The auditors might be market participants, in the case of a dispute; auditing firms conducting their regular reviews; or regulators.

Transactions often have multiple components that are relevant to different providers. A real estate or auto transaction may involve banks, insurance companies, and government agencies, each of which needs to track certain information about the transaction. Properly recording the deed in the land registration office does not guarantee that the mortgage bank, the title insurer, or the local taxing authority will do so. Each of these organizations uses its own system, its own data format, and its own staff. There are a plethora of opportunities for something to go wrong in synchronizing and reconciling all these records. And whenever that happens, it imposes additional costs and delays.

The same problems emerge in the compliance function. Regulations for banks require that certain transaction information be sent to regulatory agencies, who can examine all sides to evaluate systemic risk. For example, both counterparties must report over-the-counter swaps to the Commodity Futures Trading Commission (CFTC). Yet according to Neepa Patel, chief compliance officer at R3 and former bank examiner for the Office of the Comptroller of the Currency, the information that two counterparties send the regulators for the same transaction does not match up to 40 percent of the time.[35] These are typically administrative errors or incompatibilities between systems, such as inconsistent entity names or time stamps. These issues must be reconciled manually to produce accurate data.

The gaps between different recording systems for the same transaction also open up the potential for fraud. BigChainDB CEO Bruce Pon relates a story from his prior career providing information technology services for the automotive industry.[36] Cars are often used as collateral for loans. If a dealer sells a car but does not notify the bank issuing it a loan, and then the dealer goes bankrupt, the bank has no way to recover the funds. Unscrupulous car dealers in Russia would sell tens of millions of dollars of inventory that they were simultaneously using as collateral for bank loans. Similar issues occur with uncertified parts. Even when licensed dealers attempt to use only authorized parts when repairing cars, they have no control over other points in the supply chain where counterfeit parts may enter.

What is needed is a way to track the car all the way through the chain, from manufacturing to sale to aftermarket repair. Manufacturers, financial services firms, and intermediaries in the automotive industry could come together to create a unified view of the supply chain and financial chain around a car. In the blockchain model, says Pon, "there is one shared immutable truth, which everyone sees immediately. If there is a change, it is propagated immediately."[37] This would allow additional services, such as insurance and predictive pricing algorithms, to be applied on top of the common data set. The blockchain itself would not guarantee the accuracy of the information recorded, nor would it force all the companies to participate. However, by creating a common platform, it would make it easier to address those challenges. Toyota joined the Enterprise Ethereum Alliance to help develop such an industrywide platform.

One of the more prominent pilot projects for permissioned distributed-ledger technology is Walmart's food-safety trial with IBM. Walmart is the world's largest retailer and one of its most sophisticated supply-chain managers. Yet even Walmart cannot easily keep track of the many thousands of suppliers around the world whose products eventually wind up in its stores. Food safety is an important area in which better supply-chain visibility could save lives. And according to Walmart food-safety executive Frank Yiannas, even a modest percentage reduction in foodborne disease would produce billions of dollars of savings to the economy.[38]

When a foodborne illness occurs, the biggest challenge is identifying the source, so products from the originating farm can be removed from shelves quickly. Walmart's pilot project, initially for mangoes grown in the U.S. and pork sourced from China, recorded information on a distributed ledger using bar codes every time that a product moved from one point to another. There is no way even Walmart could get every pig farm in China onto one centralized ledger, though. In addition to the logistical challenges, many suppliers work with Walmart's competitors and would be hesitant to give Walmart open access to all their operations. The distributed ledger allowed them to share information without giving up control.

To test the system, Yiannas challenged his team to identify which farm produced a package of mangoes sold in one of Walmart's stores using conventional supply-chain mechanisms. It took a week. With the blockchain-based system, he was able to get the answer in just over two seconds. In a foodborne disease outbreak, that could be a matter of life and death.

Based on the success of the initial trials, Walmart has expanded the pilot program to other partners, including Unilever, Nestlé, Tyson, and Dole Foods.[39] The distributed nature of the system means that more companies, even Walmart's competitors, could contribute to the same platform in a way that simply wouldn't work with traditional databases.

Walmart's food-safety initiative is not going to disrupt the retail industry. It does not represent an exotic new business model or an economic shift from state-issued currency. Yet it is the kind of innovation that could not easily occur without blockchain-related technology. And it promises real economic and social benefits by eliminating duplicative records and reconciliation.

Translucent Collaboration

If there is no trust, encryption can allow anonymous exchange, but the arrangement lacks the scale economies of networks. If trust is plentiful, there is no need for burdensome checks and balances. Much of the time, however, especially in business contexts, communities interact under conditions of limited trust. They wish to share data, but they still maintain control. I call this "translucent collaboration."

A 2017 IBM survey of three thousand high-level executives across the globe found that firms exploring blockchain adoption viewed the technology as a kind of "trust accelerator," enhancing collaborative initiatives.[40] This model is being adopted in a diverse range of cases. For example, the broadband and media company Comcast is currently developing a new advertising platform using this approach, in partnership with other major media companies in the U.S. and Europe.[41] Comcast's system will allow marketers to better target advertising by connecting their audience segmentation data with that of television networks. Such data sharing is limited today because neither side wants to give up control over its information. A distributed ledger provides a secure platform on which everyone can benefit from a common pool of information without having to worry about how a potential competitor or intermediary will handle proprietary data.

Similarly, there are also many contexts in financial services where parties have to share information with potential rivals. In syndicated loans (a $4 trillion annual market), a number of lenders join together to share in a loan arrangement. Doing so helps spread risk and allows smaller lenders access to transactions that they could not support alone. The difficulty with syndicated loans is that, given the amounts of money at stake, the allocation of rights and obligations among the parties must be specified precisely. According to Caitlin Long, a former Morgan Stanley executive who became President and Chairman of the distributed-ledger start-up Symbiont, syndicated loans were considered a backwater until interest rates collapsed, suddenly making them a hot area for yield-hungry investors. The back-office infrastructure to support them was not designed for this level of activity.[42]

With a loan involving a single lender, the transaction can be processed on that lender's systems. A syndicated loan must be tracked on the system of every lender, and those systems do not interconnect. Therefore, manual processes are used to share information. These typically involve paper faxes; in 2008, twenty-five million faxes were sent just to manage syndicated loans.[43] Major investment banks literally employ hundreds of people (typically offshore, in lower-wage countries such as India) to collect those faxes as they come in and enter the data into their systems. Even though the loan typically specifies the same interest rate for all members of the syndicate, each calculates it independently. None of them would trust another lender, or a third party, to perform this essential function.

The fractured nature of the syndicated loan process imposes significant costs and creates many opportunities for errors and inconsistencies. These must be reconciled every time, which creates further costs and delays. Placing the loan on a distributed ledger and executing its terms through smart contracts circumvent all that. Each of the lenders, as well as the borrower, sees exactly the same information at all times. Yet no one has to give up control.

Symbiont is developing a syndicated loan solution, working with major financial services firms including Credit Suisse, Barclays, State Street, U.S. Bank, Wells Fargo, KKR, and AllianceBernstein.[44] As these companies gain more experience with blockchain-based approaches, they will find many other opportunities to apply them. Almost every aspect of modern finance involves digital transactions involving multiple parties, where a distributed trust model could improve efficiency and create new opportunities.

As a permissioned system, the syndicated loan network still requires a baseline level of identity among the providers. A similar application on a public blockchain might allow any entity that could demonstrate sufficient capital reserves through a smart contract to participate in a loan syndicate. Established financial services providers would probably resist opening up the market in this way. The same application, therefore, could have two very different value propositions, depending on the structure of the distributed-ledger platform. A public blockchain could take advantage of translucent collaboration to create entirely new financial markets. A permissioned network helps the current universe of players function more efficiently. Both could coexist in theory, although legal and regulatory considerations, which will be taken up in part II of this book, loom large.

Tokens of Value

The final opportunity for blockchain systems is the direct exchange of value through virtual economies. The traditional way to make something valuable is to make it scarce. Gold and diamonds are worth more than copper and granite because there is less supply in the world, with high demand. The Internet economy, by contrast, is governed by the economics of abundance. *Wired* editor Chris Anderson's concept of the "long tail," first introduced in a 2004 article, captured how the dramatically lower costs of storing and transacting in digital goods shifted the structure of markets.[45] In a physical bookshop, shelf space is scarce. The costs of production and distribution make a book that sells 500 copies much less profitable than one that sells 500,000. As a result, markets in physical goods concentrate on a small number of hit products. Digital markets can exploit the long tail of demand for products that sell small numbers individually but large volumes in aggregate. It costs Amazon virtually nothing to list another item. In addition to providing direct revenue, the data that Amazon accumulates through its huge inventory feeds back to improve its service.

The tension between the Internet's economics of abundance and the physical world's economics of scarcity drove many of the great controversies in Internet law. When it became virtually costless to make a perfect digital copy of content and distribute it around the world, the creative industries feared that their business model would break. This led to a series of copyright law battles that still rage today. When users started taking advantage of "all-you-can-eat" broadband pricing, the response from network operators touched off a giant fight over network neutrality rules to prevent unreasonable discrimination. And when companies such as Google and Facebook figured out how to target advertising to make free services highly profitable, it led them down a path of intensive personal data collection, giving rise to ongoing privacy controversies. Revelations in spring 2018 that the political consulting firm Cambridge Analytica surreptitiously acquired millions of Facebook user profiles and employed them to target voters in the U.S. presidential election knocked over $100 billion off of Facebook's market capitalization and sparked growing calls for stronger regulation.[46]

The blockchain is a technology of artificial scarcity. It combines the benefits of digital transactions with assurances that digital resources cannot be copied. Content owners use cryptography in the form of digital rights management to prevent unauthorized copying of audio and video files. Cryptocurrency tokens achieve the same result on decentralized networks.[47] To establish a viable currency, Bitcoin had to make it impossible to double-spend or to overwhelm the validation network with Sybil attacks. Once a token represents scarce value, however, it can be used as more than money. It becomes a cryptographically secured digital asset, or "cryptoasset."[48]

Cryptoassets can represent physical goods, as in the automobile-lending example earlier in this chapter. They can represent scarce digital entities, like the CryptoKitties collectibles described in chapter 2. Alternatively, they can represent the utility of the network itself. For Bitcoin, money is the core application, so the network value is simply the price of all available bitcoin. For Ethereum, the value is its ability to create decentralized applications (Dapps) using ether to pay for the necessary gas to execute computations. More demand for Ethereum smart contracts, given limits on the supply of ether tokens, should increase the token price. The same is true for Dapps themselves.

Civic, for example, offers blockchain-based identity verification services.[49] Users who provide personal information, validators who verify it, and large service providers who connect their user profiles to the system all receive compensation in the form of Civic's CVC tokens. These tokens can be used to pay for validating information (such as an employer checking a college transcript or a bank performing anti-money laundering checks) and other Civic services. The more activity on the network, the more the tokens are worth. When tokens can be traded on independent exchanges, their value will fluctuate based on traders' expectations, but over time, the total value of tokens should converge to the value of the Dapp.[50]

A Dapp, therefore, is similar to a corporation. It is a platform for activity that generates value. Just as a company can sell stock to the public to finance its operations, a Dapp could sell tokens. For a network, these could be created by "premining" a set number of coins, with additional coins created through a proof-of-work or similar process. Any desired set of rules could be established around the tokens with smart contracts, such as the four-year vesting schedule typical of stock options in private companies. By analogy to an initial public offering (IPO) of stock, token sales are often called "initial coin offerings (ICOs)."

The first project to launch an ICO was Mastercoin, a system for creating new application coins—or appcoins—on the Bitcoin network.[51] It generated $5 million in bitcoin back in 2013. Ethereum followed in mid-2014, raising approximately $18 million well before it mined its first block of ether. The next two years saw a slow trickle of additional ICOs raising amounts in a similar range.

As the price of bitcoin surged from $400 to nearly $20,000 between mid-2016 and late 2017, there was a flurry of ICO activity, raising ever-greater amounts. Ethereum created a standard called ERC20, as previously mentioned, which simplified the process of creating tokens based on Ethereum smart contracts. And a network of service providers, hedge funds, legal experts, and others emerged to help projects structure and execute token sales. Over $4 billion worth of cryptocurrency was raised through hundreds of ICOs in 2017.[52] Media interest ramped up correspondingly.

At one point in 2017, every week seemed to set a new ICO high-water mark. Brave, the web browser developer described in chapter 3, offered Basic Attention Tokens (BATs), which can be used to pay publishers in lieu of advertisements. The token sale sold out in a matter of minutes, raising ether worth $35 million at the time. Bancor, which makes it easier to exchange cryptocurrency tokens for one another, raised the equivalent of more than $150 million a few days later. Tezos, which developed a new blockchain network based on flexible governance, topped that with an ICO generating more than $230 million at the time. And Filecoin, which is building a distributed cloud storage network, raised more than $250 million between tokens sold to the public and presold at a discount to partners. All told, there were more than 50 ICOs in 2017 that raised at least $30 million.[53]

The ICO frenzy was so intense that investors began to expect a token from any company connected to the blockchain. OpenBazaar, a well-known, cryptocurrency-powered decentralized marketplace, even felt obliged to issue a blog post explaining why it was not doing an ICO.[54] Among the reasons given were the economic and legal uncertainty of the concept and the absence of any need for a token in the company's business model. Six months later, its CEO announced plans for an OpenBazaar Token at the Token Summit conference.[55]

While the ICO market at its peak was an order of magnitude smaller than the overheated IPO market for Internet start-ups at the end of the 1990s, there were striking similarities. Projects with little or no code written were suddenly achieving billion-dollar valuations, the justification for which was often difficult to find. "[C]ompanies are issuing tokens when the same tasks can be achieved with existing blockchains," argues former Ethereum CEO Charles Hoskinson. "People are blinded by fast and easy money."[56]

In a hot market where there is tremendous excitement about cryptocurrencies, a limited inventory of investments available to the public, and great uncertainty about the future, it is easy for the market price of a token—what someone will pay for it—to become detached from any rational assessment of its real worth—the discounted value of future activity on the network. Such gaps are endemic to financial markets. Market-makers and arbitrageurs use breaks between trading and real values as money-making opportunities, and in so doing move markets toward the "correct" price, a process known as "price discovery." That is how things work in theory. In practice, though, there are many opportunities for abuses that harm investors, giving rise to a large body of financial regulation. The legal and regulatory status of token sales will be discussed in chapter 9.

Token sales could offer a new means of funding innovative technologies that circumvents the limitations of the traditional venture capital model.[57] Protocols need a critical mass of users to generate positive network effects. For a new protocol, it may be difficult to compete against incumbents or simply to get off the ground. Venture capitalists are looking for businesses that can scale fast and produce "home run" returns, which isn't always the right model for a start-up. "The biggest challenge of building a network business is the bootstrap problem," says venture capitalist Chris Dixon.[58] Brave and Civic both received traditional venture capital funding, but they also issued tokens to capitalize on their other benefits.

When traditionally structured businesses are successful, the value generally accrues not to the users, but to the operators. Some 2 billion people contribute their attention and content to Facebook, but they receive none of the economic benefits that Facebook generates as a result. If Facebook were organized around an appcoin, users could share the benefits as token prices appreciated—at least in theory. The potential value of a token could also provide incentives for users to engage with what could become the next Facebook. Early adopters and strong believers in new platforms would be encouraged to get in early, when the token price was low. In contrast to traditional venture capital funding, which does not provide a "liquidity event" until the company is sold or goes public, the token sale model allows immediate translation of investments into a currency.

At this early stage of development of the cryptocurrency market, few platforms other than Bitcoin itself are operating on a sufficient scale to drive the value of their tokens based on actual utility. Most of the ICOs launched so far are for services that are not yet operational. Some will never succeed in launching a production network. Even the ones that reach that point may not attract a substantial number of users. Just because something *can* be tokenized does not mean that it *should* be. Where the model makes sense, however, it has the potential to change the way that start-ups are funded and grow.

A tokenized business is actually two economic systems linked together: an internal cryptoasset marketplace tied to an external cryptoeconomic security system (the blockchain network). Most Dapps outsource the cryptoeconomic verification by operating on top of an infrastructure platform such as Ethereum. That still leaves significant challenges. In OpenBazaar's case, the biggest reason for forgoing an ICO was that it does not need an internal token to motivate behavior. As an eBay-like marketplace, it already has an economy: exchanging goods for money.

Running a business as a token economy benefits from specialized expertise.[59] Before ICOs, the primary example of services powered by user-owned private currencies were online games that offered virtual coins to purchase goods or gain abilities.[60] The virtual goods model powered the rapid growth of gaming companies such as Zynga and Supercell. But it also created problems, such as overreliance on high-spending "whales" and vulnerability to fickle user tastes, as shown when Zynga's usage (and subsequently the stock price) collapsed. Operating a company in thrall to a market price that you do not control is not a simple matter. Token issuers typically have some power to adjust the exchange rate of tokens for services on the platform, but if they go too far in devaluing the tokens, users will revolt.

After all, if token economies are such a great model, why has Facebook not adopted it? Facebook could issue virtual credits that users could purchase as an alternative to viewing advertisements. In fact, Facebook did try to do this. In 2009, Facebook Credits was created as a token system for virtual goods in games operating on Facebook. It shut down in 2012 because Facebook did not see the advantage of operating its own internal currency.[61] Users also found it simpler to purchase virtual goods in the native virtual currencies of each game, on which Facebook could still charge a tax.

At the end of the day, moreover, a centralized firm such as Facebook makes money by extracting value from its network. Its business model is incompatible with a fully tokenized structure, in which value resides in the network. This creates opportunities for competitors built around token economies. However, those competitors face the same trade-offs. And while Facebook would have to change its business model, established platforms such as Amazon Web Services that already charge for services might have an easier time coopting the token model if competitors show its value.

There are also dangers to the token model. The flood of ICOs, many of questionable value, is spurring legal and regulatory debates that will be discussed in chapter 9. And the balancing act between nonprofit entities overseeing token-based protocols and the financial interests of developers or users can be challenging. Tokenized networks are vulnerable to attacks, bugs, and disagreements about future development. Governance mechanisms are needed, as will be explored in chapter 7.

Despite the risks, the potential of tokenization, like the potential for the other three blockchain value propositions, is extremely exciting. One need not believe that hyperbitcoinization will soon overthrow fiat currencies and central banks to view the blockchain as the most significant tech trend since the Internet. With trust seemingly in retreat on every front, the potential of blockchains is tantalizing.

If all Bitcoin did was to establish a viable, decentralized privacy currency, it would constitute an important, potentially epochal, development in the history of finance. But it has achieved much more than that. Bitcoin was the start of a wave of similar systems and supporting work, now stretching to every corner of the world and virtually every sector of the economy. At its core, money is a trusted form of information that conveys value. Decentralized, networked digital money therefore represents a new form of communication. That makes its implications almost unimaginably broad.

In time, systems based on blockchain technology's foundational innovations could influence all aspects of business, government, and human communities. It would be premature to label the blockchain a revolution with similar impacts as the printing press, the telephone, or the Internet, but it belongs in the same conceptual category.

II Ledgers Meet Law

5   Unpacking Blockchain Trust

Something from Nothing

A good way for a computer to determine if a web page is interesting is to see if interesting pages link to it. The problem with this approach is that the computer cannot decide if a page is interesting without knowing if other pages are interesting. But those pages are only interesting if interesting pages link to them. And the cycle continues. The circularity seems impossible to resolve.

As it happens, two solutions to this circularity problem for web search were identified around the same time. One was developed by a Cornell professor visiting at IBM Research, and the other by a pair of unknown Stanford graduate students. The latter two were Larry Page and Sergey Brin, who used their approach to create the Google search engine.[1] Needless to say, it worked. And even though the other solution, CLEVER, had the backing of the mighty IBM, Google triumphed and supercharged the development of the Internet. Sometimes, in a networked environment, with certain limiting conditions, math allows something to be created out of nothing.

The conceptual challenge of the blockchain is similar. Bitcoin or other cryptocurrency tokens are valuable because everyone agrees that they are. Such creation of value *ex nihilo* seems illogical. Surely, it appears that there must be someone, or something, standing behind the ledger. The genius of trustless trust is that there need not be. Yet this realization only begins the inquiry. As described in chapter 1, the blockchain represents a reinvention of trust, not its elimination.

Just as Google's algorithms for finding information wound up shaping both the online marketplace and the ways that we encounter knowledge, the attributes of blockchain technology will structure the particular kind of trust it creates. Blockchain networks are distributed, in that they do not have any central control points. They rely on cryptoeconomic constraints that combine the mathematical guarantees of cryptography with the power of economic incentives. They record information immutably, making it difficult (if not impossible) to change information once recorded. They make the contents of the ledger transparent to participants. And they maintain trust through software algorithms rather than procedures.

Each of these characteristics offers both benefits and limitations. The particular shape of blockchain trust also frames the ways that blockchain systems interact with the law.

Distributed

First and foremost, trustless trust is distributed.[2] The blockchain replaces trust in individuals or institutions with trust across a system as a whole.[3] Trust in the conventional financial system means faith in individual actors such as banks or regulators. With the blockchain, by contrast, no distinct party—not miners, those running blockchain nodes, creators of the code, or users—is necessarily trusted. Every single full node has a complete and accurate copy of the blockchain; there are no administrative nodes or hierarchical relationships.[4] Everyone has access to the same software. So long as they do not control a majority of the mining power, no untrustworthy actor can undermine the integrity of the system. That is the "trustless" dimension of the blockchain.

Permissioned ledgers relax this constraint somewhat, but they do not abandon it. A permissioned distributed ledger system grants control over access. It may also grant parties different levels of visibility into transactions compared to the fully transparent approach of public blockchain systems. Once participants are on the network, however, no one has the power to alter or control the ledger. There are still multiple nodes negotiating consensus, rather than having a master copy. Participants in Symbiont's syndicated loan trial or Walmart's food-safety pilot trust the ledger more and each other less than they would in the traditional arrangements.

The core property of a distributed trust architecture is that it makes it possible to trust the output of a system without necessarily trusting any of its individual components. Normally, these two go together. You would not trust a bicycle to carry you safely if you could not trust the integrity of the wheels and the brakes. The problem is that assessing the trustworthiness of components is costly and often impossible. How confident are you in the security of the encryption that your bank uses to move money from your checking account to a merchant? Are you sure that chicken you bought at the market was not contaminated with salmonella at the slaughterhouse? Could you even find out? It is unlikely. Yet people happily use their banks and eat their chicken without a second thought.

That is where the trust architecture comes in. You trust your bank and the brand of chicken that you buy, partly out of prior experience, but mostly because if something bad happens, you have recourse. That recourse might involve voluntary responses, regulatory intervention, or private legal action. You do not need to evaluate the hygiene procedures of the slaughterhouse because you trust the meat company and government regulators to do that for you.

In these examples, the trustworthiness of the system still depends on the trustworthiness of the components. A slaughterhouse owner who cuts corners may result in contaminated chicken getting to market, even if all others in the supply chain do their job responsibly. The same might be true if the slaughterhouse did its job, but the butcher at the market did not. What if a few untrustworthy actors did not necessarily undermine the trust of the system as a whole? It would be as if the slaughterhouse allowed the meat to become contaminated, but the market automatically rejected it. The blockchain trust architecture seeks to produce just such a result. Users can be confident about transactions without having confidence in the counterparty or any intermediaries.

The blockchain's architecture distributes trust similarly to how the Internet's architecture distributes traffic routing. Packets of data are only entitled to "best efforts" on the part of the network. No router is guaranteed to deliver information. That is not a problem because the Internet's protocols detect and resend missing packets so quickly that no one notices. Eliminating the need for centralized trust in traffic delivery meant that every new system could focus on its own services without depending on or seeking approval from someone else.[5] The blockchain promises to create an "Internet of Value" by taking aspects of the digital economy that are traditionally centralized and replacing them with distributed trust. It allows users to pay for things or make enforceable commitments in the same way that they send packets across the network.

The blockchain's diffuse form of trust is not entirely orthogonal to traditional conceptions. In Francis Fukuyama's analysis, trust is an expectation arising within communities of shared norms.[6] Trust is not merely a disposition between distinct parties; it is a collective state of a system. The basis of Fukuyama's argument, as well as Robert Putnam's research on social capital, is that societies vary (between themselves and over time) on the strength of trust relationships they support. High-trust societies develop powerful private firms and government institutions because of their strong bedrock of interpersonal trust, not the other way around. Centralized trust in specific transactions depends on a more distributed baseline trust as an expression of social norms.

In the same way, a centralized relationship such as a digital-wallet provider holding a customer's stash of bitcoin can be built on top of the distributed computational activity of the blockchain. Few ordinary users run full Bitcoin nodes or obtain their bitcoin through mining; most interact with the blockchain through an intermediary such as Coinbase. Furthermore, as noted earlier, although the blockchain is physically distributed, it functions as a logically centralized record.[7] The blockchain can *seem* like a central source of truth, even when it is actually decentralized.

Cryptoeconomic

Cryptoeconomic security is the distinctive feature of public blockchain networks.[8] It means that the parties engaged in validation of the ledger are motivated through economic incentives. In the case of Bitcoin, this is the opportunity to win the block reward every ten minutes by being the first to solve the hashing puzzle. Permissioned ledgers generally do not use this mechanism. They rely on cryptography for security, but they do not employ Satoshi Nakamoto's incentive inversion to turn potential attackers into honest transaction validators. The importance of cryptoeconomic security is, therefore, one of the key dividing lines between public and permissioned-ledger networks.

The public blockchain architecture does not assume any participant in the network will be trustworthy; to the contrary, it assumes that some will not. If one could reasonably believe that all validation nodes will record information truthfully, achieving consensus would be simple. Conversely, if most participants consistently cheated, trusting the system would be foolhardy. In other words, if you can trust all of the people some of the time, or some of the people all of the time, is a reliable consensus possible? This is a basic question in sociology and political theory. After all, in the real world, people are generally honest only part of the time. In the language of economics, they behave opportunistically, violating rules when the perceived benefits exceed the costs.

All the traditional trust architectures overcome this problem through the same mechanism: sanctions. If you violate the law or break a contract, you will be subject to recourse through the mechanisms of the Leviathan state. If you violate the norms of an effectively governed community, you will be ostracized or punished by the community itself. If you violate your terms of service with an intermediary, it can cut you off or impose fees.

The traditional approaches differ in where they find the power to sanction, but they share the belief that sanctions are necessary to promote trust. A system of sanctions, however, also has costs. There are the costs of the sanctions themselves, both to the individual sanctioned and to the fabric of the community. Even more significant, there are monitoring and enforcement costs to operating the sanctions system.

If opportunistic behavior could be prevented without sanctions, that would create significant new opportunities. The cryptographic element of blockchain networks prevents some forms of brute-force cheating. However, as the prior failed digital cash efforts demonstrated, that level of protection was insufficient. Here, Satoshi once again found a solution through inversion.[9] Instead of making cheating costly, Bitcoin made it costly to behave honestly. After all, mining is expensive. It requires expensive computer hardware and electricity. That is terribly wasteful, which is why blockchain networks are exploring proof of stake and other consensus protocols that express cost in different ways. But it is actually not a disincentive in the way it might appear.

For the purpose of building a trust architecture without sanctions, costliness is actually a benefit. Mining is *reliably* expensive. Only those who can prove that they did the work can earn the benefits of the block rewards and transaction fees. The costs of the system become "skin in the game" for inducements rather than the deadweight loss of punishments.

It is entirely possible that the total costs expended by the miners will exceed the rewards that the software spits out. Proof-of-work systems periodically adjust the difficulty of their hashing puzzles up or down depending on the amount of computing power in the network. Miners rationally decide what investments to make based on expected returns at the current cryptocurrency price. The miners bear those costs, not a central operator of the blockchain.

And ultimately, if the system works, it creates a positive-sum game. The value of the cryptocurrency increases because it is more trusted. If users are willing to pay more for bitcoin, that bitcoin becomes a more valuable reward for the miners. Greater investment produces greater returns. The more mining activity there is, the more secure the blockchain becomes because it takes more power to overwhelm it with a 51-percent attack. Self-interest actually improves the security of the network for all.

Now the indefiniteness of the enforcement mechanism becomes a benefit. With sanctions, the possibility of not getting caught leads some to break the rules. With proof of work, however, the randomness of the block reward is what causes miners to invest. The difficulty of the hashing puzzles is a well-defined mathematical property. Miners know how much computation they bring to the table and can weigh the investment of hardware and energy against the likely benefits.

The economist Frank Knight in 1921 developed the critical distinction between risk and uncertainty.[10] Much of the future is unknown to us, and some of it is simply unknowable. Yet we cannot simply live by Yogi Berra's maxim: "It is tough to make predictions, especially about the future."[11] Knight pointed out that the scenarios that we can reliably model are fundamentally different than those that we cannot. If I know that there is a 20 percent chance it will rain today, I can make a judgment whether to bring an umbrella, even though I am not sure what will happen. On the other hand, if I have no idea whether it will rain, I have no basis to decide. Knight labeled the first category "risk" and the second "uncertainty." Economics is the formalized study of responses to risk. It has little to say about uncertainty, which is better addressed by fields such as psychology and religion.[12]

The blockchain takes the uncertainty of the Byzantine generals problem and turns it into risk. The participants in the network are modeled as rational economic actors, responding to incentives. They want to earn the greatest profits on their investments, whether through honest behavior or cheating. The system is structured to align those investments to make honesty the winning strategy. Cheaters must compete against the bulk of the network, which winds up being less worthwhile than behaving honestly and earning the rewards that the system doles out. That is the theory, at least. Bitcoin's real-world success showed that the theory could actually work.

Immutable

Immutability represents the time dimension of blockchain trust. The cryptoeconomic design of the distributed verification network ensures that information is accurately and consistently recorded. However, that does not guarantee that what was recorded yesterday is what you see today.

Your bank balance is just a set of numbers in a database stored in the bank's data centers.[13] In theory, someone with the proper authorization could go in and move money from one account to another, or the person could add a few zeros to an account balance. That typically does not happen, though. Banks enforce security measures, internal controls, and reconciliation processes to flag unauthorized transactions. These systems work well the vast majority of the time—but not always. In 2016, hackers stole $81 million from the central bank of Bangladesh by exploiting connections to the SWIFT system, the central network for international payments between banks.[14] Many other records are less secure.

Centralization inevitably creates points of failure. To trust that the information currently displayed in a database is the information originally recorded, one must trust the goodwill and procedures of each intermediary. That is what the blockchain addresses by decentralizing trust. Even in such a system, however, information is reliable only if it is highly resistant to tampering. Distributing the verification process actually increases the potential for manipulation of the ledger because it puts more people in a position to do so.

The blockchain addresses this problem by making transactions immutable. It is essentially impossible to alter a recorded value, so long as the network is functioning as intended. This is one function of the costly computation in the proof-of-work system. The Bitcoin mining process requires that every valid block be signed with a hash of the prior block. The blockchain is the longest sequence of blocks. Changing anything prior to the current block means forking the entire chain back to that point. Because every block is linked in a specific sequence, such an action will be rejected without a majority of total mining power (a 51-percent attack).[15] One can therefore be confident that what is recorded on the blockchain has not been altered.

A blockchain is, at some level, nothing more than a historical record of transactions organized using the Merkle tree data structure. Bitcoin does not even natively have the concept of an account with balances, or what computer scientists call "state": a representation of the present status of the system. Figuring out how much bitcoin you have requires adding up all the previous transactions. Ethereum and some other systems emphasizing smart contracts allow for accounts, but there is still no mechanism to edit those accounts directly. Making a change requires a transaction that automatically increments a counter to prevent duplication.

Immutability is an important factor in making ledgers trustworthy in a decentralized way. With any of the traditional trust architectures, trust in information is really a proxy for trust in the actors maintaining that information. You are not trusting your bank's database so much as trusting your bank. If the ledger is immutable, there is nothing standing behind it but the cryptoeconomic or other type of security of its software. Similarly, immutability allows cryptocurrency tokens to function as bearer instruments. The value is directly resident in the asset because there is no way to break its connection to the information recorded on the ledger.

Immutability, however, is not always well defined. There are several interpretations of what immutability means. Furthermore, it is not always clear that the most immutable system is the best one. As one poster on a Reddit online discussion thread about the topic sarcastically mused, "The concept of immutable, as applied to blockchains, seems quite mutable."[16] Legal scholar Angela Walch identifies the "haze of confusion" around immutability as a problem for two reasons: It creates overconfidence that records can never be changed or rolled back, and it produces uncertainty when legislators or courts refer generically to immutable ledgers.[17]

Part of the reason is that immutability, like trust, is not binary. Blockchain trust is immutable in a probabilistic sense.[18] Distinguishing untrustworthy chains from the consensus is not an all-or-nothing decision. The more subsequent blocks added following the one in question, the more processing power is required to fork the chain back to that point. Over time, therefore, trust in prior transactions increases. Nick Szabo uses the analogy of a fly trapped in amber. As more and more layers cover it, the fly becomes more fully stuck. A fly encased in a thick block of amber has clearly been there a long time.[19]

Blockchain trust is thus not instantaneous.[20] A new block is verified on the Bitcoin blockchain roughly every ten minutes.[21] Each block has a fixed size, so transactions often must wait until the next block. The requisite confidence level (and thus delay) to accept a block as valid depends on the risk profile of the activity. Someone with little at stake will prioritize speed over small, incremental robustness, while one engaged in a large, important transaction will be willing to wait for more confirmations. In theory, the benefit of probabilistic trust is that anyone can decide the level of assurance they want by tolerating additional delay. In practice, though, it is not so simple. A Bitcoin transaction six blocks deep is commonly described as immutable. However, this is just an arbitrary convention.[22] Users (and even businesses) may not be able to judge how much confidence they need relative to the amount of delay.

The immutability of a blockchain is also not absolute. There are at least two groups of actors in a distributed ledger network with the power to unwind recorded transactions: developers and verification nodes. Most public blockchain networks, such as Bitcoin and Ethereum, are structured as open-source software projects. There is a core group of developers, under the auspices of a nonprofit foundation, who provide the official software to the verification nodes. Developers who want to move the project in a different direction can fork the code to their own modified version and create their own network of verification nodes. For example, JPMorgan's Quorum is a fork of Ethereum software that incorporates identity and privacy features.

Alternatively, the core developers could update the code of the network to fork the blockchain itself. If most of the nodes are running software code that specifies a prior transaction as invalid, it will no longer be included in the blockchains they recognize. Such a systemwide software update is known as a "hard fork." If one side of a hard fork disregards a previously verified transaction, it directly breaks the immutability of the ledger.

A hard fork is a rare and difficult occurrence. For one thing, it forces the verification node operators, and everyone else in the network, to choose sides. There are now two incompatible versions of the chain. Each treats the other as invalid, as though someone maliciously added illegitimate transactions. If everyone agrees to go down one fork, it becomes the real chain. That happened to Bitcoin on a few early occasions, when serious technical flaws were discovered that allowed people to give themselves a virtually infinite amount of the currency. Things get more complicated, though, if the hard fork is contentious. Both sides might then consider their chain the "real" one. The Ethereum fork following The DAO hack, covered in chapter 3, is a good example.

Hard forks are troublesome for blockchain trust because they are a reversal of the famous parable about the Emperor's new clothes. The creators of a blockchain network declare that they are *not* emperors. They do not have the power of the operator of a centralized network to manipulate information, so the network can be trusted independent of the creators. But developers have more power than they let on. To some degree, trusting a network means trusting its developers' judgment. And even in an open-source project, a single individual can exercise significant authority. The much-vaunted immutability starts to sound less than ironclad. Thus, when Ethereum project leader Vitalik Buterin tweeted off-handedly in response to security concerns about a new consensus algorithm, "We can just delete the attackers' deposits and keep going,"[23] one commenter called that "the most dangerous statement anyone in crypto has ever made."[24]

The network software developers are not the only ones who can initiate a hard fork. The operators of the verification nodes could independently choose to update their software to fork the chain. Mining pool operators threatened to do so during the Bitcoin block size controversy, discussed in chapter 7.

Finally, immutability is not always beneficial for trust. It can create a false confidence. The blockchain guarantees that a transaction was recorded accurately and only once, but it does not guarantee whether the person making that transaction is the rightful owner of the relevant private key, nor does it control for other factors. And sometimes a more trustworthy relationship can benefit from the ability to alter prior commitments.

The theory of relational contracts emphasizes that contracts may be dynamic arrangements that necessarily contemplate renegotiation to better address mutual needs. If a relationship evolves over time, knowing that prior commitments are set in stone may not always maximize mutual trust. And when government is involved, "immutability" may mean that systems are resistant to legitimate political authority.

The fact that blockchain immutability is not absolute does not necessarily undermine the trust value of these systems. Recall that trust involves vulnerability. Trusting people in the real world implies the possibility, even if remote, that they will betray your trust. We are comfortable imagining such scenarios because we intuitively understand human psychology. Not so with blockchains. Many of the most serious debates about the viability of distributed ledger systems involve messy questions about immutability. For these reasons, some blockchains build in governance mechanisms under which transactions can be reversed or the rules for the network changed. We will examine these in more detail in chapter 10.

Transparent

With the Bitcoin system and similar networks, every transaction is public. Anyone can download the entire blockchain back to the genesis block mined by Satoshi. The parties involved are identified only by cryptographic keys, which are associated with transactions rather than accounts. So, without further analysis, it is not obvious who owns how much bitcoin. Given control over the keys, however, no one can dispute that a given transaction occurred. Without transparency, even if the ledger were trustworthy, users could be misled about its contents. The transparent ledger also allows third parties to provide analytics services that examine transaction patterns across the network.

A second level of blockchain transparency is that the software powering the major networks is open source.[25] The algorithms of the blockchain are not hidden like those of Google or Facebook; they are available for inspection by all participants in the ecosystem. Bitcoin, Ethereum, and the Hyperledger consortium are based around nonprofit foundations that manage and distribute software source code. Anyone can review or suggest improvements to the code. Trusting the efficacy of the consensus mechanism on these networks, therefore, is not just a matter of reputation or legal enforcement; it can be backed by direct inspection and analysis of the algorithms.

Traditional trust architectures often reinforce trust through secrecy. A bank stores assets in an impressive vault. Lawyers declare their conversations with clients privileged. Coca-Cola zealously hides its secret formula. There is an assumption sometimes that something transparent is inherently untrustworthy. Yet this is often a confusion of trust with reputation, or with privacy. A bank will not show you its full transaction ledger because it would reveal the actions of other customers, not because it would make you question the accuracy of its records. Google does not reveal its search algorithms because competitors would copy them and advertisers would game their system.

Open-source blockchain software, by contrast, is freely available to copy and modify. (Although, as an aside, there has been a flurry of patent activity around blockchain technologies, raising fears about infringement lawsuits against widely used approaches.) And the designers of blockchain networks *assume* that these systems will be gamed. In fact, that is the essence of their cryptoeconomic trust model. Blockchains overcome strategic behavior through game theory, not through obfuscation.

One of the great insights of modern cryptography and software development is that the traditional solution of "security through obscurity" is often misguided and can be replaced with security through structured transparency. Most of the critical software programs underpinning the Internet, including the Linux operating system and Apache web server, are open source. More developers having access to the source code means that more people can identify bugs. Similarly, security flaws are easier to spot when code is out in the open. With effective cryptography, even if the formula used to encode information is known, it cannot be decoded easily without possession of the key. With public key cryptography, moreover, the public key can be distributed because it reveals nothing without possession of the secret private key.

In other ways, the blockchain's notion that trust can emerge from transparency is not new. Public companies are required to report detailed information about their financial performance every quarter, as well as any events that investors would consider material at any time. They are also required to submit to regular audits by independent firms. This auditing is designed to ensure that the information that firms report is accurate and that the conclusions they draw about their performance match the underlying reality. It is an imperfect process. Cases such as Enron and Worldcom show how auditing can fail, especially when the auditors' incentives are misaligned with investors'. As cryptoeconomic systems, distributed ledger platforms are structured to align incentives with trustworthiness.

There may be good reasons not to make all transactions public, even without identifying the parties. In a supply-chain environment, transaction flows may have significant competitive value. Participants may not want their competitors to know their exact transaction patterns, or secrecy may be particularly important to the user or the application. As a result, most permissioned blockchains do away with Bitcoin's transparent ledger. They tend to be established by organizations or networks of organizations that want to maintain a greater degree of secrecy. They also do this for convenience because removing the "flooding" requirement to broadcast every transaction throughout the network significantly improves performance.

On public blockchains, a new form of cryptography called "zero-knowledge proofs" is being used to achieve similar or even greater secrecy.[26] A zero-knowledge proof makes it possible to verify encrypted information without actually decrypting it. Systems such as ZCash and Monero use this to make Bitcoin-like cryptocurrency transactions fully private.[27] Zero-knowledge proofs are now being incorporated into Ethereum, as well as into the Quorum permissioned-ledger system.[28]

The appropriate transparency level of blockchain systems is still subject to debate. The right balance is likely to vary by application. It is also possible to have multiple levels of transparency in the same network. One approach is to allow audit nodes, which have deep visibility but no ability to initiate transactions. Corporate auditors today expend a great deal of effort obtaining access to books and records for their reports, but these generally give them only a retrospective view. Government regulators are another group that would value having real-time audit visibility into transaction networks. Central banks and other financial regulators, for example, could use audit nodes in a blockchain network to evaluate systemic risk. This bird's-eye regulators' perspective could be securely separated from the ground-level visibility available to market participants. Different networks are likely to explore various transparency structures to meet their needs.

Algorithmic

Finally, blockchain trust is algorithmic. An algorithm is just a recipe for solving a problem. If you want to create banana nut pancakes, the recipe will spell out the steps so you do it correctly each time. You cannot eat the recipe, but you use it to make something edible. Computers use algorithms written in software to guide their actions. Some algorithms are quite simple. Humans can retrace their steps and understand exactly why they do what they do. Other algorithms are inscrutably complex.

The algorithms that Facebook uses to decide which of billions of posts to place in your newsfeed weigh hundreds of signals and are constantly being tweaked. Facebook's decision to display a post, therefore, is quite different from the decisions that the *New York Times* editorial board makes every morning about what to put on the front page of the paper. Someone at Facebook could not explain every decision, because the choices are not made by people. The best the company could do would be to explain the goals and structure of the algorithm, and then suggest the inputs that produced the outputs you saw.[29] That is why, for example, Facebook had such difficulty responding to charges that it manipulated voters in the 2016 U.S. Presidential election. Facebook's seemingly innocuous goal was to maximize revenues from advertising. The algorithms, which third parties exploited, did the rest.[30]

In an algorithmic system, therefore, what is being trusted is not the people, but the machines. For the blockchain, that means the software and underlying math of the consensus process. Computer security expert Andreas Antonopoulos, author of the book *Mastering Bitcoin*, calls it "trust-by-computation."[31] It is like the trust you have when you ask a calculator to compute the square root of 3 and it responds with 1.7320508. You would not expect anyone to challenge that answer because it is a simple calculation for a machine to perform. But what if you are using an online calculator written as a project by a computer science student, who made some programming mistakes? Or what if you are asking for a more complex calculation, like the future price of a stock or the chance that a felon will commit another crime if let out early on parole? You might not be so confident.

The algorithms for a blockchain network are set out in the software that runs on the verification nodes. In many cases, especially for public chains, the source code is freely accessible. Anyone can examine that code and review the mechanisms used to generate trustworthy results. Often, there are whitepapers or other documents that step through how the system seeks to ensure reliable consensus. One of the reasons that Bitcoin got off the ground was that experts could review its algorithms, discuss potential flaws, and model its implications. Developers have expanded and revised the code in response to these findings. As a result, even when a block is mined by a company based in China that you've never heard of, it makes sense to trust the contents. You do not need to trust the company itself in the way that you trust your bank.

Algorithmic trust is related to decentralization. Vitalik Buterin distinguishes objective and subjective cryptoeconomic systems. In objective systems, "the protocol's operation and consensus can be maintained at all times using solely nodes, knowing nothing but the full set of data that has been published and the rules of the protocol itself."[32] Subjective systems require some additional knowledge. That has to come from somewhere—typically a central authority. Both systems in Buterin's model use crypto-economic security. With smart contracts, knowing that a transaction was recorded properly is not enough. A valid transaction may require information beyond the four corners of the agreement itself.

An objective system sounds desirable. And indeed, the edifice of block-chain trust rests on the belief that the machines, not fallible and opportu-nistic humans, are driving the bus. But there is a catch. Machines may be running the code, but humans are acting on it. A subjective system might differentiate between legitimate and illegitimate transactions in a way that an objective one could not. As Buterin notes, "Concepts like manipulation, takeovers, and deceit, not detectable or in some cases even definable in pure cryptography, can be understood by the human community surrounding the protocol just fine." Buterin highlighted the distinction in early 2015. It became the basis for an existential threat to Ethereum with The DAO hack the following year, as discussed in chapter 3.

Algorithmic trust can also incorporate human decision-makers explic-itly. One example built into Bitcoin is multisig, short for "multiple signa-tures." In a basic Bitcoin transaction, the recipient of the currency must provide his or her private key to receive the funds. Multisig allows the sender to specify that some fraction of a larger number of keys is required. The most common multisig arrangement requires two of three keys. This allows a simple arbitration process. If both parties agree, their keys are sufficient to consum-mate the transaction. If they disagree, the holder of the third key breaks the tie. That third key-holder would typically be a neutral party selected in advance of such a situation. Multisig thus allows the blockchain to connect with human-based trust because an arbitrator can break the tie between adversarial parties.

Moving in the opposite direction, blockchain systems can also use algo-rithmic decision-making to take humans out of the loop more thoroughly. That can be a double-edged sword, though. There are also significant dangers in the rise of what legal scholar Frank Pasquale labels the "black box soci-ety."[33] Algorithmic systems can undermine privacy, manipulate people into decisions that they did not intend, reinforce societal biases embedded in their source data, and occasionally fail spectacularly.[34] We assume that algorithms are neutral, but they encode the aims of those who create them or hidden biases in the data that feeds them.[35]

Algorithmic trust is especially dangerous when these systems incorporate machine learning, or as it is popularly termed, "artificial intelligence (AI)." With machine learning, the system evolves in response to data. The power of such systems is extraordinary.[36] Advances in machine learning are behind the rapid improvements in everything from the Siri and Alexa intelligent agents to autonomous (driverless) cars. The problem is that the algorithm's machine learning comes from abstract statistical correlations that are difficult for humans to interpret and audit. Trusting an AI-trained system, therefore, adds another degree of risk over trusting a system based on a hard-coded algorithm.[37]

With smart contracts, a blockchain network gains the power of automated decision-making and execution. That capability can be used to create a new algorithmic organizational form: the decentralized autonomous organization, or DAO.[38] (The crowdfunding service that nearly took down Ethereum, confusingly named "The DAO," was one implementation of this general concept.) A DAO is a business, conceived as a nexus of contracts, built entirely in software.[39] The standard corporate arrangements of equity, debt, and corporate governance can be encoded as a series of smart contracts based on cryptocurrencies. As self-executing software running on a distributed blockchain, a DAO need not have any owners in the traditional sense. It simply operates and interacts with the world according to its algorithms. The concept was first articulated in 2013 by Dapp developer Dan Larimer, and it was expanded by Vitalik Buterin, who went on to create Ethereum.[40]

The DAO idea sounds like science fiction, but early versions of the concept are already being implemented. Aragon, an Ethereum-based platform, raised $25 million in a token sale for its system to make it easy to create and manage smart contract–based organizations. Specifically, that means corporate governance functions such as issuing shares, setting roles and permissions for shareholders, payroll, accounting, and voting on corporate bylaws.

As discussed in chapter 1, from the dominant transaction-cost economics perspective, firms know that their trust in employees and business partners may be violated through opportunistic behavior. The expenses of forming, monitoring, and enforcing agreements therefore shape their decisions, as well as organizational structures. Aragon's vision is that smart contracts can reduce the transaction costs of these corporate functions.

Originally promoted as a platform for DAOs and "unstoppable companies,"[41] Aragon shifted to focus on managing traditional, human-owned corporations through blockchains using smart contracts. It acknowledges that it "need[s] to solve multiple issues" in order to build truly autonomous organizations.[42] Some of those issues are technical. For example, the contracts that systems like Ethereum can handle with acceptable performance today are relatively simple; self-owned organizations interacting with the world through machine learning are still just conjectures. Others, though, relate to difficult problems of law and governance. The most advanced example in practice, The DAO, was a spectacular failure.

In sum, the very attributes that make blockchain systems algorithmically trustworthy also give us reason to distrust them. That should not come as a surprise. Trust, as we have seen, implies vulnerability. Only with the possibility of betrayal can true trust be realized. Blockchain networks are dangerous because they are so valuable. And their dangers, like their value, are already starting to manifest themselves.

6   What Could Possibly Go Wrong?

Vision and Reality

Ken Thompson, the co-creator of the Unix computer operating system, received the Association for Computing Machinery's prestigious Turing Award in 1984. In his acceptance speech, he did something odd. He chose not to talk about Unix at all; instead, he spoke about trust.[1] Computer security can never be proven indisputably, Thompson pointed out, because those who write the software can embed malicious code that is invisible to outside observers. "You can't trust code that you did not totally create yourself," he concluded. Instead, you must trust the people who wrote the code. Humans are always in the loop.

Three decades later, that principle remains true. With Bitcoin, Satoshi Nakamoto created a new decentralized trust architecture. He did not overcome the need for trust. Just as a map is not the same as the territory it covers, a computer system implemented in the real world never matches its idealized description. Many ideas that sound great on paper wither in the face of real-world complications. Most people do not change their behavior overnight. Building technology platforms that work at scale and integrate with existing systems takes time and often involves false starts. Sometimes the true problems are not ones that the blockchain can solve. Sometimes the adoption incentives are not as strong as it seems within the bubble of blockchain enthusiasts. Incumbents have significant advantages and do not necessarily stand still in the face of innovation. Success is far from guaranteed.

Several much-hyped examples of revolutionary blockchain opportunities have failed to meet expectations. A pioneering initiative to register land titles on a blockchain in Honduras, thereby empowering individuals, failed amid disputes with local officials.[2] A company that observers said could "transform the music industry"[3] with blockchain technology offered singer/songwriter Imogen Heap's song "Tiny Human" on Ethereum with great fanfare ... and generated sales of $133, as reported by blockchain critic David Gerard.[4] A prominent, well-funded blockchain start-up promising to cut the cost of remittances between immigrants and their families took two years to launch in its first country, and had less than seventy-five users per day a year later.[5] None of these examples mean that the companies involved, or the use-cases they promoted, are doomed to failure. Perhaps they were simply too early. But they should be cautionary notes for those who view the triumph of the blockchain as inevitable.

Furthermore, the Internet experience should give pause to those making confident predictions about the blockchain's social impacts. The Internet is an extraordinary tool for free speech around the world but also is the mechanism that repressive governments now use to control their populations.[6] Social media brought people together but also nurtured communities of hate and state-sponsored disinformation campaigns.[7] Uber provides people around the world with efficient access to transportation but also gives one company tremendous power that it has repeatedly abused.[8] The blockchain has similar potential to be used for good and ill. The same corrosive forces that gave rise to the modern trust crisis could undermine or corrupt its solutions.

Just because the blockchain provides a better mousetrap does not mean that it will restructure the world. Major established systems are typically more resilient than they appear. For example, longitudinal research by New York University (NYU) professor Thomas Philippon concluded that "the unit cost of financial intermediation appears to be as high today as it was around 1900."[9] Despite the introduction of the telephone, the computer, the Internet, the cloud, and all the other technological innovations of the past century, it costs about the same in real terms to transact in financial markets as it used to. The volume and sophistication of activity have grown dramatically, but so have the transaction costs represented in the financial services sector. Philippon speculates that as basic services commoditize, new, more expensive products emerge, such as asset management, in a continual effort to beat the market.

One interpretation of this result, from fellow NYU professor David Yermack, is "that there really is a desperate need for technology to come, reduce the cost of financial intermediation, probably by orders of magnitude."[10] He posits this as the opportunity for financial technology (fintech) innovations including distributed ledger technology. The question, though, is why these innovations would be any more likely to change these dynamics. Recording financial transactions on a distributed ledger could be much cheaper than doing so through a collection of reconciled databases and could give rise to many new services.[11] But the same was true of moving from paper to computerized records, and from room-sized mainframes to Internet cloud storage. Today's financial services colossus JPMorgan Chase is light years more sophisticated than the firm that John Pierpont Morgan created in 1895. Yet it occupies a similar role in the interstices of finance.

What would really change the economics of financial services—and other sectors—is a fundamental change in industry structure. The tokenization model described in chapter 2, in which value resides in the network rather than its controlling operator, offers just that potential. If big players in the middle no longer gained comparative advantage from their bigness, it might actually produce the dramatic power shifts that blockchain boosters describe. Entrepreneurs with great ideas would no longer be at the mercy of venture capitalists and other financial gatekeepers. Musicians and authors would not have to give over control, and most of the profits, to music labels and publishers. Developers of innovative technologies would overcome the inertia of less-efficient incumbent approaches. Economic opportunity would be open to more individuals around the world, especially in low-income regions. Governments would be more effective in serving their citizens, while at the same time intruding less in their lives. Incumbent firms could benefit as well, but they would need to become more transparent and more dedicated to serving their users.

All these potential transformations are tremendously exciting. But they are not inevitable. And as the finance industry illustrates, even technological transformations that preserve market structures can produce massive innovation. The proper response to the blockchain, therefore, is not to get out of the way of inexorable disruption, but to engage. What matters are not the industries that the technology might conceivably transform, but the markets and practices that it will actually change. The way to separate the two is to dive below the surface commotion of press releases, funding announcements, and cryptocurrency prices.

Even when distributed ledger technology is applied in contexts where it can add significant value, there are substantial uncertainties and dangers. Satoshi Nakamoto came up with a novel and valuable approach to distributed trust, but it is far from a perfect solution. Certain challenges cannot be overcome by any technology. The same wave of hype that produced the Whoppercoin (as discussed in chapter 4) leads many to think that blockchains cannot fail. In reality, even if the foundational security of a distributed consensus remains intact, many things can go wrong. And there are many reasons why pilot projects or start-ups announced with great fanfare do not achieve their stated goals.

To reach their potential, systems built around blockchain technology will need robust trust. The blockchain vision treats trust as a public good rather than a source of private advantage. Participants on public blockchains will need to trust in a decentralized model in which no one—seemingly—is in charge. Companies on permissioned distributed ledger networks will need to trust that they can share control. And across the board, governments will need to trust that their citizens will be protected, taxes will be paid, and abuses can be policed. This means that blockchain-based solutions will need to engage with the mechanisms of governance and law.

Satoshi's Error

In the words of Nick Szabo, "There is no such thing as a fully trustless institution or technology."[12] When Satoshi Nakamoto wrote in his Bitcoin whitepaper that he "proposed a system for electronic transactions without relying on trust," he actually meant something much narrower. Electronic transactions in bitcoin can be trusted as valid without a discrete trustworthy third party, such as a government or bank, to verify them. That is indeed a dramatic change. There are a surprising number of situations in which the need to trust certain parties creates inefficiencies, conflicts, and failures. What unites Bitcoin and the distributed ledger platforms it inspired is a commitment to limiting the scope of that trust. Perversely, reducing the necessarily trust in some parts of a system may make the whole most trustworthy. Yet that is very different than saying that trust is absent. Just ask the customers of QuadrigaCX.

QuadrigaCX is the largest cryptocurrency exchange in Canada. It allows customers to trade fiat currencies for cryptocurrencies such as bitcoin and ether. In May 2017, ether worth about $14 million at contemporary exchange rates became inaccessible due to a programming error.[13] No foul play was involved, and the ether did not disappear. Anyone could still view the records identifying the currency on the Ethereum distributed ledger. Yet for the customers involved, it was as if a stack of $100 bills were locked in an impenetrable safe, with no key.[14] If this were traditional money sitting in a vault or the electronic records of a bank, there would be no problem. The bank by definition would have custody over the funds. It would have the ability— even if it were reluctant or legally restrained in exercising it—to release the funds. But that is exactly the form of "relying on trust" that Satoshi negated.

The point here is not just that QuadrigaCX's customers trusted the exchange, which let them down. They did, and it did. Those customers also trusted a system that made it impossible for QuadrigaCX to recover their funds once they are cryptographically locked away. This is the dark side of immutability. Banks and governments and others do not change transactions after the fact because they simply cannot. Where reliance on others is a cause for concern, this minimization of third-party trust makes participants more willing to transact. Perversely, though, that requires more trust on the part of participants. It is a leap of faith to engage in valuable transactions where no one has the ability to exercise control, like sitting in a self-driving car with no ability to operate the brakes or steering wheel.

The degrees and directions of trust involved in distributed ledger systems are design choices. They can be dialed up or down depending on the context. A digital cash system allowing anonymous cross-border payments has a different risk profile than an online ad-targeting solution for a network of publishers and advertisers. Design decisions, though, impose trade-offs. There is no such thing as a free lunch, even if you are paying in a virtual currency. And the trade-offs are not always clear.

The second biggest misunderstanding of Satoshi's legacy, after the belief that trust is a solved problem, is the belief that humans are a solved problem. Even when the guts of the system involve rigorously logical computers interacting through precise machine transactions, people are not irrelevant. Blockchains exist to solve human problems and power human activity. They can never fully escape human messiness. Nor should they want to.

The blockchain was developed in response to trust failures, but it can also be the cause of failure. The early stage of distributed ledger development accentuates these difficulties. In the cryptocurrency world today, a great deal of infrastructure development is happening in parallel with the creation of applications that depend on that infrastructure. It is like decorating the upper floors of a building while the ground floor is still just a frame. Bitcoin is by far the most mature piece of distributed ledger infrastructure, and even it still struggles with basic scaling and governance challenges. Many of the other infrastructure components are at trial stages or are just concepts under development.

On the one hand, it is remarkable how successful the growth of cryptocurrencies and distributed ledgers has been despite the immaturity of their foundations. On the other hand, things have gone spectacularly wrong. And they will again. Vlad Zamfir, one of the core developers of Ethereum, created a stir when he tweeted in May 2017, "Ethereum is not safe or scalable. It is immature experimental tech. Do not rely on it for mission critical apps unless absolutely necessary!"[15] He is to be commended for urging realism about the technology. But then again, his warning was too late. The asset value of Ethereum at that point exceeded $10 billion. And his warning was in vain. Seven months later, when he declared, "I can't think of a single blockchain/cryptocurrency project that is ready for production,"[16] Ethereum's asset value was nearing $70 billion.

Blockchain-based systems are not invulnerable. At the most general level, distributed ledgers depend on modern cryptographic techniques such as secure hashing algorithms. Basic vulnerabilities in these mechanisms cannot be ruled out, especially with advances in computing power. Quantum computers, for example, might be able to break encryption methods that the most powerful conventional computers cannot crack. If such flaws exist, however, they will apply at least as strongly to the existing online transactional systems, which rely on the same cryptography. And the blockchain world has attracted some of the world's foremost computer scientists, who are working actively to prevent such failures. Platforms such as Ethereum, for example, are already incorporating quantum resistance into their designs, even though workable quantum cryptographic computers are still some way off.

A more likely danger is flawed implementation of cryptographic techniques, such as reliance on random number generators that are not actually random. Blockchain technology, like any system built on computer code, is not perfect. There have been significant bugs discovered in the open-source Bitcoin code, although they were addressed prior to any lasting damage. MIT researchers found a potentially catastrophic vulnerability in the IOTA cryptocurrency network, which was forced to conduct a hard fork that made the network inaccessible to exchanges for three days.[17]

Proof-of-work and similar consensus mechanisms have some explicit limitations. Most notably, they can be overcome by a 51-percent attack.[18] The processing power of the Bitcoin and Ethereum networks today is equivalent to that of hundreds of the world's fastest supercomputers, running nonstop, making it quite difficult for someone to match it. Estimates are that just the hardware involved would cost several hundred million dollars. Nonetheless, because most mining is now handled through pools in which many participants aggregate their activity, it is not inconceivable that a pool could cross the threshold.[19]

The danger of a 51-percent attack increases when mining network power decreases.[20] That tends to occur when the price of bitcoin falls, reducing the incentives for miners, or at the halving points, when the algorithm automatically reduces the award to slow the flow of new currency into the system.[21] The dramatic rise in the price of bitcoin and other cryptocurrencies in 2017 made a decrease in mining power seem unlikely, but that could change if the price crashes. The rapid growth of the blockchain market belies its immaturity. According to a group of leading researchers in 2015, "[w]e do not yet have sufficient understanding to conclude with confidence that Bitcoin will continue to work well in practice...."[22]

The Limits of Decentralization

Blockchain decentralization has limits. This is true even for Bitcoin, perhaps the purest decentralized cryptocurrency. Bitcoin users trust the code issued by the core developers, and that code incorporates hard-coded elements such as "checkpoints," beyond which the blockchain cannot be forked. And bitcoin holdings are actually quite concentrated. According to an analysis in late 2017, just 1,000 accounts held 40 percent of the currency, and 100 held over 17 percent.[23] The concentration of some initial coin offering (ICO) tokens is even more extreme. Brave raised $35 million, but two-thirds of the tokens went to just twenty holders.[24]

The biggest points of residual centralization for public blockchains, however, are the miners and the core developers. Bitcoin works because Nakamoto Consensus aligns the economic interests of miners and network users. The vision of the Bitcoin whitepaper was that mining would be a relatively low-intensity activity that ordinary users could engage in. There would be millions of miners around the world, all putting processing power to work for the hope of earning rewards. Indeed, for the first few years of Bitcoin's existence, this was a relatively accurate description.

However, as the price of bitcoin—and the corresponding rewards from mining—increased, competition among miners revved up. Dedicated mining companies began creating specialized hardware that was optimized for Bitcoin's hashing puzzles. Ultimately, they moved to designing their own custom chips, called application-specific integrated circuits (ASICs), to power massive racks of mining computers. The performance of these ASICs was so much greater than the alternatives that for all intents and purposes, mining became a scale game. Operators such as Bitmain and Bitfury gained a sustained advantage through their mastery of ASIC design.

Mining pools accelerated this trend. Each Bitcoin miner was supposed to compete with others to earn block rewards, but groups of mining operators realized that they could achieve better results by pooling their earnings. Instead of each miner receiving nothing most of the time and a windfall when it successfully solved a block, pools split their payouts in proportion to the hashing power contributed. This made payouts steadier and more predictable, further accelerating the commercialization of mining. The fact that ASIC developers could outsource some of their hardware obsolescence risk to small-scale miners was another incentive.

The final step toward mining consolidation was the shift in mining economics as processing power increased. Hardware costs and bandwidth became a smaller percentage of total expenses than electricity to power the intensive computing and to keep the machines from overheating. So those with access to cheap or free electricity, especially in locales that made it easy to operate and cool massive server farms, had an advantage. Relationships with local or national authorities who control electricity supplies became a competitive differentiator for miners.

Fewer than ten groups dominated Bitcoin mining by 2017.[25] Most were Chinese mining pools. (Bitfury, which operates its own data centers and sells hardware only to large purchasers, is the primary exception.) Ethereum mining is also highly concentrated, even though its consensus algorithm is designed to be ASIC-resistant.[26]

The concentration of mining calls into question the basic premise that public blockchains are decentralized. Collusive miners could, like the Japanese keiretsu networks of major corporate groups, create an outwardly competitive market that actually serves a small coalition of private and government interests. As the price of cryptocurrencies increases, the money to be made through proof of work goes up as well. The mining operations for Bitcoin and Ethereum now generate several million dollars per day in revenue from their block rewards. And with the scaling challenges Bitcoin has faced, transaction fees have ramped up as well. Mining pool operators can be expected to maximize their profits. There is no reason for them to promote decentralization of the Bitcoin network if doing so conflicts with their economic interests.

Ethereum and other networks hope to limit the power of miners by switching the consensus algorithm to proof of stake. Proof of stake replaces computationally intensive mining with the staking of tokens. Even if it succeeds, though, proof of stake could promote centralization of a different kind by giving large holders of the cryptocurrency—who have more available to stake—greater power over its development.

The miners are not the only concentrated blockchain interest group. The developers working on the core software also tend to be small groups wielding a great deal of power. Satoshi Nakamoto and a few colleagues created the original Bitcoin implementation in 2009, but it has been significantly revised and extended since then. Implementing a scalable, reliable, bug-free network takes ongoing efforts. Hyperledger and R3 follow a more established model for open-source software projects of interest to major companies. They have corporate members who contribute funding and code, along with established governance structures for those members.

Coinbase cofounder Fred Ehrsam estimated in mid-2017 that there were only about fifteen primary developers each for the Bitcoin and Ethereum platforms.[27] Important infrastructure projects such as Lightning Network, which hopes to create a new application layer that greatly improves the performance of the Bitcoin network, run on shoestring budgets. For projects managing cryptocurrencies with asset values in the tens of billions of dollars, on which companies around the world have staked their futures, those are tiny numbers. The small number of core developers keeps these projects nimble, but it raises the question of whether they can handle the load. Both projects have much larger communities of engaged developers, but they depend on the work of the core group.

On the Bitcoin side, although there is a Bitcoin Foundation with the mission of promoting the protocol, most of the key developers are paid by third parties such as the MIT Digital Currency Initiative, the venture-backed startup Blockstream, and the self-funded ChainCode Labs. The Bitcoin Core developers are actually a very loosely connected group, who often disagree.

Only a handful of them have "commit" access to update the official Bitcoin Core software repository, and there is no formalized process for granting that power.

The Ethereum Foundation has a stronger position in the Ethereum ecosystem. Thanks to its 2014 crowdsale, it has resources to fund core developers. It also has a "benevolent dictator" who shepherds the project, in Vitalik Buterin. Finally, Ethereum's community norms tend to be more collaborative than Bitcoin's. This model parallels that of other successful open-source projects, most notably the Linux Foundation led by Linus Torvalds, but it creates some tension with the notion of Ethereum as a truly decentralized system.

The distributed trust model of blockchain systems is based on power being concentrated in the network itself. Validators are incentivized to participate but not guaranteed any control over transactions. Dapps engaging in token sales replicate this structure on the next higher layer. The value of the network resides in the currency, which is distributed among users and other token holders. It is not centralized in the network operator, in contrast to centralized information and social media platforms. The network is the infrastructure, which creates value for all.[28] Yet no one is automatically responsible for funding that infrastructure.

This creates the potential for a tragedy of the commons. Developers, users, and token holders of applications benefit from good engineering of the blockchain platforms, but they do not necessarily contribute to it. Networks that held lucrative token sales during the ICO boom were able to monetize to support development prior to launch. Then again, they face expectations commensurate with the scale of their crowdsales.

The fact that miners and core developers can exert influence over the direction of a blockchain system does not invalidate the basic claim of decentralization. There is no one entity that can throw a magic switch and alter the network. Power to alter the protocol, such as changing the block size, is different from power to change the information recorded on the ledger. Immutability holds up so long as the network collectively is more powerful than an attacker.

What the limits of blockchain decentralization mean is that questions of governance and regulation cannot be dismissed. These systems depend on trust, and trust depends on the collective decisions of those who shape the platform.

Centralization has benefits. In 2013, an update to the Bitcoin Core software accidentally triggered a potentially catastrophic hard fork. The Bitcoin community quickly recognized that the best course of action was to downgrade to the earlier version, destroying the fork.[29] The core developers were able to reach consensus in less than an hour through online chatroom conversations. The fix was quickly implemented because the mining pool BTC Guild, which then controlled 20 to 30 percent of Bitcoin mining power, threw its weight behind the change. A more decentralized community might not have been able to respond in time to stave off a crisis.

On the other hand, if a country wants to crack down on blockchain-based activity, it has ways to gain purchase. It could not completely shut down the network if enough nodes were outside its borders. It could, however, effectively threaten local users, miners, and the exchanges converting cryptocurrencies into and out of fiat currencies. China did just that in mid-2017. It banned Bitcoin exchanges and token offerings, out of concerns about financial fraud and capital flight.[30] Yet shortly thereafter, Yao Qian, the head of the People's Bank of China's Digital Currency Research Institute, called for the Chinese central bank to issue its own cryptocurrency.[31]

From all indications, Chinese leaders understand very well how economic soft power, embodied in mechanisms such as the Marshall Plan after World War II and Treasury Bills as the global reserve currency, helped make the U.S. the world's lone superpower. Tokenizing the Chinese renminbi before other major fiat currencies is one potential path toward similar soft power in the twenty-first century. Russia appears to have similar designs.[32] Cryptocurrency mining could even become a strategic technology for major nations, like atomic physics during World War II or supercomputing during the Cold War.

These are speculative scenarios today. Whatever happens, the bedrock assumption that public blockchain networks are inimical to centralized private or public control needs to be qualified. If cryptocurrencies become more significant in either financial or political terms, those in charge today will not be powerless to shape them.

Not-So-Smart Contracts

While the fundamental failure of a blockchain platform cannot be ignored, a greater concern lies in the software and services on top of the distributed ledgers. As noted previously, even though the integrity of the distributed ledger is a purely mathematical phenomenon, that is only one aspect of the blockchain trust system. The software layer that translates distributed consensus into applications and services gives the blockchain its transformative power, but it also creates risks and challenges that no fancy math can overcome.

The next layer, beyond the blockchain itself, is the smart-contract code that implements transactions.[33] The Bitcoin scripting language is intentionally quite limited, in order to prevent flawed or malicious scripts. It basically allows for moving currency between users, with a few additional features such as multiple-signature confirmation ("multisig"). Using the Bitcoin blockchain to do anything else requires what could be considered clever hacks, such as encoding tokens for other assets as colored coins.

Ethereum and other general-purpose blockchain platforms offer full-blown application functionality through their smart-contract systems. A smart contract can have errors and security flaws, like any other software code. And indeed, vulnerabilities have already been identified in high-profile Ethereum smart contracts.[34] Errors or security exploits in smart contracts are particularly dangerous because the blockchain directly carries value or rights to assets. There are significant practical limitations in replacing human enforcement of agreements with software running on the blockchain. Things simply do not always go according to plan.

The QuadrigaCX example described earlier is a real-world case in which a simple error in smart-contract coding caused roughly $14 million of ether to, well, disappear into the ether. The currency balances are recorded on the Ethereum blockchain, but the ether is irretrievably wrapped in an inaccessible smart contract. Because the contract itself was immutably recorded, it cannot be edited to correct the mistake.

Ironically, the root of the QuadrigaCX problem was the resolution of the earlier crisis of The DAO, described in chapter 3. To reverse the theft of ether from contributors to The DAO crowdfunding system, Ethereum forked into two chains. Cryptocurrency exchanges had to add "splitter" code to account for the fact that all prefork Ethereum holders now held Ethereum Classic (ETC) as well. QuadrigaCX was one of them. A bug in the splitter code was what froze its customers' funds in an inaccessible smart contract. This incident illustrates the interdependencies that inevitably arise when software code automates decision-making and enforcement.

Even without bugs or attacks, there are reasons to doubt that smart contracts will always operate as desired. First, they require the reduction of human-readable language to machine-readable code. This limits their scope to those subjects and activities that can readily be specified precisely. A contract that my connected car will be unlocked upon presentation of a certain cryptographic key can be encoded through a programming language such as Ethereum's Solidity. The network address for the car lock, the desired key, and the action to be taken are all subject to precise definition. On the other extreme, some contractual terms simply cannot be expressed through formal logic because they imply human judgment. A machine has no precise way to assess whether a party used her or his "best efforts," for example.

In the case of The DAO, the difference between a legitimate transaction and theft came down to intent, which is something that computers cannot determine under the terms of a smart contract. As Lightning Labs chief executive officer (CEO) Elizabeth Stark puts it, "The DAO was a fascinating example when the implied meaning of the code differs from the actual execution of the code."[35] Shortly after the hack, an anonymous letter was posted, allegedly written by the attacker:

> I have carefully examined the code of The DAO and decided to participate after finding the feature where splitting is rewarded with additional ether.... I am disappointed by those who are characterizing the use of this intentional feature as "theft." I am making use of this explicitly coded feature as per the smart contract terms and my law firm has advised me that my action is fully compliant with United States criminal and tort law. ... I reserve all rights to take any and all legal action against any accomplices of illegitimate theft, freezing, or seizure of my legitimate ether, and am actively working with my law firm.[356]

The posting was almost certainly a hoax, but it was nevertheless instructive. It highlighted exactly the subjectivity problem that Vitalik Buterin identified a year earlier—only now the consequences were real.

Despite great advances in machine learning, computers do not have the degree of contextual, domain-specific knowledge or subtle understanding required to resolve contractual ambiguity. Even worse, it may be difficult to be sure what the smart contract will do until it runs.[37] Formal verification methods can be applied to check smart contracts before they are encoded on the blockchain. These can be automated systems or, for more significant smart contracts, bespoke auditing by expert teams. There are already consulting firms playing a role analogous to financial auditing firms today.

However, even if these steps are taken, there are some smart contracts that cannot be formally proved to achieve the desired results.

And even if the smart contract operates as designed, it may produce suboptimal outcomes. Facts may change between the ex ante specification of contract rights and the ex post adjudication of legal effects. Parties to smart contracts can try to hedge against such changes by incorporating qualifying language or "act of God" (force majeure) clauses, but those are the kinds of imprecise terms that are difficult to specify in computer code. In other cases, parties may wish to enter into a mutually advantageous alteration of a contract prior to performance.

Under standard contract law, such modifications are unproblematic. For smart contracts, however, they pose a difficulty. Upon agreement, the contract is locked into place. To enable an intermediate step before execution, the smart-contract code would need to incorporate the possibility of modification explicitly. As a technical matter, this would increase the complexity of the process. It would also introduce difficulties about how to encode when and how parties might be permitted to modify the set terms of a smart contract. Developers are working on creative solutions, such as allowing users to vote on the best version of a smart contract, but even if effective, these will involve tradeoffs.

Finally, as cultural critic Ian Bogost points out, the power of smart contracts could be abused.[38] The lack of human intervention in their execution and enforcement makes smart contracts potentially more efficient, but it removes them from the domain of judicial oversight. Contract law is fundamentally a remedial institution.[39] It is concerned less with changing how parties act when entering into an agreement than with achieving the right result after the fact. In incorporates a variety of doctrines—unconscionability, mutual mistake, illegality, capacity, consideration, fraud, duress—that allow a party to escape from even clearly specified contractual obligations. These exceptions do not undermine trust in contract enforcement because judges supervise their application.

With smart contracts, there are no judges. The parties specify the terms at the outset, and the blockchain network automatically enforces them once the contract is activated. This can produce the scenario found in The DAO, where a contract is executed in a way that none of the parties intended. Or it can give one party extraordinary power over the other, without judicial restraints. Smart contracts thus represent the same threat as digital rights management technology, which overrode the carefully balanced safeguards of copyright.[40] Content owners were able to use technology to impose limitations that the law would not support.

As Nick Szabo suggested, an auto lease encoded as a smart contract could allow the lender to disable the car remotely if the borrower fails to pay. That might be seen as a decentralizing alternative to the capriciousness of regulated financial services providers. But it also could be a tool for the arbitrary exercise of private power. The borrower in this scenario is in thrall to the lender far more than under the current system. Without regulatory and governance mechanisms to constrain them, blockchain-based systems can easily become means of central control. Bogost notes that this pattern, open decentralization leading down the garden path to private power, is exactly what happened with the Internet, now dominated by a few platforms such as Amazon, Google, and Facebook.

Trusting the Token Issuers

A popular slogan in the Bitcoin community is "Vires in numeris," a rough Latin translation of "Strength in numbers." Sometimes, though, that turns into "Caveat emptor": Let the buyer beware. Traditional trust architectures allow for sanctions when parties violate the rules of the game. Trustless trust comes with no such protections. The distributed ledger verifies that information is recorded accurately, but not the legitimacy of that information.

The ICO gold rush illustrates both the benefits and dangers. Companies can raise money in new ways and support new kinds of applications. Investors around the world who would not otherwise have opportunities to fund start-ups can do so with the click of a mouse. Those investors can receive tokens offering both independent investment value and utility on the platform. Those are the positives. The negative side is that those contributing to the token sales enjoy none of the legal protections that have long been the norm for securities offerings.

Polybius launched an ICO in June 2017 "with little more than a 22-page 'prospectus' and a promise that 'Polybius Bank will become a fully digital bank accessible everywhere at any time.'"[41] A "blockchain share" issued by Polybius "represents the right to receive a part of company's profit," just like a stock. But instead of selling stock, a highly regulated activity in most of the world, the company made the offering online, to anyone, through an Estonian foundation. It stated that it would announce the country of registration for the new Polybius Bank only after the ICO. Investors did not seem to mind. They quickly snapped up $31 million worth of the tokens.

Those purchasing Polybius tokens in most ICOs were not primarily interested in the immutability of the transaction, without central control. They would have been just as happy buying equity through a traditional private offering of stock. What they were betting on was some combination of excitement about the venture itself and a belief that the tokens will appreciate in value. The latter depends only indirectly on the viability of the blockchain. Investors trusted Polybius much more than the distributed ledger technology.

And Polybius built its trust on the traditional method of individual reputation. The ICO materials discussed the founders' expertise (developed through a prior Bitcoin mining hardware business), and the whitepaper sought to demonstrate their technical and business acumen.[42] Banking is highly complex, highly regulated industry, however. The Estonian financial regulator issued a press release stating that Polybius had no license to offer financial services in its home country, a worrisome fact for an erstwhile global bank.[43] A start-up such as Polybius trying to enter the banking market would face long odds without the backing of experienced players.

Polybius touted an association with Ernst & Young (EY), one of the Big Four global audit and accounting firms. A press release said that EY partner Daniel Haudenschild and two others were "collaborating to lead the Polybius project team on banking operations, technology, and legislation," and noted that "[m]any of EY's activities involve advisory support to financial institutions."[44] The institutional reputation of EY, a pillar of centralized trust, no doubt enhanced investors' willingness to take a risk on an unproven and as-yet-unbuilt business.

On closer inspection, it is not so clear that it should have. The Polybius project's website listed the three EY employees among fifteen "advisors," who presumably were granted tokens ahead of the ICO as compensation.[45] It does not identify any formal partnership, investment, or consultancy relationship with the auditing firm. If one is trusting Polybius in part by trusting EY, that trust could well be misplaced. Indeed, shortly after the launch of the ICO, EY told the *Financial Times*, "Daniel Haudenschild is no longer with EY and his comments concerning EY's Blockchain strategy are incorrect."[46]

None of this proves that Polybius is a scam, or otherwise in violation of legal obligations. Yet would likely give most investors pause. Perhaps Polybius will succeed in building a global virtual bank and its token holders will profit handsomely. Or perhaps they will lose everything—after the developers pocket some of the ICO proceeds. Token offerings of this sort represent a sudden, grand experiment in "anything goes" securities offerings, targeting retail investors all around the world. Given all the uncertainties and technical complexities of blockchain technology, most investors are unlikely to understand what they are getting into, even with extensive financial disclosure. Without it, they are at the mercy of the offerors and investment promoters. A system that invites abuse on this scale will be abused.

As with many blockchain-based activities, boundaries and best practices need to be worked out. Different countries may come up with different answers. That is the normal way that the law evolves. A baseline set of disclosure and accuracy requirements, however, seems essential to a well-functioning market. The blockchain may dramatically improve the efficiency and liquidity of funding companies. But it will not change human nature.

Centralized Edge Providers

The final significant vulnerability for blockchain-based activity lies at the edges of the ledgers. Even when value is encoded into decentralized systems, the access points may be through centralized edge services. For example, an individual who stores bitcoin with a consumer-oriented wallet service such as Coinbase, Blockchain.info, or Xapo must trust that provider in the same manner as with a bank. The wallet provider stores the private cryptographic keys for its customers, which allows them to access their cryptocurrency through a standard user name and password. However, if the wallet provider is hacked, the keys become vulnerable. The fact that the wallet is connected to a distributed ledger does not make the wallet service itself inherently more decentralized than a traditional web-based service, nor does it make the wallet itself any more secure. As Nick Szabo tweeted, "Bitcoin is the most secure financial network on the planet. But its centralized peripheral companies are among the most insecure."[47] It is estimated that 10 percent of the ether raised in ICOs has already been stolen, mostly from wallets.[48]

A particular point of vulnerability at the edge of blockchain networks lies in exchanges that trade cryptocurrencies for dollars or other government-backed money. With Bitcoin, the only two ways to obtain cryptocurrency are through mining or by exchanging with someone else. End users today cannot compete as miners, so at some point, they have to buy their bitcoin or other cryptocurrencies with existing currency. A number of exchanges have sprung up around the world to serve this need. They also allow institutional traders to create markets. Well-functioning exchanges, like traditional stock exchanges, can further the price-discovery process and promote efficient capital formation.

Unfortunately, cryptocurrency exchanges often prove insufficient to the task. In 2014, the most prominent bitcoin exchange, Mt. Gox, collapsed after hackers were able to steal a significant amount of currency, then worth about $400 million, in a series of thefts.[49] Another major exchange, Bitfinex, was hacked in 2016, losing cryptocurrency valued around $70 million at the time. All told, there have been at least fifteen incidents in which cryptocurrency worth at least $1 million was stolen, with a total value exceeding $600 million at the time of the thefts. That number would be at least an order of magnitude higher at peak bitcoin valuations.

It is much easier to build the basic technology platform of an exchange than to ensure that it is robust against security vulnerabilities and is able to maintain sufficient liquidity as trading volumes grow. Although there has been some effort to require the licensing of cryptocurrency exchanges, the global nature of the market means that many exchanges are essentially unregulated today. A site converting euros into bitcoin may look similar to a traditional currency exchange converting euros into dollars or yen, but it is not nearly as secure.

Even without foul play, exchanges and other edge providers are vulnerable to bugs. The QuadrigaCX problem mentioned earlier in this chapter was a case in which a simple coding error cost $14 million that could not be recovered. More recently, the Parity wallet service revealed that more than $160 million worth of ether was trapped after a user (apparently) accidentally issued a command that made all smart contracts using a certain version of the software inaccessible.[50]

Like QuadrigaCX, Parity introduced the bug when it updated its wallet software to fix an earlier flaw. That original problem allowed hackers to steal $30 million worth of ether raised in token sales. And Parity is not a company of blockchain neophytes. It was cofounded by Gavin Wood, the former chief technologist of Ethereum. Like exchanges, wallets are a centralized concession to make it convenient for ordinary users to handle cryptocurrency. Wallet-security practices will improve over time, but so long as people depend on edge providers, the risk will remain.

The other aspect of the trust in edge providers is that those providers can decide whether to police transactions. A Bitcoin transaction for drugs, or gambling, or a contract killing will be processed the same way as one for a pizza. With traditional financial transactions, the payment processors (such as Visa and Mastercard members) are control points that governments can pressure to block illegal transactions. If the payment is in bitcoin, there is no one involved in the payment itself to pressure, just a distributed network of miners. If, however, the transaction goes through an edge provider, it can be subjected to legal enforcement. That might be difficult depending on where the service is located and whether it hides identities of its management, but it is not impossible. The most famous example was Silk Road, discussed in chapter 2.

Different levels of security and robustness are needed depending on the context. A bank will be more concerned about certain risks than a merchant engaged in a small-value consumer transaction. Medical records on the blockchain will have different risk profiles than supply-chain records for diamonds. Such variation is not unique to the blockchain; it is part of trust and security with existing centralized systems. Given the novelty of distributed ledgers, though, it will take some time to sort out the appropriate security models.

Rules of the Road

The fact that blockchain networks and the activities on top of them can cause harm does not undermine the value of distributed ledgers. It just shows the naïveté of believing that Satoshi Nakamoto's invention solved the problem of trust once and for all. Many things that provide significant benefits also produce substantial dangers. A car can kill its owner if the brakes fail through a defect, can kill others if the owner drives while drunk, and can be used as a weapon if driven into a crowd. But no one suggests that cars should be outlawed. Rather, rules such as driver's licenses, automobile registration, traffic laws, insurance, and tort liability balance the desire for safety against the benefits of driver or manufacturer autonomy.

Taking the analogy further, autonomous (driverless) vehicles promise to solve problems such as drunk driving by replacing human drivers with machines. The machines, however, create new challenges. What if your autonomous vehicle has a bug, or someone hacks it to drive off a cliff? What if it strikes and kills a pedestrian?[51]

As with ordinary cars, the choice is not between outlawing self-driving-car technology and accepting unlimited harm. Various rules will be designed to strike the best risk/benefit trade-off. Who is responsible when an autonomous vehicle crashes and what approval procedures should be necessary to put one on the road are two examples of the questions that are now under discussion. Blockchain systems pose the same types of challenges and deserve the same type of scrutiny. They are likely to be extremely beneficial on balance. That should not lead us to ignore their potential downsides, however.

The next several chapters of this book examine how laws and regulations could address these harms, making blockchain-based systems both more trusted and more trustworthy. Chapter 7 considers the ways that government-defined legal rules, as well as private means of controlling behavior, can influence activity on blockchain networks. Chapter 8 shows how the blockchain's software code relates to traditional forms of legal enforcement. Chapter 9 looks at how governments can, will, and should oversee those networks themselves.

7   Blockchain Governance

Vili's Paradox

Vili Lehdonvirta, an economic sociologist at the Oxford Internet Institute, could hardly be called a Luddite. An expert on digital markets and former videogame developer, he was one of the first to take seriously the organizational dynamics of virtual worlds and the gig economy. He cowrote the definitive book on virtual economies. A *New Yorker* article even flagged him as a potential Satoshi Nakamoto.[1] (He laughed and offered a convincing denial.) Yet Lehdonvirta is something of a cryptocurrency critic. He describes himself as being "very skeptical of the claims that blockchain will fundamentally transform the economy or government."[2]

Lehdonvirta argues that distributed ledgers face a governance paradox.[3] If they truly have no means of collectively resolving disputes other than voluntary agreement, they will fail. On the other hand, Lehdonvirta asserts, when these networks adopt formal or informal governance structures, they are no longer truly decentralized. If Ethereum succeeds because Vitalik Buterin and its core developers are wise leaders who can enforce decisions by changing the code, how is that any different than centralized development projects such as Linux, or Facebook for that matter? At that point, the advantages of decentralization, which must be weighed against the overheads it imposes, disappear. With governance, Lehdonvirta suggests, there is no longer decentralization. But with decentralization at any interesting scale, there must be governance. Hence the paradox.

Vili's Paradox is the starting point for any serious discussion of the blockchain's future as a trust architecture. External forces of law and regulation will shape the blockchain economy, but the real success of blockchain-based systems will depend on their internal capacity to instantiate new forms of governance. Without functional governance, the best that blockchain networks can do is revert to the traditional foundations of peer-to-peer (P2P), Leviathan, or intermediary trust. They run the risk of creating the worst of all worlds, and failing spectacularly.

Lehdonvirta distinguishes enforcing rules—which is the function of the blockchain—from making rules, which he calls "governance." The distributed ledger takes care of the problem of third-party enforcement. It cannot do the same for third-party rule-making, however, because it is itself a product of rules. There is no way to bootstrap a rule system like the blockchain into existence: It must be designed by someone. Unless the initial rules are perfect, now and for all time, they will eventually need to be modified. And that will require centralized third parties.

Lehdonvirta has a point. Those who believe that the blockchain heralds a revolutionary decentralized economic order, which will necessarily triumph over established arrangements, have placed their faith in a false god. But his account is incomplete. It may be true that, as he concludes, "once you address the problem of governance, you no longer need blockchain." You may, however, still want it. Blockchain governance is not an oxymoron. As with law and regulation, though, it will take multiple forms, involving multiple actors, and using multiple tools for coordination.

The response to Vili's Paradox lies in examining the subtleties of distributed ledger adoption. To use Brian Behlendorf's formulation, shifting the point of minimum viable centralization makes a difference, even when that point is nonzero. Again we return to the gap between what Satoshi Nakamoto claimed to create—a system that worked "without relying on trust"—and the more limited, yet actually more significant, reality. What Bitcoin actually eliminated was the need for trusted third-party validation of transactions, which is only one element of trust. Adam Ludwin, CEO of the blockchain technology firm Chain, made the same mistake with the admittedly pithy statement, "Cryptocurrencies do not *have* governance mechanisms, they *are* governance mechanisms."[4] A more accurate statement is that cryptocurrency networks are technologies of governance.[5] The blockchain decentralizes the rule-enforcement aspects, but not necessarily rule creation.

Where this account can be supplemented is in the definition of governance. Lehdonvirta equates governance with private rule-making, and elsewhere defines public rule-making as regulation.[6] Yet the two cannot so easily be separated. Legitimacy arises from the interplay of internal and external rules.[7] If blockchain networks and Dapps were clearly subject to legal obligations, they would have more leeway in establishing exotic governance arrangements. Law would serve as a backstop. Conversely, if the smart contracts provide strong protections, as with some well-designed initial coin offerings (ICOs), there might be less need to apply traditional legal frameworks.

As Elinor Ostrom emphasized in her work, governance is polycentric: "The humans we study have complex motivational structures and establish diverse private-for-profit, governmental, and community institutional arrangements that operate at multiple scales to generate productive and innovative as well as destructive and perverse outcomes."[8]

The blockchain world will be no different.[9] Successful blockchain governance cannot be merely an idealized design question, just as successful smart contracting cannot rely entirely on ex ante coding.[10] It requires careful attention to the ways that real-world systems develop and interact. Blockchain networks will be subject to overlapping governance structures, with varying degrees of centralization.

This perspective calls into question Lehdonvirta's sharp distinction between rule-making and enforcement. A mere expression of preferences is not governance. Anyone can make up a set of rules. Getting people to comply with those rules is the hard part. Compliance may be achieved in various ways. Hard-edged enforcement mechanisms can force people to behave in certain ways. As discussed in chapter 5 in connection with the cryptoeconomic trust design of public blockchains, sanctions are not always the best—or even an effective—solution. The level of punishment is not the primary determinant of whether people obey the law, as Tom Tyler's work illustrates.[11]

The Power of Consensus

Blockchain technology at its core creates not money, but agreement. As described in chapter 2, the protocols that Satoshi created were designed to drive networks to consensus. Yet a consensus is an odd thing. It represents something more than a majority and something less than unanimity. And it some ways, consensus is more powerful than both. According to the sociologist Edward Shils:

> Where it exists, consensus is a counterforce against the fulfillment of the divisive potentialities of divergent "interests" and beliefs. Consensus facilitates

collaboration: it reinforces the cooperation which arises from coincidences of interest, limits the range of the divergence of interests by defining ends in a way which renders them more compatible, and circumscribes the actions injurious to cooperation which might arise from the divergent interests.[12]

What exactly, then, is a consensus? Webster's dictionary gives two definitions: "general agreement" and "group solidarity in sentiment and belief." They have very different implications. The first says nothing about the emotional or psychological status of the community reaching consensus; the second definition makes the community's views the whole meaning. Blockchain networks, it appears, promise to replace the second definition with the first. Computers have no "sentiment and belief," but they can be very effective at reaching "general agreement" if that concept is defined precisely enough.

Every participant need not agree in order for consensus to be reached. In a distributed ledger environment, consider a situation where one participant is untrustworthy and attempts to add double-spend transactions. The system might still be said to be in consensus. The one bad actor would be outweighed by the rest of the participants, and its transactions rejected. On the other hand, if 51 percent of participants want to reject a transaction and 49 percent want to accept it, there is a majority, but not necessarily consensus. The level of disagreement is so high that trust in the majority result will be weak.

In this way, consensus is deeply connected to trust. As one political scientist puts it, "If there is a consensus on 'consensus' ... it is that it occurs where there is a high degree of 'trust' amongst members of a political system."[13] Consensus is achieved when those who disagree with the outcome agree to be governed by those who do. The erstwhile opponents do not continue as an active minority, as happens in a democratic system. They become indistinguishable from the community that always supported the consensus. The dissenters' willingness to join the consensus requires them to trust that they will not be exploited by the majority.

Where there is healthy consensus, trust follows. When the consensus holds, it gives participants confidence that the system is working. It reinforces the belief that if they give way to the will of the community, so will others when the time comes.

There is a long history of consensus being a preferred means of dispute resolution among technologists. Unanimity is often impossible when engineers have different views about the best technical approach to pursue. At the same time, the formalism of majority voting feels constricting to those used to letting their code do the talking.

The famous mantra of the Internet Engineering Task Force (IETF), as stated by MIT researcher David Clark, is: "We reject: kings, presidents, and voting. We believe in: rough consensus and running code."[14] Clark expressly included voting as something to be avoided. Centralized power, even if implemented through fair and democratic means, was to be avoided. The challenge of getting fractious participants to agree sufficiently was mediated by two qualifiers. The consensus need only be "rough," and existence proofs in the form of working software were privileged over abstract ideas.

Satoshi Nakamoto never referenced Clark's mantra, but his system embodied its key principles. Bitcoin and its descendants allow imperfect consensus. In fact, they are built around the expectation that some participants in the network might be untrustworthy or unreliable. And cryptocurrencies made running code king. Functions that traditionally were executed based on democratic procedures or governmental institutions were built into the system and automated. As we shall see, that does not mean that the blockchain's software always trumps government-based legal regimes. The blockchain's code operates in the first instance as a different kind of law.

Bitcoin's money supply illustrates this approach. Monetary policy, which influences the rate of inflation, is traditionally the domain of expert central bankers. The politicians who appoint those bankers, however, are answerable to a democratic electorate. Satoshi's design fixed the total supply of currency at 21 million bitcoin, and established an automatic process for issuing that currency at a gradually slowing rate. Every Bitcoin validator and user accepts this regime as an attribute of the currency. The limit on supply could, however, be removed through a hard fork that gained sufficient support.

Bitcoin's approach may or may not have been a good idea. Some finance experts argue that the fixed supply of bitcoin means that it will inevitably be deflationary and lose out to fiat currencies, where governments can print money at will.[15] Not all cryptocurrencies take the same approach; Ethereum, for example, has no absolute limit on the number of coins. In either case, the network's algorithmic rules function as governance mechanisms to coordinate behavior toward consensus. Those who diverge from the consensus rules of a blockchain network can work to forge new technical consensus or create their own network.

Even when that consensus is implemented through immutable smart contracts, therefore, there is always an ongoing governance process in the background. Vitalik Buterin captures this by defining governance as equivalent to "coordination flags."[16] Institutional actors operating within established norms signal for a certain action. Participants determine whether to comply *based on whether they think everyone else will.* They may look to multiple indicia of consensus to make such decisions. This conception bears a striking similarity to Ostrom's description of trust creation: "It is not only that individuals adopt norms but also that the structure of the situation generates sufficient information about the likely behavior of others to be trustworthy reciprocators who will bear their share of the costs of overcoming a dilemma."[17]

There are a variety of alternative methods to govern behavior without formal enforcement. Incentive structures may make the desired behavior the rational choice, even though people retain the option in theory to do otherwise. Behavioral "nudges" may produce similar results, even when not based on rational self-interest, by shaping the "choice architecture" of decisions.[18] And community norms backed with community-based sanctions may be strong enough to promote compliance. Each of these mechanisms involves trade-offs. Choices made in the rule-making process are necessarily about compliance structures.

Blockchain networks do more than just enforce consensus over distributed ledgers. They incorporate a variety of formal and formal governance mechanisms. The results will be different when the same dispute occurs on Bitcoin, Ethereum, Ripple, or R3 Corda. One benefit of the proliferation of blockchain networks is experimentation with governance models. So, while Lehdonvirta is correct that decentralized enforcement is not tantamount to decentralized governance, it could stimulate significant governance innovations.

Governing the Governors

The new institutional economist Avner Greif showed in a series of papers how Jewish merchants operating in the Muslim world of the tenth century built an effective reputation system without the support of formal law or modern communications.[19] It was an excellent example of P2P trust. Agents who defrauded one of these Maghribi traders would find themselves shut out from other opportunities throughout the western Mediterranean. The Maghribis could trust those they did business with because their institutional structures reined in opportunistic behavior. They had created an effective governance structure, which Oliver Williamson describes as "the institutional framework within which the integrity of a transaction is decided."[20]

Looking at governance more broadly, Greif sought to explain why some countries today are rich and stable, while others are poor and lack effective political order. He identified two essential institutional functions: contract enforcement and coercion constraints. Scholars have focused primarily on the former, he noted, because they define "the range of transactions in which individuals can commit to keep their contractual obligations."[21] However, credible enforcement institutions, following Thomas Hobbes's logic, rest on the potential for coercion. And that is itself a threat to markets. How can one trust a private deal when the agents of the state can, at any moment, abrogate it for their personal benefit? So, as Greif detailed, mechanisms such as separation of powers and checks on the state's authority are equally important to the development of confidence in markets. Trust at scale requires institutions, and institutions require governance.

One of the key attributes of permissioned ledgers is how they support governance rules to constrain the power of network participants, compared to traditional trusted intermediaries. According to Hyperledger executive director Brian Behlendorf: "You can do markets a lot of good if you take a player who acts at the center as message-passing hub (essentially as God) and turns them into somebody more like a referee on a football field."[22] A referee has strong powers, but they are confined in scope and subject to well-defined rules.

Conversely, the fiasco concerning The DAO (described in chapter 3) is a good example of what happens when enforcement institutions develop without coercion-constraining ones. The hack itself suggested that the blockchain could not be trusted to distinguish among illegitimate transactions. A system that enforces theft, even unintentionally, is no different than one that unreliably enforces legitimate contracts. The response to the theft was equally problematic.[23] The decision to roll back through a hard fork was made by the Ethereum Foundation and adopted by a majority of mining nodes.

Various unofficial polls during the hard fork debate notwithstanding, the foundation had no democratic processes for decision-making. The CEO and COO of Slock.it were the former chief tester and chief communications officer of the Ethereum project, respectively, raising questions about whether they received special treatment to reverse the drain of funds. The process was halting and chaotic.

As Vitalik Buterin ruefully observed, "I think prior to 2015 people naively thought 'blockchains do not need governance.'"[24] It is an open question how widely that naive view persists. For those involved in The DAO episode and the subsequent Ethereum fork, however, there could be no question that governance mattered. Once the fork occurred, there were two Ethereum chains. They were identical in every respect, with one exception: Ethereum Classic (ETC) adopted the governance rule that nothing could justify reversing an executed, immutable smart contract. The main Ethereum chain took the position that sometimes such a drastic step was called for.

Law can foster trust because it is an institution, not just a set of formal rules. The legal system can adapt to changing circumstances or to edge cases not contemplated in the drafting of the rules. And law is implemented through processes—court decisions, legislation, administrative actions, and the like—with various formal and informal bases for legitimacy. All that flexibility and process makes law imperfect and often inefficient. Yet as we have seen, translating rules into smart-contract code and cutting out the human enforcement mechanisms create their own problems.

The blockchain's algorithmic architecture does not eliminate the role of humans in fostering trust. The proof-of-work systems behind the major blockchain platforms depend on miners, responding to economic incentives, in order to validate transactions. Decisions about investment in blockchain hardware and software, as well as whether to accept cryptocurrencies in lieu of traditional money, are also made by humans rather than machines. Even The DAO, which was the epitome of an automated, leaderless, software-based organization, had explicit roles for humans to serve as contractors and curators to authorize certain actions.[25] This is significant because human systems are more easily subject to legal enforcement than software code. Governments have difficulty directly regulating algorithms, but they can regulate individuals and organizations that design or implement those algorithms.

A subtler reason for the persistence of human involvement in the trust architecture of the blockchain is the impossibility of eradicating subjectivity. The attack on The DAO provided a perfect illustration. The attacker exploited a bug to drain a substantial amount of currency away from users into its own account. However, it used a valid, self-executing smart contract to do so. Under The DAO's terms of service, the functionality of the code expressly superseded any human-readable terms:

> [T]o the extent you believe there to be any conflict or discrepancy between the descriptions offered here and the functionality of The DAO's code at 0xbb9bc244d798123fde783fcc1c72d3bb8c189413, The DAO's code controls and sets forth all terms of The DAO Creation.[26]

Unsurprisingly, the victims of the attack proved unwilling to accept this result. The problem was that the difference between a legitimate crowd-funding transaction and unauthorized theft came down to intent, which was not something that the smart contracts could evaluate. On the other hand, this is the sort of thing that courts tease out all the time. They marshal evidence and use judges or juries to evaluate the expressed intent of the parties.

Without such human-based governance and dispute resolution mechanisms, smart contracts on the blockchain will sometimes execute in ways that are inconsistent with the desire of the parties. Given the extraordinary scope of activity that could be tied into distributed ledgers, this is potentially a very worrisome proposition. The issue is not just financial loss, as with The DAO. Blockchain registries will control many physical assets and systems. Widespread failures of smart contracts to achieve their intended results could not only undermine trust in the blockchain, they could produce the kinds of damage anticipated (but largely unrealized) from the Y2K bug in the year 2000.

As with the historical narratives explored in Greif's work, the success of distributed ledger systems is ultimately a matter of effective governance. "It's naive to think we can we get ourselves out of the need to regulate ourselves," observes Behlendorf.[27] Blockchain networks cannot rely solely on their consensus rules to resolve conflicts that operate above the level of basic transaction validation.

The Social Contract

Stating that blockchain networks need governance begs the question of how those governance systems can develop. Sometimes the answer will be straightforward. The relevant entity may use a traditional organizational structure, even if its trust model is based on distributed ledgers. Silk Road, Mt. Gox, and AlphaBay were centralized systems. Someone controlled the keys. When the keys were stolen or those operators were arrested, they shut down. All these markets used cryptocurrency as a means of transacting, but they themselves were not decentralized.

The 2017 WannaCry ransomware attacks were similar. The malware demanded payment in bitcoin to a specified address in order to decrypt users' hard drives. Cryptocurrency was a supporting mechanism, in the same way that a robber may use a gun as a supporting mechanism. The essence of the cybercrime was tricking users into installing harmful software. There are clear points to assign legal responsibility.

The same analysis holds true for governance questions. Coinbase, one of the largest cryptocurrency exchanges, is regulated as a money transmission agent under state and federal laws in the U.S., where it is based. Coinbase benefits from the distributed networks of Bitcoin, Ethereum, and other cryptocurrencies. However, Coinbase itself is not a distributed network. It has a board of directors and shareholders. It is subject to the same governance processes as a financial exchange trading stocks or other conventional instruments.

Blockchain networks and Dapps work differently. No one holds a master key, even if some actors wield more influence than others. The level of structure varies. The Bitcoin Core developers are a loosely defined and shifting group, who struggle to reach consensus even among themselves. Most blockchain networks and Dapps involve a defined organization at the core, such as the Ethereum Foundation. Those organizations, however, depend on community adoption. They cannot just impose top-down rules. So, then, what makes decisions legitimate?

For all the technical wizardry of Nakamoto Consensus and Turing-complete smart contracts, the essential questions are quite familiar. They date back to Enlightenment figures such as Hobbes and John Locke, with precursors in ancient times. These philosophers focused on a basic question: Where does government come from? The standard pre-Enlightenment answer was the divine right of kings. Authority could originate only from God. Any other answer seemed circular, just like building trust and governance on a foundation of trustlessness. Locke and Hobbes argued that government could emerge out of nothingness with the consent of the governed, or what they called a "social contract." The leaders of the American Revolution took these ideas to heart.

Hundreds of years later, Bitcoin achieved the same feat of self-creation. And when blockchain networks face governance crises, they can fall back on the same philosophical concepts. Ethereum's Vlad Zamfir advocated for the post-DAO hard fork in Lockean terms: "The Ethereum community has an implicit, constantly evolving social contract that describes which changes to the Ethereum protocol and platform it would consider adopting."[28] The great danger, he warned, was something that "puts the platform at risk of being gamed by motivated parties."

This was also a paramount concern of the framers of the U.S. Constitution.[29] They wanted to create a democratic system, but they worried about giving excessive power to self-interested factions or politicians who might manipulate voters to gain power. The framers' response was to institutionalize formal systems, such as checks and balances, a bicameral legislature, and separation of powers, as a dynamic counterweight to majoritarianism. These mechanisms add friction to governance. That can be a drain on efficiency, but it also makes it harder for the system to go completely off the rails. Such governance structures operate as the coercion-constraining rules that Greif emphasized.

Public blockchain governance can be described in terms of three major interest groups subject to checks and balances: developers, validators (miners), and token holders.[30] Application software developers (e.g., wallets) and exchanges may also be relevant. Ideally, governance processes would balance the interests of these groups and offer them pathways to resolve their differences. The Bitcoin scaling debate and the Ethereum post-DAO hard fork furnish two examples of blockchain network governance in action.

Governance in Practice

Economists describe money as having three properties: It is a medium of exchange, a store of value, and a unit of account. The trouble is that the first two of those are sometimes in conflict. Buying an espresso at the local coffee shop and saving for retirement are both uses for money, but they are quite different. If you are using the currency for transactions, you want its value to remain stable. If an exchange charged $1 for one bitcoin last week, and it charges $2 today, you will spend twice as much on a cup of coffee denominated in bitcoin. That might not be a problem if the whole economy ran on bitcoin, because the price of everything would be pegged to it rather than dollars. But we are unlikely to get to that point any time soon. Conversely, if you are holding bitcoin in an investment account and the exchange rate with the dollar doubles, so does your investment.

If one group of Bitcoin users is interested in transactions and another is interested in investment, their interests are not aligned. Both want Bitcoin to succeed, but success means different things to each group. As Paul Vigna and Michael Casey explain in their book *The Age of Cryptocurrency*, this tension harkens back to a long-standing debate. "Metallists" value money as a thing of inherent value, which emerges from the bottom up from user activity or the inherent worth of coins, while "chartalists," following Georg Friedrich Knapp, see money as a product of rules and social relationships.[31] Is a cryptocurrency valuable because of what it is used for, or is it used for things because it is valuable? This book, focused on the collective phenomenon of trust, takes the latter perspective, but the debate is instructive.

Many early Bitcoin enthusiasts emphasized transactions rather than trust, because they wished for a currency not dependent on governments or social interactions. Yet so far, most of the activity in the market involves Bitcoin as a store of value rather than a cashlike instrument for routine payments. In 2015, Wences Casares, a well-known Bitcoin entrepreneur and CEO of the digital wallet firm Xapo, stated that 96 percent of the coins on Xapo were held as investments rather than for use in purchases.[32] And this was before the 2017 run-up in bitcoin prices. Only three of the top five hundred online retailers in 2017 accepted bitcoin, a number that actually fell from the prior year.[33] Most companies that take payment in bitcoin immediately convert it to dollars or another traditional currency to avoid the price fluctuation. For Bitcoin or other cryptocurrencies to become viable as payment mechanisms, they will need to become trusted in a broader sense than offering secure ledgers and limited supply.[34]

In the early days of bitcoin, there were very few things to spend it on. Even now, most of the situations where bitcoin is accepted as a payment mechanism could be handled more easily by traditional money, with the possible exception of illegal activity. For most of those currently holding bitcoin, the currency is an investment in bitcoin itself rather than a means for transactions. An increasing bitcoin exchange rate also increases the effective value of rewards to miners, which brings more of them into the game and enhances the security of the system.

An increase in the value of bitcoin is thus a positive for the legitimacy of the currency. However, it creates the impression that bitcoin's success is entirely a function of its exchange rate in dollar terms. That is not entirely true. Bitcoin is not a stock; it is a currency. If it is going to become useful *for* something rather than merely *as* something, the price fluctuation is a problem rather than a benefit. The online game marketplace Steam announced in December 2017 that it would no longer accept bitcoin payments because of the high fees and volatility driven by trading activity.[35]

Today, you can still use bitcoin to pay on online sites such as Overstock .com, Dish Network, Microsoft's Xbox gaming service, and Expedia.com, as well as an eclectic collection of small retailers. Alternatively, you can buy and hold bitcoin as an investment. (The mantra of Bitcoin enthusiasts is "HODL," based on a misspelling of "hold" in an early message-board poster's drunken rant.) Yet Satoshi Nakamoto's dream of Bitcoin as a ubiquitous, low-cost, high-speed global transaction currency remains unrealized. And with transaction speeds dropping and fees increasing in recent years, it seems more distant than ever.

This tension is at the heart of Bitcoin's recurrent governance controversies. Satoshi's original idea was that for some time, the primary means of incentivizing verification nodes would be the automatic reward that miners earn when successfully mining a new block. Transaction fees voluntarily added by senders would grow in significance later, as the block rewards decreased. In practice, however, transaction fees scaled up more quickly. The growing level of traffic overwhelmed the Bitcoin network. Those who wanted their transactions to be processed in a reasonable amount of time were forced to tack on larger and larger transaction fees to move to the head of the queue. By 2017, Bitcoin transaction fees routinely were several dollars per transaction, and sometimes much more, making small-value "micropayments" impractical.[36] And the slow speed of Bitcoin transactions became an increasing drag on many applications.

The question was how to scale the network. The small group of core developers who oversee Bitcoin's code debated what to do for several years. One faction wanted to allow larger block sizes, meaning that each validated block would include more transactions. Others worried that this would destabilize the network. Some wanted to move fast, others to change slowly over time. The faction opposed to increasing the block size eventually coalesced around a technical upgrade called "segregated witness (Segwit)," which would process blocks more efficiently. It also made possible a feature called Lightning, allowing some transactions to be processed off the block-chain and validated as a group. There were several attempts to resolve the debate, but none succeeded in gaining sufficient support.

Technical fights among developers are nothing new. The IETF is legend-ary for its many conflicts over the years. Yet the Bitcoin community failed to match the IETF's success in achieving "rough consensus." One of the key reasons why is that the developers are not the only ones whose voices matter. They create the software, but it is the miners and other full-node operators who run it. With most cryptocurrencies, there is no way to force a miner to run a particular software version.[37] The accurate blockchain is the one that most of the computing power in the validation network considers the longest chain. If enough miners choose to run different software, the network will fork. There will be two blockchains, which diverge over time.

In some ways, forks are a beneficial feature of blockchain networks. They mean that no group that somehow achieves a majority of voting rights (in the form of mining "hashing power") can force a minority to accept its decisions. The two sides will go their own ways, and users will decide which blockchain they value and trust. Forking is a well-accepted practice in the open-source world. Splinter groups take software projects in particu-lar directions without forcing everyone to accept their vision. The anony-mous cryptocurrency Monero, for example, originated in a fork due to a developer revolt. It now has significantly higher adoption than Bytecoin, the blockchain from which it forked.

However, forks can also create confusion, reduce the level of cryptoeco-nomic security, and weaken trust. Sometimes changes to the protocol can be executed through "soft forks," in which the chain splits but the two vari-ants remain compatible. Those nodes running one version of the software cannot use the features that the other version offers, but both still record the same set of transactions. Significant changes such as adjusting the block size require a clean break, known as a "hard fork."

Some miners preferred larger blocks, because that meant more transac-tions, and therefore more fees. The core Bitcoin developers were split, but they were generally more concerned about network integrity than transaction volumes. The solution that maximized bitcoin's stability as a store of value independent of governments was not necessarily the one that made it easiest to use bitcoin for large-scale retail payments. Token holders represent the third interest group alongside miners and developers. They too can decide which blockchain is the real one by their choice of client software. Many activist bitcoin holders and wallet providers weighed in on the scaling debate, on both sides.

So far, Bitcoin has managed to avoid a decisive break. A compromise called the New York Agreement allowed the implementation of Segwit in mid-2017. At the same time, a splinter group executed a hard fork to create a parallel currency with larger blocks, known as Bitcoin Cash.[38] Bitcoin Cash is not universally supported. It trades at a significantly lower price than bitcoin. If nothing else, though, it demonstrated that the Bitcoin network could go through a hard fork and not collapse. A plan to execute another hard fork to increase the block size on the main Bitcoin chain, envisioned under the New York Agreement, was called off due to lack of support.[39]

The positive spin on the Bitcoin scaling fight is that Bitcoin's diffuse governance promotes stability. It takes a lot to line up sufficient support for any significant change. That puts pressure on those proposing changes to do the spade work necessary for community support. Users and other network participants can rely on Bitcoin not being captured by one particular group's agenda, and they can be confident that risky new features will receive substantial vetting prior to adoption. Slow development at the protocol layer opens the door for more innovation to shift to the application layer, through mechanisms such as Lightning payment channels.

The negative perspective is that Bitcoin governance is broken, making necessary changes excessively difficult. One person's stability is another's rigidity. After years of controversy, it is difficult to imagine the Bitcoin community coalescing and quickly responding to a crisis today in the way that it did during the 2013 accidental fork described in chapter 6. Moreover, compared to Ethereum and other blockchain projects, the pace of new code and new features for Bitcoin has slowed thanks to the tension over scaling proposals. As brilliant as Satoshi's design was, and as much good work has gone into Bitcoin since then, the network will ultimately need to evolve as technology and the marketplace change.

Ethereum has a more close-knit development community based around the Ethereum Foundation. Yet it too struggles when governance is put to the test. After the collapse of The DAO, there was a period of weeks in which the community debated potential responses. The hard fork that was eventually adopted generated significant opposition, which eventually coalesced around ETC. Whether future catastrophic losses of ether would trigger similar hard forks was not decided.

At the time of the hard fork, Ethereum's Vlad Zamfir rejected any formal mechanisms to implement the network's social contract: "It is paramount that the social governance process, rules, or principles that govern hard forks do not become institutionalized. ..."[40] A year later, however, he sang a different tune, stressing the need for governance based on something other than economic incentives: "It is a matter of identifying (nascent) governance institutions, their formal rules, and the tacit/ad hoc norms/culture around them."[41] As with the move from the close-knit technical community of the IETF to the larger world of business and state actors for Internet governance, the trust that established the network was insufficient to support it at scale.

For Ethereum, perhaps unintentionally, the legacy of the DAO experience reinforced trust in the platform's governance processes. After the hard fork, the price of ether tumbled as trust in the currency was shaken. Yet slowly at first, and then, quite rapidly, it rebounded. At the time of the QuadrigaCX incident a year later, ether had risen from $10 after the hard fork to nearly $300. When asked to explain their confidence in the currency, many traders pointed to the successful fork as evidence that Ethereum could be counted on to resolve significant problems.[42] Its community faced an existential threat and responded decisively. It had leaders, and at least the rudiments of processes for them to direct the community.

Ethereum's successful rebound from the fiasco of The DAO illustrates the importance of governance. Its processes are far from perfect. Even the more-established blockchain networks are still experimenting to find the right balance of flexibility and formality. How successful they are will go a long way to deciding which platforms thrive.

8 Blockchain As/And Law

Vlad's Conundrum

Surveying the landscape at a time of significant legal controversies around blockchain-based projects, Ethereum core developer Vlad Zamfir remarked on Twitter: "I think there is a direct conflict between some widely adopted policy goals and the 'real success' of blockchain tech."[1] Asked by Ethereum project leader Vitalik Buterin to elaborate on those policy goals, he listed sanctions, anti–money laundering (AML), terrorist-financing restrictions, preventing tax evasion, capital controls, copyright, and rules against the publication of certain kinds of information. These are not marginal elements of public policy. Most governments would consider them nonnegotiable.

Zamfir's statement squarely frames an essential question: is the blockchain compatible with law? If the "real success" of blockchain technology means that the only rules are those embodied in the consensus process, it would seem that is not. Public blockchain networks are often described as censorship-resistant. Yet one person's censorship may be another person's rule of law. Just as smart contracts cannot tell the difference between a thief and a legitimate user, they cannot, on their own, distinguish legal from illegal transactions. Blockchain decentralization appears to throw out the baby with the bathwater when it comes to the enforcement of government-defined law.

Even if blockchains are not necessarily used for illegal activity like Silk Road's drug marketplace, perhaps they make it impossible to stop those who choose to engage in such activities. We might call this "Vlad's Conundrum." Some would view freedom from state-based law enforcement as an unalloyed good. Zamfir, however, was expressing concern. The rule of law is essential to functional societies. And even if one holds deep skepticism toward government power, the blockchain will not achieve "real success" in mainstream adoption as a technology of lawlessness.

Fortunately, the conundrum can be resolved. The blockchain does operate as a kind of law, but that does not mean that it will—or should—trump other regulatory modalities. Appreciating blockchain software code as law is the start of the inquiry, not the end.

Many would cheer the use of blockchain technology by activists in North Korea to publish illegal prodemocracy manifestos. But it would not stop there. In a truly decentralized network, there is no way to impose limits on money transfers to known terrorists, transactions selling children into modern slavery, or movement of funds known to be stolen. Universal freedom, at the outer limits, is tantamount to anarchy: Thomas Hobbes's war of all against all. At minimum, any legitimate policy choices on a truly distributed network would require a majority vote of participants. Even such a pure democratic mechanism would require new governance technologies that, if they are feasible at all, have significant limitations.

Law and morality are contextual. Individuals can decide which actions to deem permissible. So can communities of individuals exercising legitimate power, such as religious organizations or nation-states. The world cannot. The fundamental problem is not technical. A perfect real-time global voting system could not determine the proper treatment of abortion or the ideal solution for online privacy. On some issues, people simply cannot agree. They will accept a disagreeable solution only if they are willing to cede ultimate authority to some trusted institution. Blockchain decentralization cannot make this problem go away.

Political philosophers such as John Rawls and business ethicists such as Tom Donaldson and Tom Dunfee have wrestled with the question of how to establish stable rules in a world of diverse perspectives.[2] For example, what should multinational firms do if bribery is expected where they do business but illegal or considered unethical in their home country? The basic idea of the republican form of government is that even if citizens disagree about the proper policy decision, they agree to follow the decisions of the democratically elected legislature and properly appointed judges. When everyone is not a citizen of the same nation, that rationale breaks down. Philosophers offer various approaches in response, but none can be coded into an algorithm.

The Augur prediction market platform illustrates the conundrum. A "prediction market" allows participants to bet on predictions by buying and selling them like stocks.[3] Those betting on outcomes that turn out to be wrong lose their money, which goes to those making the correct predictions.[4] Because the participants have "skin in the game" and aggregate their predictions with others through pricing signals, prediction markets often produce quite accurate odds. They are a commonly cited illustration of the "wisdom of crowds" in action.[5] Companies such as Google use prediction markets internally as forecasting devices.[6]

Prediction markets seem like a perfect fit for the blockchain. They involve bringing buyers and sellers together, a currency of value, and shared record-keeping to track predictions. There is just one problem: Unregulated real-money prediction markets are generally illegal in the United States. With a few exceptions, such as the Iowa Electronic Market to predict political campaigns, which limits accounts to $500, prediction markets are considered either a form of prohibited gambling or derivatives exchanges, which must receive approval from the Commodity Futures Trading Commission (CFTC). The largest commercial prediction market, the Ireland-based Intrade, was sued by the CFTC and forced to stop serving U.S. customers in 2012. It closed down entirely in 2013 amid acknowledgments of "financial improprieties."[7] A further concern is the possibility of predictions that might encourage illegal activity.[8] Despite this, Augur raised $5 million in a crowd-sale. It is developing a decentralized platform to create prediction markets on Ethereum.[9]

Don and Alex Tapscott, in their best-selling book *Blockchain Revolution*, are enthusiastic about Augur's potential. After mentioning that centralized prediction markets such as Intrade were shut down, they note the concerns about "assassination markets and terrorism futures." They state briskly, however, that this will not be a problem for the blockchain-based version: "Augur resolves the issue of unethical contracts by having a zero-tolerance policy for crime."[10] That entirely begs the question: When laws governing the contracting parties, the developers, and the other participants in the prediction market disagree, what is a crime? Deciding what counts as unethical is even more difficult.

And what does zero tolerance even mean here? The Augur developers do not control what questions can be posted on the prediction market. On Facebook and Reddit, administrators have the ability to delete illegal, offensive, or harassing material that users post. Not so on a decentralized platform such as Augur. Its predictions are smart contracts processed without human intervention. If someone listed a criminal contract for an assassination, who would stop it? As Zamfir suggested, there seems to be an inherent conflict between the innovative scope of something like Augur and legitimate public policy considerations.

One solution is for the distributed applications simply to ignore the legal system. As one of the creators of OpenBazaar, a decentralized online marketplace based on cryptocurrency, put it:

> [I]f we allowed people to be accountable towards traditional courts and law, we're opening up pandora's box in letting governments interfere by making their own laws about what's "cheating in a transaction" and what is not, which leaves room for censorship....[11]

Censorship resistance, the argument continues, is the sine qua non of blockchain-based systems. The problem is when no legal accountability means no accountability at all. "Anything goes" quickly breaks down when networks scale, necessitating complex rule structures. That was the lesson of every Internet-based community, from eBay to Wikipedia to Reddit.[12] It was a very clear lesson of The DAO. And governments will act effectively against excessive illegal activity, as the Silk Road takedown demonstrated. AlphaBay and Hansa, two cryptocurrency-fueled dark marketplaces that sprung up in Silk Road's place, were similarly shut down by law enforcement in 2017.[13]

Pockets of extralegality can persist. There are many "darknet" communities for online file sharing, distributing malware tools, and drug transactions that launched after peer-to-peer (P2P) services like Napster were shut down and before the rise of Bitcoin. But they rarely became big enough to dent the legitimate, regulated markets. And when they did, as with the Megaupload file locker service run by the notorious New Zealand–based playboy Kim Dotcom (né Kim Schmitz), arrest and prosecution were eventually the result. More decentralized systems such as OpenBazaar may make legal enforcement harder, but they will not prevent it.

There are also plenty of healthy small communities that do not engage in illegal activity, where "Let the buyer beware" works well enough. However, extrapolating from that to large global marketplaces is a categorical error. Law is necessary not because of limitations in technology, but limitations in people. People behave differently when protected by the anonymity of the crowd. As the Internet essayist Clay Shirky writes, "a group is its own worst enemy."[14]

Fortunately, the conflict between government-imposed regulation and unconstrained blockchains need not be so stark. The blockchain is not the first networked technology offering the potential to escape law and the power of the state altogether. Neither are its acolytes the first to ponder the tensions that freedom creates with morality and social order. They can learn from history. They can also leverage the blockchain's decentralized technology to promote accountability in new ways. Augur, for example, is developing an innovative mechanism of computational juries to address illegal or unethical prediction contracts. These will be discussed in more detail in chapter 10.

The relationship between the blockchain and law is indeed fraught. There will be systems such as Silk Road that go too far in promoting illicit activity, and there will be governments that go too far in cracking down on valuable technologies. However, the two roads of machine-powered ledgers and human-powered law need not diverge.

Things That Cryptoregulate

Renowned cyberlaw scholar Lawrence Lessig's aphorism, "Code is law," is frequently invoked to justify the domination of technical approaches such as the blockchain over legal enforcement. Yet that perspective is a fundamental misreading of Lessig's statement. He did not say "Code always disrupts law" or "Code is superior to law." His point was that software code and legal enactments are both mechanisms that can govern human behavior. Code is *a form of* law…and not necessarily the best one.

Lessig's New Chicago School framework,[15] elaborated upon in his seminal 1999 book, *Code and Other Laws of Cyberspace*,[16] holds that actually, four regulatory forces are commonly used to constrain human actions: *the law, social norms, the market, and architecture.* The last of these, in a technological environment, is defined through software code. A critical insight of Lessig's book and other early Internet scholarship, including my own,[17] was that technology should be studied as a regulatory modality in its own right. Software is not the end of regulation; it is a different kind of regulation that coexists with other mechanisms.

In the subsequent years, scholars have examined the technological architecture of Internet-based systems in great detail. Significant public policy

Table 8.1
Things that Regulate in the Blockchain Environment

	Rules	Motivation
Formal language	Cryptography	Self-interest
Human language	Law	Trust

fights over file sharing, network neutrality, intermediary liability, and digital privacy were all, at some level, battles about architecture. So were many of the business transitions that eventually elevated Apple, Google, Facebook, Amazon, and Microsoft into five of the world's most valuable and influential companies as other formidable competitors, both new and old, faltered.

The blockchain is a new form of software-based architecture. Just as it was wrong at the time Lessig wrote to view the Internet in purely technical terms, it is a mistake today to see the blockchain from only one perspective. However, blockchain-based systems have attributes that Lessig's code categories do not fully capture. A modified framework, illustrated above in table 8.1, offers a more accurate picture.

The distinctive architectural element for blockchain networks is cryptography. Distributed ledger systems enforce decisions based on the difficulty of reversing cryptographic mathematical transformations. In the place of markets is self-interest, or what economists would call "incentives." Many of the relevant decisions, such as whether to contribute computing power to mining a cryptocurrency or which chain to follow after a fork, do not involve market transactions. Moreover, the term "self-interest" captures the surprising aspect of Nakamoto Consensus—namely, that miners' single-minded greed can contribute to the public good of a trusted shared ledger.

The parallel to norms is trust. Trust can be thought of as a social norm, but it is more accurately the factor that makes norms possible. These three categories, taken together, describe the essential characteristics of blockchain consensus. The fourth "thing that regulates" remains law. It is the one regulatory dimension that is by nature external to blockchain software, networks, and communities because it comes from governmental actors. These "New New Chicago School" categories for blockchain systems can be organized along two axes: whether they are expressed in formal mathematical terms or in human language, and whether they describe a system of rules or an expression of human motivation.

Cryptography creates formal rules that are not subject to debate. A private key is mathematically connected to a certain public key, but one cannot be determined from the other without expending unrealistic levels of computing power. A hash function proves that someone had a particular document, even if the document itself cannot be reconstructed from the hash. When built into a software system such as Bitcoin or Hyperledger Fabric, such cryptography effectively limits behavior.

Economics is also grounded in math, but it focuses on how humans make constrained choices. Specifically, economics builds a formal theory around how people can be expected to respond to incentives. Someone theoretically could choose a lump of coal over a large stack of hundred-dollar bills, but self-interest (and common sense) strongly suggest they will not. From this simple premise comes a large body of knowledge. Especially relevant for the present purposes is game theory, which applies self-interest analysis to adversarial interactions.

It is quite common and quite tempting to evaluate blockchain-type systems purely in terms of the first row of the table. The bundling of cryptography and self-interest into cryptoeconomics is widely identified as Satoshi Nakamoto's central innovation.[18] Formal systems are neat and precise. They seem to do away with the ambiguities and abuses that cause suffering and limit freedom in human societies. The architecture of cryptography tantalizingly offers a way to instantiate the economics of game theory in binding rules.

Yet it is a mistake to ignore the human side of the ledger. A story about systems governing people, organizations, and societies cannot be written entirely in mathematical notation. Cryptoeconomics influences, and is influenced by, both trust and the law. Although it is expressed in terms designed to be read by humans rather than machines, law is also a structure of rules that define the scope of possible behavior. Where cryptography rests on the deep symphony of mathematics, law rests on the power of institutions and processes. Similarly, trust is not something that can be stated in precise economic terms. It is a leap of faith. Without that leap, society as we know it could not thrive. As humans, we are somehow driven to trust each other, just as we are driven to maximize our personal welfare. Even when our instructions are carried out automatically by computers, it is we who program those computers to serve our ends.

Blockchains regulate. A full accounting of the blockchain story must therefore consider all four factors. Blockchain-based solutions that ignore any element will produce unintended and undesirable outcomes. In particular, those that focus only on internal consensus dynamics to the exclusion of external law run the risk of going astray. Some already have.

This does not mean that law will remain untouched. It must adapt as well. Ideally that evolution will go hand in hand with development of new technological and cryptoeconomic models. The blockchain could foster innovation, wealth creation, economic development, equality, free expression, more trustworthy markets, and more effective government, all of which are also goals of the legal system. But it could just as well lead to rampant illegality, intractable disputes, abuse of power, and authoritarian control. Law—or blockchain systems acting as a form of law—could play an important role in addressing such challenges.

One of the most important lessons from Lessig's analysis was that law and code are not binary alternatives. In the early days of the Internet, entrepreneurs and technologists argued that because software-based networks could create communities that transcended territorial boundaries, those communities could disregard state-made law in favor of technologically enforced rules.[19] That proved to be an incomplete assessment at best. There were some examples of online self-governance, but there were more cases where law reasserted itself or the two mechanisms interacted, with norms and markets also having an impact.

The same story will play out with blockchain technology. Cryptography, self-interest, and trust may in limited circumstances take the place of law, but more often they will coexist with it. That coexistence may be synergistic or it may result in conflicts. The challenge for both governments and blockchain communities is to achieve the best results in a hybrid environment.

This Time It's Different?

The argument that the blockchain disrupts law has a familiar ring. In the late 1990s, it was fashionable to see the Internet as a technology that undermined regulation through decentralization. The cyberactivist John Perry Barlow wrote in his 1996 *Declaration of the Independence of Cyberspace* that governments "have no sovereignty where we gather" and do not "possess any methods of enforcement we have true reason to fear."[20] It captured the spirit of a movement that included not just traditionally committed libertarians, but also innovation-focused developers and legal experts. Scholars wrote of online communities freed from the strictures of territorial sovereigns.[21] Some cyberactivists went so far as to claim an abandoned British naval platform in international waters as the independent territory of Sealand, believing that they could operate servers completely outside legal restrictions.

These visions of an unregulable, decentralized cyberspace all met the cold hard limits of reality. As Jack Goldsmith and Tim Wu explained in their 2006 book *Who Controls the Internet*, governments around the world were able to impose their will on online activity.[22] Utopian initiatives like Sealand collapsed amid internal squabbling, with little or no adoption. China built a "Great Firewall" that monitored all Internet traffic in and out of the country. And geolocation technology allowed courts to impose sanctions on activity that touched citizens of their jurisdictions. Efforts to circumvent legal regimes, whether through P2P technology or online gambling services located in island jurisdictions where the conduct was legal, were repeatedly thwarted. The Internet did represent something big and new. But the legal system was able to incorporate and adjust to it, as it did with every technology since at least the printing press.

It turns out that while the Internet is nowhere, the people and companies and systems that deliver Internet services are very much somewhere. There are any number of control points, from the Internet service and hosting providers that manage the flow of bits to the financial-services firms that control the flow of money, which regulators can target to control online activity. The Internet is a regulated space. That is not to say, of course, that it is regulated in the same way everywhere, nor that online transactions are regulated identically to their offline analogs. Working through the practicalities of Internet regulation has been a twenty-year global process so far, with no end in sight. But a key point has been established: Internet regulation is not a contradiction in terms.

The blockchain has rekindled the cyberlibertarian flame. There are two ways to frame a discussion about blockchain and law: *Can* these technologies be subject to legal and administrative oversight? And *should* they be? Many blockchain developers and advocates, especially those that cut their teeth on Bitcoin in its earlier years, see the answer to the second question as obvious, and the first nearly so. Cryptocurrency, they argue, was created as a solution to the problem of government oversight of value-based transactions. Satoshi Nakamoto's breakthrough was to invent money that escaped the prison of regulation.

On this view, the decentralized architecture of blockchain networks is a firewall against government intervention. The blockchain is not just immutable; it is censorship-resistant. No higher authority can command a blockchain to do something, any more than it can control activity around the Internet. There is no "there there" to regulate. Verification nodes can be distributed around the world such that no territorial government has legal authority over a majority of the network. Government regulation and the blockchain are antithetical.

Proponents of distributed ledgers are taking up this banner. Legal scholars Aaron Wright and Primavera de Filippi draw a direct connection between the blockchain's "Lex Cryptographia" and the "Lex Informatica" of software code described in a 1997 article by Fordham law professor Joel Reidenberg.[23] They argue that the blockchain "could make it easier for citizens to create custom legal systems, where people are free to choose and to implement their own rules within their own techno-legal frameworks."[24] Self-executing smart contracts and decentralized autonomous organizations (DAOs), they argue, could implement private legal systems without regard to territorial states, much as Bitcoin created a private global currency.

Some take this idea even further. "Thanks to the Blockchain technology, we have the chance to not only re-invent governance, but fundamentally replace the Nation State."[25] So say Bitnation founders Susanne Tarkowski Tempelhof and James Fennell Tempelhof. Founded in 2014, Bitnation intends to create a borderless, virtual nation-state, featuring a constitution, democratic governance, and a variety of civic services, all managed on the Ethereum blockchain.

The experience of the past twenty years suggests that governments and powerful private institutions will not so easily be disintermediated.[26] Where they had a strong desire to regulate online activity, they found ways to do so. A similar pattern seems likely for activity on the blockchain: Where the stakes are high enough, governments will not simply defer their authority. Even when transactions are entirely digital, P2P, cross-border, and cryptographically secured, providers on the network can be identified and subject to territorial legal obligations. Moreover, outside of activity that is illegal or in need of extreme security, the incentives are lacking for most users to adopt custom legal systems where the existing ones are functional.[27] And as the creators of The DAO discovered, taking the place of law is not as easy as it may seem.

Wright and De Filippi acknowledge this fact. They suggest that the blockchain might expand the scope of regulation by code relative to other regulatory modalities. While this could be the case, the fact that distributed ledgers can be employed to develop customized extralegal rule-sets for communities and organizations does not mean they will be. Given the experience of the past twenty years, the burden is on those arguing that the outcome will be different this time. It bears noting that while distributed ledgers based on Nakamoto Consensus are new, smart contracts and digital currencies are not. Nick Szabo described the mechanism for private regulation by smart contracts in the early 1990s. There has not, however, been widespread adoption of cryptographically based, private law.

Governments could also employ blockchain technology themselves to expand their power. The universal visibility of transactions in a distributed ledger is an authoritarian regime's dream. China, for example, has banned unlicensed Bitcoin exchanges at the same time as its central bank is looking at tokenizing its currency through a permissioned blockchain. A digital currency issued by a central bank would do away with the anonymity of cash transactions. And tokenized systems to track personal information and associated metadata, even if decentralizing control to individuals, could radically centralize the availability of that data to governments and dominant private platforms. Describing this scenario, the technology critic Adam Greenfield observes that "blockchain technology enables the realization of some very long-standing desires on the part of very powerful institutions."[28]

Again, Lawrence Lessig's point was that code—along with markets and norms—is just one coequal modality of regulation. Hence the title of his book, describing code "and other laws of cyberspace." Whether it is superior or inferior depends on the context. For example, digital rights management software can limit the use of content more tightly than copyright law because it ignores safety valves such as fair use and the first sale doctrine.[29] Regulation by code or cryptography might actually be worse for freedom and innovation.

If there is to be a Lex Cryptographia, therefore, the salient challenge is to identify its strengths and weaknesses. As discussed in chapter 4, the blockchain may prove more trustworthy than conventional law when it overcomes reliance on untrustworthy intermediaries or authorities, or it eliminates transaction costs and errors from synchronizing multiple ledgers. As chapter 6 detailed, it will be less trustworthy (or even dangerous) if the ledger infrastructure fails, the rigidity of smart contracts produces unintended consequences, it promotes a narrow reliance over richer relationships of trust, or else the enduring power asymmetries are too strong.

Beneath these examples lies a deeper divide between law and the blockchain as regulatory institutions. They take fundamentally different approaches to enforcement. Legal systems establish mechanisms to enforce rules, such as courts or administrative agencies. Blockchain systems focus instead on designing rules to be enforced automatically. As Satoshi Nakamoto explained, with Bitcoin, "there's no reliance on recourse. It's all prevention."[30]

Ex Ante Design vs. Ex Post Dispute Resolution

Blockchain code as an alternative to law would be implemented through smart contracts, which seem superior to the messy process of legal enforcement. When parties agree on contractual terms, why rely on slow, potentially inaccurate or biased, and jurisdictionally limited courts when a distributed network of machines can execute the agreement perfectly each time? This view is prevalent among blockchain promoters.[31] The flaw in this reasoning is the failure to distinguish contractual execution from enforcement. Carrying out the specified steps in an agreement is the easy part. And in reality, it is not a particularly novel phenomenon. Billions of dollars of derivatives trades are executed each day with no human intervention. Computers are programmed with the contractual terms and perform the trades when specified circumstances occur.

The important question is whether doing automated transactions on a distributed ledger is fundamentally different than doing them on a centralized trading platform. The answer is that, with current "computable contracts," to use a term from law professor and software engineer Harry Surden, execution of the agreement is automated, but enforcement is not.[32] The parties involved can revise the agreement before performance, and a court can reverse it afterward. Smart contracts automate contractual enforcement by ceding all power to the decentralized network maintaining the ledger. Everything beyond the code is just an explanation. Or to quote The DAO's terms of service, it is "merely offered for educational purposes."[33]

Automating contractual enforcement is not as neat as automating execution. There are certainly large potential benefits to eliminating the legal system from the contractual process. An unstoppable contract does not operate at the whim of some confused judge, or corrupt local official, or greedy government, or deceitful counterparty. The efficiency gains of taking lawyers out of the enforcement loop are what might allow for functional DAOs and other major classes of activity encoded as smart contracts.

Yet anyone who has seen the 1983 movie *WarGames* should be feeling some anxiety at this point. In the movie, the U.S. cedes control over its nuclear-launch decisions to a superpowerful computer, the War Operations Plan Response (WOPR), which it believes will make better decisions than fallible politicians. Predictably, things do not go according to plan, as a teen computer whiz (Matthew Broderick) gains access to the system and wreaks havoc. In the end, Broderick narrowly avoids nuclear war (and gets the girl, to boot). He shows the WOPR, through rounds of tic-tac-toe, that some games have no winning solution. Its animating belief shattered, the machine gives up. While *WarGames* was a fictional comedy-drama—albeit one that greatly raised concerns about hacking among real-world law enforcement officials— there is actually a serious insight here: No matter how fast they calculate, there are some things that computers cannot do as well as humans. The same is true for smart contracts.

Even when smart contracts fully execute agreements, parties aggrieved at the results will still resort to litigation. Judges who believe an injustice or legally cognizable injury has occurred will not simply throw up their hands and defer to a distributed ledger. There may be practical difficulties in identifying pseudonymous or anonymous counterparties, as well as in bringing legal actions against actors in other countries. On the former, there is almost always some known entity to sue, whether the action succeeds or not. Had contributors to The DAO not received their money back through the Ethereum hard fork, some of them doubtless would have sued Slock.it (the developers of the Dapp) and the Ethereum Foundation. On the latter concern, cross-border contractual disputes are a staple of modern business among multinational firms. There are certainly some parties to smart contracts who will refuse to appear in court, but established firms are unlikely to do so. Issues of jurisdiction and choice of law are challenging, but not insoluble.

Litigation over smart contracts will reverse the position of the parties. Rather than seeking to have alleged promissory obligations fulfilled, complaining parties will now seek to undo or reverse completed transactions. In doctrinal terms, claims of breach will transform into claims for restitution. This will affect legal standards such as causes of action and burdens of proof, with unpredictable consequences. It may lead to a greater focus on the practicalities of executing a legal judgment transferring cryptocurrency or rights recorded on a distributed ledger. For example, plaintiffs could seek court orders directing defendants to give up private keys in order to execute reverse transactions. Even where such efforts fail, the confusion and expense involved could create problems for smart-contract platforms.

The extensive academic literature on incomplete and relational contracts emphasizes that contracts are often more than a one-shot interaction between parties, followed by performance or judicial resolution of a dispute. Oliver Hart, Bengt Holmstrom, Jean Tirole, and other incomplete-contracts theorists showed how the business practices around contracts assume that scenarios can materialize that the contract does not clearly contemplate.[34] Relational-contracts scholars such as Ian Macneil explored how contracts are often manifestations of ongoing relationships.[35] Ex ante, parties to a relational contract must anticipate later renegotiation, and ex post, courts must determine how to fill any gaps in the agreed-upon contract.[36]

Smart contracts attempt to atomize the contractual process.[37] They formally strip away both the time dimension of interactions among the parties and the uncertainties of future judicial resolution. Yet in the real world, they bind real people, who have real relationships, and their performance unfolds in real time. This makes it impossible to avoid some of the messiness that accompanies traditional contracts.

Ironically, when two of the major distributed ledger technology companies struck a deal to pay for services with cryptocurrency, they chose not to use a smart contract.[38] In September 2016, Ripple granted R3 options to purchase up to 5 billion XRP—Ripple's cryptocurrency—over a three-year period. In return, R3 agreed to provide Ripple with access to its network of financial services partners and to help promote Ripple's technology. A year later, Ripple attempted to terminate the agreement, claiming that R3 failed to deliver on its side of the bargain. In the interim, the price of XRP had risen twenty-fold, making R3's options briefly worth over $15 billion. R3 sued to protect its windfall.

Had the deal been formulated as a smart contract, it would only have made the problems worse. R3's obligations under the deal are exactly the kinds of vague commitments that automated execution through smart contracts struggles with. At the time of the agreement, R3's exercise price for the options was actually higher than the market price of XRP. The idea was that R3 would be incentivized to promote Ripple to its partners because that would increase the price of the currency. Neither party likely expected the wild increase in the XRP price in 2017, for unrelated reasons.

Even distributed ledger companies themselves, it seems, have a hard time anticipating how circumstances might change. Law still has a role to play. Perhaps over time, parties will get better at coding to adapt to uncertainty. Relying on smart contracts, however, will remain a bet on ex ante formalizations, which can never match the flexibility of ex post human decision-making.

Law as a Technology of Trust

How, then, does law promote trust? In truth, trust and law have an ambiguous relationship. A promise lacking the required attributes of contract law may still be sufficient to engender trust, even though it is not enforceable. Conversely, untrusting enemies may enter into legally binding transactions if they see a mutual advantage. Yet the two domains are clearly connected. The question, which numerous scholars have engaged, is whether law is more likely to promote or undermine trust.[39]

On the one hand, law may enhance confidence and channel relationships in trust-enhancing ways. The legal system provides redress for violations of agreements, which may give the parties additional confidence when entering those relationships. This was essentially Thomas Hobbes's argument in *Leviathan*. Legal enforcement is not perfect, but trust necessarily involves some risk. The legal enforcement mechanism may reduce the possibility and magnitude of loss from untrustworthiness enough to induce trust-based relationships. Moreover, law formalizes relationships. Knowing the scope of expectations on both sides, as well as placing the entire arrangement within a structure, can limit misunderstandings. Thus, even though legal enforcement rests on the Leviathan of state power, law may create necessary space for the informal arrangements of P2P trust. In the formulation from chapter 1 of trust as confident vulnerability, the prospect of legal redress makes the actor feel less vulnerable, thus expanding her or his confidence to interact.

On the other hand, legal enforcement may actually reduce trust. Critics of the American legal system argue that the expansive use of law and lawyers undermines social cohesion.[40] The formalization that law imposes may replace the fluidity of normal human relationships with dry commitments.[41] And while legal redress may make trust less risky, it may also stifle trust-enhancing actions, leaving the parties worse off.[42] In fact, trusting purely on a calculating basis may not be trust at all.[43] In this view, trust inures in relationships. Contracts and other legal formalities may memorialize aspects of those relationships, but they are separate from trust.[44] Researchers have shown that if the trusting party is relying on the competence of the other, as opposed to its goodwill, reducing that competence to detailed contractual language can arouse suspicion.[45] Too much focus on what happens if something goes wrong can undermine confidence that things will go right. It suggests distrust, which may beget distrust in response.[46]

However, the choice is not necessarily so stark. When parties have the option, legal enforcement through either private contractual agreement or regulation can offer a backstop where interpersonal trust is insufficient. Over time, as confidence in relationships increases thanks to legal risk mitigation, affective trust may expand as well.

Both the virtue and the limitation of law as an instrument of trust amount to the fact that it is an apparatus of the state. Legal authority supersedes that of the parties. Law arises from territorial sovereignty, which gives it a defined geographic scope. It operates through bureaucratic mechanisms or adversarial processes, both of which have well-understood flaws. And law must treat everyone equally, rather than offering unlimited customization for particular parties. While each of these offers correlative benefits, there is a gap in the possibility space.

One of the important functions of lawyers is to ask, "What if something goes wrong?" No large-scale computer-based system is perfect. Sometimes the flaws are technical, sometimes they are human, and most of the time they are a combination of both. The legal system exists as a mechanism to address those flaws and to align private interests with public goals.

Both the legal system and software code can promote trust. Both can also undermine it. As distributed ledgers become more prominent, the simplistic view that they obviate the need for law will become increasingly untenable. The Silk Road saga showed that the blockchain is not an impermeable shield against legal enforcement, and the attack on The DAO showed the limitations of purely algorithmic systems. Both governmental actors and the technologists developing the new distributed platforms must take affirmative steps to engender trust. They can work together to do so.

Modes of Interaction: Supplements, Complements, Substitutes

In most cases, blockchain-based technical enforcement mechanisms and traditional legal structures will have no direct contact. Law shapes behavior only in limited circumstances. There is a vast domain of activity that blockchain-based ledgers can structure, where law is indifferent. Even when there is some potential for overlap, the two systems often serve different objectives. If an American citizen makes a profit of $1 million buying and selling cryptocurrencies, the U.S. tax code specifies what they are obliged to pay to the government. The fact that smart contracts could be used to funnel a percentage of those profits automatically to government programs that the individual supports in no way mollifies the tax collectors.

Sometimes, however, blockchain-based systems can directly shape compliance with legal obligations. In those situations, there are three possible forms of interaction: supplements, complements, or substitutes.

The blockchain acts as a supplement when it takes law as the basic means of enforcement. In these situations, the primary value proposition of the distributed ledger is the efficiency gain of a shared data record. Even though the blockchain creates its own enforcement mechanisms for transactions and smart contracts, they are structured in such cases to reinforce the established legal rules. Supplemental scenarios illustrate that blockchain-based systems do not necessarily replace legal arrangements, even when they operate as an alternative compliance mechanism.

The blockchain acts as a complement when the legal regime is flawed. Law can fail for many reasons, even in jurisdictions with sophisticated and well-established legal systems. Sometimes the volume of activity scales beyond the capacity of legal mechanisms to regulate it. Sometimes the legal system needs a better way to keep track of the things it regulates. Sometimes it needs a better way to keep track of the people it regulates. And sometimes enforcement lags because incentives are improperly aligned. A blockchain consensus can step in to fill gaps in enforcement through traditional means.

The blockchain acts as a substitute when it replaces law entirely as the enforcement mechanism. This is perhaps the most widely described scenario in popular discussions on law and the blockchain, but it will likely be the least common in practice. There are, however, significant opportunities in all three categories.

Blockchain as Supplement to Law

There are many situations where blockchain-based systems can reinforce traditional government-defined law by offering new pathways to achieve legal objectives. For example, when companies issue shares, as described in chapter 1, the established legal regime is based around central securities depositories such as the Depository Trust & Clearing Corporation (DTCC).[47] These record holders maintain shares on behalf of beneficial owners (the actual shareholders). The legal arrangements are clear, but there can be practical difficulties in implementation. Distributed ledgers offer a different model: a single real-time record that tracks ownership directly. This mechanism can be integrated into the established securities regime without displacing existing legal relationships.

The Delaware Blockchain Initiative (DBI) is an ambitious effort to enhance the existing corporate law regime through distributed ledgers. The problem with a clearinghouse such as the DTCC is that records can go out of sync. In 2015, former shareholders of Dole Foods won a class-action lawsuit that entitled them to $2.74 per share in damages.[48] The company had approximately 37 million shares outstanding. Yet somehow, the court received claims representing 49 million shares. There were two reasons for the discrepancy. Arbitrageurs traded heavily in the days leading up to the merger. Some of those trades had not cleared through the DTCC when the merger officially closed, so both the sellers and buyers claimed ownership. And some trades involved illegal, naked short-selling, where investors in effect sell shares that they never actually held.[49]

If companies could issue their stock on a distributed ledger, such discrepancies (and others, such as errors in capital tables and in recording proxy votes) would be prevented. It would always be possible to see how many shares a company had outstanding and who owned them. The DBI seeks to make this vision a reality.

Tiny Delaware is the state of incorporation for a majority of Fortune 500 firms, as well as many smaller ones. Corporate franchise fees and other associated activity constitute a significant element of Delaware's state budget—something that it does not wish to lose. Delaware sees distributed ledger technology as a valuable tool for both its own state services, as well as for companies subject to its authority. The state changed its law to authorize official corporate record-keeping on distributed ledgers. Upon approval of an incorporation filing, a state agency would transfer cryptographically signed shares to the company, which could distribute them as transactions on the blockchain. Delaware is working with the blockchain technology start-up Symbiont to implement the system.

The DBI is a good illustration of the power of ledgers described in chapter 3. The shift from P2P exchange of stock certificates to the DTCC clearinghouse model of intermediary trust cleared the way for significant financial innovation based on the new, more liquid record-keeping foundation. Moving corporate stock tracking and other foundational aspects of finance to a fully digital, real-time environment through distributed ledgers could have similar impacts in time. And the same kinds of record-keeping issues appear throughout all sectors of the economy.

Companies that issue shares on a blockchain are still following the requirements of corporate law. They are just doing so in a different way. The fact that Delaware had to modify its statutes to accommodate distributed ledger shares illustrates that steps may still be necessary to validate the legal supplements. Here, though, law is not being disrupted or replaced by code; it is evolving in the way it always has.

An experiment in Illinois is applying the same thinking to land registration. American real property records are already quite blockchain-like. Most major countries use a process called "title by registration," in which an accepted transaction registration becomes the official land title. In the U.S., the records maintained in local property offices around the country are structured as a "chain of title," sometimes going back over a century. They list conveyances of the property between owners in sequence. Like the blockchain, records can only be added, not changed or deleted. Immutability is important because so much value depends on the accuracy of recorded

DIGITAL LAND ABSTRACT

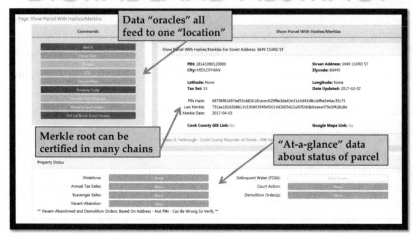

Figure 8.1
Cook County blockchain-based land records.

records. And unlike many financial applications, fine-grained control over who sees what information is not necessary. Government-operated property ledgers, like public blockchain ledgers, are transparent by design.

Cook County, Illinois, the municipality that encompasses Chicago, launched a proof of concept for a blockchain-based property registry in 2016.[50] It tested colored coins on the Bitcoin blockchain to represent transactions. As shown in figure 8.1, every property transfer or other activity—such as new mortgage or an easement—is represented through a cryptographic hash. All the hashes are then linked in a Merkle tree structure on a blockchain. The makes it possible to track any changes reliably.

This system makes the property records more reliable because any change is automatically reflected in the parcel's listing. It also improves transparency because anyone can view the ledger and the full stream of transactions. And in the future, it could be augmented with smart contracts to incorporate more complex transactions.

A blockchain-based system for real property registries, like one for corporate stock registries, could significantly reduce errors and improve efficiencies of systems that are central to the economy. Another aspect of both these examples is that they involve official records. Despite their Cypherpunk roots, blockchains can be tools for government just as much as alternatives to it. "Censorship resistance" turns into "unhackable official records" when government is the one responsible for the information. In addition, the public records form the basis for significant private industries. One offshoot of the American system of land registration is the need for expensive private title insurance for even routine real estate transactions. Goldman Sachs estimates that moving to distributed ledgers could reduce title insurance costs in the U.S. by $2 billion to $4 billion annually, thanks to improved efficiency and reduced risk.[51]

Despite the potential benefits, implementation of blockchain-based solutions to enhance legal regimes will not always be easy. The intermediaries that benefit from the existing arrangements may resist change. In Delaware, for example, a new gubernatorial administration put the brakes on rollout of the DBI, even after the necessary software and legal changes were in place.[52] Registered agents, whose services the new system could make unnecessary, complained about the loss of business. The delay may only be temporary, but it illustrates that a successful pilot project or proof of concept is not the same as a full-scale deployment. Over the long run, however, the efficiency gains of blockchain-based ledgers for stock ownership—and many other functions—will be difficult to ignore.

Blockchain as Complement to Law

A second class of applications involves situations where trust based on the legal system is breaking down or insufficient. Blockchain-based solutions can help address problems that stymie the enforcement of legal rules. In such situations, the blockchain ledger serves not as a parallel approach to traditional records, but as the mechanism that introduces workable legal compliance.

Consider the challenge of orphan works under copyright law.[53] These are works whose rights-holders cannot be located. They may well be in the public domain, but there is no easy way to tell. Those hoping to use these works, such as documentary filmmakers incorporating archival footage, cannot negotiate a license even if they want to. Orphan works are thus in legal limbo. The risk of statutory damages for copyright infringement— up to $150,000 per work regardless of actual harm—is a severe threat that scares away potential users of the material. The marketplace envisioned by copyright law fails to develop, and creativity is chilled. And this is not a small problem. When librarians at Carnegie Mellon University attempted to digitize their collection of books, they could not find the rights-holders for roughly a quarter of the works sampled.[54]

Orphan works are a good opportunity to use a shared registry to create a new market.[55] A blockchain-based registry would be available to all and would not give excessive gatekeeper power to any intermediary. It could keep track of efforts to engage in the diligent search for rights-holders that is required under copyright law.[56] Smart contracts could ensure that those who use orphan works pay licensing fees to legitimate rights-holders who come forward (most likely vetted by an arbitration mechanism). The distributed ledger here would not take the place of standard copyright law, but it would extend it in a direction that it cannot easily go today.[57]

Sometimes the problem with legal enforcement involves misaligned incentives. The legal system has what it needs to operate effectively, but the participants in the activity do not actually promote compliance. Incentives are a human problem rather than a technical one. Just having trustworthy records on a ledger does nothing to shift incentives. However, blockchains create valuable assets, which can be distributed in a manner that changes the incentives among the parties in the network.

In the online advertising world, fraud is a huge problem. Advertisers lost an estimated $16 billion in 2017 to fraud, and the amount continues to grow.[58] Over the past ten years, online and mobile advertising has grown rapidly, catching up to the rate of spending on traditional media. Led by companies such as Google and Facebook, the online market moved from static banner ads to programmatic systems that manage advertising flows among marketers and publishers. Tens of billions of dollars of online advertising each year now flows through intermediaries that match advertisers with sites and set prices dynamically.

Advertisers generally pay for these ads based on the number of times that they are displayed (impressions) or the number of times that users click on them. The problem is that it can be difficult to distinguish a real human clicking on an ad from a software bot. Fraud perpetrators have built large "clickfraud" networks of computers that automatically request ads that no one actually views. The fraudsters are clearly abusing the system, but there is no easy means of legal recourse or policing.

The incentive alignment issue arises from the economic structure of the online advertising industry. Advertisers pay, and publishers generate revenues, based on the volume of ads displayed or clicked on. It is in the interest of publishers to see those numbers go up. As a result, publishers do not always actively police fraudulent activity. It is not worth it for them to expend time and money to take actions that may reduce their revenues. All the actors in the online advertising market agree that clickfraud is illegitimate. Yet the problem continues to get worse. Unlike some of the prior scenarios, the problem is not scaling or keeping track of all the relevant information; it is getting participants to take enforcement action.

To address this problem, the start-up MetaX, the Ethereum technology development studio ConsenSys, and the Data and Marketing Association (a trade group for advertisers) announced a solution in 2017 called adChain.[59] With this system, advertisers and publishers will be able to purchase cryptocurrency tokens. Sites that wish to receive advertising will put up the tokens to join a "whitelist" of nonfraudulent publishers. Advertisers will vote, using tokens, on whether the site is legitimate. A better and more complete whitelist will make the tokens more valuable, which incentivizes everyone to participate honestly in the system. Once the whitelist is established, advertisers can factor it into their decisions about which advertising bids from sites to accept. The token economy is designed to replace the existing market with one based on a better set of incentives.

Blockchain-based systems that function as legal complements still face the normal adoption challenges of any start-up or new solution. Overcoming a gap in legal enforcement doesn't necessarily mean solving a business problem well enough to gain traction. Complements illustrate pathways for law and blockchain technology to work together, with both playing a role.

Blockchain as Substitute for Law

Where legal enforcement is weak or nonexistent, the blockchain can take its place in some cases. Contrary to the views of some blockchain proponents, costly mechanisms of intermediation and legal enforcement cannot be dispensed with entirely. As in the early days of the Internet economy, the conceptual possibility of self-defined rules outside traditional law does not overwhelm the power of territorial sovereigns and private intermediaries. However, where trust and the rule of law do not hold sway, such as in conflict zones or parts of the developing world, the blockchain may allow for a viable substitute. These extralegal trust regimes are likely to emerge from the bottom up in surprising places, but they could grow to a substantial scale.

When the Argentinian government in Buenos Aires blocked credit card companies from accepting Uber ride-sharing transactions, the company switched to a debit card transacting in bitcoin.[60] This example resembles Silk Road and other uses of bitcoin for illegal activity. The difference is that the underlying activity is not per se illegal, merely subject to a regulatory dispute. The cryptocurrency gave Uber leverage against the government by establishing a trusted payment option outside traditional centralized channels.[61] As with the orphan works example, blockchain trust potentially shifted the legal power dynamics.

In many parts of the world, land title records are incomplete and difficult for ordinary citizens to interact with. As mentioned in chapter 1, the Peruvian economist Hernando de Soto argues that the absence of well-functioning land registration systems in the developing world is a major impediment to economic development.[62] Initiatives are underway in various parts of the world to use the blockchain as a solution, along the lines of the proof of concept in Cook County, Illinois. De Soto is supporting one, led by the cryptocurrency mining and services firm Bitfury, operating initially in the Republic of Georgia.[63] Similar efforts are underway in places such as Sweden and Dubai.

Where government services such as land title registration are largely functional, a blockchain approach may improve efficiency, but its benefits relative to traditional database architectures are still somewhat limited. The great opportunity lies in using the blockchain to establish trusted registries where none previously existed. The hurdle is the human actors outside the ledger. A corrupt local land office that refuses to record information accurately on a blockchain, or that disregards the information it reports, can still do so. One of the first initiatives to record land titles on a blockchain, an effort in Honduras involving the start-up Factom, never got off the ground because of difficulties with the local partners.[64] Bitland, a start-up based in Ghana, is taking a bottom-up approach in parts of Africa without working land registries.[65] It sends surveyors to interview farmers and identify the boundaries of their properties, which it records on a private blockchain-based registry that banks can use in granting loans.

Most of the successful efforts to employ the blockchain in areas without functional legal regimes, are, like Bitland, relatively small in scale so far. Humanitarian aid is often delivered in environments lacking legal enforcement, leading to substantial fraud and inefficiencies.[66] Seeing an opportunity to use the blockchain as an alternative, the United Nations World Food

Programme (WFP) conducted a pilot project with 10,000 Syrian refugees in a camp in Jordan.[67] The refugees have no legal form of identity, so the project used retina scanners at stores in the camp. Transactions were then recorded on a permissioned fork of the Ethereum blockchain. The pilot was successful and will be expanded by the end of 2018 to all 500,000 Syrian refugees in Jordan. It represents an exciting demonstration case. However, the system is not truly decentralized, with WFP operating the only validation node, and it has not been deployed further across WFP's global footprint. As with many enterprise distributed ledger systems, moving from trials to production is a difficult process.

When blockchain systems substitute for law, the critical element is that there is no state-backed enforcement mechanism to fall back on. This will create pressure to develop a secondary layer of trust-enhancing mechanisms, similar to the way that reputation scores and identity systems developed on the Internet to enhance trust in e-commerce. Distributed online arbitration mechanisms, discussed in chapter 10, are one example of what might stand in for courts or other traditional enforcement vehicles. Replacing law with decentralized solutions based on blockchain technology does not make the challenges of fair and efficient enforcement go away, though it could open up new pathways to address them. There is a balancing act here: The opportunity must be large enough to justify implementation of trust-enhancing mechanisms, but small enough that state actors do not feel compelled to crack down.

In the end, the choice between decentralized private blockchain systems and centralized government-defined legal regimes turns out to be less stark than it appears. Both are mechanisms of trust. Governmental institutions can fail, but so can technological ones. And the formal attributes of both are often less important than the human arrangements necessary to put them into practice. The challenge for the coming years will be to work out which approaches function most effectively in which contexts. To be sure, there will be conflicts and misunderstandings. Successful blockchain-based solutions, however, need not come at the expense of successful legal ones.

9 We're from the Government, and We're Here to Help

We Need to Begin Somewhere

It was an inauspicious start. In 2015, the State of New York became one of the first jurisdictions in the world to adopt a regulatory regime for cryptocurrencies. Its Department of Financial Services began requiring virtual currency businesses to obtain a BitLicense in order to operate or serve customers in the state.[1] "We want to promote and support companies that use new, emerging technologies to build better financial companies," said Superintendent of Financial Services Ben Lawsky when announcing the rules. "We just need to make sure that we put appropriate regulatory guardrails in place.[2] He continued: "Regulators are not always going to get the balance precisely right. ... But we need to begin somewhere."

The BitLicense was controversial from the beginning. Bitcoin entrepreneurs and technologists argued that the threat of overbroad regulation, as well as the costs of compliance, would chill start-up activity. During the yearlong comment period on the draft rule, more than four thousand comments were filed, most of them critical.[3] And when the regulations went into effect, a substantial number of Bitcoin-related start-ups left New York, including the exchanges Kraken, Shapeshift, Bitfinex, and Poloniex.[4] "The 'Great Bitcoin Exodus' has totally changed New York's Bitcoin ecosystem," declared the *New York Business Journal*.[5]

The BitLicense requirement applies to any "virtual currency business activity," defined as "storing, holding, or maintaining custody or control of virtual currency on behalf of others" and "controlling, administering, or issuing a virtual currency."[6] All these categories are subject to uncertainty. Are software wallets required to register like full-blown exchange operators?

Does it matter whether services have control over cryptocurrency they handle? What exactly does the exception for transmission in "non-financial" contexts mean?

Lawsky had a point that regulators had to start somewhere. And the idea behind the BitLicense—that custodial financial exchanges transacting in cryptocurrencies should be treated similarly to comparable exchanges transacting in traditional currencies—was largely sound. If a consumer provides dollars to be traded for another currency or sent across borders, they are exposed to the same kinds of risks when cryptocurrency is involved.

The problem lay in the execution. The BitLicense requirements for covered entities were onerous. The regulations were drafted in a way that seemed to cover many cryptocurrency businesses other than custodial exchanges. And the certification process was cumbersome.[7] As of early 2017, only three BitLicenses had been granted, out of nearly two dozen applications.[8] The recipients—Circle Internet Financial, Ripple, and Coinbase—were three of the best-funded start-ups in the space, reinforcing concerns the BitLicense would crowd out small players. If the goal was, as Lawsky asserted, to "promote and support" cryptocurrency innovation, the BitLicense failed. Although a number of jurisdictions in the U.S. and around the world have subsequently adopted rules related to cryptocurrencies, few have followed New York's model.

Two years after the Great Bitcoin Exodus, the exchanges had not rejoined the New York blockchain scene. But others had. R3, the financial industry distributed-ledger consortium with more than $100 million in funding, is headquartered in New York. As one might expect, so are a number of finance-focused blockchain start-ups such as Digital Asset Holdings, Symbiont, and Axoni. And the activity is not limited to financial services. Consensys, the leading venture-development studio building around Ethereum technology, grew from one hundred to more than four hundred employees during 2017 alone in its Brooklyn headquarters, and it is working on dozens of innovative projects around the world. Blockstack, a high-profile start-up that hopes to build "a new internet for decentralized apps" on blockchain foundations, is located in New York as well. The New York Bitcoin and Ethereum meetups each have more than five thousand members.

The BitLicense, for all its flaws, did not kill off cryptocurrency activity in New York. Then again, neither did it create the model for regulatory innovation that its creators intended. In fast-moving areas, regulators inevitably face a dilemma. If they move too soon, subjecting new technologies to old rules without good cause, they risk killing off innovation or pushing it to other jurisdictions. If they wait too long, the public will be harmed, and the costs of imposing requirements on now-substantial industries will become even greater. Where regulators see clear evidence of the harms that they were established to prevent, they will need to act. Unclear requirements like the BitLicense create uncertainty, but so does the absence of any definitive regulatory statement.

The idea that blockchain-based systems are immune from regulation is even more of a myth than the idea that they are fully trustless. The companies trying to build substantial legitimate businesses around distributed ledgers are not hard to find. The more difficult issue is what that regulation should look like. When New York began considering the question in 2013, Bitcoin was by far the dominant cryptocurrency network, smart-contract engines like Ethereum did not exist, and permissioned ledgers, with the primary exception of Ripple, were not in the picture. Mining and exchanges were small-scale operations that many start-ups and individuals were pursuing. The market today looks very different. Coming up with rules that last seems like an impossible challenge.

Then again, the world of finance has changed radically in the eighty years since the U.S. adopted the basic frameworks that still govern securities transactions. If written thoughtfully, old rules can address new developments. Smart regulators can encourage innovation even as they protect against abuses.

When the Federal Communications Commission (FCC) received a petition in 1994 to ban "the provision of ... telecommunications service via the 'internet' by non-tariffed, uncertified entities,"[9] it faced a challenge similar to New York confronting Bitcoin in 2013. The voice over Internet Protocol (VOIP) start-ups springing up to provide services were not subject to the pricing, universal service contribution, consumer protection, emergency service, and other requirements that traditional phone companies faced. The FCC managed to steer a course between chilling innovation and abandoning its mission, gradually bringing VOIP services within a set of obligations.[10] Today, a majority of Americans who have landline phones in their homes use VOIP technology without even knowing it. At the same time, real-time voice and video messaging on services such as Skype, Facetime, and WhatsApp has been a hotbed of innovation and adoption, with offerings that look very different than traditional phone service.[11] If regulators can follow the FCC model, they will support the realization of the full potential of cryptocurrencies.[12]

Regulatory Controversies

Bitcoin demonstrated that the software code of Nakamoto Consensus could successfully regulate behavior to create a valuable digital currency. With years of secure operation and growth to an asset value in the tens of billions of dollars, there is no longer any doubt that distributed ledger technology can function as law. That leaves open the question of how ledgers and the law differ in their regulatory approaches.

Where legal enforcement is the superior means of achieving generally accepted public policy goals, it should be made consistent to the extent possible with the requirements of distributed ledger technology. Where the software code is an inherently superior mechanism, law should gradually give way. The transition in either case is unlikely to be so smooth. Even the basic issues about which regulatory modality is preferable may be contentious. The answers surely will change depending on the jurisdiction and the state of the technology. However, this approach is the best means to find the happy medium between the social stability of law and the power of code.

Broadly speaking, there are three major categories of regulatory controversies involving cryptocurrencies and distributed ledgers: illegality, validity, and classification. The first involves using cryptocurrencies to break the law, or theft of cryptocurrencies through hacking and similar means. The fact that bitcoin can be used to pay for drugs does not by itself raise legal problems for the cryptocurrency; Chinese yuan, dollars, or bars of gold can do the same. The challenge is that a private, decentralized currency that is pseudonymous or anonymous makes it easier to engage in such illegal activity without consequence. Contrary to fears, no major Western government has attempted to ban the possession or use of cryptocurrencies on this basis. Those that did tended to be smaller nations such as Bolivia and Bangladesh. Even countries such as China that now bar bitcoin trading do not make the possession and use of cryptocurrencies illegal.

While nothing inherently leads cryptocurrency transactions to illegal activity, Vlad's Conundrum is that the same code that makes it difficult to engage in censorship or tampering also makes it easier to engage in drug trafficking or ransomware. A related concern is that blockchain technology, by creating decentralized digital bearer instruments, creates an attractive target for thieves. These two problems, typified in Silk Road and Mt. Gox respectively, were the most prominent legal questions during the early years of Bitcoin prior to 2015. They remain significant today, with newer dark marketplaces for illegal transactions springing up and major ransomware attacks demanding contributions in bitcoin.

These are real challenges. However, they are the kinds of challenges that law enforcement can tackle. Silk Road operator Ross Ulbricht was arrested, convicted, and sentenced to life in prison. The alleged mastermind of the Mt. Gox theft, Alexander Vinnik, was arrested in Greece four years later at the request of U.S. authorities. As these examples show, the global scale of blockchain networks does not prevent nations from enforcing their laws. Coordination among law enforcement and mechanisms such as extradition can be used to bring criminals to justice. And courts in major countries like the United States have little difficulty applying conventional doctrines of jurisdiction in order to exert their authority when the interests of their citizens are implicated.[13] The Federal District Court in New York rejected arguments by Arthur Budovsky, who founded a pre-Bitcoin digital currency provider called Liberty Reserve, that it was not subject to U.S. jurisdiction because it was based on Costa Rica and served a global market.[14]

The supposed anonymity of the blockchain is also not an absolute bar against legal enforcement. Firms such as Elliptic and Chainalysis work with law enforcement agencies to track down criminals by analyzing cryptocurrency transaction patterns. That process is an arms race. Criminals are starting to use transaction-scrambling services called "tumblers," as well as anonymous cryptocurrencies such as ZCash and Monero, in order to avoid being tracked. Analytics technology is evolving as well. Most of the time, however, such measures are unnecessary. Users generally obtain and hold cryptocurrencies through wallet applications that require anti-money laundering/know your customer (AML/KYC) checks upon sign-up. Those that do not, such as Vinnik's BTC-E, face fines and shutdown orders from regulators. Law enforcement agencies can be expected to tighten rules on wallet providers as cryptocurrency adoption increases.

Finally, while the level of criminal activity involving cryptocurrencies should not be dismissed, neither should it be exaggerated. The WannaCry ransomware attack, in which computers around the world were rendered inaccessible and the perpetrators demanded payment in bitcoin to unlock them, created huge disruptions for major services such as the National Health Service in the United Kingdom. However, the Bitcoin accounts specified for payment received only about $140,000, which can be tracked if it is ever changed into fiat currency.[15]

The second broad regulatory question is how other legal structures recognize distributed ledgers. The issue of what information counts as legally valid appears in a variety of contexts, ranging from financial regulations to evidentiary rules in court. The relevant definitions are embodied in a large number of federal, state, and local rules. Many of these presume that valid information exists in a defined place, under the control of a defined entity, neither of which is meaningful in the blockchain context.

States are beginning to move toward treating blockchain-based information analogous to more traditional records. As part of the Delaware Blockchain Initiative (DBI) discussed in chapter 8, the state of Delaware adopted legislation authorizing distributed ledgers for both government records and regulatory functions such as tracking corporate shares and liens.[16] Arizona passed a law declaring that blockchain-based digital signatures were legally enforceable.[17] And Vermont made blockchain-based information admissible as evidence in court.[18]

The biggest challenge in giving blockchain ledger records equal treatment is usually definitional. There is no formal definition of what counts as a blockchain, cryptocurrency, distributed ledger, or smart contract. Industry groups such as the Chamber of Digital Commerce and organizations such as the Uniform Law Commission, a group of experts that proposes model laws to state legislatures, are working on proposed definitions, but the proper formulation will vary depending on the circumstances. The attributes that make a corporate record valid on a blockchain are different from those relevant for evidence in court. For example, the Delaware legislation does not mention blockchains at all, referring simply to "distributed electronic networks or databases."[19] There are so many legal contexts involving records and validity of information that working through them, jurisdiction by jurisdiction, will be a slow process.

In the analogous context of digital signatures, the U.S. Congress passed a federal law in 2000, the E-SIGN Act, mandating that a signature "may not be denied legal effect, validity, or enforceability solely because it is in electronic form."[20] This automatically preempted state laws requiring paper signatures, removing the need to change them case by case. It left open the question of whether a digital signature was enforceable in any specific case by requiring only that the electronic form could not be the sole reason for invalidation. Thus, some electronic signatures must be cryptographically secured, while in other cases, typing one's initials on an electronic form is sufficient. This matches the variation with physical signatures. Some documents can just be signed with the parties' initials, while others require witnesses, notaries, and other formalities.

The solution to the blockchain validity issue could not be as simple as the E-SIGN Act. There is no clean dividing line analogous to electronic versus nonelectronic signatures that applies across the board to the entire range of applications. However, the general approach of validating blockchain and distributed-ledger records as a category, so long as they meet the security and other requirements of the particular legal application, would speed the process of adoption. As with digital signatures, blockchain validity is relevant both for private law matters, such as contract enforcement, and for public law issues, such as regulated industries (healthcare and financial services, primarily), government services, and government-maintained records.

A third category of regulatory controversies involves activity that is generally legitimate, but not structured according to the legal requirements for the nonblockchain equivalent. Is the sale of tokens an "investment contract" under Securities and Exchange Commission (SEC) rules, and are those doing the issuing investment managers? Does a cryptocurrency exchange qualify as a derivatives marketplace subject to regulatory requirements issued by the Commodity Futures Trading Commission (CFTC)? Are profits on appreciation in cryptocurrencies subject to income tax as commodities, currencies, or neither?

Blockchain technology can be used to perform services functionally quite similar to regulated activities. Mere resemblance should not be enough to impose the full weight of regulations designed for an entirely different environment. On the other hand, if blockchain technology is used to implement the same functions, raising the same issues, as other technologies, it should not be automatically exempt from regulation.

This was the kind of problem that the BitLicense was designed to address. The New York Department of Financial Services concluded that existing definitions were not sufficiently broad to cover cryptocurrency activity that raised similar issues to traditional money transmission. It created a new classification and a targeted set of obligations for those that met it. Another potential basket is "no regulation." A final one is "no regulation yet."

Such debates are likely to make up the bulk of the regulatory controversies over blockchain-based activities. The treatment of token offerings under securities laws represents a major test case that is being addressed in real time.

The Token Offering Test Case

Modern securities regulation developed after the Great Crash of 1929, when numerous small investors fell victim to scams. The foundational principle of securities regulation is disclosure. Investment involves risk, and no one is entitled to legal protection against a bad decision. However, without regulation, there is a strong information asymmetry between investors—especially retail investors—and investment promoters. Without an opportunity to evaluate the risks, investors are easily exploited.

In the U.S., beginning with the 1933 Securities Act and the 1934 Securities and Exchange Act, the government mandated detailed registration and disclosure terms for securities offerings.[21] With defined exceptions, private offerings can be made only to accredited investors with the financial resources and sophistication to take on the risk. All offerings, especially public offerings, require detailed financial information and risk disclosures. Misstatements, and omissions of material information in many cases, can be sanctioned. There are significant timing and communication limits designed to ensure that investors are treated equally and that issuers do not artificially stimulate investor excitement. The SEC and other regulators have the authority to enforce these rules and prosecute violators.

What constitutes a "security" or "investment contract" subject to this regulation is broadly defined under U.S. law. Whereas in Europe, most regimes enumerate categories of covered investment products, the guiding light in the U.S. is the *Howey* test. This test, derived from a case in which an orange grove owner sold interests to guests at his Florida resort, includes four elements:

1. The contribution of money;

2. To a common enterprise;

3. With the expectation of profits;

4. Derived from the efforts of others.[22]

The multi-billion-dollar question is whether initial coin offerings (ICOs) fit within this rubric. If they do, and they are either offered in the U.S. or sold to American citizens, they must comply with the strictures applicable to traditional securities offerings.[23]

ICOs clearly involve contributions of money. The fact that purchasers contribute cryptocurrencies rather than fiat currencies is no barrier. They generally involve a common enterprise to which the money is contributed, in the form of the application or blockchain platform. The remaining two prongs are the challenging ones. Many online games, such as Clash of Clans and Candy Crush, sell users digital tokens for real money. Yet these tokens are clearly not securities because their primary purpose is to aid in the game. Purchasers have no expectation that they can sell them back to make money. Even if there is intent to profit, an offering may not be a security when the purchasers are active participants in the success of the venture. The regulatory protections are designed for classic passive investors that investment promoters may take advantage of.

The SEC first applied the *Howey* test to a token offering in connection with The DAO crowdfunding scheme, which spectacularly failed, as described in chapter 3. The SEC concluded that The DAO offered a security, which should have been registered and regulated as such.[24] It was clearly marketed as an investment opportunity, with purchasers of tokens entitled to returns based on the performance of the projects funded. And the SEC concluded that, for all the hype about The DAO being a distributed, autonomous entity, The DAO token purchasers were essentially relying on the managerial activities of Slock.it, the software developer. Its employees wrote the code, oversaw the operations of the system, and delegated curator functions to coordinate with projects seeking funding. Token holders' ability to influence the operation of The DAO were limited. When the hack drained a substantial portion of the funds, investors had no recourse but to turn to Slock.it and the Ethereum Foundation to make them whole.

Whether a truly autonomous and collectively managed organization would be treated the same is an interesting question. The operational smart contract–based systems today labeled as distributed autonomous organizations (DAOs) still leave primary management functions in human hands. If DAOs ever do reach the point of full autonomy, that will raise a host of legal questions well beyond securities regulation. Even so, setting baselines and expectations for more conventional enterprises will make those thorny challenges easier to confront.

In its report on The DAO, the SEC made three other important statements. First, it made clear that ICOs operating globally and headquartered outside the U.S. can still be subject to U.S. securities laws if they market to American investors. This was a well-established legal principle. Many activities in modern securities markets have global reach, and it would make no sense if offerors could escape responsibilities simply by where they locate their operations.

Second, the SEC referred to Ethereum as a currency, not a security, even though Ethereum also launched by selling tokens that appreciated in value. The agency did not explicitly step through the analysis, and it still could reconsider this classification in the future. A key distinction is likely that ether has significant utility above and beyond being a way to invest in the success of the Ethereum Foundation's efforts. Just as the primary function of bitcoin is to buy things, the primary function of ether is to obtain the gas necessary for executing smart contracts. Ether purchasers are active contributors to the success of the enterprise in a way that DAO token purchasers were not. Especially when Ethereum launched its crowdsale in 2014, well before the 2017 ICO gold rush, purchasers were not necessarily focused on profit. And the Ethereum Foundation is a nonprofit that only holds a small amount of the total ether in circulation. The facts and circumstances of offerings, such as the content of marketing materials, can make the difference in the classification exercise.

Third, the SEC emphasized that those who exchange or resell cryptocurrencies classified as securities are also subject to its rules. That was an important warning to financial intermediaries beyond the token issuers themselves. The major reason that some ICO tokens are so highly valued is that, in addition to whatever utility they have within their platform, they can be traded for other cryptocurrencies or fiat. The option to cash out new tokens, however, depends on the willingness of exchanges to list them. Most cryptocurrency exchanges were not set up as regulated secondary markets in securities, and thus have strong incentives to avoid listing tokens that might subject them to regulatory sanctions. Or they might suddenly stop selling tokens to American users, as the Bitfinex exchange did.[25]

The Shapeshift cryptocurrency exchange responded to the SEC report on The DAO with a blog post stating that it might have to delist some tokens likely to be considered securities. While that decision was understandable, the company's explanation was not. "At their most fundamental level," the post asserted, "tokens (a colloquial term for blockchain ledger entries) are speech: they are inscriptions of meaningful information into a communal record."[26] By this definition, stocks and titles to cars or land would also be speech, presumably insulated from regulation. The fact that cryptocurrency assets enable innovation is simply not a sufficient reason to isolate them from rules.

Some exchanges have begun to move in the opposite direction. While registering as a regulated Alternative Trading System (ATS) is an expensive and drawn-out process, it provides legal protections for those platforms that wish to trade tokens classified as securities. Templum and TZero were among the first to launch cryptocurrency exchanges with ATS certification, and established competitors such as Poloniex and Coinbase seem likely to follow suit.

Those most threatened by the SEC's conclusion (since repeated in several other contexts) that most token offerings likely constitute securities, are issuers of already-completed ICOs. Some responded to the SEC guidance on The DAO by abandoning planned offerings, or even refunding tokens already issued. Protostarr, which hoped to allow celebrities to solicit funding from their fans through cryptocurrency tokens, returned its ICO proceeds and shut down after receiving an exploratory call from the SEC. The company raised only about $47,000, and it was never charged by the agency. "We're just a couple guys who are tech nerds in our basement," chief executive officer (CEO) Joshua Gilson told *Forbes*. "It did not occur to us that the model everyone else in the world is using would have any specific laws here that would apply to us."[27]

Gilson's honesty was refreshing. On the other hand, his naïve assumption that his company could solicit funds from investors around the world without meeting any legal standard shows how far blockchain fever has spread. There are in fact a number of exceptions that allow small companies to raise money without the full restrictions of securities registration. Protostarr might not be able to raise hundreds of millions of dollars that way, but it did not do so through its token offering either.

Polybius, introduced in chapter 6, further illustrates the problem with the "anything goes" attitude prevailing for token sales. A company executive acknowledged that its token met the *Howey* test and would be classified as a security in the U.S.[28] This was given as a reason why the token was not listed on U.S.-based exchanges. However, Polybius apparently took no steps to register its securities offering or to exclude American investors. The company merely stated the following in its Frequently Asked Questions (FAQ) section:

> Joining the investors board is open to all countries with some exceptions. These exceptions lay within the regulations that are present in some jurisdictions, like the US. We encourage our investors to be prudent with their decisions so not to create legal disputes.[29]

Whatever happens to Polybius, this is an untenable situation. If law means anything, a company should not be able to take actions that seem clearly contrary to legal requirements, and then explain them away by putting the burden on its investors. Polybius is hardly the only ICO issuer in this position. And the issue is not just one for U.S. regulation. Other major jurisdictions hosting ICOs, such as Switzerland and Singapore, also have securities-regulation regimes, as do the other major countries with investors purchasing tokens. The particulars vary, but none allows companies to raise tens of millions of dollars without any disclosure requirements or fraud protections. The potential problems are so severe that China and South Korea banned ICOs entirely.[30]

Viewing ICOs as primarily a technical hack around the restrictive regulation of securities law is the Napster error. The backers of the Napster peer-to-peer (P2P) file-sharing application believed that the benefits it offered—easier access to music, better availability of rare content, and lower transaction costs than the traditional distribution process—would allow it to overcome objections that it was facilitating copyright infringement. They were wrong. And Napster's arguments that it could have created a better music-distribution service for both creators and consumers were significantly stronger than unregulated ICO offerors' arguments against disclosure obligations.

In the case of ICOs, the investor-protection rationale behind the structure of securities regulation is no less relevant when the asset being sold is a token than when it is a stock. On the other hand, ICOs do not *necessarily* operate like securities. They can be structured in many different ways, and their appeal to purchasers varies based on the nature of the system in question. Some token distributions, known as "airdrops," raise no money at all; they are purely designed to get tokens into the hands of users.[31] And many projects that raise funds through unregulated ICOs voluntarily disclose information and work with legal experts to put in place reasonable protections for their purchasers.

The issue comes back to classification. Two important distinctions are whether the tokens are offered primarily for fund-raising purposes or to provide utility on the application platform, and whether the project is operational at the time of the offering. For all the high-minded analysis by venture capitalists and technology thought leaders about how token offerings overcome the barriers to decentralized innovation, most of the conversation around ICOs among both offerors and purchasers centers on making money. To the general public, token sales are a hot new investment scheme.

Companies such as Brave and Filecoin, which create token economies as their core business model, have colorable arguments that their primary goal is to create users rather than investors. The tokens are necessary for the operation of their networks. Users need to participate by spending the tokens or taking actions such as viewing ads and providing storage. Such coins, being predominantly based around utility, could be outside the *Howey* requirements. However, even if something is labeled a "utility token" and offers functionality on a software platform, it still constitutes a security if marketed primarily as a passive investment. The SEC made this clear in its enforcement action against the ICO of a restaurant review start-up called Munchee.[32] Munchee actively promoted the tokens based on potential price appreciation as adoption grew, rather than as a way to participate actively in the network. A good regulatory scheme would need to provide some guidance so that offerors understand the boundaries of the category.[33] And there would still be some baseline requirements, even for unregistered utility coins. Fraud is fraud.

The second distinction, not directly drawn from the *Howey* test, is between functional and prefunctional services. Companies can offer tokens before they operate an application that can accept them. Doing so can allow early-stage projects to gain needed funding for software development, and to raise capital more easily than through traditional angel and early-stage venture capital channels. As of October 2017, fewer than 10 percent of token networks with completed ICOs were operational.[34] This is both a blessing and a curse. Ethereum might never have had the resources to finish developing its network without the opportunity to launch a preoperational token sale. Early token offerings help promote platforms and create networks of interested supporters and contributors.

On the other hand, companies raising funds based on their potential, sometimes before they have written even one line of code, present a recipe for risk. Fraud and manipulative practices such as pump-and-dump schemes are widespread. Even well-meaning projects may never launch due to technical, management, or competitive issues. Having too much money up front can be a problem for start-ups because it encourages them to be profligate or to feel insufficient pressure to hit the next milestone. The ease of issuing tokens for prefunctional networks, and the associated market frenzy, has also invited arrangements in which institutional participants such as venture capitalists and hedge funds can obtain "premined" tokens at a discount, giving them a structural advantage over retail investors.

From a legal perspective, a prefunctional token cannot have utility, almost by definition. There is nothing at the time of sale to use it for. As a result, these offerings are more likely to meet the *Howey* requirements for regulated securities offerings. There are a number of initiatives allowing ICOs to address regulators' concerns. We will examine some of these in chapter 10. There will likely be a period of regulatory experimentation in both the public and private sectors until standard approaches to ICOs are defined. Such as process is healthy, so long as those seeking to raise funds are willing to work with those seeking to protect the public.

The need for investor protection does not end once the tokens are issued. ICO projects need to establish legal and corporate governance frameworks to manage their activities. Someone needs to decide whether and/or when to convert the cryptocurrency received from contributors into fiat currency, whom to hire, and how to run the project. Many high-profile ICOs are structured as nonprofit foundations, which provides tax benefits and legal certainty. However, it also creates obligations, especially if the original developers of the technology operate a for-profit company that transacts with the foundation.

Tezos was the largest-ever ICO, after raising more than $230 million. It established a Swiss foundation to oversee the network, which would contract with the for-profit firm developing the technology. A few months later, the leaders of the development team were in a legal battle seeking to remove the executive they hired to run the foundation.[35] Issuance of the Tezos tokens and development of the network was put on hold for several months, until the impasse was resolved with the restructuring of the foundation board.[36] Ironically, the selling point of the Tezos blockchain technology is dynamic management of network governance. It is designed to avoid the technical stalemates that have paralyzed the Bitcoin community. Coordinating policy changes on an operational network, however, is very different from coordinating a development process involving human teams, with large sums of money at stake.

The freedom to operate projects globally and avoid the scrutiny of regulated offerings also opens the door to problems. Compliance with a regulatory regime may be costly, but the social benefits can exceed those costs.

Regulation and Innovation

Regulation is often characterized as the antithesis of innovation. To many, it seems obvious that government involvement in the development of cryptocurrencies and blockchain-based systems will slow and corrupt the development of new systems. If government were only necessary because people could not trust each other without the fear of the Leviathan, then perhaps Satoshi Nakamoto solved that problem.

Here too, however, there is reason to question the old cyberlibertarian view. Regulation of the Internet was actually an important step in its widespread adoption. Many things that "just worked" in the early days turned out to be the consequences of a small, close-knit, homogeneous online community. As the Internet began to look more like society, it faced the same political and economic challenges as offline communities.

For example, when Microsoft used its monopoly power in the late 1990s to threaten Internet-based start-ups, the U.S. government restrained it through antitrust enforcement. The Internet might look very different today if there were no independent market for web browsers, or if Microsoft had sufficient leverage to implement its plan to charge a small fee for all e-commerce transactions.[37] Moreover, the knowledge that governments were operating to police abusive practices helped promote trust in the new and unfamiliar word of virtual transactions. Later, Internet advocates began to call for government intervention to enforce network neutrality rules, to prevent broadband access providers from discriminating against unaffiliated services, and privacy protections.

Something similar is likely to occur for distributed-ledger technology. The notion that activity on a blockchain cannot be subject to legal enforcement died with the arrest of Ross Ulbricht, if not before. Particularly with the rise of permissioned ledgers and enterprise-grade systems on top of public ledgers, regulation as a facilitator of blockchain development is gaining currency.

Not that the path forward will be easy. The Internet offers a largely positive model of governments in the main acting thoughtfully and nascent industries in the main acting responsibly. There were plenty of counterexamples, but enough cases of regulators and the regulated cooperating to allow growth and innovation have survived. There is no guarantee that the same will be true for the blockchain—but the potential is there.

To be sure, there are important questions about where to draw lines around surveillance and permissible uses of technology. Criminals and terrorists will try to exploit the blockchain, just as they exploit other technologies whenever possible. Governments will overreact and propose rules that cause collateral damage to legitimate operations. The point, however, is that these are not new challenges. Calls for regulation do not represent the end of cryptocurrency innovation; they signal the blockchain's ongoing maturation.

As described in the previous section, much of regulation is a classification exercise. The rules establish status categories, and the regulators police who is subject to those categories. Sometimes the classification is obvious. Verizon and AT&T do not dispute that in completing conventional, circuit-switched, landline telephone calls, they are operating as "telecommunications carriers" under the Communications Act of 1934. Sometimes, though, the classification is more difficult. Does Comcast, which historically did not offer telephone service and now does so over specialized packet-switched data networks using Internet technologies, fit in that box? Does Vonage, which owns no network facilities itself but provides voice calling as an application for broadband users? Does Amazon, which now supports voice messages on its Echo personal assistant devices?

The simple answer is that services that look like a duck and quack like a duck should be regulated as ducks. If ducks are overregulated, the rules should be adjusted for everyone. The practical implications of these principles for Internet-based voice communications services involved more than a decade of contentious debate. That was not necessarily a bad thing. The FCC was sensitive to concerns about preemptive and overexpansive regulation dampening innovation. There was literally no way that the classification controversy could have been resolved quickly in the 1990s because the technology was too immature and its implementation too limited.

Regulators today face a similar challenge in classifying the flock of young cryptoducks.[38] In 2015, FinCEN, the financial crimes enforcement office of the U.S. Treasury Department, announced a civil enforcement action against Ripple, one of the first successful non-Bitcoin cryptocurrency networks. Ripple was designed to support international transactions between different currencies. Where bitcoin was created to serve as a currency, Ripple's currency, XRP, was created as an intermediary among dollars, euros, yen, and so forth.

The problem, in FinCEN's eyes, was that Ripple was operating without registering as a regulated money-services business. There was nothing wrong with processing money transfers; the issue was doing so without having to meet the obligations of existing players in that industry. In particular, Ripple failed to follow the AML/KYC rules for its users. These are designed to prevent criminals and terrorists from using the banking system to support their activities. In response to the FinCEN action, Ripple agreed to a $450,000 fine and committed to establish an AML/KYC compliance regime.

The Ripple sanctions were a turning point for the cryptocurrency industry. Unlike Bitcoin, which is a protocol implemented on a distributed network, Ripple is a company. Its business model depends on its ability to develop partnerships with financial institutions around the world, so that it could exchange XRP back and forth with their local currencies. FinCEN sanctions are a big deal. The AML/KYC process, which typically requires financial-services operators to verify physical identity documents such as passports and check against blacklists of individuals, can be onerous, especially for fast-moving and highly computerized service providers.

Some companies saw the FinCEN action as a signal that the U.S. was not a hospitable jurisdiction for cryptocurrency companies. Xapo, a venture-backed Bitcoin wallet start-up, relocated its headquarters from California to Switzerland ten days after the decision. The BitLicense went into effect in New York a few months later, causing further consternation about regulators killing the golden goose of cryptocurrency innovation. Yet in the end, those concerns proved overblown. If anything, U.S. regulators taking the initiative, even if they at times went too far, helped market participants evaluate their priorities. By adjusting its practices to comply with the FinCEN requirements, Ripple became a more trusted network. It saw adoption of its technology and currency rise dramatically over the following two years.

One difference between the regulatory debates in the dot-com and distributed-ledger era is that the U.S. is no longer the dominant source of activity. In the 1990s, usage and start-up creation were heavily centralized in the U.S. The Internet today is highly globalized, and distributed-ledger activity is even more so. In addition to New York and Silicon Valley, London, Berlin, Zurich, and Singapore are major hubs, with significant centers in China, Canada, South Korea, Estonia, and Hong Kong as well.[39] Vitalik Buterin, leader of the Ethereum project, is a Russian who grew up in Canada, heads a foundation headquartered in Switzerland, and now lives in Singapore. If he had created an early Internet start-up, he likely would have headed to Silicon Valley.

The global distribution of blockchain-development activity encourages jurisdictional competition. American dominance of the early Internet industry produced major benefits for the country, both economic and in terms of global soft power. Hoping to be the Silicon Valley of the crypto-economy, countries ranging from Gibraltar to Russia are creating new legal frameworks to attract blockchain start-ups, coin offerings, and other activity. The early leader is the canton of Zug, Switzerland, which combines a stable government, a central location in Europe, a welcoming environment for cryptocurrency companies, and favorable tax policies. It is bidding to be the cryptocurrency equivalent of Delaware for U.S. incorporation. (Although the real Delaware, as we have seen, hopes to be a player as well.)

The U.S. is still a very important driver of blockchain activity. A significant portion of core Bitcoin development occurs there, and New York is one of the primary centers for distributed-ledger technology in financial services. Many of the most significant investors in blockchain start-ups are located in the U.S. And American technology and services firms such as IBM, Microsoft, and PWC are at the forefront of most large-scale enterprise implementations of distributed-ledger applications. The technical talent and technology start-up ecosystems in the U.S. remain unmatched.

It bears repeating that major Internet companies did not locate themselves in Sealand or island tax havens; they went to where the developers and customers were. Organizations do not just seek the least regulation; they seek the best regulation, among a slate of other factors. A reliable and stable regulatory environment will be important for building trust in blockchain platforms that seek a large user base. Similarly, even jurisdictions eager to attract entrepreneurial businesses in fields such as cryptocurrency do not simply engage in a race to the bottom.

Singapore is a hotbed of blockchain activity, due in part to its permissive regulatory attitude. However, the Monetary Authority of Singapore (MAS) made clear in an August 2017 announcement that ICOs there would be subject to money-laundering and terrorist-financing restrictions.[40] They would also be regulated as securities offerings when they "represent ownership or a security interest over an issuer's assets or property." Some small territories focused on generating revenues may take an "anything goes" attitude, but ICOs based there will eventually be less trusted—and therefore less successful in attracting capital. Moreover, the countries where that capital comes from will not be shy about exercising jurisdiction. These are the same reasons why all companies today do not domicile in offshore tax havens.

While the BitLicense may have given the U.S. a poor regulatory reputation in some cryptocurrency circles, more recent initiatives were more thoughtfully drawn. The Uniform Law Commission, which creates model codes that are widely adopted by state legislatures, issued a model cryptocurrency law in 2017 that carefully limits the scope of regulation. Peter Van Valkenburgh, research director at the generally deregulatory cryptocurrency think tank Coin Center, declared it "a big win for Bitcoin and cryptocurrencies."[41] The CFTC created a LabCFTC group to study cryptocurrencies and engage with the nascent industry. The SEC's investigative report on ICOs and The DAO was widely praised as measured and technically knowledgeable. And bitcoin prices jumped after the chairs of the SEC and CFTC testified on cryptocurrency regulation before Congress in February 2018, apparently out of relief at their measured approach.[42]

The regulatory race is still at an early stage. The Internet of Value is embryonic. Decisions made in the coming years will shape where it contributes new opportunities for efficiency, innovation, and freedom. The future is far from clear. Some governments will try to stifle the blockchain or force it into ill-fitting legal regimes. Developers and entrepreneurs will employ the powerful general-purpose capabilities of smart contracts in unpredictable ways. All this uncertainty means that the dividing lines between the old and new trust architectures will be fluid. Yet positive steps can be taken to promote the benefits of the blockchain and limit its potential for harm.

The important yet paradoxical lesson from Thomas Hobbes's *Leviathan* is that in order to gain freedom of action, we must also give up some freedom. (In modern behavioral economic terms, the Leviathan is the ultimate example of a commitment device.) Legal enforcement backed by the power of the state is just one example. In today's Internet economy, we give up a great deal of power and control to intermediaries such as Google and Facebook to create a low-cost and low-friction environment for communication and commerce. That is the trust trade-off described in chapter 1. Satoshi Nakamoto's revolution makes it possible to reconsider many of those arrangements. It does not itself ensure trust in every sense, however.

The combination of law and software code can be a powerful means of changing social relations. To take one example, legal advocates and technologists came together to develop open-source and Creative Commons licenses, in order to expand the scope of digital rights in software and creative works online.[43] Open-source licenses contractually ensure that those who utilize open-source software in commercial projects preserve the open elements, and in some cases, they make their own additions available as open source. Creative Commons is a set of licenses that can easily be added to content online to allow reuse with attribution, which otherwise would require formal permission under copyright law.

Both of these "legal hacks" today are widely accepted, and even encouraged, by major businesses. They make content and software available more freely, without overly limiting opportunities for those who wish to monetize or control them. Similarly, fulfilling the potential of distributed ledgers will require a new set of approaches that incorporate both law and technology to promote trust.

A Framework for Regulation

Regulation is not a unitary activity. The process for regulating derivatives trading will be different than for preventing cross-border money transfers that evade capital controls or fund terrorist groups. Different regulators within major countries such as the U.S. may not take exactly the same approach, let alone those in different countries. However, there are some common themes among the various stories about the potential and actual regulation of decentralized blockchain projects. Regulators can ask the following three questions to guide their decisions about whether to act.

1. Was the system created for a legitimate purpose?

The legal battles over P2P file-sharing services, referenced in chapter 8, were some of the early defining moments for cyberlaw. After Napster, the first major such service, was found liable for contributory copyright infringement because it maintained a central list of all content, developers created distributed file-sharing networks with no point of central control. In *MGM v. Grokster*, the Supreme Court unanimously held that this made no difference.[44] The file-sharing services in this case were so clearly designed to evade copyright law that they could fairly be said to induce lawbreaking. The *Grokster* inducement test is controversial as a point of copyright law. As a rule of thumb for regulators, it creates a sensible starting point: focus on the bad actors first.[45]

Some services allow violation of legal or regulatory obligations as an accidental by-product of a technical innovation. In other cases, it is no accident. Silk Road and AlphaBay were dark marketplaces based around illegal transactions such as drug sales. Their operators knew this, capitalized on it, and used cryptocurrencies and anonymity primarily as a means to avoid legal enforcement. OpenBazaar, like the second-generation file-sharing services, seems to be a distributed extension of these banned marketplaces.[46] It allows buyers and sellers to transact in a fully decentralized manner. The OpenBazaar software running on each user's computer connects P2P with other users to support transactions using bitcoin or other cryptocurrencies.

Yet unlike Silk Road, OpenBazaar operates in the open. Its developers are known, and leading venture capitalists such as Union Square Ventures and Andreessen Horowitz have invested in it. These backers acknowledge that, as with the Internet's core protocols, the benefits of decentralization necessarily allow abuse to happen. But they argue that, in contrast to Silk Road and the file-sharing services in *Grokster*, OpenBazaar's creators have no incentive to encourage illegal activity.[47] They make no money from transactions. Further, OpenBazaar incorporates a reputation and rating system that it believes will help police illegal activity.[48] And it should be noted that while OpenBazaar employs cryptocurrencies to avoid restrictions by traditional financial intermediaries, the service itself does not employ a distributed ledger. It is a P2P software network.

None of this is definitive. It gives law enforcement a basis to evaluate OpenBazaar's intent, as well as the level of illegal activity in practice. As we saw with The DAO, assessing intent is tricky. It needs to be implied from the weight of evidence. To use the famous line from the movie *Casablanca*,

Silk Road's and Grokster's creators were shocked, shocked to see this illicit activity going on. OpenBazaar's creators take a different tack. They and their investors realize that they will need to convince regulators of their integrity. Augur, discussed in chapter 8, faces a similar burden for its blockchain-based prediction market. And in the case of ICOs, token sellers need to make good on their claims that the value proposition extends beyond evading the investor protections of securities law.

At some point, there will be case law, analogous to *Grokster*, defining limits for services like OpenBazaar. The touchstone in copyright law is the *Sony* "substantial non-infringing use" test, under which the Supreme Court refused to find videocassette recorders guilty of secondary infringement. Something similar might need to be devised for cryptocurrency-based activities.

2. Are there alternative means to achieve public policy goals?
The point of regulation is actually not to regulate. It is to achieve societal objectives, such as preventing illegal conduct, protecting the public, or promoting fair competition. Just as blockchain-based services should not be willfully ignorant about potentially illegitimate consequences of their technology, regulators should not be willfully blind to technological solutions that reach the same objectives.

When the online retailer Overstock.com launched the first offering of shares registered on a blockchain, it worked to ensure that its actions were fully legal. That required an extended process of dialogue with the SEC, which regulates securities offerings. Overstock.com, a longtime Bitcoin proponent, established a subsidiary called TZero to implement distributed-ledger technology for capital markets. It filed a registration statement with the SEC to offer the securities through TZero's platform.

The question for the SEC was whether the Overstock.com offering met the requirements of securities law, even though it operated in a very different manner from traditional offerings. As a pioneer, it had to expend significant resources to work through the issues with the SEC, and in some cases, it modified its plans to satisfy its concerns. One challenge was that the securities laws incorporate requirements for clearing and settlement: the processes of establishing reciprocal obligations, and then transmitting the corresponding funds or securities. These steps have no analogue with a distributed-ledger system. Clearing is an inherent part of a transaction, not a separate step. And transactions are settled as soon as a block is validated.

Overstock.com had to use a conventional transfer agent to, in effect, create a shadow set of duplicate records in order to satisfy the regulators that the transactions were processed correctly.

In the end, the SEC approved the Overstock.com offering. The company sold approximately 125,000 shares in a special blockchain class through its trading platform.[49] It subsequently gained approval for TZero's platform as a regulated ATS, which will allow it to trade ICO token securities in compliance with U.S. legal requirements. Similarly, the start-up LedgerX gained approval from the CFTC for a regulated, blockchain-based derivatives-trading platform.[50] On the other hand, the SEC rejected a proposed exchange-traded fund (ETF) tracking bitcoin because it was concerned about inability to police fraud and manipulation influencing the price.[51] The important variable is not the technology involved, but whether regulatory objectives can be met.

Augur CEO Joey Krug notes that when it comes to prediction or derivatives markets, the bulk of existing regulation covers issues such as storage of customer funds, fair trade execution, and settlement that may not raise the same concerns in a blockchain context. On the other hand, the potential for flawed smart contracts is a new threat that the traditional regulatory regime does not address. He speculates that "[t]he CFTC isn't likely to start doing smart contract audits anytime soon, but honestly, if you asked me to bet against it happening in the next 20 years, I probably wouldn't bet against it."[52]

There may be opportunities to assuage governmental concerns through means outside the regulatory system itself. Some high-profile, ICO-focused investment groups, including Pantera Capital and Blockchain Capital, are supporting the ICO Governance Foundation (IGF), a global self-regulatory initiative for token offerors. Based on a Swiss foundation, the IGF is developing a standard registration form for ICOs, a registration database for investors, and certification of custodial organizations to handle funds contributed to ICOs. The registration form would provide the kind of information about how projects are structured and how funds will be used that appears in government-required filings such as the SEC's S-1 for initial public offerings (IPOs). It would be designed as a schema for online submission, allowing easy search and analysis.

The IGF recognizes that its voluntary self-regulatory process is not a substitute for legal compliance in relevant jurisdictions. However, the group is looking to work with regulators to establish best practices and standards. If it can establish a good track record, investors may come to value token sales that go through the IGF process in more detail. And the IGF is not alone. For example, Cameron and Tyler Winklevoss, major early bitcoin investors who founded the Gemini cryptocurrency exchange, have proposed the Virtual Currency Association (VCA) as a self-regulatory body to police trading of cryptocurrencies once they are issued.[53]

Securities laws in the U.S. expressly recognize that self-regulatory organizations, most notably the Financial Industry Regulatory Authority (FINRA) for broker-dealers and the National Futures Association (NFA) for futures traders, can oversee compliance with legal and ethical standards. Organizations along the lines of the IGF and the VCA might provide a bridge between regulators and the private sector. A number of other self-regulatory initiatives have been floated to address concerns associated with ICOs.

All these examples show that regulation is not a light switch; it is an ongoing series of conversations between and among regulators and the private sector. Both sides will need to view the regulatory toolkit broadly to find the best solutions for the novel challenges that cryptocurrencies raise.

3.   What are the costs and benefits of regulatory action?

Finally, regulators must always assess the consequences of their activities. This occurs more than technology innovators realize. In an environment of regulatory competition, regulators are aware that overly restrictive decisions can push activity to other jurisdictions. They have limited resources for enforcement action. And regulatory agencies want to align themselves with the forces of innovation. Nonetheless, when market developments are uncertain, as in the blockchain case, evaluating costs and benefits is often more of an art than a science.

Regulators can choose where and when to intervene. Blockchain proponents who say that "the regulators can't arrest everyone" neglect that there are pressure points at the edges of networks where regulators can focus their attention. Rather than attempt to shut down a network or a protocol, for example, they can focus on the onboarding points, which are typically centrally managed. So long as the operators of those edge services are responsible actors, there are opportunities to work with regulators.

The SEC's approach to securities-regulation questions around ICOs illustrates a careful balancing. The agency's strategy of addressing The DAO first was as important as its substantive conclusions. The SEC knew that ICOs were opening the door for significant innovation and did not want to spook the market. It understood that the *Howey* dividing line would be difficult to apply to some projects. So it picked one that was not only a clear case, but already dead. The DAO already had returned all contributions after the hard fork and shut down. There was no need for the SEC to take any enforcement action. But its analysis could serve as a warning shot to the market, giving guidance for those uncertain about its views. Even as the agency began taking subsequent enforcement actions, its chair, Jay Carney, put out a statement emphasizing that "ICOs—whether they represent offerings of securities or not—can be effective ways for entrepreneurs and others to raise funding, including for innovative projects."[54]

Going forward, the SEC and other regulators will need to take more active steps to address ICO activity and abuses. The SEC has formed a Cyber Unit dedicated to enforcement challenges around online activity, including ICO-related misconduct.[55] In addition to informal conversations such as the one that led Protostarr to shut down, the SEC has already begun filing charges against unscrupulous ICO promoters. The most difficult questions will involve offerings like The DAO, where failure to register, rather than fraud, is the primary violation. Fraud involves clear harm and illegitimate conduct. An unregistered security might still be offered in a way that affords reasonable protections to investors and information to the market.

To address such challenges, regulators will need to calibrate their actions in the way that the FCC did with VOIP services. The agency knew that mindless application of its rules to ban all unregulated, Internet-based telephony would stifle innovation and prevent new competitive alternatives. Where it could, the FCC identified activities clearly outside its rules to eliminate uncertainty about future regulation.[56] On the other hand, where companies used the technology for regulatory arbitrage without any consumer benefits, it stepped in.[57] It handled policy issues individually, such as how to ensure that calls to 911 emergency services went through, to avoid unnecessary spillover effects. And when there were good reasons to apply the traditional rules to services using new technologies, it worked with those providers to help them comply.

The SEC's initial actions suggest that it intends to steer a similar course for ICOs. Other major securities regulators, such as the Singapore MAS, the Financial Market Supervisory Authority in Switzerland, and the Federal Financial Supervisory Authority in Germany, have indicated that they understand the need to tread carefully, but act when needed. One of the benefits of the global nature of ICOs is that regulators can compare notes. Effective approaches in one jurisdiction can be copied elsewhere. The biggest challenge is that this process will take time. Cryptocurrency projects that decided to issue tokens first and ask questions later may find themselves in a difficult spot. Where existing laws and regulations fail to offer an effective pathway, changing them may involve an agonizingly slow process for entrepreneurs caught up in the rush of cryptocurrency market development.

Nonetheless, governments will have to adapt if they wish their citizens to enjoy the benefits that distributed ledgers can bring. There are many important legal questions to resolve, just as there were for the Internet. Often, there will not be a single correct approach. The coming years will witness significant experimentation around both the business and the legal models for distributed-ledger systems. The measured pace of regulatory evolution is both a feature and a bug. Moving too quickly on the basis of developments that turn out to be passing fads can have costs as well. The greatest reason for optimism that regulatory concerns will be resolved is that while governments are not going away any time soon, neither is the blockchain.

III Building the Decentralized Future

10 Connecting the Legal and the Technical

The Education of Nicholas Szabo

Nick Szabo insists that he is not Satoshi Nakamoto. Yet it is easy to see why he is commonly identified as the mysterious creator of Bitcoin.[1] Szabo, an experienced cryptographer and information-security researcher, created BitGold, a predecessor to Bitcoin that shares several of its attributes. He invented the concept of smart contracts in the 1990s. His libertarian politics match those in Satoshi's writings, and his eclectic blog shows a fascination with the history of money. Speculating on whether Szabo or anyone else is the real Satoshi is something of a parlor game, but Szabo clearly appreciates the foundations of blockchain systems as well as anyone.

Given his interests, what Szabo did in the early 2000s is notable. It was an unusual step for a cryptographer: He went back to school to earn a law degree at George Washington University.[2] To truly comprehend the issues involved in developing digital currencies and smart contracts, Szabo concluded, he needed to understand the law. Perhaps he was on to something.

"A legal contract is code executed on the brain of a lawyer," Szabo now says.[3] The fact that smart contracts can function without the machinery of legal enforcement does not make the law irrelevant. It means that developers should study the law to identify where the "dry code" of smart contracts can match the functions of the "wet code" of legal practice. This is one illustration of how cryptographic mechanisms and the law can be connected to build effective distributed ledger solutions. Governance by code alone has serious limitations, as we have seen. Law has its own flaws. Successful systems will need to draw from both.

There are several mechanisms to link the blockchain's distributed, algorithmic trust structures with the human-interpreted, state-backed institutions of law. In some contexts, no legal involvement will be needed. In others, where the blockchain is purely supplemental, existing legal arrangements function normally without any special integration. In many cases, however, affirmative steps must be taken to combine the best aspects of distributed ledgers and centralized law. The two strategies to fuse legal and crypto-graphic enforcement are to make the law more code-like, and to make the code more law-like. Both are being explored.

Making Law More Code-Like

Law is not just a set of rules on a page. It is a dynamic enterprise with a complex and varied toolkit. New challenges call for new mechanisms of legal activity. Expert regulatory agencies, for example, were introduced in the 1930s to deal with the complexities of a technology-driven, industrial econ-omy. Constitutional law scholar Bruce Ackerman suggests that these changes were significant enough to represent a sub rosa amendment of the funda-mental governance structure in the U.S.[4] The blockchain will not produce so dramatic a change, but it will stimulate innovative solutions to make law operate more consistently with governance through software code. Some examples now under development are regulatory sandboxes, safe harbors, modular contracts, and information fiduciaries.

Safe Harbors and Sandboxes

Safe harbors and sandboxes are express mechanisms to forestall legal enforce-ment. A safe harbor excludes certain activities from legal obligations. When firms can take sufficient steps to police themselves, a safe harbor incentivizes them to do so. It also defines what specific conduct is necessary. Perhaps the best-known safe harbors in the technology world are § 230 of the Telecom-munications Act of 1996 and § 512 of the Digital Millennium Copyright Act of 1998.[5] Both shield online intermediaries from liability for content flowing across their systems. Section 230 says that online services will not be treated as publishers, meaning that they are generally not liable for con-tent created by their users. Section 512 offers similar protection for copy-right infringement, so long as the online platforms take down infringing material when notified.

The breadth of these safe harbors, created in the early days of the com-mercial Internet, is problematic. They can make it difficult to restrict clearly harmful activity, such as online harassment, because the intermediaries have no incentive to take an active role. On the other hand, the twin safe harbors from the 1990s were a significant factor in the rapid growth of Internet-based applications. They were particularly important to the spread of user-driven Web 2.0 services and social media. The safe harbors encourage innovation by giving services the assurance that they will not face crushing liability for user-generated content.

These safe harbors recognize that the volume of user-contributed material for an online service may be so large that case-by-case review is impractical. Facebook simply cannot consider whether to accept every update to a user's newsfeed in the same way that the *New York Times* considers what to put on its front page. And to the extent that there are technical means of policing content, they will more likely be deployed if service providers have immunity. Otherwise, their steps to regulate content will open them up to more liability every time something slips through the cracks. The safe harbors, therefore, create an online content environment more suited to the code-based world of the Internet than the traditional world of print publishing.

Coin Center, a think tank for cryptocurrency regulatory questions, advocates a new, legislative safe harbor for blockchain-based start-ups.[6] It would bar the imposition of state and federal rules requiring licensing or registration, such as money transmission laws, on blockchain-based services that lack control over user funds. "Control" would be defined as the "power to execute unilaterally or prevent indefinitely a transaction on a blockchain network." A custodial exchange, which holds users' private keys and creates risks for users analogous to money transmitters, would still be subject to regulation.

Sandboxes are similar to safe harbors, but limited in time or scale. A regulatory sandbox exempts certain companies or activities from regulation as a means to foster experimentation and start-up activity. Unlike a safe harbor, a sandbox is not necessarily permanent, and it usually applies only to new companies. One of the concerns about the Internet safe harbors is that they were designed to help nascent firms without the resources to police content on their platforms, but wound up helping titans like Google and Facebook. A sandbox can be constructed to apply to organizations at early stages of development, but disappear when they mature.

Like safe harbors, sandboxes allow legal regimes to operate in a manner more hospitable to software-directed environments. The term "sandbox," suggesting a well-bounded space for play and experimentation, is also used in computer science. A software sandbox allows code to execute in a walled-off environment without risk to the larger system.

In the United Kingdom, the Financial Conduct Authority (FCA), the primary financial regulator, established a Fintech Sandbox program that allows companies to experiment with new services.[7] Companies apply to operate in the sandbox, and if approved, they gain permission to introduce services without being subject to certain regulatory obligations for a period of time. The companies' activities are closely monitored by the FCA, which gains a better understanding of these new platforms. The largest percentage of companies accepted into the first round of the sandbox were blockchain-related. In the FCA's report on the initial cohort, it noted that issues with "execution time uncertainty, volatility in the value of digital currencies, liquidity requirements, transaction fees, and the availability of exchanges" emerged in its tests, and it required firms to guarantee refunds to customers who lost their money in the conversion to cryptocurrencies.[8] These insights can be the basis for informal guidance or formal rules in the future.

There is nothing quite comparable in the U.S. at this time, although the Commodity Futures Trading Commission (CFTC) recently established a LabCFTC program to allow experimentation with blockchain-based systems for derivatives trading.[9]

Modularizing Contracts

Private law can be made more code-like as well. Most business contracts are essentially modules that lawyers string together and customize. Some sections describe business terms and what should happen under defined circumstances. Such operational aspects are the kind that can often be automated in smart contracts.[10] Other parts of contracts are nonoperational or legal terms, such as limitations on damages, indemnification, confidentiality, and choice of law or forum. Lawyers often reuse standard clauses, which they adapt and negotiate for the particular transaction.

To make this contract-drafting process more analogous to the formalized coding that goes into a smart contract, the contractual clauses can be represented as components that are assembled into a digital document using a markup language. Templates could be created from these modules to provide baseline agreements for common scenarios. Lawyers would still play a role in customizing the templates, deciding which variations to use, and negotiating contentious terms. The skills required of lawyers would have to change, with the field becoming more like legal engineering.[11] Legal code audits could also be implemented to ensure that the contracts match the parties' intent, analogous to the security audits widely used by firms engaged in software development.[12]

Several initiatives are developing exactly this sort of system. These include OpenLaw, a project of Ethereum development studio Consensys;[13] the start-ups Clause.io and Agrello;[14] the smart-contract templates group of the R3 consortium;[15] and the CommonAccord and Legalese projects.[16] Some of these are focused more on the nonoperational side, making the process of legal contract drafting more efficient. Others are concentrating more on operational templates that can be incorporated into smart-contract systems. By standardizing the elements of smart contracts ahead of time and making them easier to review, such mechanisms should cut down on the errors that led to failures such as the hack of The DAO.

There are also initiatives to create specialized model contracts, most notably for initial coin offerings (ICOs). The Simple Agreement for Future Tokens (SAFT) is a standard agreement designed by the law firm Cooley LLP, the angel investment group Angelist, and Protocol Labs, the parent company of the Inter Planetary File System (IPFS) distributed-storage project.[17] It was first used in the Filecoin token sale by Protocol Labs, which raised more than $250 million in the largest ICO to date.[18] It quickly became the dominant mechanism for U.S.-based ICOs, because it seemed to offer a path to fit token offerings into existing securities laws.

The distinctive feature of the SAFT is that it splits the promise of future tokens (which is treated as a regulated security offering) from the distribution of operational tokens. The initial transaction is typically handled under SEC Regulation D or Regulation Crowdfunding, two of the exceptions to the registration requirements for securities offerings. These come with significant limitations. A Regulation D offering can be made available only to accredited investors (those verified to have more than $1 million in net worth, or income in excess of $200,000 individually or $300,000 for a household). A Regulation Crowdfunding offering can only raise slightly more than $1 million. Filecoin's success at attracting huge sums of capital despite the accreditation hurdle suggests that these are not insurmountable restrictions, but they do move away from the concept of ICOs as a global fund-raising tool that gives all individuals freedom to invest in new instruments. A significant chunk of Filecoin's funding, and that raised through other major SAFTs, came from venture capitalists and hedge funds granted preferential terms.

The biggest concern about the SAFT is that it does not guarantee that once a network is operational and tokens are issued, they can be resold into the public market and not treated as securities.[19] As the Securities and Exchange Commission (SEC) made clear in its Munchee enforcement action, a token can still constitute a security even if it has utility for a cryptocurrency application. Issuers who rushed to employ the SAFT have had to reconsider what happens when the initial purchasers seek a return on their investment. As the SEC offers further guidance on ICOs, different standardized contracts could replace the SAFT as the favored tool.

As the SAFT story demonstrates, modular contracts do not necessarily resolve hard legal issues. Where these approaches add value is in separating blockchain functionality from more conventional aspects of activities. By defining more concretely the scope of traditional contracts, they can provide clarity on where smart contracts may have room to operate.

Information Fiduciaries

In May 2017, the Kraken cryptocurrency exchange experienced a flash crash.[20] A large Ethereum sell order exceeded the buy orders pending in its order book. Following standard procedure, the exchange automatically lowered the trading price until it could complete the sell order. The price of ether on Kraken dropped from nearly $100 to $26 in a matter of seconds. Shortly thereafter, someone launched a distributed denial of service (DDOS) attack that overwhelmed Kraken with spurious network traffic, preventing customers from accessing their accounts for roughly an hour.

Many customers had issued stop loss orders for Kraken to liquidate their position if the price of ether fell below a certain point. Others had purchased ether on margin, also subject to liquidation conditions if the price fell. During the period of the DDOS attack, these customers could not access their accounts, and their ether was sold at an artificially low price.

Similar flash crashes have occurred on other exchanges. Some have voluntarily reimbursed customers for losses. Kraken did not do so for traders holding ether on margin. A class-action lawsuit was filed two months later, accusing Kraken of failing to take sufficient steps to prevent the liquidation, and of being unavailable during the DDOS attack.[21] It sought damages in excess of $5 million. The facts involved were exotic, but the legal claims were pedestrian: negligence and breach of contract.[22]

The interesting aspect is that this case was filed at all. To Silver Law Group, the law firm behind the class action, the fact that cryptocurrencies were involved was insignificant. Customers suffered losses. Someone should be held legally responsible. Whether or not the Kraken lawsuit succeeds, this line of thinking will appear elsewhere. If a jury believes a defendant caused an injury, it will not be concerned that the money involved is not "real."

Kraken is a centralized exchange, not a blockchain. However, there is no reason that the same logic would not apply when participants in distributed systems experience legally cognizable injuries. Had the hack of The DAO not been reversed by the Ethereum hard fork, those who lost money would likely have sought legal recourse. The DAO itself was just software, with no management team. However, there was a group of developers at Slock.it that wrote and published that software, along with the companion website. In its investigative report, the SEC concluded that Slock.it was legally responsible for the structure of The DAO's token offering under securities laws.[23] The same analysis would likely apply in a private lawsuit as well. The Ethereum Foundation might also have been sued for helping to promote The DAO, or for the limitations in the Solidity programming language, although those theories would be more difficult to establish.[24]

There are many other situations where organizations involved in blockchain-based projects might be exposed to legal liability. For example, a number of Dapps are using the blockchain for digital identity systems. These systems are designed to verify identity credentials and record information on a distributed ledger that allows attestations without release of information. In other words, a website or financial-services provider could verify that a customer was over eighteen years old, a U.S. citizen, and not on a terrorist-funding watch list, all without actually seeing any of the customer's personal information.

The issue with such systems is what happens when something goes wrong. If a bank accepts a customer it should not because of its reliance on the blockchain-based digital identity provider, is the bank legally liable when something illegal happens? Is the identity provider? In conventional business-to-business arrangements, such issues are covered through contracts between the parties. These almost always contain representations and warranties, indemnification clauses, and other mechanisms to allocate responsibility in case of a breakdown. When access to the identity attestations is through a smart contract acting on records stored on a blockchain, such provisions may not be so clearly spelled out, nor are they easy to implement.

Some of these legal questions, like those in the Kraken lawsuit, will be relatively straightforward. Others will not. The more decentralized and autonomous the entity directly providing the service at the core of the lawsuit, the more challenging the situation. The legal system will need to evolve new practices and doctrines. Historically, tort law had to change with the growth of retail commerce in the nineteenth and early twentieth centuries. Old requirements such as privity of contract—the requirement that an injured customer sue only the dealer, not the manufacturer, even if the manufacturer were at fault—went by the wayside. New legal doctrines, such as strict liability for product defects, came into being. The same process will occur in the distributed ledger world.

In particular, something equivalent to fiduciary duties is likely to arise for public blockchain networks. Legally, a fiduciary is someone in a position of special responsibility. This includes directors and officers of corporations, trustees managing trusts, executors of wills, lawyers, and doctors. A fiduciary has to put the other party's interests ahead of its own. It must do more than act in a truthful way; it must take an appropriate degree of care and avoid conflicts of interest. The class of fiduciaries is not fixed. It expands to cover new relationships that exhibit the same dependencies.

Legal scholars Jack Balkin and Jonathan Zittrain have suggested, for example, that dominant Internet-based platforms such as Google and Facebook should be treated as "information fiduciaries" because they have such strong control over personal information online.[25] Many financial-services providers are treated as fiduciaries because of the degree to which investors rely on them and the strong incentives to leverage the relationship for personal gain.

Those developing public blockchains bear many indicia of fiduciaries. Permissioned networks are limited to identified entities who can generally enforce their rights through contractual relationships with the network operator. On a public network, however, participants have less leverage. A holder of bitcoin or ether depends on the network for the integrity of its tokens. Law professor Angela Walch argued after the attack on The DAO that blockchain developers should be treated as legal fiduciaries.[26] A fiduciary needs to be in a special relationship of trust that makes the other party uniquely vulnerable. Given the absolute control that blockchain networks exert over users' currency holdings and the potential for arbitrary governance decisions, that test might well be met.

Following the hack, the Ethereum Foundation had to decide whether to propose a hard fork, thus returning the currency held by the attacker. In that context, there was no dispute who was the thief and who was the legitimate currency-holder, but in other situations, the distinction might not be so clear. And there are other ways that the network might take advantage of its users. The software developer could collude with miners to implement advantageous consensus rules for certain mining hardware in return for a kickback, for example. In the Bitcoin scaling debate, there were many accusations about certain core developers who were employees of Blockstream, a venture-backed start-up created to commercialize Bitcoin technology.

To talk about fiduciary responsibility, there has to be an identifiable fiduciary. The Ethereum Foundation is a legally constituted entity. The Bitcoin core development process is more scattered. Even with Ethereum, however, miners do not have to use the code produced by the foundation. Ethereum Classic (ETC) was born when a splinter group chose to reject the update reversing the hack of The DAO. The degree of control that any entity exerts over the blockchain network will depend on the circumstances. Several ICOs, such as Tezos, NEO, Qtum, and EOS, are planning blockchains that compete with Ethereum, and their decisions structuring the token sales frame the economic model for the network. The viability of these networks is tied to trust, so if they take advantage of users, those users are likely to exit.

The information-fiduciary concept could align the locus of legal responsibility with the locus of code on blockchain networks. The obligations involved might be considerably less than for traditional fiduciaries because blockchain network operators lack the ability to engage in many forms of harmful behavior. For example, they cannot easily abscond with user funds, even though they establish the network, because those are records on an immutable blockchain.[27] How exactly such a regime would operate and how it would be implemented legally remain to be worked out. Information fiduciaries might simply be a conceptual model for self-defined governance rules of blockchain networks. They illustrate how old legal doctrines may still help address very novel situations.

Making Code More Law-Like

Just as regulators and lawyers can adapt to the blockchain environment, distributed ledger systems can become more hospitable to legal enforcement. The three main pathways being explored are to integrate the terms of legal and smart contracts, to integrate traditional legal enforcement mechanisms into smart contracts, and to integrate law-like governance processes into blockchain platforms.

Templates and Contractual Integration

The simplest way to make blockchain-based systems more consistent with legal enforcement is literally to connect the two. Even if smart contracts can be enforced in court under the basic principles of contract law, they serve a different function than the fundamentally remedial institution of contracts.[28] Smart contracts are good at setting forth anticipated conditions and consequences ex ante, and then ensuring the consequences occur upon fulfillment of the conditions. Legal contracts are good at cleaning up the mess when, as inevitably occurs, things do not go according to plan. There is no reason, however, that the two mechanisms cannot coexist. Difficulties arise when the smart and legal contracts disregard one another, as in the collapse of The DAO.

The alternative approach is to pair smart contracts and legal contracts explicitly. Information security expert Ian Grigg first explored this idea in 2004, before the advent of cryptocurrencies, as part of the Ricardo digital transaction platform for financial instruments.[29] Ricardo defined its contracts as having three components: legal code (the human-readable text of a contract), computer code (the executable steps of a smart contract), and parameters (the variables that influence how the computer code executes). The legal code included the cryptographic hash string of the computer code, which guaranteed that it was referencing the proper smart contract. In parallel, the smart contract included the cryptographic hash string of the legal contract text. Thus, the two were definitively linked. If there was a problem with the smart contract, one could turn to the legal contract for resolution. Grigg called this structure the "Ricardian contract" because it was developed for the Ricardo system.

Like Szabo's original notion of smart contracts, Ricardian contracts were largely a theoretical construct prior to the blockchain, and in particular,

Ethereum's successful implementation of blockchain smart contracts.[30] The approach has since been rediscovered. Several groups are building solutions using the mutual hashing of smart and legal contracts, including a subgroup of the R3 consortium led by the British bank Barclays,[31] the Monax Burrow software now part of the Hyperledger open-source initiative,[32] and OpenLaw.[33]

With this approach, the human and smart contracts explicitly reference one another through digital signatures. In contrast to The DAO's terms of service, which privileged the algorithmic contract over the human-readable explanations, this approach makes each dependent on the other. A court or other decision-maker can use the conventional contract to understand the intent of the smart contract, which handles execution of the agreement.[34]

Not every smart contract will require a bespoke, human-negotiated contract alongside it. As with the contract system today, forms will be widespread for business-to-consumer and low-value agreements. In many cases, the costs of dispute resolution will so far exceed the potential recovery that "quick-and-dirty" reliance on the naïve actions of machines will be sufficient. Regulation of intermediaries such as registries may obviate the need to specify legal terms for every associated smart contract. As blockchain-based systems become more familiar, a combination of custom, common law, and model legislation is likely to develop to address common situations.

Arbitration, Oracles, and Computational Courts

Contractual integration links the substantive terms of a legal agreement with those of a smart contract. A different approach is to take some aspects of enforcement out of the automated system of the smart contract. In other words, a smart contract can be self-executing but not fully self-enforcing, thus avoiding the ambiguities and limitations of automated, code-based enforcement.

Many smart contracts will already need to interface with the outside world. For example, a call option to buy a security at a certain price can be executed algorithmically on the blockchain, with payment made in bitcoin or another cryptocurrency. The blockchain, however, does not know stock prices. That information must be provided to the smart contract through an external connection, either to an automated data source or a human arbiter. Those external sources are called "oracles."[35] Some oracles are just traditional data feeds designed with interfaces for smart contracts to process them in an automated way. Thompson Reuters, one of the largest business publishing firms, is making some of its data feeds available in a manner designed to function as smart-contract oracles.[36] Oraclize is a start-up focused entirely on turning data feeds into oracles.[37]

As Wright and De Filippi point out, oracles could be extended to dispute resolutions by courts or private actors.[38] Oracles can also be humans. Consider a simple smart contract in which each of the parties has a private key and a third key is given to an expert arbitrator. The smart contract requires two of three keys in order to execute, known as a "multiple signature (multisig)" arrangement. If the parties agree that the contract has been fully performed, they provide their keys and the smart contract executes. If there is a dispute, the parties turn to an arbitrator, who either provides a key along with that of the party seeking to enforce the contract, or refuses it, therefore preventing completion of the transaction. The system has just mimicked a legal arbitration process.

Smart contracts could by default incorporate arbitration mechanisms or rollback provisions. They could be designed to operate only in extreme cases, with high barriers through the design of the multisig process. This would help address extraordinary cases such as the attack on The DAO. Alternatively, they could be used to create a regular outlet for private dispute resolution, in the way that so many business-to-consumer form contracts today push disputes into arbitration. Balaji Srinavasan, a blockchain investor and founder of the start-up Earn.com, suggests optimistically that "over time blockchains will provide 'rule-of-law-as-a-service' as an international, programmable complement to the Delaware Chancery Court."[39]

The distributed nature of the blockchain may call for new enforcement mechanisms that are themselves distributed.[40] For example, new international arbitration networks might need to be developed that are tuned to the needs of blockchain disputes, much as the World Intellectual Property Organization created the Uniform Dispute Resolution Process (UDRP) to handle trademark disputes over Internet domain names.[41] However, because arbitration decisions could in some cases be directly executed on the blockchain and would apply on a peer-to-peer (P2P) basis, blockchain arbitration systems would be different from any current example.[42] Andreas Antonopoulos and Pamela Morgan proposed a decentralized arbitration and mediation network (DAMN) for funding to The DAO in May 2016.[43] Although the collapse of The DAO prevented consideration of their proposal, others are proposing similar ideas. For example, Mattereum, a project from block-chain entrepreneur Vinay Gupta, hopes to establish a private network of arbitrators tied to proprietary smart-contract templates.[44]

The trade-off of an arbitration regime is that it reintroduces intermediation to the decentralized blockchain environment. As Internet law scholar James Grimmelmann and computer scientist Arvind Narayanan put it, "[A]n arbitrator who can give you back your car is also an arbitrator who can take your car away from you. He's an intermediary of precisely the sort the block chain was supposed to eliminate."[45] Once again we run into Vili's Paradox: a well-governed blockchain system is not truly decentralized, and a truly decentralized blockchain system will not be well governed.

Computational courts and juries are a further extension of decentralized dispute resolution with the purpose of overcoming this challenge. They attempt to automate the process and avoid the need for predefined decision-makers or laws. Instead of arbitrators resolving disputes, these mechanisms employ the wisdom of the crowd through structured voting mechanisms implemented through smart contracts.[46]

Augur is trying to implement the computational jury approach. Augur, introduced in chapter 8, is a platform for creating markets in which users can stake real money (in the form of cryptocurrency) to trade on the outcome of predictions. As noted earlier, one reason that real-money prediction markets such as Intrade were shut down by regulators is that they could be used in illegal or unethical ways. A prediction market for the murder of one's mother-in-law, for example, would be troublesome.

Augur uses a system in which participants in the marketplace purchase a token, called REP. When someone creates a market, such as a prediction that the president will be impeached within a certain period of time, they post a bond in REP. They get the bond back if the market is legitimate. (Those who wish to bet on the outcome of the prediction do so in ether or some other cryptocurrency.) A randomly selected group of "reporters"—analogous to a jury—is tasked with verifying the outcome. Those reporters must also post a REP bond. The reports can be challenged, and if a second, randomly selected jury agrees with the challenge, the reporter providing incorrect information loses her or his bond.[47]

Augur hopes to produce verified outcomes without having to trust a central authority. Even for an agreed-upon fact, such as who wins the World Series, Augur itself need not assess whether a prediction is accurate. It can decentralize that step, potentially making its system more scalable and over-coming controversies around less-definite outcomes. Like the real-world jury system, helping to decide cases for fellow community members becomes an obligation of "citizenship."

If this mechanism works, Augur could turn into a kind of self-organizing oracle for anything. And as its founder points out, financial derivatives are essentially just complex bets on the future. Through eliminating transaction costs of intermediation, Augur hopes to "democratize and decentralize finance" by "enabling anyone, anywhere, at anytime in the world to create and speculate on derivatives at a low cost for the first time."[48] Like Bitcoin, it promises to take activities that traditionally required central authorities and spread them across a community motivated through incentives.

Augur uses the same system to police illegal or unethical activity. Reporters can mark contracts as "undeterminable/unethical." If this option achieves a majority, perhaps after a second round of reporting, the contract can be ter-minated and the REP deposit returned. Reporters are incentivized to make good ethical judgments in the same way that they are incentivized to make accurate factual assessments: Otherwise they risk losing their REP. In the-ory, Augur does not need to define community standards; the community self-defines them.[49] Augur chief executive officer Joey Krug acknowledges that this will likely apply to a limited category of conduct: "In practice, I think the [commonly agreed-upon standard] for 'what is unethical' will only be things that are considered unethical in a majority of cultures around the world."[50]

Augur's computational juries are a fascinating effort to re-create some-thing like a legal system entirely on cryptoeconomic principles. But there are plenty of reasons for skepticism. A majority of participants may believe that something is ethical—such as using certain illegal drugs—that is nonetheless illegal in the relevant jurisdictions. Whether something is ethical may be much harder for a reporter to decide than whether it is factually correct. The risk of losing REP if their decision is successfully challenged may make report-ers shy about selecting the "undeterminable/unethical" option. And those two categories are actually quite different from one another. At minimum, though, Augur's system could provide data to build other decentralized dis-pute resolution platforms. The Aragon project, described in chapter 5, has a similar concept for decentralized courts governing blockchain-based corpora-tions, including multiple levels of appeal up to a Supreme Court.[51]

Any of these voluntary mechanisms could be baked into blockchain applications, or even legally mandated in some cases. The full range of incentives and governance mechanisms could be used to encourage compliance with desirable approaches. For conventional disputes, the Federal Arbitration Act directs U.S. courts to accept private arbitration decisions when fraud is not involved, and the New York Convention extends reciprocal recognition of arbitral awards worldwide. National legislation and international agreements could create similar legal force for appropriately designed blockchain dispute resolution systems.[52]

On-Chain Governance

One of the biggest problems with blockchain networks as governance institutions is the difficulty of changing foundational rules. This is Vili's Paradox once again. Systems that have well-structured mechanisms for considering and implementing changes to consensus rules or other attributes are not fundamentally decentralized. The ultimate solution to the paradox would be to have a governance system that is as decentralized as blockchain consensus mechanisms themselves.

Even though Bitcoin lacks a formal governance structure, its developers have rigged a voluntary signaling mechanism for technical changes, BIP 9,[53] under which miners can broadcast their willingness and readiness to adopt changes. A similar process was used for the Segwit upgrade. Segwit automatically activated on the Bitcoin network after a threshold of 80 percent of network hashing power signaled for it.[54] While signaling thus enables a crude voting mechanism for controversial Bitcoin protocol upgrades, it leaves much to be desired as on-chain governance. The thresholds for approval are arbitrary. They are set centrally by those who propose the upgrades. Even more important, BIP 9 only signals; it does not enforce policies. Debates about scaling Bitcoin still require agreement among a critical mass of network participants.

There are several efforts underway to create true on-chain governance. A project called Rootstock is trying to create a smart-contract layer on top of Bitcoin.[55] It incorporates a built-in process giving both miners and users the power to make binding votes on network changes. Projects such as Decred, Dfinity, and Tezos are building entirely new blockchains with governance mechanisms baked in.[56] These systems use algorithms to allow network participants to vote on changes to the protocol. Proposals receiving sufficient support are automatically implemented. Decred successfully executed a change to its algorithm for allocating these voting tokens using the governance mechanism in the spring of 2017. Tezos, a more ambitious project, held one of the largest ICOs based on its governance concept.

There are limitations to these systems; they do not fully overcome Vili's Paradox.[57] They internalize many aspects of the rules governing distributed ledger systems. However, they generally rely on hard-coded rules for democratic voting to carry out changes. And they advantage large holders of tokens over other constituencies such as miners, developers, and active users. This may be a very good way to govern; it may even be, to paraphrase Winston Churchill, the best possible choice from a set of bad options. It is not perfect. Any governance structures that are imperfect will eventually need to be modified by someone. Moreover, humans need to define the rule changes that network participants vote on and code the software to implement them if adopted. The on-chain governance systems make the blockchains operate more like a human-based legal or governance regime, but they still leave gaps that traditional institutions will fill.

How successful these various approaches to law and the blockchain will be is far from clear. Old and new trust architectures will be fluid. Governance mechanisms and hybrids of code and law are the ways forward, but most of the details remain to be worked out. If they can be, the door is open to solving a wide variety of economically and socially significant problems in new ways.

Fusions of Cryptogovernance

Recall the diagram of things that cryptoregulate presented in chapter 8. Each of the four modalities—cryptography, law, self-interest, and trust—is a form of governance. Blockchain-based systems incorporate all of them into hybrid solutions, as illustrated in table 10.1.

This framework for cryptogovernance expands upon Vitalik Buterin's distinction between subjective and objective cryptoeconomic systems, discussed in chapter 5. Cryptography and law govern by constraint: they limit what people can do. Self-interest and trust shape people's choices so that they choose voluntarily to act in a certain way. Cryptography and economics are forms of applied mathematics whose effects, over a sufficiently large

Table 10.1
Forms of Blockchain Governance

	Governance by Constraint	Governance by Action
Objective governance	Cryptography	Self-interest
Subjective governance	Law	Trust

data set, can be modeled objectively. Law and trust are human-erected systems that always involve some measure of judgment and values.[58]

The governance challenge for blockchain-based systems is to merge these modalities. Each form of governance is imperfect by itself. Vili's Paradox reflects the separation of cryptography and self-interest. Economic incentives operate through decentralized decision-making, but they must be shepherded through centrally defined, cryptographically enforced rule sets. Vlad's Conundrum—that true freedom will be abused to cause harm—describes the separation of cryptography from law. Computer code neither knows nor cares whether it enables illegal behavior. Cryptographic constraints alone cannot ensure effective governance of distributed ledgers because they cannot comprehend human motivation. Humans will inevitably find ways to exploit the vulnerabilities of the system because they are motivated substantially by self-interest. Whoever attacked The DAO followed the rules of the smart contracts and the consensus mechanism. Bitcoin mining pools insisting on block sizes that maximize their income are doing nothing inconsistent with Nakamoto Consensus.

The economics of self-interest can explain such behavior. It can also help create responsive institutional structures. Yet economics cannot say, "Thou shalt not steal" or "Take one for the team." As critical technology theorist Adam Greenfield observes, governance through cryptocurrencies embodies a worldview in which everything has a price and can be traded in a market.[59] While that could lead to cooperative arrangements of mutual assistance, it could also give the cryptowealthy all of the power and none of the limits of a liberal democratic society.

Economic predictions have bite because most people respond rationally to incentives. However, economics cannot enforce obligations in the way that unbreakable cryptography can. Where incentives are misaligned or something other than economic rationality influences behavior, it hits its limits.

Bitcoin brought cryptography and self-interest together through the cryptoeconomic structure of proof of work. However, the fusion is imperfect. It operates on the microscale of consensus, not the macroscale of the networked system. Although there are interesting experiments to extend cryptoeconomic principles to governance of communities, all have risks or weaknesses. And none has yet been adopted in a system operating at scale, where there is significant money at stake.

Connecting law and trust poses similar challenges. As discussed in chapter 8, sometimes the two forces are well aligned, and other times they act in opposition. Once again, the problem involves levels of analysis. On the microscale of individual interactions, too much legal formality is a threat to trust. It implies that enforcement is necessary, which in turn implies that trust is insufficient. That dynamic can itself undermine trust. One reason that blockchain-based systems are effective in creating distributed trust is that instead of law, they rely on cryptography and can avoid such problematic legal oversight.

At the macrolevel of governance, however, things look different. Too much legal formalism can be troublesome in small groups with strong interpersonal trust, but in larger and more diverse communities, it creates fewer concerns. Formalized legal institutions such as democratic representation structures and judicial enforcement processes create a low-transaction cost environment for social interaction. Private exchanges and financial intermediaries replace handshake deals with systematized rules. The Nobel Prize–winning economic historian Douglass North traced how the growth of such institutions bridged the gap between small, family-based clusters and the large national and international transaction environments of modernity.[60]

The challenge is to create legal regimes based on more than coercive sanctions. One reason is that those sanctions are not always effective. Tom Tyler's work showed that deterrence is not the primary reason that people obey the law.[61] Instead, it is the sense that law is implemented in a fair and thus legitimate way that determines compliance rates. Legal sanctions also require a community operating within the territorial boundaries of a sovereign actor. Mechanisms to enforce laws outside a country's physical geography, such as extradition, are cumbersome. And they tend to work only when both jurisdictions have consistent legal regimes.

In the blockchain context, the problem of legal compliance is magnified. Those who do not trust the law can more easily relocate to a more favorable jurisdiction, as in the response to the BitLicense in the State of New York, or they can use cryptography to hide from it. Nonetheless, as Ross Ulbricht and Alexander Vinnik discovered, the law will pursue. However, such legal enforcement involves cost, uncertainty, and collateral damage. It is far better to write laws that are actually followed. This is often easier said than done, though. There is much work to be done in developing trusted legal rules for distributed ledger activities, as discussed in the previous chapters.

In liberal political theory, the social contract and democratic mechanisms provide a bridge between law and trust. Yet, as we have already seen in the motto of the Internet Engineering Task Force (IETF), which rejected voting in the same breath as kings and presidents, the cyberlibertarianism that animates the original Bitcoin community finds that solution unacceptable.[62] When the long-running Bitcoin scaling debate became particularly contentious in 2015, the administrator of the Bitcoin.org website and discussion forums refused to allow open debate on proposed alternatives. He declared, "One of the great things about Bitcoin *is* its lack of democracy."[63]

The four-quadrant cryptoregulation model reveals additional potential fusions. On the diagonal, the integration of law with incentive-based models represents a well-trod path. Using economic techniques to assess legal rules and regulatory requirements can fairly be called the mainstream analytic approach in law today, at least in the U.S. Even most of the criticisms of the law and economics consensus adopt its language, incorporating behavioral economics, capabilities theory, or post–Chicago School insights around market failure to criticize the approach on its own terms.

The opposite diagonal, cryptography and trust, is also very familiar. It is largely the way that security is implemented for digital systems today. People and organizations place their data on the Internet, and engage in transactions there, because of the robustness of cryptographic methods of protection. As with law and economics, there are limitations to cryptography and trust. For example, the most secure cryptography in the world will not protect against a user volunteering a password in response to a misleading "spearphishing" email. Hillary Clinton's campaign chair, John Podesta, trusted incorrectly, and as a result he allowed Russian hackers to circumvent the cryptographic locks on his email history and access all his messages.

On the vertical dimension, the gap between cryptography and law lies in the difference between how we express ourselves to each other and how we program our computers. Law can never be reduced fully to objective rules. Portions of it certainly can be, with significant benefits. Yet that only makes the parts that cannot more important. Hard-edged, cryptographically secured code can never fully encompass human intentions. This is the problem of smart-contract expression discussed in chapter 6.

More generally, because it is expressed in finite systems, the cryptographic dimension of distributed ledger systems cannot bootstrap itself as law can. Legal systems incorporate both the rules themselves and the institutional processes of rule-making. Law is not just an exercise of reading predefined codes; it is inherently dynamic.[64] It incorporates both of Vili Lehdonvirta's functions: rule making and rule enforcement. Another necessary dimension of blockchain governance, therefore, is the fusion—imperfect though it may be—of cryptography and law. Such mechanisms were discussed earlier in this chapter.

That leaves trust crossed with economics. Such a fusion must explore behavioral motivations that go beyond economic incentives. The affective dimension of trust—what Oliver Williamson described as noncalculative behavior—may be impossible to account for in transaction-cost economics, as Williamson argued.[65] It has significant value in the larger framework of governance. Successful distributed ledger systems are ones in which trust structures are aligned at the governance level. Ironically, one of the basic reasons to adopt distributed ledger technology is the limited trust among participants in a network.

The heart of the governance problem with Bitcoin scaling relates to Frank Knight's definitions of risk and uncertainty, as discussed in chapter 5. Mining bitcoin involves risk: the returns may not exceed the expense involved. However, the risk is calculable, so miners can rationally decide whether to invest. Similarly, users can decide whether to trust the blockchain because the risks involved are comprehensible. The code, which defines the governance rules for consensus, is public. And there is now a history upon which to base empirical decisions.

Changing the consensus algorithm in fundamental ways, however, opens up significant uncertainty. Even a simple expansion of block size could threaten the stability of the system, according to many Bitcoin core developers. How any change will affect the various interested communities over time is a difficult question to answer. The more decisions change the shape of the distributed ledger network over the long run, the harder it is to evaluate

commitments, which may be costly to unwind. In transaction-cost economics, these are known as the problems of asset specificity and bounded
rationality.

Governance is a fundamentally hard problem. Blockchain technology
addresses a particular governance challenge—consensus about the status of
the ledger—in a new way. That does not by itself resolve the higher-level
coordination challenges that blockchain networks face. Effective solutions
will need to draw upon the best aspects of legal and technical trust.

11 An Unpredictable Certainty

As Speculative as They Are Rich

In 1994, the National Research Council (NRC) of the United States assembled a blue-ribbon panel of business and technology leaders to consider the future of what was then still called the National Information Infrastructure. The group issued its final report in 1996. The title, *The Unpredictable Certainty*, captured perfectly the prospects for the Internet then, and for the blockchain today.[1]

Observing that "[t]he opportunities presented by the evolving information infrastructure are as speculative as they are rich ..."[2], the report's authors nonetheless expressed confidence that "the technology and its uses will advance steadily,"[3] and that the Internet was "an extraordinary platform for innovation, one that is perhaps unique in human history."[4] That the nascent digital network of networks would change the way people lived, worked, and communicated was a certainty. How and when, however, were unpredictable beyond a short time horizon.

"As speculative as they are rich" is an apt caricature of the cryptocurrency millionaires piling their bitcoin and ether profits into initial coin offerings (ICOs). It is also a good description of the opportunities that the blockchain and distributed-ledger technologies present. The development history of the Internet provides useful guidance for the blockchain's future in two ways: It shows how the promise of decentralization can be undermined as systems scale. And it suggests a path for blockchain technology to reinvigorate the immense promise of the open Internet.

By 1996, when the NRC published its report, companies such as eBay, Amazon, and Yahoo! were already established. The first graphical web browser,

NCSA Mosaic, had been released three years before, and the first major commercial browser, Netscape Navigator, a year after that. Bill Gates had issued his famous internal memo declaring that the Internet was now the top focus of Microsoft, the world's most powerful technology company.[5]

Yet popular adoption of the Internet was quite limited. AOL, the online service that most people used to access the Internet, had 5 million members, and the total U.S. online audience was about 20 million. On average, these users spent about thirty minutes per month on the web.[6] (Today, Americans average about four hours online per *day*.)[7] Social media, messaging, mobile Internet access, and streaming media as we know them did not exist. Pundits of the era could still describe the Internet as a "trendy and oversold" fad.[8] What looks in hindsight like an inevitable march toward user adoption, corporate engagement, and global diffusion seemed deeply speculative twenty years ago.

If specific technology developments were not foreordained, neither were legal responses. The U.S. government could have strangled the Internet in its crib. It nearly did. Congress in 1996 passed overbroad criminal penalties for "indecent" content online, which could have killed off search engines and other services due to fear of liability. Instead, the harmful portions of the law were struck down in court, and an amendment granted intermediaries broader immunity for user-provided content than traditional content publishers or distributors. The Federal Communications Commission (FCC) could have authorized onerous per-minute charges for Internet access and banned Internet-based voice communications; instead, it embraced the technology. The U.S. could have used its control over the root of the Internet's domain name system to impose all sorts of restrictions; instead, it transitioned oversight to the Internet Corporation for Assigned Names and Numbers (ICANN), an international, privately run, multi-stakeholder body.

Any of these steps—and many others—could have slowed and perverted the growth of the open Internet. The cyber libertarians of the 1990s were wrong that the Internet could escape the clutches of territorial legal regimes, but they were right that governments and courts should take the Internet's potential seriously.

The blockchain is today's unpredictable certainty.

The genie of decentralized trust is out of the bottle. Bitcoin demonstrated that trustworthy record-keeping and value exchange were possible on a distributed ledger. Ethereum showed that smart contracts could automate complex transactions. Even if every major platform and Dapp in operation today failed, others would take up the mantle. Decentralization and shared truth have powerful applications in so many contexts that technical capabilities will eventually match market needs. Yet there are serious unanswered questions, as discussed throughout this book.

Inevitably, at a time of boundless enthusiasm about the potential of blockchains and distributed-ledger technologies, most discussions focus on the benefits rather than the risks. It is more exciting to describe how systems are supposed to work than to speculate about what would happen if they did not. Intoxicating talk of revolution, disruption, and changing everything is in the air. Those who question the upbeat narratives are usually skeptics of the whole enterprise. Many influential commenters have explained all the reasons why Bitcoin could not possibly work, would not replace cash, was a Ponzi scheme, and would never be of interest to the general public. More recently, critics argue that regulators will never allow blockchains to succeed, that Bitcoin is the only viable blockchain, and that established companies will never use the technology.

The cheerleaders and the naysayers make the same mistake: They confuse parts of the story for the whole. Years of real-world experience involving thousands of people, hundreds of companies, and billions of dollars of investment show that blockchain consensus actually works. At least, it works as much as one could say the Internet works.

On the other hand, the jury remains out on whether this innovation will amount to more than an interesting new asset class for specialized investors and a tweak to enterprise database architectures. A great deal of business activity and experimentation is occurring. There are some real-world success stories and validated use-cases. There is not yet a Yahoo! or Netscape of the blockchain economy, let alone a Google or Wikipedia. Perhaps such a company is operating today, but not yet at the same level of impact. Even if blockchain adoption reaches Internet scale, there is no guarantee that systems will retain the protean openness and decentralization that make projects like Bitcoin and Ethereum so exciting.

Participating in the blockchain universe, as either a buyer of coins or a user of systems, requires a leap of faith. So much of the technology involved is complicated and unproven. Both individuals and organizations have to make investments based on imperfect information and trust a world that they do not fully understand. Appropriately enough, that leap of trust is precisely how blockchain technology itself operates. It constructs a reliable truth on unreliable foundations.

The blockchain took hold, at least in part, as a response to the global trust crisis. It does not offer a complete solution to that crisis; nothing could. The most one can say is that in areas such as financial services, data protection, and surveillance, where trust in private and public authorities is experiencing the greatest tension, blockchain technology can contribute to effective responses. The blockchain offers particular promise as a counterweight to the creeping centralization that has undermined the original vision of the Internet.

Decentralization Cannot Hold

Many influential technologists and investors, including MIT Media Lab director Joichi Ito and venture capitalist Marc Andreessen, have compared Bitcoin and the blockchain to the Internet in its early days.[9] As Andreessen framed the analogy in 2014:[10]

> A mysterious new technology emerges, seemingly out of nowhere, but actually the result of two decades of intense research and development by nearly anonymous researchers. Political idealists project visions of liberation and revolution onto it; establishment elites heap contempt and scorn on it. On the other hand, technologists—nerds—are transfixed by it. [Eventually] its effects become profound; and later, many people wonder why its powerful promise was not more obvious from the start.

Not so long ago, the Internet was what the blockchain is today: a crazy idea about decentralizing power that just might change the world. It too was attacked as both a toy and a tool for criminals to exploit. It too was misunderstood as a technology of ungovernability when it was really a technology of governance. Comparing the blockchain to the Internet is valuable for two reasons. Looking backward, studying the Internet's history provides a template for how distributed ledger technology will evolve. Looking forward, blockchain-based systems could reinvigorate the Internet as an open, decentralized platform.

The blockchain world could use a dose of institutional memory. Distributed ledgers took off as a broad, worldwide business phenomenon around 2015, almost exactly twenty years after the similar ignition point for the Internet. Cryptocurrency developers in their twenties—a healthy percentage of most major projects—do not remember a world before personal computers tapped into a global communications network; many do not remember a world before smartphones and social networking. Vitalik Buterin, the preternatural genius behind Ethereum, was born the same year that Marc Andreessen released Netscape Navigator. The global nature of Blockchain development also cuts against awareness of history. Teams in Singapore or Berlin are less likely to be familiar with the stories that played out in Silicon Valley and Washington, D.C. But they should be. The blockchain's growth is both a replay of the Internet's great success and an opportunity to rectify its greatest failure. The Internet too began as a rebellion against institutional power, and it became in many ways a tool of institutional control.

The Internet started in the 1970s with a mundane use-case: sending electronic files between users on different university or government computer networks. Over the next forty years, it swept the world, leaving few communities and businesses untouched. It did so in part because it was designed as an open foundational technology infrastructure. Many proprietary innovations are built on top of the Internet, ranging from Airbnb to YouTube. The Internet supports all of them.

Wikipedia did not need to ask permission to start a grand experiment in creating the world's greatest collection of user-curated knowledge. Netflix and Spotify did not need to ask permission to change the way that people around the world interact with and consume media. Salesforce did not need to ask permission to move enterprise software from the desktop to the network. Amazon did not need to ask permission to create the world's largest store, or, a few years later, to create the world's largest virtual-computing cloud. WhatsApp, Instagram, WeChat, and Snap did not need to ask permission to alter the way that billions of people communicate every day. All of this happened because no one owns the Internet. Those who might feel threatened by innovation lack the power to stop it.

For all its success, though, the Internet has failed to realize many of the dreams and expectations it provoked. A handful of broadband and wireless network operators today control access in most of the world. A small number of companies dominate search, social media, advertising, e-commerce, and many other major functions. They keep users as much as possible within their own walled gardens. Economies of scale and network effects—the fact that networked services become more valuable as they offer connections to more people—accentuate this consolidation. Individuals have little control over the torrent of personal data that firms aggregate to deliver services. Some governments have found ways to limit the free flow of information online and to exploit the network for the purpose of surveillance. User empowerment and permissionless innovation are significantly constrained.

The trust crisis in business, government, and media described in chapter 1 is also hitting the Internet economy because Internet-based organizations are no longer countercultural alternatives to those establishment institutions: They *are* the establishment. And they are facing a major trust gap. Salesforce CEO Marc Benioff declared at the World Economic Forum annual meeting in 2015, "The digital revolution needs a trust revolution."[11] And Internet Society CEO Kathy Brown has described the "global erosion of trust amongst users" as an "existential threat to the future of the Internet."[12]

Trust is especially important in the online world. On the Internet, there is no face-to-face contact, and interactions are necessarily mediated by computer hardware, software, and service providers. A user who clicks a "Buy" button on eBay or responds to a post on Facebook trusts in who or what is on the other side of the transaction. That trust requires more than just technical reliability and good intentions on the part of online providers. Francis Fukuyama correctly pointed out that enthusiasts for information technology often ignore the importance of trust: "Trust does not reside in integrated circuits or fiber optic cables. Although it involves an exchange of information, trust is not reducible to information."[13] The successful growth of the digital economy required the development of a trust layer on top of the Internet.

In the early days of e-commerce, many users refused to transact because they were afraid that their credit cards and other information would be stolen. The primary technical response was a security protocol, Transport Level Security (TLS), which verifies the connection between a user's browser and a website's server.[14] By greatly increasing confidence that what Internet users saw on their screens were actually legitimate sites, TLS formed a basis for mainstream trust in e-commerce. Standing behind TLS is public key infrastructure (PKI). As discussed in connection with the DigiNotar incident in chapter 4, PKI is a centralized trust architecture. A website is trustworthy if it has the proper certificate. It obtains that certificate from an organization called a "certificate authority (CA)," which signs it with its own cryptographic private key. The CA may, in turn, gain authority from a higher-level CA.

Verifying the integrity of information transmitted over the network is just part of online security. Even when users have sufficient confidence in the platforms they interact with, there is often a buyer, seller, or other provider at the other end of the transaction. Companies such as Amazon.com and eBay quickly found that users needed ways to gain trust in the products they were offering, as well as the third parties offering them. As these intermediaries became increasingly large, they turned into beacons of trust for their users. Trustworthy service providers became the guarantors of a trustworthy Internet. This helped to promote centralization of those platforms. As the MIT Digital Currency Initiative's report on redecentralizing the web explains: "Even though the Internet was built on distributed protocols, the web needed to consolidate around a few curated service platforms in order to become practical for everyday people to use."[15]

Services such as Google, Facebook, Amazon, Tencent, and Alibaba now reach billions of users, control a disproportionate share of advertising and transaction revenues online, and have market capitalizations among the highest of any companies in the world. They use the Internet's open protocols, but their value accrues from keeping users within their own walled gardens as much as possible.

The major online platforms achieve this lock-in through their control of users' digital identities. A user cannot transfer her Facebook activity to another service, or choose what data she provides. This identity control can even extend to applications beyond Facebook. With "social log-in," other services allow their users to log in through their Facebook, Google, or Twitter credentials. This process is convenient for both users and the other services, but it entrenches the control of these major online intermediaries.

Reputation systems were the other major response to the need for trust online. These systems, which first gained notice with eBay's seller ratings, are now common elements of online services, using a variety of designs. They are especially important for overcoming trust barriers that hinder new forms of interaction. In recent years, the sharing economy, as typified by Uber and Airbnb, has seen rapid adoption thanks to successful reputation systems. Users are willing to get into strangers' cars and stay in strangers' apartments because the intermediary platforms offer ratings and verification systems that they believe are reliable.[16] However, malicious actors can game these systems.[17] The proliferation of automated bots designed to influence public opinion on services such as Twitter became a major problem during the 2016 U.S. presidential election. Ironically, perhaps, the low cost of creating fake accounts to overwhelm reputation systems produced a variant of the Sybil attacks that Bitcoin's proof of work system was designed to combat, as described in chapter 2.

The core problem is that today's Internet security, identity, and reputation infrastructures impose a hierarchical architecture of trust. For example, TLS is secure so long as the hierarchy of intermediaries successfully manages their digital certificates. Users are trusting the hierarchy of CAs rather than those they are transacting with directly. And because TLS is a point-to-point security protocol, it is not optimized for end-to-end trust. Similarly, the intermediaries and platforms control the identity and rating systems. Identities and ratings are generally not portable across sites, and therefore they do not function as a personal representation of reputation. Today's trusted Internet may not be so trustworthy after all.[18]

There has been a dramatic shift in perceptions of major Internet platforms as they grew to positions of dominance in the information ecosystem. Technology companies were seen as disruptive entrants breaking the stranglehold of monopolistic companies in communications, media, financial services, and other sectors. They stood for freedom of expression and empowerment of users. Now, antitrust experts worry openly about Amazon's power in retail,[19] while start-ups and content creators bemoan Google and Facebook's duopoly over online advertising.[20] Instead of making us smarter by offering access to the world's information, these platforms are accused of turning us into thoughtless automatons[21] and opening the door for political manipulation and fake news.[22] Cornell information security researcher Emin Gün Sirer sums up the danger as follows: "Code monocultures are dangerous. Centrally controlled services pose an existential threat to our democracies and social lives."[23]

The worrisome centralization of the Internet is not limited to the major platforms. Behind the scenes, Internet traffic routing has consolidated into a small number of backbone providers, many of which are associated with broadband access services. These backbones and online services increasingly connect directly to improve performance, moving away from the Internet's originally decentralized design. Content providers rely on overlay networks such as Akamai and Cloudflare, which potentially add a further layer of centralization. When Cloudflare, which provides protection against denial of service (DOS) attacks that overwhelm websites, decided to drop the neo-Nazi site The Daily Stormer as a customer, following similar actions by major domain name registrars, it effectively took the site off the Internet.[24] That decision was warranted—Cloudflare is under no obligation to take on a customer that promotes hate and violence—but it illustrated that the Internet is no longer quite the permissionless environment it once was.

Overcoming the Trust Trade-Off

The phrase "With great power comes great responsibility" embodies a time-less truth. Perhaps that is why it has been attributed to sources as varied as Winston Churchill, Jesus, the French government in the aftermath of the 1789 revolution, a nineteenth-century British politician, and the *Spider-Man* comic books. Those with power, whether they sought it or not, cannot disclaim its correlative obligations. In the technology world, many prefer to ignore the ways that software architecture grants the authority to shape behavior. The power of courts and regulatory agencies is easy to see; that of code and its masters, less so. Yet both are powerful regulators. Poorly designed code can be as harmful as poorly designed law.

Power does not necessarily make intermediaries untrustworthy. Market forces and internal norms can push even dominant firms not to be evil. How-ever, centralized control enables them to act in ways that may not be in the interests of those who trust them, or that do not promote equity, innovation, and other values.[25] It shifts the dynamics of speech, creativity, and innova-tion, and even absent deliberate efforts to stifle competition. And it makes it easier for governments to expand surveillance or limitations on digital free-dom because they need only piggyback onto the new control points.[26]

Regulation and antitrust enforcement are the traditional responses to the excessive power of trusted intermediaries. Legislation is the traditional route to contain government surveillance activities. None of these has been particularly successful for the Internet. The blockchain offers another route. Distributed ledger technologies, and especially public blockchain networks, embody an orientation toward openness and decentralization that is more like the early Internet than today's more controlled environment.[27]

Decentralization is a strategy to address the problem of power. Democ-racies replaced fallible kings with the distributed authority of voters and representatives. Dividing responsibilities among different branches of gov-ernment further dilutes potentially dangerous concentrations of power. As Satoshi Nakamoto recognized in his original Bitcoin whitepaper, the same dynamics apply to the private power of intermediaries in financial transactions, such as banks. The need to trust someone or something creates a power imbalance. The widely trusted actor becomes powerful in ways that it can exploit. Google is trusted as the most useful information source, and Facebook is trusted with personal information, which gives both sites the ability to lock out potential competitors and extract additional revenue.

There have been prior movements to move the Internet to a more truly distributed model. Most efforts, such as the Diaspora decentralized social network, simply failed to gain traction.[28] Most notably, in the late 1990s, peer-to-peer (P2P) technology took off as a way to connect Internet users directly, bypassing controlling intermediaries.[29] Unfortunately, though it was employed for a variety of services and offered significant technical advantages, P2P was largely associated with illicit file-sharing systems such as Napster.[30] When those platforms collapsed under legal onslaught from the music industry, the broader movement also faltered. Improvements in bandwidth and processing power, plus the reluctant agreement of the music industry to allow affordable licensed downloads, also took the wind out of the P2P movement's sails.

P2P technology is still widely used in important Internet functions such as content delivery. Mainstream user-facing Internet services, however, have gone in the opposite direction. The great Internet architectural shift of the twenty-first century so far is the rise of cloud computing.[31] Companies such as Google, Amazon, Apple, Microsoft, and Facebook now run massive data centers that function as platforms for network activity. Cloud computing makes possible tremendous advances in the capability and scalability of services delivered to users and businesses. However, it is a scale game. Only a few companies have the resources and expertise to compete, and they are always looking for ways to leverage their platforms into other market opportunities.[32]

In light of the growing power of cloud supergiants, as well as the revelations about extensive government surveillance over online activity, a growing number of technologists and entrepreneurs are talking about redecentralizing the Internet.[33] World Wide Web creator Tim Berners-Lee is a prominent advocate.[34] A Decentralized Web Summit in June 2016 featured Berners-Lee, Transmission Control Protocol/Internet Protocol (TCP/IP) cocreator Vint Cerf, Internet Archive head Brewster Kahle, and other influential figures.[35] The basic challenge to such efforts is not just the entrenched power of public and private interests, although that is a significant hurdle. It is the Internet's fundamental structure.

The Internet was designed to support trustworthy communication on a distributed network of networks.[36] Users can rely on the network to deliver data, even though no one manages the end-to-end flow of traffic and the system is extremely heterogeneous. This works through the use of a "spanning layer": the Internet Protocol (IP).[37] Everyone agrees to support IP; what people do at higher and lower layers is up to them.[38] This structure promoted tremendous innovation, competition, and creative freedom because users and services were not locked into a particular network technology. They could build whatever they wanted on top of the transport network and leave the details of moving packets to the lower layers.

The Internet architecture has been unimaginably successful. It allowed the Internet to scale up from a small collection of research networks to a global platform that influences the lives of billions of people each day. There is a problem, however. By establishing the IP spanning layer at the level of basic transport, it allows for proprietary solutions and concentration of power at higher levels.

Best-efforts IP transport is available to all from anyone who wishes to provide it, but reliable delivery with quality of service, security, identity management, content, searching, and other important functionalities is subject to lock-in by dominant providers at the top. Facebook today enjoys great market power because the social graph—the network of relationships and data around online identities—is a proprietary asset rather than a common resource. The same goes for Google with searching, Apple with mobile apps, and Uber with local transportation provisioning.

So long as the spanning layer of the network sits below the trust layer, trust will be a force for centralized control. Secure communication, reputation, and identity are services that intermediaries and service providers offer for their own advantage, not network primitives available to all.

The Internet's designers explicitly placed such functionality above the spanning layer because they were focused on the goal of data transmission across a decentralized network of networks.[39] The vision of an "end-to-end" network was that transport providers should not embed unnecessary functionalities that could be delivered in a more open and evolutionary way at the edges of the network.[40] The problem is that the former edges have become new centers at a higher level of the network stack. A new spanning layer is needed, this time focusing on trust: an Internet of Value, operating on top of the Internet of Communication.

Blockchain as Spanning Layer

The excitement about the blockchain as a "new Internet" reflects its potential to return to the Internet's decentralized roots.[41] As Lawrence Lessig has suggested, the blockchain provides an opportunity to revisit the foundational decisions of cyberlaw, and this time, perhaps, produce a more open environment.[42] If blockchains succeed in becoming widely adopted as trustworthy ledgers, a key opportunity for proprietary control would be removed.

As venture capitalist Chris Dixon observes, "If I'm building on Ethereum, I'm not worried about Ethereum kicking me off, the way I would if I were building on Facebook and Twitter."[43] Ethereum is run by a nonprofit foundation, supported through a network of independent miners and available as open-source software, which allows anyone to fork both the code and the prior transaction history. All those features make it very different from the private information platforms dominating the web. It would be significantly harder (and less valuable) for the Ethereum Foundation to twist the platform to benefit some users over others.

To be sure, a redecentralized Internet will still have large providers and experience government engagement. Although the blockchain is already being used to create decentralized search engines, marketplaces, social networks, and other analogues to today's dominant platforms, the incumbents retain extremely strong institutionalized advantages. The challenge is not to defeat Facebook, but to open the door for the next Facebooks, which will operate in a distributed manner that empowers users.

As with the Internet, the key lies in the separation of functionality at the point of the spanning layer.[44] The Internet separates the data structure (IP) from the traffic management (TCP). Everyone can use IP and assume the interoperability of the data plane. At the same time, everyone can innovate around the control plane. For the blockchain, the distributed ledger is the data plane, and the smart contract is the control plane. Both are important. Confidence in the basic integrity of the ledger is essential. Yet it is insufficient for the richer, more relational interactions that reflect trust. Technical innovation, standardization, and legal facilitation will all be required to cross this chasm.

The walled gardens of today's Internet took the open platform of TCP/IP networks and privatized the layer of data above it through proprietary interfaces. Public distributed ledger networks such as Bitcoin and Ethereum are different, in that all information is available to anyone. No one owns the database of Bitcoin transaction records the way that Google owns its database of search queries. Moreover, the software for these networks, as well as for major permissioned-ledger projects such as Hyperledger and R3, is open source. That means that anyone can take it apart, evaluate its operations, create extensions to it, or even create a modified version of it. This can lead to fragmentation, but it also promotes innovation.

The concepts of "open data" and "open source" reflect only one dimension of blockchain openness. The reason that dominant Internet platforms soaked up so much of the value in online activity is economic as much as technical. Facebook sits between users looking to interact and advertisers looking to market to them. In 2017, it generated more than $30 billion in revenue from these interactions. Users provide the data and attention that feeds this profit machine, but they receive none of the financial benefits. Network effects help to lock in Facebook's control. A competitor, even one offering a far superior service, cannot offer the same value proposition because what people want is access to their friends. And Facebook keeps tight control over the identity information for its users.

There is nothing inherently wrong with companies such as Facebook making money in this way. Facebook and other online intermediaries are phenomenally innovative companies, which have helped to connect the world and in many ways changed life for the better. Yet their power is inherently corrupting. Intermediaries necessarily shape markets to serve their own interests. In 2017, for example, the European Union imposed a $2.7 billion fine on Google for manipulating online-shopping search results to benefit its affiliates.[45]

Distributed ledger networks operate differently. A cryptocurrency token can be used to monetize that ownership value. For example, the Inter Planetary File System (IPFS) offers a blockchain-based, distributed cloud-storage technology. Instead of storing files in a particular location, accessible through a uniform resource locator (URL) address, IPFS stores multiple copies of files, in pieces, across many hard drives throughout the network. It is designed to use the Filecoin token to incentivize users to contribute storage space. The token provides the intermediation by establishing incentives on both sides, analogous to the way that Google brings together advertisers and viewers. Those who upload files contribute tokens (which they can purchase for other currencies) and those who store them earn tokens. IPFS, the company, provides the technology, but it has no control over the content stored on the network. And the value of the tokens depends on supply and demand.

Blockchain-based start-ups that monetize through ICOs rather than traditional venture capital and public markets plan to flip the economic model of traditional proprietary platforms. They offer users the ability to accrue value directly from the success of their protocols. This could help overcome the network effects trap, which makes it so difficult for a new platform to get to scale.[46] With the ICO model, projects may have easier access to capital because they can tap into individuals around the world rather than the small collection of early-stage venture capitalists and angel investors. Their investors receive something of potentially immediate value—tokens that can either be used for services on the platform or translated into other currencies through exchanges. And if a protocol takes off, those tokens still belong to the purchasers. The platform cannot centralize the value creation in the way Facebook does.

At least, that is the theory. A substantial percentage billions of dollars raised by ICOs since 2016 was from investors simply looking to get rich from projects that they did not intend to participate in, and often did not understand. The absence of regulation allowed some offerings to stack the deck against ordinary investors, not to mention engage in outright scams. And the blockchain does not necessarily overcome the incumbency benefits of existing intermediaries. There is no reason to think that a distributed Facebook competitor would be any more successful built on a distributed ledger than previous efforts such as Google+ and Diaspora were. Steem.it, a blockchain-based online discussion network that lets users reward high-quality content using cryptocurrency, is a nice proof of concept, but it shows no signs of dethroning Reddit or Facebook. The overheated predictions that the blockchain will necessarily transform the economy and overthrow incumbents need to be tempered.

Even so, the influx of capital into Dapps is spurring a flood of creative innovation. There were plenty of failures during the early days of the

Internet market as well. And some of the new blockchain-based solutions are taking direct aim at the proprietary underpinnings of the existing Internet ecosystem. Blockstack and the Ethernet Name Service are creating distributed, blockchain-based alternatives to the Internet's domain name system for access to online resources.[47] Blockstack has gone farther, proposing a fully tokenized and decentralized version of the Internet's core protocols.[48]

The blockchain also supports a decentralized approach to identity that returns control to individual users. With "self-sovereign identity," users control their profiles and what information services can access.[49] A collection of enterprise providers, start-ups, and nonprofits, including Microsoft, Evernym, Tierion, Uport, and the Sovrin Foundation, are working to create an identity infrastructure in which users are no longer tied to dominant platforms or centralized intermediaries such as credit bureaus. The Decentralized Identity Foundation, the ID2020 public-private partnership, and the World Wide Web Consortium are shepherding the creation of open standards to make this vision a reality.[50] Such efforts are still at a relatively early stage, and important concerns remain, such as the legal responsibility for errors mentioned in the previous chapter. However, there is demand from both major private firms and government agencies for reliable identity frameworks that avoid single points of failure.

The blockchain could overcome a key problem that doomed prior decentralized digital identity efforts. Once users have private keys representing identity information, they need somewhere to store them. In the past, that wound up being a centralized provider like Facebook. Blockchains allow the verification and management of keys without ceding control. "Now we have a way that I can create an ID, I can put it somewhere, I can prove I own it, and they can't take it away from me," says Kaliya Young, a digital identity advocate who cofounded the Internet Identity Workshop in 2005.[51]

Self-sovereign identity would also make it easier to provide only the information needed for particular interactions. Using advanced cryptographic techniques, it is possible to verify the truth of a claim—such as whether someone has more than $100,000 in liquid net worth or is over twenty-one years old—without actually storing that private information on the blockchain. Such verified claims would, for example, allow a prospective lender to obtain a financial transaction history, while a prospective employer would get verification of any educational degrees earned, but no data that was not necessary for the transaction at hand. Users could create a different key pair for each business relationship, so the theft of one would not expose other information. Government agencies are starting to support these development efforts as a way to combat fraud, inefficiencies, and security breaches such as the recent hacks into the Office of Personnel Management and Equifax. The State of Illinois has launched a pilot project to issue digital birth certificates on a blockchain based on this approach.[52]

Interoperability could further reconstitute the Internet on a distributed ledger foundation. The meaning of interoperability in the blockchain context is still uncertain. The Internet created a mechanism for distinct computer networks, called "autonomous systems," to talk to one another and form a coherent metanetwork. There are still many private networks not fully integrated into the collective. Some use Internet technologies but restrict access; others continue to use incompatible networking standards for certain aspects of their communications; still others are physically disconnected from the Internet for security. In the distributed ledger world today, there are private networks that exchange no data with other ledgers, altcoin networks that are built on a shared but distinct platform (such as Bitcoin, Ethereum, or Tendermint), and various crude connectors to share data and smart-contract logic across platforms.

In the future, the various islands may grow more independent, or they may merge. One quite possible scenario is for bitcoin to dominate as a reserve currency and store of value, while Ethereum dominates as the platform for distributed applications and private consortia remain independent. Another is that the network effect of public platforms ultimately wins out, and even the closed consortia run on top of an open platform. This is the way that the Internet works today. Another is that there are a number of public blockchain networks for different regions and applications, but they talk to each other seamlessly. A variety of projects, including Cosmos, Ripple's Interledger Protocol, and Polkadot, hope to deliver cross-chain interoperability so that users need not worry about which coin or which blockchain powers the application they interact with.[53]

A decentralized Internet of blockchains could replace the current Internet economy with one that more strongly empowers individuals and fuels innovation. Such a future would open up opportunity more broadly around the world. It is, however, far from a certainty. The blockchain, like the Internet, was born as a technology of openness. It will not remain so without solid governance mechanisms that produce robust trust.

12   Conclusion

Mike Hearn's Odyssey

The British software developer Mike Hearn is one of the most controversial figures in the blockchain world. As a senior engineer at Google's office in Zurich, Switzerland, he worked on systems such as Google Maps and Gmail. He discovered Bitcoin in 2009, a few months after the release of Satoshi Nakamoto's whitepaper, and immediately began exchanging email with him about how the network might scale. He soon began contributing to the Bitcoin development project. Eventually, he quit his lucrative job at Google to work on Bitcoin full time as one of the small group of Bitcoin core developers.

In 2013, Hearn gave a mind-blowing talk at the Turing Festival in Edinburgh on blockchain-based, autonomous agents.[1] He foresaw a world in which self-driving cars used a decentralized autonomous organization (DAO), which he called TradeNet, to find riders and bid for space on roads. No one would own the cars. They would own themselves and be programmed to maximize productivity, including investing in the creation of new cars when their revenues exceeded costs, all without human intervention or central management. Another entity, MatterNet, would coordinate the delivery of physical objects through autonomous quadcopters. All of this could be implemented through smart contracts. New arrangements built around cryptocurrencies might replace not only the financial system, but also taxation as a means of funding the creation of public goods.

For many, this talk was an eye-opener about where Bitcoin could lead. At the time, the Bitcoin community was still largely a collection of volunteer software developers and digital cash enthusiasts. Vitalik Buterin had not yet proposed Ethereum. Paul Vigna and Michael Casey, in their book *The Age of Cryptocurrency*, call Hearn's talk "the most far-reaching forecast of [the] potential in blockchain technology."[2] Hearn was the visionary who appreciated the blockchain's radically transformative potential early on.

Given his enthusiasm, therefore, it was a shock when, two and a half years later, Mike Hearn publicly declared in an extraordinary blog post that Bitcoin had failed. He was ceasing his involvement in Bitcoin development and selling all his bitcoin. Hearn was a strong advocate of increasing the Bitcoin block size to improve performance. He was frustrated at other core developers who blocked these efforts, in particular a proposed fork called Bitcoin XT. At the same time, Bitcoin mining power had consolidated into a few pools. Hearn's conclusion was that Satoshi's grand experiment in decentralization had come to an end: "What was meant to be a new, decentralised form of money that lacked 'systemically important institutions' and 'too big to fail' has become something even worse: a system completely controlled by just a handful of people."[3]

At the root of the conflict was a disagreement about the relationship of scaling and decentralization. Hearn's nemesis among the core developers, Greg Maxwell, argued that as the Bitcoin network supported more activity on-chain, a few large corporations would be the only ones that would be able to operate the network nodes.[4] Hearn believed the opposite: growth was the only way to break the oligopolies of miners and core developers.[5]

Whatever the technical merits of the particular proposals for Bitcoin scaling, this debate implicates the themes at the heart of this book. The traditional understanding is that trusted systems must either be small enough for interpersonal peer-to-peer (P2P) trust or give up power to the Leviathan of centralized authority or to dominant intermediaries. What Hearn perceived was that distributed ledgers allowed a third option. They created a common truth without assuming the trustworthiness of any central actor. The blockchain's trust architecture offered the solution to the very problem Bitcoin was experiencing.

Yet there was a catch, which lurked in Hearn's earlier visionary explorations. In his 2013 Turing Festival talk, Hearn recognized that the most powerful applications of the blockchain created a public goods problem. A self-organizing marketplace of self-managed, autonomous vehicles would be superior to the status quo in every way but one: no one could own it, so who would be incentivized to build it? Hearn suggested assurance contracts, under which developers would be compensated automatically, but only once a threshold of support or implementation was reached.[6]

Crowdfunding services such as Kickstarter use this approach to great effect. However, the mechanism still requires someone to define the rules and objectives for the contract. For most of the assurance contracts that economists theorize, that entity is assumed to be the government—the very thing that Bitcoin was created to escape. Even if a private actor makes the rules, it needs some legitimate mechanism to create and enforce them. This brings us back to Vili's Paradox of governance: The mechanisms to make decentralized systems effective seemingly make them no longer decentralized.

Hearn was convinced that Bitcoin was doomed to recreate the flawed patterns of centralized governance that Satoshi hoped to overcome. He saw that if Bitcoin could not effectively govern itself, governments would step in to protect their citizens:

> Over the years governments have passed a large number of laws around securities and investments. Bitcoin is not a security and I do not believe it falls under those laws, but their spirit is simple enough: make sure investors are informed. When misinformed investors lose money, government attention frequently follows.

Hearn believed that Bitcoin's valiant experiment in decentralization had ended in failure. He abruptly left and took a new job with a very different distributed-ledger project. He became the lead platform engineer for R3 and the primary architect of Corda, its distributed-transaction platform for regulated financial-services firms.

When asked why he made the move, Hearn told *The New York Times*, "I want to be in a professional environment again where people are grounded in some sort of business reality."[7] To his critics, it appeared that Hearn was retreating to the familiar bureaucratic corporate world and turning his back on the transformational opportunity of the blockchain.

Following Hearn's dramatic announcement, the Bitcoin community continued to work slowly and contentiously toward resolution of the scaling debate. In fall 2017, with the implementation of Segwit and the price of bitcoin many times what it was when Hearn sold in December 2015, it could be said that facts had proven Hearn wrong. "There are some individuals like Hearn that are not capable of understanding the potential of Bitcoin," suggested an article in *CoinTelegraph*, a major cryptocurrency news site.[8] That would have been quite a shock to anyone who had watched Hearn's visionary 2013 talk.

In reality, those who equate the blockchain's success entirely with the spot market price of bitcoin and other cryptocurrencies are the ones demonstrating a failure of imagination. There are many factors that cause the exchange rate between dollars and bitcoin to fluctuate over the short to medium term, but the one that matters in the long run is trust. Hearn might have been wrong that Bitcoin's governance failures were insoluble—that remains to be seen— but he was absolutely correct that governance is crucial to distributed ledger technologies, including public blockchain networks.

Hearn's career arc describes the two poles of the distributed ledger world. Corda's network is permissioned, where Bitcoin is public; transmits information only between transacting parties, where Bitcoin broadcasts the full ledger to all; employs familiar relational databases for its information stores, rather than a blockchain structure; and does away with the native cryptocurrency entirely. Advocates of public blockchains dismiss permissioned systems such as Corda as uninteresting. They are, they say, just a tool for existing enterprises to operate a bit more efficiently, rather than a means to restructure markets. Hearn is widely reviled among Bitcoin true believers for wrongly declaring Bitcoin a failure and joining the established banks Satoshi Nakamoto hoped to destroy.

One could not build TradeNet or MatterNet as Hearn envisioned them on Corda because someone always has to decide who can operate on the network. The fact that the same man is behind both, though, should lead one to question this simple dichotomy. Hearn left Bitcoin because he believed that for all the rhetoric of decentralization, Bitcoin had become a centrally controlled system, and a poorly managed one at that. Whether history judges him prescient or a fool for declaring the Bitcoin experiment a failure in January 2016, his story illustrates that significant technologies implemented in the real world are never as pure as their creators intend.

Building real systems used to provide real services for real people involves trade-offs. The right set of trade-offs depends on the context, as well as on the relevant objectives. A venture capitalist willing to accept ten failed investments for a single big success makes different trade-offs than a retail investor deciding where to put her life savings. A start-up looking to transform existing markets thinks differently than a huge corporation, even the best and most innovative ones. What works for users in Silicon Valley probably won't work in Somalia, and vice versa.

The distributed architecture of trustless trust first made real in Satoshi Nakamoto's whitepaper is a way of thinking, not a recipe. It will be implemented in different ways along multiple tracks. Some will prove to be dead ends, and some will merge over time. Some will be abused. Some will shave a few percentage points off corporate transaction costs. And some just might change the world significantly for the better.

A Matter of Trust

Roy Amara was the futurist's futurist. He spent eighteen years at the legendary Stanford Research Institute (SRI), helping shape the concept of computing as we now know it. Along with Paul Baran, one of the creators of the packet-switching technology that made the Internet possible, he helped found and lead the Institute for the Future, a legendary Palo Alto think tank. Among many other projects, he led studies on the social impact of computers in 1973 and on what we now call "climate change" in 1978, decades before those topics reached the mainstream. He is best known today for a remarkably perceptive aphorism: We tend to overestimate the impact of technologies in the short run but underestimate them over the long term.

The personal computer, the Internet, the web, social media, the smartphone ... almost all transformative technologies over the past fifty years illustrate Amara's Law. In all likelihood, the blockchain is no exception. Today, with small teams raising hundreds of millions of dollars in ICOs with little more than a whitepaper, and the price of cryptocurrencies surging overnight, it is easy to get ahead of reality. Delays, crashes, and detours are inevitable. For the blockchain to reach its potential as a worldwide platform may take a decade, or two, or five. Those investing in blockchain-based assets for a financial return need to be successful over their defined time horizon. But those seeking to identify critical trends and take advantage of them need only be directionally correct. At some point, we will likely wonder how anyone doubted the potential of distributed-ledger technology—or whatever we call it then—but those who moved too fast or picked the wrong vehicle will still miss out.

Distributed ledgers are the first advance in information technology (IT) in twenty years whose potential impact matches that of the Internet. They are, however, still relatively early in their development. Further growth of the blockchain will depend partly on technical advances, partly on adoption patterns, partly on the business innovations built on top of distributed ledger platforms, and partly on the resolution of the legal and governance challenges to the blockchain's trust architecture.

At a time when trust in centralized power structures is waning, the blockchain's trustless trust offers a compelling alternative. There is, however, no substitute for the hard work of ensuring that the affordances and constraints of technological systems match the expectations and needs of the individuals, organizations, and communities that adopt them. Even if the grandiose predictions about transforming finance, government, commerce, and more prove ill advised, the blockchain has already produced important discoveries. Its potential is far greater. Like the Internet, the blockchain is a foundational technology whose impacts could reach into every corner of the world. To move forward, though, law and distributed ledgers need one another.

How the story plays out will be a matter of trust.

Notes

Introduction

1. Charles R. Geisst, *Wall Street: A History*, revised and expanded ed. (Oxford: Oxford University Press, 2004), 13.

2. John D'Antona, Jr., "Who Safeguards the Industry?" *Traders Magazine*, April 2, 2017, http://www.dtcc.com/news/2017/august/02/who-safeguards-the-industry.

3. The gross world product, a measure of global economic activity, was estimated to be $119 trillion in purchasing power parity terms in 2016. *World Factbook*, Central Intelligence Agency (CIA), https://www.cia.gov/library/publications/the-world-factbook/geos/xx.html. This number is smaller because it is a static measure of output, whereas the DTCC number is a measure of financial transaction flows, many of which move in offsetting directions.

4. This was the date that the first block of Bitcoin transactions was validated. Timothy B. Lee, "Five Years of Bitcoin in One Post," *Washington Post*, January 3, 2014, "The Switch" section, http://www.washingtonpost.com/news/the-switch/wp/2014/01/03/five-years-of-bitcoin-in-one-post. The whitepaper describing the Bitcoin architecture was released approximately two months earlier.

5. Scott Rosenberg, "Bitcoin Makes Even Smart People Feel Dumb," *Wired*, August 9, 2017, https://www.wired.com/story/bitcoin-makes-even-smart-people-feel-dumb.

6. Mitch Tuchman, "Heed Warren Buffett's Warning: Bitcoin Is Pure FOMO," *MarketWatch*, https://www.marketwatch.com/story/heed-warren-buffetts-warning-bitcoin-is-pure-fomo-2017-12-26.

7. Paul Krugman, "Bitcoin Is Evil," *The New York Times*, December 28, 2013, "Opinion Pages" section, https://krugman.blogs.nytimes.com/2013/12/28/bitcoin-is-evil.

8. Luke Graham, "Governments Will Close Down Bitcoin and Cryptocurrencies If They Get Too Big, Warns Jamie Dimon," CNBC, September 22, 2017, https://www.cnbc.com/2017/09/22/bitcoin-jpmorgans-jamie-dimon-lays-into-bitcoin-again

.html. With the price of cryptocurrencies soaring, Dimon expressed regret for this statement a few months later.

9. Naval Ravikant (@naval), Twitter, June 22, 2017, 6:36 p.m., https://twitter.com /naval/status/878018839044161536.

10. Everett M Rogers, *Diffusion of Innovations* (New York: Free Press, 2003).

11. Garrick Hileman, "State of Blockchain Q1 2016: Blockchain Funding Overtakes Bitcoin," *CoinDesk,* May 11, 2016, https://www.coindesk.com/state-of-blockchain -q1-2016/.

12. James Schneider, Alexander Blostein, Brian Lee, Steven Kent, Ingrid Groer, and Eric Beardsley, *Profiles in Innovation: Blockchain—Putting Theory into Practice* (Gold- man Sachs, May 24, 2016), https://www.finyear.com/attachment/690548.

13. Sam Smith, "Nearly 6 in 10 Large Corporations Considering Blockchain Deploy- ment," Juniper Research, July 31, 2017, https://www.juniperresearch.com/press /press-releases/6-in-10-large-corporations-considering-blockhain.

14. Marco Iansiti and Karim R. Lakhani, "The Truth about Blockchain," *Harvard Business Review* 95, no. 1 (2017): 118–127, https://hbr.org/2017/01/the-truth-about -blockchain.

15. Carlota Perez, *Technological Revolutions and Financial Capital: The Dynamics of Bubbles and Golden Ages* (Cheltenham, UK: Edward Elgar, 2003).

16. Barton Swaim, "'Trust, but Verify': An Untrustworthy Political Phrase," *Wash- ington Post,* March 11, 2016, http://www.washingtonpost.com/opinions/trust-but -verify-an-untrustworthy-political-phrase/2016/03/11/da32fb08-db3b-11e5-891a -4ed04f4213e8_story.html.

17. Albert Wenger, "Bitcoin: Clarifying the Foundational Innovation of the Block- chain," Continuations, December 15, 2014, http://continuations.com/post/1052720 22635/bitcoin-clarifying-the-foundational-innovation-of.

18. Also, the fact that the Bitcoin ledger has not been hacked does not mean that all cryptocurrencies are similarly secure.

19. Interview with author, October 24, 2017.

20. Nick Szabo, "More Short Takes," Unenumerated, July 1, 2012, http://unenum erated.blogspot.com/2012/07/more-short-takes.html. ("[Q]uantum thought, as I call it—although it already has a traditional name less recognizable to the modern ear, scholastic thought—demands that we [simultaneously] consider often mutually contradictory possibilities.")

21. See "Cryptocurrencies with Tim Ferriss, Nick Szabo, and Naval Ravikant," *Medium,* June 6, 2017, https://medium.com/@giftedproducts/cryptocurrencies-with-tim-ferriss

-nick-szabo-and-naval-ravikant-51a99d037e04. As it turns out, the connection between Szabo's approach and legal analysis is no accident. See chapter 10.

22. For one useful resource, see *The Chicago Blockchain Center Manual of Style*, https://docs.google.com/document/d/1AHnrM9h8k-bqaTS1HNDws6ipcuR0Zbn__heM0ZTg-J0/mobilebasic.

23. Dong He, Karl Habermeier, Ross Leckow, Vikram Haksar, Yasmin Almeida, Mikari Kashima, et al., "Virtual Currencies and Beyond: Initial Considerations: IMF Staff Discussion Note," International Monetary Fund (IMF), January 2016, https://www.imf.org/external/pubs/ft/sdn/2016/sdn1603.pdf.

24. "Digital Currencies," Bank for International Settlements, November 2015, https://www.bis.org/cpmi/publ/d137.pdf.

Chapter 1

1. Satoshi Nakamoto, "Bitcoin: A Peer-to-Peer Electronic Cash System," Bitcoin.org, October 31, 2008, https://bitcoin.org/bitcoin.pdf.

2. Nathaniel Popper, "Decoding the Enigma of Satoshi Nakamoto and the Birth of Bitcoin," *New York Times*, May 15, 2015, https://www.nytimes.com/2015/05/17/business/decoding-the-enigma-of-satoshi-nakamoto-and-the-birth-of-bitcoin.html; Joshua Davis, "The Crypto-Currency," *The New Yorker*, October 3, 2011, https://www.newyorker.com/magazine/2011/10/10/the-crypto-currency.

3. To be fair, perhaps what Satoshi Nakamoto intended to say was that Bitcoin requires no trust in third-party authorities to create value.

4. "The Trust Machine," *The Economist*, October 31, 2015, https://www.economist.com/news/leaders/21677198-technology-behind-bitcoin-could-transform-how-economy-works-trust-machine.

5. "2017 Edelman Trust Barometer: Executive Summary," Scribd, https://www.scribd.com/document/336621519/2017-Edelman-Trust-Barometer-Executive-Summary.

6. Michael Dimock, "How America Changed During Barack Obama's Presidency," Pew Research Center, January 10, 2017, http://www.pewresearch.org/2017/01/10/how-america-changed-during-barack-obamas-presidency; Jim Norman, "Americans' Confidence in Institutions Stays Low," Gallup.com, June 13, 2016, http://news.gallup.com/poll/192581/americans-confidence-institutions-stays-low.aspx.

7. Ron Elving, "Poll: 1 in 5 Americans Trusts the Government," NPR.org, November 23, 2015, https://www.npr.org/2015/11/23/457063796/poll-only-1-in-5-americans-say-they-trust-the-government. This problem is by no means limited to America. Across the thirty-five countries in the Organisation for Economic Cooperation and Development (OECD), only 43 percent of citizens report that they trust their

government. "Trust in Government," OECD, https://www.oecd.org/gov/trust-in -government.htm.

8. Connie Cass, "Poll: Americans Don't Trust One Another," *USA Today*, November 30, 2013.

9. Robert D. Putnam, *Bowling Alone: The Collapse and Revival of American Community* (New York: Simon and Schuster, 2001).

10. Francis Fukuyama, *Trust: The Social Virtues and the Creation of Prosperity* (New York: Free Press, 1995).

11. Annette Baier, "Trust and Antitrust," *Ethics* 96, no. 2 (January 2, 1986): 231, 232, http://www.jstor.org/stable/2381376 (arguing that "any form of cooperative activity ... requires the cooperators to trust one another...."); Kenneth J. Arrow, "Gifts and Exchanges," *Philosophy & Public Affairs* 1, no. 4 (1972): 343, http://www.jstor.org /stable/2265097 (stating that "[v]irtually every commercial transaction has within itself an element of trust."); G. Richard Shell, "Opportunism and Trust in the Negotiation of Commercial Contracts: Toward a New Cause of Action," *Vanderbilt Law Review* 44, no. 2 (March 1991): 225–226 (observing that "social psychologists, sociologists, economists, philosophers, and legal scholars all have recognized that trust is central to the efficient coordination of human goals").

12. Niklas Luhmann, *Trust and Power* (Chichester, UK, and Toronto: Wiley, 1979).

13. Fukuyama, *Trust*.

14. Roger C. Mayer, James H. Davis, and F. David Schoorman, "An Integrative Model of Organizational Trust," *Academy of Management Review* 20, no. 3 (July 3, 1995): 709–734, https://doi.org/10.2307/258792.

15. Fukuyama, *Trust*; Putnam, *Bowling Alone*; Frank B. Cross, "Law and Trust," *Georgetown Law Journal* 93 (2005): 1457.

16. Eric A. Posner, *Law and Social Norms* (Cambridge, MA: Harvard University Press, 2009); Margaret M. Blair and Lynn A. Stout, "Trust, Trustworthiness, and the Behavioral Foundations of Corporate Law," *University of Pennsylvania Law Review* 149, no. 6 (2001): 1745.

17. Ronald H. Coase, "The Nature of the Firm," *Economica* 4, no. 16 (1937): 386–405.

18. Rachel Botsman, "The Changing Rules of Trust in the Digital Age," *Harvard Business Review*, October 20, 2015, https://hbr.org/2015/10/the-changing-rules-of-trust -in-the-digital-age.

19. Oliver E. Williamson, "Calculativeness, Trust, and Economic Organization," *Journal of Law & Economics* 36, no. 1 (1993): 453–486. Kenneth Arrow, another economics Nobel Prize winner, offered a more favorable assessment of trust as an externality

with "real, practical economic value," but that nonetheless, it is not a commodity "for which trade in the open market is technically possible or even meaningful." Kenneth J. Arrow, *The Limits of Organization* (New York: W. W. Norton, 1974), 23.

20. Satoshi Nakamoto, "Bitcoin Open Source Implementation of P2P Currency," Satoshi Nakamoto Institute, November 2, 2009, http://satoshi.nakamotoinstitute .org/posts/p2pfoundation/1/.

21. Ray Dillinger, "If I'd Known What We Were Starting," LinkedIn, September 20, 2017, https://www.linkedin.com/pulse/id-known-what-we-were-starting-ray-dillinger/.

22. LaRue Tone Hosmer, "Trust: The Connecting Link between Organizational Theory and Philosophical Ethics," *Academy of Management Review* 20, no. 2 (1995): 379, 380; Blair and Stout, "Trust, Trustworthiness, and the Behavioral Foundations of Corporate Law," 1745; Mayer, Davis, and Schoorman, "An Integrative Model," 709.

23. Cross, "Law and Trust," 1459 ("Much has been written on trust in various academic disciplines, such as philosophy, business, psychology, political science, and law.").

24. Putnam, *Bowling Alone*. Historian Geoffrey Hosking makes a similar distinction, adding an orthogonal division between thick and thin trust based on the level of knowledge supporting the decision to trust. Geoffrey A. Hosking, *Trust: A History* (Oxford: Oxford University Press, 2014).

25. Fukuyama, *Trust*.

26. Jay B. Barney and Mark H. Hansen, "Trustworthiness as a Source of Competitive Advantage," *Strategic Management Journal* 15 (1994): 175–190.

27. Robert C. Solomon and Fernando Flores, *Building Trust in Business, Politics, Relationships, and Life* (New York: Oxford University Press, 2001), 20.

28. Cross, "Law and Trust," 1466 ("Cognitive trust requires an assessment of the probability and magnitude of that risk of harm.").

29. Williamson, "Calculativeness, Trust, and Economic Organization."

30. Williamson, in fact, thinks that it is not part of trust at all.

31. Harvey James, "The Trust Paradox: A Survey of Economic Inquiries into the Nature of Trust and Trustworthiness," *Journal of Economic Behavior & Organization* 47, no. 3 (February 2002): 291, 303–304. In the classic prisoner's dilemma, two players do best when both trust one another. However, the rational strategy for each is not to trust. Therefore, they wind up with the worst possible outcome.

32. Bo Rothstein, *Social Traps and the Problem of Trust* (New York: Cambridge University Press, 2005).

33. Fukuyama, *Trust*, 11.

34. Rachel Botsman, "We've Stopped Trusting Institutions and Started Trusting Strangers," TED Talk, June 2016, https://www.ted.com/talks/rachel_botsman_we_ve_stopped_trusting_institutions_and_started_trusting_strangers/transcript?language=en.

35. Zipcar cofounder Robin Chase, one of the pioneers of the sharing economy, says, "I always thought with Zipcar that people would treat our cars well *if* we treated them well. ... If you think Zipcar treats you fairly and well, you will do the right thing by the company likewise." Interview with author, October 30, 2017.

36. Cross, "Law and Trust," 1464; Karen Jones, "Trust as an Affective Attitude," *Ethics* 107, no. 1 (1996): 5–6.

37. Baier, "Trust and Antitrust," 235. ("When I trust another, I depend on her good will toward me.")

38. J. L. Morrow, Jr., Mark H. Hansen, and Allison W. Pearson, "The Cognitive and Affective Antecedents of General Trust within Cooperative Organizations," *Journal of Managerial Issues* 16, no. 1 (2004): 50. Cf. Larry E. Ribstein, "Law v. Trust," *Boston University Law Review* 81 (July 2001): 553.

39. Lawrence C. Becker, "Trust as Noncognitive Security about Motives," *Ethics* 107, no. 1 (October 1996): 43–61; Tom Tyler, "Trust and Law Abidingness: A Proactive Model of Social Regulation," *Boston University Law Review* 81 (April 2001); Blair and Stout, "Trust, Trustworthiness, and the Behavioral Foundations of Corporate Law," 1751.

40. J. David Lewis and Andrew Weigert, "Trust as a Social Reality," *Social Forces* 63, no. 4 (June 1985): 967–985.

41. Andrew C. Wicks, Shawn L. Berman, and Thomas M. Jones, "The Structure of Optimal Trust: Moral and Strategic Implications," *Academy of Management Review* 24, no. 1 (January 1999): 99–116; Cross, "Law and Trust," 1464.

42. Putnam, *Bowling Alone*, 137.

43. Fukuyama, *Trust*, 26. Cf. William A. Galston, "Trust—But Quantify," *Public Interest*, no. 122 (1996): 129.

44. Herman Melville, *The Confidence-Man: His Masquerade* (New York: Penguin Books, 1990), chapter 16.

45. Denise M. Rousseau, Sim B. Sitkin, Ronald S. Burt, and Colin Camerer, "Not so Different after All: A Cross-Discipline View of Trust," *Academy of Management Review* 23, no. 3 (July 1998): 393–404.

46. Baier, "Trust and Antitrust," 240.

47. Jeremy A. Yip and Maurice E. Schweitzer, "Trust Promotes Unethical Behavior: Excessive Trust, Opportunistic Exploitation, and Strategic Exploitation," *Current Opinion in Psychology* 6, Suppl C (2015): 216–220.

48. Russell Hardin, "Trustworthiness," *Ethics* 107, no. 1 (October, 1996): 26-42, https://doi.org/10.1086/233695; Avner Ben-Ner and Louis Putterman, "Trusting and Trustworthiness," *Boston University Law Review* 81 (2001): 523-551.

49. Samuel Johnson, *Rambler*, No. 79 (December 18, 1750): 147.

50. Maurice E. Schweitzer, John C. Hershey, and Eric T. Bradlow, "Promises and Lies: Restoring Violated Trust," *Organizational Behavior and Human Decision Processes* 101, no. 1 (2006): 1–19.

51. The enduring trust gap following the financial crisis, due to perceptions that government officials failed to act in the interest of the public, is consistent with these results.

52. Timothy J. Muris, "Opportunistic Behavior and the Law of Contracts," *Minnesota Law Review* 65 (1981): 521.

53. Shell, "Opportunism and Trust in the Negotiation of Commercial Contracts: Toward a New Cause of Action," 231–232, 265–266, 275.

54. Michael C. Jensen and William H. Meckling, "Theory of the Firm: Managerial Behavior, Agency Costs, and Ownership Structure," *Journal of Financial Economics* 3, no. 4 (July 1, 1976): 305–360.

55. Oliver E Williamson, "The Economics of Organization: The Transaction Cost Approach," *American Journal of Sociology* 87, no. 3 (1981): 548–577. Ironically, monitoring itself creates opportunities for opportunistic behavior: Employees comply when they believe they are being watched. Experimental research by Maurice Schweitzer and colleagues suggests that employers fail to realize this. They tend to trust too much. Maurice E Schweitzer, Teck-Hua Ho, and Xing Zhang, "How Monitoring Influences Trust: A Tale of Two Faces," *Management Science*, 2016: 253–270.

56. Tyler, "Trust and Law Abidingness."

57. Hernando de Soto, *The Mystery of Capital: Why Capitalism Triumphs in the West and Fails Everywhere Else* (New York: Basic Books, 2000).

58. Lily Hay Newman, "All the Ways Equifax Epically Bungled Its Breach Response," *Wired*, September 24, 2017, https://www.wired.com/story/equifax-breach-response.

59. "Privacy Fears 'Deterring' US Web Users from Online Shopping," BBC News, May 13, 2016, http://www.bbc.com/news/technology-36285651.

60. Mayer, Davis, and Schoorman, "An Integrative Model of Organizational Trust," 712. The political theorist John Dunn offers a similar definition of "trust" as "the confident expectation of benign intentions by another agent." John Dunn, "Trust and Political Agency," in *Trust: Making and Breaking Cooperative Relations*, ed. Diego Gambetta (Oxford: Blackwell, 1988), 74.

61. In a similar vein, the legal scholar Gus Hurwitz pithily defines "trust" as "reliance without recourse." Gus Hurwitz, "Trust and Online Interaction," *University of Pennsylvania Law Review* 161 (2013): 1584.

62. Rachel Botsman, *Who Can You Trust? How Technology Brought Us Together and Why It Might Drive Us Apart* (New York: PublicAffairs, 2017).

63. Kevin Werbach, "The Architecture of Internet 2.0," *Release 1.0*, February 1999, http://downloads.oreilly.com/radar/r1/02-99.pdf.

64. Rebecca Henderson and Kim Clark, "Architectural Innovation: The Reconfiguration of Existing Product Technologies and the Failure of Established Firms," *Administrative Science Quarterly*, March 1990: 9–30.

65. I use Douglass North's definition of institutions: "the humanly devised constraints that structure political, economic, and social interaction." Douglass C. North, "Institutions," *Journal of Economic Perspectives* 5, no. 1 (1991): 97–112.

66. "Will Crowd-Based Capitalism Replace Managerial Capitalism? (Full Transcript)," Reinvent, August 24, 2016, http://reinvent.net/innovator/arun-sundararajan.

67. Botsman offers a similar typology. She distinguishes among local, institutional, and distributed trust. Botsman, *Who Can You Trust?* The first is comparable to what I call peer-to-peer trust, while the second combines Leviathan and intermediary trust. I believe it is important to distinguish situations in which institutional authority supports trust among counterparties (Leviathan) from direct trust in intermediary organizations.

68. Elinor Ostrom, *Governing the Commons: The Evolution of Institutions for Collective Action* (Cambridge: Cambridge University Press, 1990).

69. Brett M. Frischmann, *Infrastructure: The Social Value of Shared Resources* (Oxford: Oxford University Press, 2013); Yochai Benkler, *The Wealth of Networks: How Social Production Transforms Markets and Freedom* (New Haven, CT: Yale University Press, 2006).

70. Thomas Hobbes, *Leviathan: Or, The Matter, Forme & Power of a Commonwealth, Ecclesiasticall and Civill* (Cambridge: Cambridge University Press, 1904). Cf. John Danaher, "Comments on Blockchains and DAOs as the Modern Leviathan," Institute for Ethics and Emerging Technologies, October 2, 2017, https://ieet.org/index.php/IEET2/comments/Danaher20160331. Danaher connects Hobbes's ideas to governance of blockchain-based decentralized autonomous organizations (DAOs).

71. Tom R. Tyler, *Why People Obey the Law* (Princeton, NJ: Princeton University Press, 2006).

72. Douglass C. North, *Institutions, Institutional Change, and Economic Performance* (Cambridge: Cambridge University Press, 1990).

73. UBS, *Building the Trust Engine* (October 2, 2017), https://www.ubs.com/microsites /blockchain-report/en/home.html; Andreas Adriano and Hunter Monroe, "The Internet of Trust," *IMF, Finance, & Development* 53, no. 2 (June 2016), http://www.imf.org /external/pubs/ft/fandd/2016/06/adriano.htm. Robert Hockett and Saule Omarova offer an alternative theory of finance in which banks function not as intermediaries, but as private franchisees of the governmental act of credit creation. Robert C. Hockett and Saule T. Omarova, "The Finance Franchise," *Cornell Law Review* 102 (2017): 1143–1218. In other words, they view it as a manifestation of Leviathan rather than intermediary trust.

74. Jordan Weissmann, "How Wall Street Devoured Corporate America," *The Atlantic*, March 5, 2013, https://www.theatlantic.com/business/archive/2013/03/how -wall-street-devoured-corporate-america/273732.

75. Hurwitz, "Trust and Online Interaction," 1580–1581 (noting how the loss of native trust among participants as the Internet was commercialized led to increased power of online intermediaries).

76. Jonathan T. Taplin, *Move Fast and Break Things: How Facebook, Google, and Amazon Cornered Culture and Undermined Democracy* (New York: Little, Brown and Company, 2017); Siva Vaidhyanathan, *The Googlization of Everything: And Why We Should Worry* (Berkeley: University of California Press, 2011); Julie Cohen, *Between Truth and Power: The Legal Construction of Informational Capitalism*, forthcoming; Shoshana Zuboff, *Master or Slave?: The Fight for the Soul of Our Information Civilization* (New York: Public Affairs, 2018).

77. Reid Hoffman, "The Future of the Bitcoin Ecosystem and 'Trustless Trust'—Why I Invested in Blockstream," LinkedIn, November 17, 2014, https://www.linkedin .com/pulse/20141117154558-1213-the-future-of-the-bitcoin-ecosystem-and -trustless-trust-why-i-invested-in-blockstream.

78. Jalak Jobanputra, "How the Blockchain Can Unshackle the World," CoinDesk, April 23, 2016, https://www.coindesk.com/blockchain-can-unshackle-us/. ("This is why the concept is often referred to as 'trustless trust.'").

79. Rachel Botsman offers a somewhat similar conception of a "trust stack." Botsman, *Who Can You Trust?*

80. Helen Nissenbaum, "Will Security Enhance Trust Online, or Supplant It?" in *Trust and Distrust in Organizations: Dilemmas and Approaches*, eds. Roderick M. Kramer and Karen S. Cook (New York: Russell Sage Foundation, 2004), 155, 162–163.

81. Joshua Fairfield, "Virtual Property," *Boston University Law Review* 85 (2005): 1047 ("Trust-minimized code means you can trust the code without trusting the owners of any particular remote computer."); Botsman, TED Talk, June 2016; "We've Stopped Trusting Institutions and Started Trusting Strangers" ("So the real implication of the blockchain is that it removes the need for any kind of third party.... [Y]ou still have

to trust the idea, you have to trust the platform, but you do not have to trust the other person in the traditional sense.").

82. Morgan E. Peck, "The Cryptoanarchists' Answer to Cash," *IEEE Spectrum* 49, no. 6 (June 2012): 50–56.

83. Philip Elmer-Dewitt, "First Nation in Cyberspace," *Time*, December 6, 1993.

84. Interview with author, October 23, 2017.

Chapter 2

1. Yuval N. Harari, *Sapiens: A Brief History of Humankind* (New York: Harper, 2015): 180.

2. Georg Friedrich Knapp, *The State Theory of Money* (London: Macmillan, 1924). Karl Polanyi argued more broadly that the transformation of labor, land, and money into "fictitious commodities" led to the development of the modern "market society." Karl Polanyi, *The Great Transformation: The Political and Economic Origins of Our Time* (Boston: Beacon Press, 2001).

3. Thomas C. Schelling, *The Strategy of Conflict* (Cambridge, MA: Harvard University Press, 1960). The creators of both smart contracts and the Ethereum network refer to these Schelling points. Nick Szabo, "Formalizing and Securing Relationships on Public Networks," *First Monday* 2, no. 9 (September 1, 1997), http://ojphi.org/ojs/index.php/fm/article/view/548; Vitalik Buterin, "SchellingCoin: A Minimal-Trust Universal Data Feed," *Ethereum Blog*, March 28, 2014, https://blog.ethereum.org/2014/03/28/schellingcoin-a-minimal-trust-universal-data-feed/.

4. Charles R. Geisst, *Wall Street: A History*, revised and expanded edition (Oxford: Oxford University Press, 2004).

5. Netting eliminates 98 percent of trades that would otherwise occur between brokerage houses. Martin Mayer, "Wall Street's Smooth Operator," *Barrons*, August 27, 2007, https://www.barrons.com/articles/SB118800153292108500.

6. For an entertaining account of this history, see Michael Lewis, *The Big Short: Inside the Doomsday Machine* (New York: W. W. Norton, 2010).

7. Paola Sapienza and Luigi Zingales, "A Trust Crisis," *International Review of Finance* 12, no. 2 (June 2012): 123–131.

8. Dodd-Frank Wall Street Reform and Consumer Protection Act of 2010, Pub. L. No. 111–203, 124 Stat. 1376 (2010).

9. Satoshi Nakamoto, "Bitcoin: A Peer-to-Peer Electronic Cash System," Bitcoin.org, October 31, 2008, https://bitcoin.org/bitcoin.pdf.

10. Arvind Narayanan and Jeremy Clark, "Bitcoin's Academic Pedigree," *Communications of the ACM* 60, no. 12 (2017): 36.

11. Bruce Schneier, *Applied Cryptography*, 2nd ed. (New York: Wiley, 2015).

12. In public key cryptography, every private key is connected to a public key that can be freely distributed. Only the holder of the secret key can read a message encoded with the associated public key. And if the message is signed with a secret key, anyone can verify who signed it using the associated public key. Simson L Garfinkel, "Public Key Cryptography," *Computer* 29, no. 6 (1996): 101–104.

13. Technically Bitcoin is pseudonymous, not anonymous, because the keys have persistent associations with transactions.

14. David Chaum, "Blind Signatures for Untraceable Payments," *Crypto* 82 (1982): 35.

15. Ken Griffith, "A Quick History of Cryptocurrencies BBTC—Before Bitcoin," *Bitcoin Magazine*, April 16, 2014, https://bitcoinmagazine.com/articles/quick-history -cryptocurrencies-bbtc-bitcoin-1397682630/. One leading text on cryptocurrencies lists nearly one hundred failed predecessors to Bitcoin. See Arvind Narayanan, Joseph Bonneau, Edward Felten, Andrew Miller, and Steven Goldfeder, *Bitcoin and Cryptocurrency Technologies: A Comprehensive Introduction* (Princeton, NJ: Princeton University Press, 2016).

16. Proceedings of FC '97, the First International Conference on Financial Cryptography, ed. Rafael Hirschfeld, February 24–28, 1997.

17. See *A & M Records, Inc. v. Napster, Inc.*, 239 F.3d 1004 (9th Cir. 2001); *MGM Studios, Inc. v. Grokster, Ltd.*, 545 U.S. 913 (2005).

18. Narayanan and Clark, "Bitcoin's Academic Pedigree."

19. The number of outstanding tokens multiplied by the market price of a cryptocurrency is often referred to as its "market capitalization." However, that term is misleading. A cryptocurrency project is not the same thing as a company, and the tokens are not shares of stock. A healthy chunk of the tokens for Bitcoin in particular are associated with lost or destroyed private keys, making them inaccessible and therefore not properly counted as value. Tim Swanson, "Eight Things Cryptocurrency Enthusiasts Probably Won't Tell You," Great Wall of Numbers, September 21, 2017, http://www.ofnumbers.com/2017/09/21/eight-things-cryptocurrency-enthusiasts -probably-wont-tell-you/. A better term is "asset value," since this number is the total value of cryptoassets in existence.

20. Leslie Lamport, Robert Shostak, and Marshall Pease, "The Byzantine Generals Problem," *ACM Transactions on Programming Languages and Systems (TOPLAS)* 4, no. 3 (1982): 382–401.

21. Joseph Bonneau, Andrew Miller, Jeremy Clark, Arvind Narayanan, Joshua A. Kroll, and Edward W. Felten, "Research Perspectives and Challenges for Bitcoin and Cryptocurrencies," *Proceedings of the 36th IEEE Symposium on Security and Privacy*, 3, July 20, 2015, http://www.jbonneau.com/doc/BMCNKF15-IEEESP-bitcoin.pdf.

22. John R. Douceur, "The Sybil Attack," IPTPS '01 Revised Papers from the First International Workshop on Peer-to-Peer Systems 251 (2002), http://nakamotoinsti tute.org/static/docs/the-sybil-attack.pdf.

23. Narayanan et al., *Bitcoin and Cryptocurrency Technologies*. Satoshi Nakamoto acknowledged that previous concepts described broadly similar mechanisms, most notably the 1998 B-Money proposal by Wei Dei and the HashCash proposal for spam filtering from Adam Back. Bitcoin was the first to implement the fusion of cryptography and game theory successfully for a digital currency.

24. This approach is analogous to the republican form of government epitomized by the U.S. Instead of empowering a king, power is decentralized to the people, who express it through voting. To mediate the potential for factionalism and mob rule, voters exercise power indirectly, by electing representatives.

25. "Bitcoin: The Magic of Mining," *The Economist*, January 10, 2015, 58, https:// www.economist.com/news/business/21638124-minting-digital-currency-has-become -big-ruthlessly-competitive-business-magic; Andreas M. Antonopoulos, *Mastering Bitcoin* (Sebastopol, CA: O'Reilly, 2015). Also cf. Kevin Werbach, "Bitcoin Is Gamification," *Medium*, August 5, 2014, https://medium.com/@kwerb/bitcoin-is-gamification -e85c6a6eea22 (explaining the significance of the motivational system to Bitcoin).

26. Narayanan et al., *Bitcoin and Cryptocurrency Technologies*, 266. Not every blockchain implements proof of work in the same manner as Bitcoin. For example, Ethereum uses a modified algorithm so that miners do not gain an advantage from using custom chips, known as "application-specific integrated circuits (ASICs)."

27. A hash function takes an input string (such as a document file) and turns it into an output string (the hash) with a specified length. Although in theory, multiple input strings could map to the same hash, cryptographic hash spaces are sufficiently large that such "collisions" are infinitesimally rare. An input string will produce the same output string every time. However, there is no known way to go from a hash back to the original, other than trying all the possibilities. Bitcoin defines parameters for the input string to limit the search space, but the possibilities are still vast.

28. Adam Back, "Hashcash—A Denial of Service Counter-Measure," http://www .cypherspace.org/hashcash/hashcash.pdf. In addition, two cryptographers independently proposed a similar approach five years before Back. Cynthia Dwork and Moni Naor, "Pricing via Processing or Combatting Junk Mail," Crypto 1992, 740 *Springer Lecture Notes in Computer Science* 139.

29. The Bitcoin network today is thousands of times more powerful than the five hundred most powerful supercomputers in the world combined. Laura Shin, "Bitcoin Production Will Drop by Half in July—How Will That Affect the Price?" *Forbes*, May 24, 2016, https://www.forbes.com/sites/laurashin/2016/05/24/bitcoin-production -will-drop-by-half-in-july-how-will-that-affect-the-price/#576083422a4c.

30. Narayanan et al., *Bitcoin and Cryptocurrency Technologies,* 65. Ethereum and most post-Bitcoin blockchain networks update blocks more frequently.

31. Narayanan et al., 88–90.

32. Narayanan et al., 59. More precisely, it is the chain with the most proof of work.

33. Some research suggests that an attacker with one-third of the mining power could disrupt the network. However, this still represents an extremely high threshold to reach.

34. Users are identified on the blockchain through private keys, so the real-world identity of the parties to a transaction may be impossible to determine. For those desiring further anonymity, there are ways to break up transactions to obscure large transfers.

35. Originally, full nodes were all miners. Today, with the proliferation of mining pools, the actual mining is generally done by specialized operators who do not verify transactions themselves.

36. A wallet holds cryptocurrency for a user and interfaces with a blockchain network or an exchange. A light client can validate transactions without maintaining a full copy of the ledger, but it does so with significantly less security.

37. Alec Liu, "Who's Building Bitcoin? An Inside Look at Bitcoin's Open Source Development," *Motherboard,* May 7, 2013, https://motherboard.vice.com/blog/whos -building-bitcoin-an-inside-look-at-bitcoins-open-source-development.

38. The only way to walk back a transaction is through a hard fork, creating a new chain without it. Ethereum took this drastic step after The DAO exploit, described in chapter 3.

39. Hence the analogy to mining for precious resources in the physical world. Eventually, the block rewards will drop to zero. At that point, the bitcoin in circulation will be fixed at 21 million. Approximately 80 percent of the total potential bitcoin have been created as of 2017.

40. Vlad Zamfir, a key developer of the Ethereum blockchain project, was one of the first to explore the concept of cryptoeconomics. He attributes the term to Ethereum leader Vitalik Buterin, although the origin moment of the word is unclear. Vlad Zamfir (@VladZamfir), Twitter, October 15, 2017, 10:49 a.m., https://twitter.com /VladZamfir/status/919576004405764096.

41. S. Herbert Frankel, *Money, Two Philosophies: The Conflict of Trust and Authority* (Oxford: B. Blackwell, 1977), 39.

42. U.S. Government Accountability Office (GAO), *Virtual Currencies: Emerging Regulatory, Law Enforcement, and Consumer Protection Challenges,* (2014), https://www.gao .gov/products/GAO-14-496; Jerry Brito and Andrea Castillo, *Bitcoin: A Primer for Policymakers* (Arlington, VA: Mercatus Center, 2016), 14–15.

43. David Yermack, "Is Bitcoin a Real Currency? An Economic Appraisal," working paper, National Bureau of Economic Research, No. w19747 (December 2013).

44. Joshuah Bearman, "The Rise and Fall of Silk Road: Part I," *Wired*, April 2015, https://www.wired.com/2015/04/silk-road-1; Joshuah Bearman, "The Rise and Fall of Silk Road: Part II," *Wired*, May 2015, https://www.wired.com/2015/05/silk-road-2.

45. *USA v. Ross William Ulbricht*, sealed complaint, September 27, 2013, https://www.documentcloud.org/documents/801103-172770276-ulbricht-criminal-complaint.html.

46. Jon Matonis, "Bitcoin Casinos Release 2012 Earnings," *Forbes*, October 4, 2017, https://www.forbes.com/sites/jonmatonis/2013/01/22/bitcoin-casinos-release-2012-earnings/.

47. Kyle Torpey, "BIP 75 Simplifies Bitcoin Wallets for the Everyday User," *Bitcoin Magazine*, April 28, 2016, https://bitcoinmagazine.com/articles/bip-simplifies-bitcoin-wallets-for-the-everyday-user-1461856604.

48. James Schneider, Alexander Blostein, Brian Lee, Steven Kent, Ingrid Groer, and Eric Beardsley, *Profiles in Innovation: Blockchain—Putting Theory into Practice* (Goldman Sachs, May 24, 2016), https://www.finyear.com/attachment/690548.

49. Daniel Krawisz, "Hyperbitcoinization," Satoshi Nakamoto Institute, March 29, 2014, http://nakamotoinstitute.org/mempool/hyperbitcoinization/.

50. Robert C. Hockett and Saule T. Omarova, "The Finance Franchise," *Cornell Law Review* 102 (2017), 1209–1210.

51. Kieron Monks, "Bitcoin Surges Past $10,000 in Zimbabwe," CNN.com, October 31, 2017, https://www.cnn.com/2017/10/31/africa/zimbabwe-bitcoin-surge/index.html.

52. Sonny Singh and Alberto Vega, "Why Latin American Economies Are Turning to Bitcoin," *TechCrunch*, March 16, 2016, http://techcrunch.com/2016/03/16/why-latin-american-economies-are-turning-to-bitcoin.

53. Todd Byrne, "Greece Reveals Plans to Adopt Bitcoin Amid Economic Turmoil," *Bitsonline*, October 27, 2017, https://www.bitsonline.com/greece-bitcoin-economic-turmoil.

54. Michael D. Bordo and Andrew T. Levin, *Central Bank Digital Currency and the Future of Monetary Policy*, No. 23711 (National Bureau of Economic Research Working Paper Series, 2017); Morten Linnemann Bech and Rodney Garratt, "Central Bank Cryptocurrencies," Bank for International Settlements (BIS), September 17, 2017, https://www.bis.org/publ/qtrpdf/r_qt1709f.htm.

55. Deloitte and the Monetary Authority of Singapore, "Project Ubin: SGD on Distributed Ledger," 2017, http://www.mas.gov.sg/~/media/ProjectUbin/Project%20Ubin%20%20SGD%20on%20Distributed%20Ledger.pdf.

56. Christine Lagarde, "Central Banking and Fintech—A Brave New World?" https://www.imf.org/en/News/Articles/2017/09/28/sp092917-central-banking-and-fintech-a-brave-new-world.

57. David Thorpe, "Bank Halts Crypto-Currency Plans over Stability Fears," *FT Advisor,* January 4, 2018, https://www.ftadviser.com/investments/2018/01/04/bank-halts-crypto-currency-plans-over-stability-fears/.

58. Leonid Bershidsky, "Authoritarian Cryptocurrencies Are Coming," Bloomberg.com, October 17, 2017, https://www.bloomberg.com/view/articles/2017-10-17/authoritarian-cryptocurrencies-are-coming.

Chapter 3

1. "Vitalik Buterin," About.me, https://about.me/vitalik_buterin.

2. "Vitalik Buterin," About.me.

3. Richard Gendal Brown, "Introducing R3 Corda™: A Distributed Ledger Designed for Financial Services," *Richard Gendal Brown Blog,* April 5, 2016, https://gendal.me/2016/04/05/introducing-r3-corda-a-distributed-ledger-designed-for-financial-services/; Paul Vigna and Michael J. Casey, *The Age of Cryptocurrency: How Bitcoin and Digital Money Are Challenging the Global Economic Order* (New York: St. Martin's Press, 2015): 124; Mark Walport, *Distributed Ledger Technology: Beyond Block Chain* (UK Government Office for Science, 2016), https://www.gov.uk/government/uploads/system/uploads/attachment_data/file/492972/gs-16-1-distributed-ledger-technology.pdf.

4. Max Weber, *General Economic History,* translated by Frank H. Knight (New York: Collier Books, 1961), 276; Werner Sombart, *Der Moderne Kapitalismus. 1. "Die" Genesis des Kapitalismus* (Leipzig: Duncker & Humblot, 1902), 23. Cf. Quinn DuPont and Bill Maurer, "Ledgers and Law in the Blockchain," *King's Review,* June 23, 2016, http://kingsreview.co.uk/magazine/blog/2015/06/23/ledgers-and-law-in-the-blockchain.

5. Stefan Thomas, "The Internet's Missing Link," *TechCrunch,* September 27, 2014, http://techcrunch.com/2014/09/27/the-internets-missing-link.

6. A few variants, such as Litecoin, took the open-source Bitcoin software and modified the consensus techniques, creating their own digital currencies in the process. While some of these are still around, none comes close to Bitcoin's scale.

7. This was a fork of the Bitcoin software to create a completely separate network, not a fork of the ledger on an established network.

8. Danny Bradbury, "Colored Coins Paint Sophisticated Future for Bitcoin," *CoinDesk,* June 14, 2013, https://www.coindesk.com/colored-coins-paint-sophisticated-future-for-bitcoin/

9. Adam Back, Matt Corallo, Luke Dashjr, Mark Friedenbach, Gregory Maxwell, Andrew Miller, et al., "Enabling Blockchain Innovations with Pegged Sidechains," October 22, 2014, https://blockstream.com/sidechains.pdf.

10. Vitalik Buterin, "A Next-Generation Smart Contract and Decentralized Application Platform," *Github*, https://github.com/ethereum/wiki/wiki/White-Paper.

11. Lisa Froelings, "Deloitte Reports More Than 26,000 Blockchain Projects Launched in 2016," *CoinTelegraph*, November 9, 2017, https://cointelegraph.com/news/deloitte -reports-more-than-26000-blockchain-projects-launched-in-2016. Only a fraction of the projects are still active, but that still represents thousands of projects.

12. "Cryptocurrency Market Capitalizations," https://coinmarketcap.com.

13. Earn.com, a well-funded start-up with high-profile backers, started as 21.co, which made consumer Bitcoin mining hardware and then went through a series of pivots as the market shifted. It was acquired by Coinbase, the leading U.S. cryptocurrency exchange, in April 2018. Robert Hacket, "Coinbase Buys Bitcoin Startup Earn.com, Hires CEO as Chief Technology Officer," *Fortune*, April 16, 2018, http:// fortune.com/2018/04/16/bitcoin-buy-coinbase-earn-com-balaji-srinivasan.

14. Christopher Malmo, "One Bitcoin Transaction Now Uses as Much Energy as Your House in a Week," *Motherboard*, November 1, 2017, https://motherboard.vice .com/en_us/article/ywbbpm/bitcoin-mining-electricity-consumption-ethereum -energy-climate-change.

15. Sebastiaan Deetman, "Bitcoin Could Consume as Much Electricity as Denmark by 2020," *Motherboard*, March 29, 2016, https://motherboard.vice.com/en_us/article /aek3za/bitcoin-could-consume-as-much-electricity-as-denmark-by-2020.

16. Ian Allison, "IOTA's Tangle Meets Internet of Things Requirements Better Than Any Blockchain," *International Business Times*, June 14, 2017, http://www.ibtimes .co.uk/iotas-tangle-meets-internet-things-requirements-better-any-blockchain -1626218. The technical term for this data structure is a "directed acyclic graph."

17. The criminals sometimes can be identified if they use intermediaries such as exchanges or through forensic analysis of their transaction patterns. See chapter 9.

18. Michael L. Rustad and Sanna Kulevska, "Reconceptualizing the Right to Be For- gotten to Enable Transatlantic Data Flow," *Harvard Journal of Law and Technology* 28 (2014): 349.

19. Paulina Jo Pesch and Christian Sillaber, "Joint Blockchains, Joint Control? Blockchains and the GDPR's Transparency Requirements," *Computer Law Review International* 18 (2017): 166–172; Michele Finck, "Blockchains and Data Protection in the European Union," Social Science Research Network (SSRN), December 6, 2017, https://ssrn.com/abstract=3080322.

20. Interview with author (October 23, 2017). The phrase alludes to the popular "lean start-up" development focus on creating an initial "minimum viable product." Eric Ries, *The Lean Startup: How Today's Entrepreneurs Use Continuous Innovation to Create Radically Successful Businesses* (New York: Crown, 2011).

21. Tim Swanson, "Consensus-as-a-Service: A Brief Report on the Emergence of Permissioned, Distributed Ledger Systems," *Great Wall of Numbers*, April 6, 2015, http://www.ofnumbers.com/wp-content/uploads/2015/04/Permissioned-distributed-ledgers.pdf. Richard Gendal Brown of the financial industry blockchain consortium R3 maps consensus along two dimensions: whom you trust, and what you trust them about. Richard Gendal Brown, "A Simple Model to Make Sense of the Proliferation of Distributed Ledger, Smart Contract, and Cryptocurrency Projects," *Richard Gendal Brown Blog*, December 19, 2014, https://gendal.me/2014/12/19/a-simple-model-to-make-sense-of-the-proliferation-of-distributed-ledger-smart-contract-and-cryptocurrency-projects/.

22. On Hyperledger, see Todd Benzies, "Tech and Banking Giants Ditch Bitcoin for Their Own Blockchain," *Wired*, December 17, 2015, https://www.hyperledger.org/news/2015/12/17/wired-tech-and-banking-giants-ditch-bitcoin-for-their-own-blockchain. On R3, see Paul Vigna, "Blockchain Firm R3 CEV Raises $107 Million," *Wall Street Journal*, May 23, 2017, https://www.wsj.com/articles/blockchain-firm-r3-raises-107-million-1495548641.

23. R3 is a member of Hyperledger, and it has discussed the possibility of contributing the open-source Corda implementation as a Hyperledger project.

24. Richard Gendal Brown, "Introducing R3 Corda."

25. Interview with author, July 19, 2017.

26. Rajesh Nair, "Why Aren't Distributed Systems Engineers Working on Blockchain Technology?" *Paxos*, August 1, 2017, https://eng.paxos.com/why-arent-distributed-systems-engineers-working-on-blockchain-technology.

27. Anthony Lewis, "Distributed Ledgers: Shared Control, Not Shared Data," *Bits on Blocks*, January 9, 2017, https://bitsonblocks.net/2017/01/09/distributed-ledgers-shared-control-not-shared-data/.

28. Interview with author, July 6, 2017.

29. Adam Ludwin (@adamludwin), Twitter, July 20, 2017, 6:52 p.m., https://twitter.com/adamludwin/status/888169713536122881.

30. Telis Demos, "J.P. Morgan Has a New Twist on Blockchain," *Wall Street Journal*, October 4, 2016, Markets section, https://www.wsj.com/articles/j-p-morgan-has-a-new-twist-on-blockchain-1475537138.

31. Interview with author, October 23, 2017.

32. Bitcoin actually uses a scripting language for transactions, meaning that every transfer is actually running software code on the blockchain.

33. To be precise, the blockchain records challenges and responses that either create or destroy bitcoin, rather than transfers of discrete tokens as such. Arvind Narayanan, Joseph Bonneau, Edward Felten, Andrew Miller, and Steven Goldfeder, *Bitcoin and Cryptocurrency Technologies: A Comprehensive Introduction* (Princeton, NJ: Princeton University Press, 2016), 75–76.

34. Intel's Sawtooth Lake system, part of the Hyperledger project, achieves decentralized time-stamping on permissioned networks by having each device use the same trusted microprocessors. Giulio Prisco, "Intel Develops 'Sawtooth Lake' Distributed Ledger Technology for the Hyperledger Project," NASDAQ.com, April 11, 2016, http://www.nasdaq.com/article/intel-develops-sawtooth-lake-distributed-ledger -technology-for-the-hyperledger-project-cm604632.

35. Interview with author, June 30, 2017.

36. Buterin, "A Next-Generation Smart Contract and Decentralized Application Platform." Cf. Vitalik Buterin (@vitalikbuterin), Twitter, August 15, 2017, 5:47am, https://twitter.com/vitalikbuterin/status/897394410589233152 ("At this point, I actually do not think 'contract' is the right term for it.").

37. Nick Szabo, "Formalizing and Securing Relationships on Public Networks," *First Monday* 2, no. 9 (September 1, 1997), http://ojphi.org/ojs/index.php/fm/article/view /548. Around the same time, Ian Grigg independently developed the related concept of Ricardian contracts, which will be discussed in chapter 10.

38. Today, many vending machines take credit cards, making them no longer the self-contained systems that Szabo was talking about.

39. D. J. Pangburn, "The Humans Who Dream of Companies That Will not Need Us," *Fast Company*, June 19, 2015, https://www.fastcompany.com/3047462/the -humans-who-dream-of-companies-that-wont-need-them; Nathaniel Popper, "Ethereum, a Virtual Currency, Enables Transactions That Rival Bitcoin's," *The New York Times*, March 27, 2016, DealBook section, https://www.nytimes.com/2016/03/28 /business/dealbook/ethereum-a-virtual-currency-enables-transactions-that-rival -bitcoins.html.

40. In practice, the computational overhead of distributed consensus places some limits on the amount of on-chain processing.

41. Olga Kharif, "CryptoKitties Mania Overwhelms Ethereum Network's Processing," Bloomberg Technology, December 4, 2017, https://www.bloomberg.com/news /articles/2017-12-04/cryptokitties-quickly-becomes-most-widely-used-ethereum-app.

42. Stan Higgins, "Enterprise Ethereum Alliance Adds 48 New Members," *CoinDesk*, October 18, 2017, https://www.coindesk.com/enterprise-ethereum-alliance-adds-48 -new-members.

43. Ethereum is working on mechanisms called "sharding" and "state channels" to overcome this limitation. How effectively Ethereum and similar blockchain networks can scale remains an important unanswered question.

44. CryptoIQ, "Rootstock—Smart Contracts on the Bitcoin Blockchain," *Medium*, March 5, 2016, https://medium.com/@CryptoIQ.ca/rootstock-smart-contracts-on -the-bitcoin-blockchain-e52b065421a8.

45. E. J. Spode, "The Great Cryptocurrency Heist," *Aeon*, February 14, 2017, https:// aeon.co/essays/trust-the-inside-story-of-the-rise-and-fall-of-ethereum.

46. Seth Bannon, "The Tao of 'The DAO' or: How the Autonomous Corporation Is Already Here," *TechCrunch*, May 16, 2016, https://techcrunch.com/2016/05/16/the -tao-of-the-dao-or-how-the-autonomous-corporation-is-already-here/.

47. Christoph Jentzsch, "Decentralized Autonomous Organization to Automate Governance," https://download.slock.it/public/DAO/WhitePaper.pdf.

48. Nathaniel Popper, "A Venture Fund with Plenty of Capital, But No Capitalist," *The New York Times*, May 21, 2016, DealBook section, https://www.nytimes.com /2016/05/22/business/dealbook/crypto-ether-bitcoin-currency.html.

49. Nathaniel Popper, "A Hacking of More Than $50 Million Dashes Hopes in the World of Virtual Currency," *The New York Times*, June 17, 2016, DealBook section, https://www.nytimes.com/2016/06/18/business/dealbook/hacker-may-have-removed -more-than-50-million-from-experimental-cybercurrency-project.html.

50. Frances Coppola, "A Painful Lesson for the Ethereum Community," *Forbes*, July 21, 2016, https://www.forbes.com/sites/francescoppola/2016/07/21/a-painful-lesson -for-the-ethereum-community/56d3a488bb24l; Joon Ian Wong and Ian Karr, "Everything You Need to Know about the Ethereum 'Hard Fork'" *Quartz*, July 18, 2016, https: //qz.com/730004/everything-you-need-to-know-about-the-ethereum-hard-fork/.

51. Miners of one chain do not recognize the validity of blocks mined by the other clients, and vice versa, even though they may otherwise use exactly the same protocols. Joseph Bonneau, Andrew Miller, Jeremy Clark, Arvind Narayanan, Joshua A. Kroll, and Edward W. Felten, "Research Perspectives and Challenges for Bitcoin and Cryptocurrencies," *Proceedings of the 36th IEEE Symposium on Security and Privacy*, 3, July 20, 2015, http://www.jbonneau.com/doc/BMCNKF15-IEEESP-bitcoin.pdf, 10.

52. Stan Higgins, "Will Ethereum Hard Fork? DAO Attack Prompts Heated Debate," *CoinDesk*, June 17, 2016, https://www.coindesk.com/will-ethereum-hard-fork/; Michael del Castillo, "Specter of Ethereum Hard Fork Worries Australian Banking Group," *CoinDesk*, June 29, 2016, https://www.coindesk.com/spectre-ethereum-hardfork-worries -anz-banking-group/

53. Ethereum is a public blockchain, like Bitcoin. Permissioned blockchains do not provide the same assurance of noninterference because access is limited to identified parties.

54. David Z. Morris, "The Bizarre Fallout of Ethereum's Epic Fail," *Fortune*, September 4, 2016, http://fortune.com/2016/09/04/ethereum-fall-out.

55. Peter Szilagyi, "DAO Wars: Your Voice on the Soft-Fork Dilemma," *Ethereum Blog*, June 24, 2016, https://blog.ethereum.org/2016/06/24/dao-wars-youre-voice-soft-fork-dilemma.

Chapter 4

1. Angela Natividad, "Burger King Just Launched Its Own Cryptocurrency, the Whoppercoin," *Adweek*, September 5, 2017, http://www.adweek.com/creativity/burger-king-just-launched-its-own-cryptocurrency-the-whoppercoin/. Others were similarly struck by the breathlessness of the coverage. See Kadhim Shubber, "WhopperCoin," *FT Alphaville*, August 29, 2017, https://ftalphaville.ft.com/2017/08/29/2192964/whoppercoin.

2. "BLT with DLT: Have It Your Way with WhopperCoin on Waves," *Waves Community*, August 25, 2017, http://wavescommunity.com/blt-with-dlt-have-it-your-way-with-whoppercoin-on-waves.

3. Chanticleer Holdings, which owns a collection of burger restaurants including several from the Hooters chain, did see its stock appreciate 50 percent after announcing that it would use a cryptocurrency in its rewards program. Tae Kim, "Chanticleer to Use Blockchain for Its Rewards Program," CNBC.com, January 2, 2018, https://www.cnbc.com/2018/01/02/chanticleer-to-use-blockchain-for-its-rewards-program.html.

4. Don Tapscott and Alex Tapscott, *Blockchain Revolution: How the Technology Behind Bitcoin Is Changing Money, Business, and the World* (New York: Portfolio, 2016).

5. World Economic Forum, *Realizing the Potential of Blockchain*, June 28, 2017, https://www.weforum.org/whitepapers/realizing-the-potential-of-blockchain/.

6. Timothy Bresnahan and Manuel Trajtenberg, "General Purpose Technology 'Engines of Growth'?," *Journal of Econometrics* 65 (1995): 83–108.

7. Paul Saffo, "Embracing Uncertainty: The Secret to Effective Forecasting," *The Long Now*, January 11, 2008, http://longnow.org/seminars/02008/jan/11/embracing-uncertainty-the-secret-to-effective-forecasting.

8. Tim Swanson, "Chainwashing," *Great Wall of Numbers*, February 13, 2017, http://www.ofnumbers.com/2017/02/13/chainwashing.

9. Christian Terwiesch and Karl T. Ulrich, *Innovation Tournaments: Creating and Selecting Exceptional Opportunities* (Boston: Harvard Business Press, 2009).

10. "Remittances to Recover Modestly after Two Years of Decline," World Bank, http://www.worldbank.org/en/news/press-release/2017/10/03/remittances-to

-recover-modestly-after-two-years-of-decline. The $30 billion figure is based on the World Bank's statistic that fees average around 7 percent.

11. Tapscott and Tapscott, *Blockchain Revolution*, 186–188.

12. Aaron van Wirdum, "Rebittance Startups Agree: Bitcoin Does Not Make Remittance Cheaper (But Does Allow for Innovation)," *Bitcoin Magazine*, October 22, 2015, https://bitcoinmagazine.com/articles/rebittance-startups-agree-bitcoin-does-not-make-remittance-cheaper-but-does-allow-for-innovation-1445528049.

13. "Does Bitcoin/Blockchain Make Sense for International Money Transfer?" *SaveOnSend Blog,* October 7, 2017, https://www.saveonsend.com/blog/bitcoin-blockchain-money-transfer/.

14. Ibrahim Sirkeci, "Would Investing in Financial Literacy Help Reduce the Use of Informal Channels?" *People Move blog,* March 2, 2016, http://blogs.worldbank.org/peoplemove/would-investing-financial-literacy-help-reduce-use-informal-channels.

15. Margins on money transfer were already down to 5 percent in most markets. Dilip Ratha, Supriyo De, Ervin Dervisevic, Sonia Plaza, Kirsten Schuettler, William Shaw, et al., "Migration and Remittances: Recent Developments and Outlook, Special Topic: Financing for Development," World Bank Migration and Development Brief No. 24, April 13, 2015.

16. Rebecca Henderson and Kim Clark, "Architectural Innovation: The Reconfiguration of Existing Product Technologies and the Failure of Established Firms," *Administrative Science Quarterly*, March 1990: 9–33.

17. The most famous illustration of decentralized and distributed networks is from Paul Baran's 1964 report for the RAND Corporation. Baran, *On Distributed Communications, I: Introduction to Distributed Communications*, August 1964, https://www.rand.org/content/dam/rand/pubs/research_memoranda/2006/RM3420.pdf.

18. Vitalik Buterin, "The Meaning of Decentralization," *Medium,* February 6, 2017, https://medium.com/@VitalikButerin/the-meaning-of-decentralization-a0c92b76a274.

19. Symbiont's chief technologist, Adam Krellenstein, draws an analogy to Conway's Law, a computer science concept that companies design system architectures that reflect their organizational structure and culture. Markets that are fundamentally P2P in organization do not lend themselves to centralized technology solutions. (Interview with author, June 30, 2017.)

20. "Toyota's Breakthrough with Blockchain and Autonomous Cars," *Blockchain Innovation Podcast,* July 27, 2017, https://itunes.apple.com/us/podcast/blockchain-innovation-interviewing-brightest-minds/id1238906492?mt=2.

21. David Schaper, "Record Number of Miles Driven in U.S. Last Year," NPR, February 21, 2017, https://www.npr.org/sections/thetwo-way/2017/02/21/516512439/record-number-of-miles-driven-in-u-s-last-year.

22. Joshua Fairfield, "BitProperty," *Southern California Law Review* 88 (2014): 805.

23. Pete Rizzo, "Toyota's R&D Division Is Building a Blockchain Consortium," *Coindesk*, May 22, 2017, https://www.coindesk.com/toyota-consortium-research -blockchain.

24. A leading biography of Madoff is subtitled "Bernie Madoff and the Death of Trust." Diana B. Henriques, *The Wizard of Lies: Bernie Madoff and the Death of Trust* (New York: Times Books, 2011).

25. Bruce Schneier, *Secrets and Lies: Digital Security in a Networked World, Fifteenth Anniversary Edition* (Indianapolis: John Wiley & Sons, 2015).

26. Josephine Wolff and Kevin Bankston, "How a 2011 Hack You've Never Heard of Changed the Internet's Infrastructure," *Slate*, December 21, 2016, http://www .slate.com/articles/technology/future_tense/2016/12/how_the_2011_hack_of_digino tar_changed_the_internet_s_infrastructure.html.

27. Blockchain-based alternatives for securing websites are discussed in chapter 11.

28. Joseph P. Bailey and Yannis Bakos, "An Exploratory Study of the Emerging Role of Electronic Intermediaries," *International Journal of Electronic Commerce* 1, no. 3 (1997), https://archive.nyu.edu/bitstream/2451/27838/2/CeDER-PP-1997-04.pdf.

29. Timothy B. Lee, "Bitcoin Needs to Scale by a Factor of 1000 to Compete with Visa. Here's How to Do It," *Washington Post*, November 12, 2013, "The Switch" section, http://www.washingtonpost.com/news/the-switch/wp/2013/11/12/bitcoin -needs-to-scale-by-a-factor-of-1000-to-compete-with-visa-heres-how-to-do-it/.

30. Nick Szabo, "Formalizing and Securing Relationships on Public Networks," *First Monday* 2, no. 9 (September 1, 1997), http://ojphi.org/ojs/index.php/fm /article/view/548; Nick Szabo, "The Dawn of Trustworthy Computing," *Unenumer- ated*, December 11, 2014, http://unenumerated.blogspot.com/2014/12/the-dawn-of -trustworthy-computing.html.

31. Interview with author, July 19, 2017.

32. This was shortened in 2017 from T+3. "SEC Adopts T+2 Settlement Cycle for Securities Transactions," Securities and Exchange Commission, press release, March 22, 2017, https://www.sec.gov/news/press-release/2017-68-0.

33. James Schneider, Alexander Blostein, Brian Lee, Steven Kent, Ingrid Groer, and Eric Beardsley, *Profiles in Innovation: Blockchain—Putting Theory into Practice* (Gold- man Sachs, May 24, 2016), https://www.finyear.com/attachment/690548.

34. "Consensus 2017: IBM Thinks Blockchain Could Save Shipping Industry 'Bil- lions,'" *CoinDesk*, May 22, 2017, https://www.coindesk.com/consensus-2017-ibm -thinks-blockchain-save-shipping-industry-billions/.

35. Interview with author, June 21, 2017.

36. Bruce Pon, "How Automakers Can Use Blockchain," *BigchainDB Blog,* June 6, 2017, https://blog.bigchaindb.com/how-automakers-can-use-blockchain-adab79a6505f.; Carly Sheridan, "Digitizing Vehicles: The First Blockchain-Backed Car Passport," *BigchainDB Blog,* March 24, 2017, https://blog.bigchaindb.com/digitizing-vehicles-the -first-blockchain-backed-car-passport-b55ead6dbc71.

37. Interview with author, July 6, 2017.

38. Jon Springer, "Walmart: Blockchain Tech a Boon for Food Safety," *Supermarket News,* June 1, 2017, http://www.supermarketnews.com/food-safety/walmart-blockchain -tech-boon-food-safety.

39. Robert Hackett, "Walmart and 9 Food Giants Team up on Blockchain Plans," *Fortune,* August 22, 2017, http://fortune.com/2017/08/22/walmart-blockchain-ibm -food-nestle-unilever-tyson-dole.

40. Veena Pureswaran, "Blockchain Explorers Are Breaking Away from the Competition," *IBM Consulting Blog,* May 18, 2017, https://www.ibm.com/blogs/insights-on -business/gbs-strategy/blockchain-explorers-breaking-away/.

41. George Slefo, "Comcast Says Marketers Can Make TV Ad Buys with Blockchain Tech," *AdAge,* June 20, 2017, http://adage.com/article/digital/comcast-marketers -make-tv-ad-buys-blockchain-tech/309486/.

42. Interview with author, June 30, 2017.

43. Edward C. Kelleher, "Loan/SERV: Automating the Global Syndicated Loan Market," DTCC, July 2, 2012, http://www.dtcc.com/news/2012/july/02/loanserv -automating-the-global-syndicated-loan-market.

44. Tanaya Macheel, "Banks Test Blockchain for Syndicated Loans with Symbiont, R3," *American Banker,* September 27, 2016, https://www.americanbanker.com/news /banks-test-blockchain-for-syndicated-loans-with-symbiont-r3.

45. Chris Anderson, *The Long Tail: Why the Future of Business Is Selling Less of More* (New York: Hyperion Books, 2008); Chris Anderson, "The Economics of Abundance," *The Long Tail—Wired Blogs,* October 25, 2006, http://www.longtail.com/the_long_ tail/2006/10/the_economics_o.html.

46. James B. Stewart, "Facebook Falls from Grace, and Investors' Stock Holdings Tumble Too, *The New York Times,* March 29, 2018, https://www.nytimes.com/2018 /03/29/business/facebook-stock.html.

47. Permissioned distributed-ledger systems generally do not incorporate a native currency.

48. Chris Burniske and Jack Tatar, *Cryptoassets: The Innovative Investor's Guide to Bitcoin and Beyond* (New York: McGraw-Hill, 2018).

49. Gertrude Chavez-Dreyfuss, "Civic Sells $33 Million in Digital Currency Tokens in Public Sale," Reuters, June 22, 2017, https://www.reuters.com/article/us-civic -blockchain-token/civic-sells-33-million-in-digital-currency-tokens-in-public-sale -idUSKBN19D200.

50. As with the valuation of any financial asset, the appropriate price reflects the discounted value of future flows.

51. Mastercoin was subsequently renamed Omni.

52. Steven Russolillo, "Initial Coin Offerings Surge Past $4 Billion—and Regula- tors Are Worried," *Wall Street Journal*, December 14, 2017, Markets section, https: //www.wsj.com/articles/initial-coin-offerings-surge-past-4-billionand-regulators-are -worried-1513235196. Most were sold prior to their networks being functional. Olga Kharif, "Only One in 10 Tokens Is in Use Following Initial Coin Offerings," Bloom- berg.com, October 23, 2017, https://www.bloomberg.com/news/articles/2017-10-23 /only-one-in-10-tokens-is-in-use-following-initial-coin-offerings.

53. See the TokenData website, https://www.tokendata.io.

54. Sam Patterson, "Why OpenBazaar Token Doesn't Exist," *OpenBazaar Blog*, June 16, 2017, https://blog.openbazaar.org/why-openbazaar-token-doesnt-exist/.

55. Pete Rizzo, "Token Summit Surprise: OpenBazaar to Launch Layer-Two Coin," *CoinDesk*, December 5, 2017, https://www.coindesk.com/token-summit-surprise-open bazaar-launch-layer-two-coin.

56. Camila Russo, "Ethereum Co-Founder Says the Crypto Coin Market Is a Tick- ing Time-Bomb," Bloomberg.com, July 18, 2017, https://www.bloomberg.com/news /articles/2017-07-18/ethereum-co-founder-says-crypto-coin-market-is-ticking-time -bomb. Ironically, Hoskinson left Ethereum because he wanted to create a for-profit company rather than operate as a nonprofit foundation.

57. Chris Dixon, "Crypto Tokens: A Breakthrough in Open Network Design," *Medium*, June 1, 2017, https://medium.com/@cdixon/crypto-tokens-a-breakthrough-in-open -network-design-e600975be2ef.; Balaji Srinavasan, "Thoughts on Tokens," News.21 .Co, May 27, 2017, https://news.21.co/thoughts-on-tokens-436109aabcbe.; Joel Mon- egro, "Fat Protocols," *Union Square Ventures Blog*, August 8, 2016, http://www.usv.com /blog/fat-protocols.

58. Interview with author, October 24, 2017.

59. There are a variety of other functions that a token-based business has to manage, on both the internal and external sides. Simple Token is a start-up creating middle- ware to help manage these processes. Jason Goldberg, "Introducing Simple Token, an Easy Way for Businesses to Issue Blockchain-Powered Tokens without the Drama," *Medium*, September 28, 2017, https://medium.com/simple-token/introducing-simple -token-an-easy-way-for-businesses-to-issue-blockchain-powered-tokens-without-the -9c911f62d874.

60. Vili Lehdonvirta and Edward Castronova, *Virtual Economies: Design and Analysis* (Cambridge, MA: MIT Press, 2014).

61. "Facebook Scraps Credits Currency," BBC News, June 20, 2012, http://www.bbc .com/news/technology-18519921.

Chapter 5

1. Google's algorithm was called PageRank. Lawrence Page, Sergey Brin, Rajeev Motwani, and Terry Winograd, "The PageRank Citation Ranking: Bringing Order to the Web," January 29, 1998, http://ilpubs.stanford.edu:8090/422/1/1999-66.pdf.

2. The concept of "trustless trust," as described here, bears significant similarities to what Rachel Botsman calls "distributed trust." Rachel Botsman, *Who Can You Trust? How Technology Brought Us Together and Why It Might Drive Us Apart* (New York: PublicAffairs, 2017). However, Botsman's notion of distributed trust differs in important ways. Botsman defines distributed trust as "people trusting other people through technology" (8), and she includes examples such as Airbnb and Uber, which promote trust through reputation systems. Blockchain-based systems, by contrast, do not make people more trusting of each other, only of the results that they observe on a distributed ledger. While they are distributed, they also minimize trust in individual actors.

3. As Aaron Wright and Primavera De Filippi state, "Trust [on the blockchain] does not rest with the organization, but rather within the security and auditability of the underlying code. ..." Aaron Wright and Primavera De Filippi, "Decentralized Blockchain Technology and the Rise of Lex Cryptographia," Social Science Research Network (SSRN), March 10, 2015, https://ssrn.com/abstract=2580664, 16. Cf. Jason Leibowitz, "Blockchain's Big Innovation Is Trust, Not Money," *CoinDesk*, May 21, 2016, https:// www.coindesk.com/blockchain-innovation-trust-money ("If each participant in the transaction trusts the blockchain itself then they do not need to directly trust each other.").

4. Jon Matonis, "Bitcoin Foundation Launches to Drive Bitcoin's Advancement," *Forbes*, September 27, 2012, https://www.forbes.com/sites/jonmatonis/2012/09/27 /bitcoin-foundation-launches-to-drive-bitcoins-advancement/37536b416bc9. These governance mechanisms have been criticized as inefficient and undemocratic. Primavera De Filippi and Benjamin Loveluck, "The Invisible Politics of Bitcoin: Governance Crisis of a Decentralized Infrastructure," *Internet Policy Review* 5 (September 30, 2016), https://policyreview.info/articles/analysis/invisible-politics-bitcoin-gover nance-crisis-decentralised-infrastructure.

5. This is known as the "end-to-end architecture" of the Internet. Jerome Saltzer, David Reed, and David Clark, "End-to-End Arguments in System Design," *ACM Transactions Computer System* 2, no. 4 (November 1984): 277–288, https://doi.org /10.1145/357401.357402. Legal scholars have traced the implications of this technical approach. For instance, see Mark A. Lemley and Lawrence Lessig, "The End

of End-to-End: Preserving the Architecture of the Internet in the Broadband Era," *UCLA Law Review* 48 (2001): 925; Barbara van Schewick, *Internet Architecture and Innovation* (Cambridge, MA: MIT Press, 2010).

6. See Francis Fukuyama, *Trust: The Social Virtues and the Creation of Prosperity* (New York: Free Press, 1995).

7. Albert Wenger, "Bitcoin: Clarifying the Foundational Innovation of the Blockchain." Continuations, December 15, 2014, https://continuations.com/post/105272022635 /bitcoin-clarifying-the-foundational-innovation-of.

8. "It is not proof of work, nor decentralized money, nor linked-list data structures, but specifically cryptoeconomics that is the single key fundamentally transformative idea that came out of Satoshi's code and whitepaper." Vitalik Buterin, "Blockchain and Smart Contract Mechanism Design Challenges," First Workshop on Trusted Smart Contracts, Malta, April 7, 2017, http://fc17.ifca.ai/wtsc/Vitalik_Malta.pdf.

9. Vitalik Buterin, "Engineering Security Through Coordination Problems," Vitalik Buterin's Website, May 8, 2017, https://vitalik.ca/general/2017/05/08/coordina tion_problems.html ("[W]e are using coordination problems to our advantage, using the friction that coordination problems create as a bulwark against malfeasance by centralized actors.").

10. Frank H. Knight, *Risk, Uncertainty, and Profit* (Boston and New York: Houghton Mifflin, 1921).

11. In truth, the quote appears to have first been used by the Danish politician Karl Kristian Steincke. "It's Difficult to Make Predictions, Especially about the Future," *Quote Investigator,* October 20, 2013, https://quoteinvestigator.com/2013/10/20/no -predict/.

12. The recent turn toward behavioral economics is all about taking psychological insights, which had been dismissed as irrelevant to economics because they could not be modeled, and showing how they represent regular and predictable biases that can be incorporated into mathematical models.

13. And there are suitable backups, of course, in the event of data loss.

14. Jim Finkle, "Bangladesh Bank Hackers Compromised SWIFT Software, Warn-ing Issued," Reuters, April 25, 2016, https://www.reuters.com/article/us-usa-nyfed -bangladesh-malware-exclusiv-idUSKCN0XM0DR.

15. Arvind Narayanan, Joseph Bonneau, Edward Felten, Andrew Miller, and Steven Goldfeder, *Bitcoin and Cryptocurrency Technologies: A Comprehensive Introduction* (Princ-eton, NJ: Princeton University Press, 2016), 71–72.

16. Textrapperr, Reddit r/Ethereum, October 27, 2016, https://www.reddit.com/r /ethereum/comments/59naa2/what_does_immutability_really_mean/d99ye84.

17. Angela Walch, "The Path of the Blockchain Lexicon (and the Law)," *Review of Banking and Finance Law* 36 (2017).

18. Vitalik Buterin, "On Settlement Finality," *Ethereum Blog,* May 9, 2016, https://blog.ethereum.org/2016/05/09/on-settlement-finality.

19. "Cryptocurrencies with Tim Ferriss, Nick Szabo, and Naval Ravikant," *Medium,* June 6, 2017, https://medium.com/@giftedproducts/cryptocurrencies-with-tim-ferriss-nick-szabo-and-naval-ravikant-51a99d037e04.

20. Michael Abramowicz, "Cryptocurrency-based Law," *Arizona Law Review* 58 (2016): 359, 375.

21. Other blockchain networks such as Ethereum offer faster confirmations. Some even promise instantaneous finality, but such architectures either make tradeoffs in the centralization of trust or have not been proven secure and scalable.

22. Joseph Bonneau, Andrew Miller, Jeremy Clark, Arvind Narayanan, Joshua A. Kroll, and Edward W. Felten, "Research Perspectives and Challenges for Bitcoin and Cryptocurrencies," *Proceedings of the 36th IEEE Symposium on Security and Privacy,* 3, July 20, 2015, http://www.jbonneau.com/doc/BMCNKF15-IEEESP-bitcoin.pdf (noting that the six-block convention "originates from the reference client and is not based on any analysis of the probability of deep forks.").

23. Vitalik Buterin (@VitalikButerin), Twitter, June 4, 2017 3:13 a.m., https://twitter.com/vitalikbuterin/status/871263595593572353.

24. That "No2X" Guy Who (@hq83bnn9), Twitter, June 4, 2017 11:33 a.m., https://twitter.com/hq83bnn9/status/871389578153914369. The reaction was overblown. Buterin was talking about proof of stake, the consensus algorithm that Ethereum hopes to adopt. In a proof-of-stake system, those validating transactions stake some of their currency on their actions. If they violate the rules of the network, they lose that stake. Those are the "deposits" that Buterin was referring to. The "we" who would delete them are the proof-of-stake algorithms governing what counts as a violation.

25. Bill Maurer, Taylor C. Nelms, and Lana Swartz, "'When Perhaps the Real Problem Is Money Itself!': The Practical Materiality of Bitcoin," *Social Semiotics* 23, no. 2 (April 1, 2013): 261–277. Open-source software means that any interested expert can verify the integrity of the code and help to identify its vulnerabilities.

26. Oded Goldreich and Yair Oren, "Definitions and Properties of Zero-Knowledge Proof Systems," *Journal of Cryptology* 7, no. 1 (1994): 1–32, https://link.springer.com/article/10.1007/BF00195207.

27. Eli Ben Sasson, Alessandro Chiesa, Christina Garman, Matthew Green, Ian Miers, Eran Tromer, and Madars Virza, "Zerocash: Decentralized Anonymous Payments from Bitcoin," *2014 IEEE Symposium on Security and Privacy* 459.

28. "'Mind-Boggling' Math Could Make Blockchain Work for Wall Street," Bloomberg.com, October 5, 2017, https://www.bloomberg.com/news/articles/2017-10-05/-mind-boggling-math-could-make-blockchain-work-for-wall-street.

29. Mike Ananny and Kate Crawford, "Seeing without Knowing: Limitations of the Transparency Ideal and Its Application to Algorithmic Accountability," *New Media & Society*, 2016: 973–989.

30. This is not to say that Facebook and similar companies bear no responsibility for the consequences of the systems they build. Algorithmic platforms can be made more robust and protective of user interests. The point here is simply that the political ideology of Facebook, the platform, is not necessarily that of Facebook's management or employees. It is the output of Facebook's algorithms.

31. Andreas Antonopoulos, "Bitcoin Security Model: Trust by Computation," *Radar*, O'Reilly Media, February 20, 2014, http://radar.oreilly.com/2014/02/bitcoin-security-model-trust-by-computation.html.

32. Vitalik Buterin, "The Subjectivity/Exploitability Tradeoff," *Ethereum Blog*, February 14, 2015, https://blog.ethereum.org/2015/02/14/subjectivity-exploitability-tradeoff/.

33. Frank Pasquale, *The Black Box Society: The Secret Algorithms That Control Money and Information* (Cambridge, MA: Harvard University Press, 2015).

34. Cathy O'Neil, *Weapons of Math Destruction: How Big Data Increases Inequality and Threatens Democracy* (New York: Crown, 2016).

35. Zeynep Tufekci, "The Real Bias Built in at Facebook," *The New York Times*, May 19, 2016, "Opinion" section, https://www.nytimes.com/2016/05/19/opinion/the-real-bias-built-in-at-facebook.html.

36. As BigChainDB chief technologist and former AI researcher Trent McConaghy explains, blockchain networks could also promote the development of AI. Trent McConaghy, "Blockchains for Artificial Intelligence," *BigchainDB Blog*, January 3, 2017, https://blog.bigchaindb.com/blockchains-for-artificial-intelligence-ec63b0284984. More data, as well as better sharing of models built using that data, are the keys to improving machine-learning performance. Blockchains promote data sharing through the mechanisms of decentralization, shared truth, and translucent collaboration described in chapter 4.

37. I credit Christian Terwiesch with pointing out this distinction to me.

38. Melanie Swan, *Blockchain: Blueprint for a New Economy* (O'Reilly, 2015); Wright and De Filippi, "Decentralized Blockchain Technology and the Rise of Lex Cryptographia."

39. Whether a DAO is a corporation in the legal sense is a harder question. Shawn Bayern, "Of Bitcoins, Independently Wealthy Software, and the Zero-Member LLC," *Northwestern University Law Review* 108 (2014): 1485–1500; Tanaya Macheel, "The

DAO Might Be Groundbreaking, But Is It Legal?" *American Banker*, May 19, 2016, https://www.americanbanker.com/news/bank-technology/the-dao-might-be -groundbreaking-but-is-it-legal-1081084-1.html; Peter Van Valkenburgh, "DAOs: The Internet Is Weird Again, and These Are the Regulatory Issues," *CoinCenter*, June 2, 2016, https://coincenter.org/entry/daos-the-internet-is-weird-again-and-these-are -the-regulatory-issues.

40. Daniel Larimer, "The Hidden Costs of Bitcoin," LTB Network, September 7, 2013, https://letstalkbitcoin.com/is-bitcoin-overpaying-for-false-security; Vitalik Buterin, "Bootstrapping a Decentralized Autonomous Corporation: Part I," *Bitcoin Magazine*, September 19, 2013, https://bitcoinmagazine.com/7050/bootstrapping-a-decentralized -autonomous-corporation-part-i/.

41. Luis Cuende, "Introducing Aragon: Unstoppable Companies," February 10, 2017, https://blog.aragon.one/introducing-aragon-unstoppable-companies-58c1fd2d00ce.

42. Aragon's frequently asked questions (FAQ) page says that the system is "everything you need to run your company on Ethereum." It also describes decentralized organizations as its "long-term vision." Aragon FAQ, https://aragon.one/faq.

Chapter 6

1. Ken Thompson, "Reflections on Trusting Trust," *Communications of the ACM* 27, no. 8 (1984): 761–763.

2. Pete Rizzo, "Blockchain Land Title Project 'Stalls' in Honduras," *CoinDesk*, December 26, 2015, https://www.coindesk.com/debate-factom-land-title-honduras.

3. Ben Dickson, "Blockchain Could Completely Transform the Music Industry," *VentureBeat*, January 7, 2017, https://venturebeat.com/2017/01/07/blockchain-could -completely-transform-the-music-industry.

4. David Gerard, "Imogen Heap: 'Tiny Human'. Total Sales: $133.20," Davidgerard.co .uk, April 22, 2017, https://davidgerard.co.uk/blockchain/imogen-heap-tiny-human -total-sales-133-20. Gerard, a Unix system administrator, offers many more examples in his book-length critique of the cryptocurrency world. David Gerard, *Attack of the 50 Foot Blockchain: Bitcoin, Blockchain, Ethereum & Smart Contracts* (Self-published, 2017).

5. Laura Shin, "Bitcoin Startup Abra Adds Gwyneth Paltrow as Advisor, Is Featured in Apple Reality TV Show," *Forbes*, August 2, 2017, https://www.forbes.com/sites /laurashin/2017/08/02/bitcoin-startup-abra-adds-gwyneth-paltrow-as-advisor-is -featured-in-apple-reality-tv-show/. The company, Abra, pivoted to offer broader mobile wallet and payment services.

6. On the Internet's potential for free expression, see Clay Shirky, *Here Comes Everybody: The Power of Organizing without Organizations* (New York: Penguin, 2008); Rebecca MacKinnon, *Consent of the Networked: The Worldwide Struggle for Internet Freedom* (New

York: Basic Books, 2013); Zeynep Tufekci, *Twitter and Tear Gas: The Power and Fragility of Networked Protest* (New Haven, CT: Yale University Press, 2017). On the dangers, see Evgeny Morozov, *The Net Delusion: How Not to Liberate the World* (New York: Penguin, 2012).

7. Alice Marwick and Rebecca Lewis, "Media Manipulation and Disinformation Online," Data & Society, May 15, 2017, https://datasociety.net/output/media-mani pulation-and-disinfo-online.

8. Benjamin Edelman, "Uber Can't Be Fixed—It's Time for Regulators to Shut It Down," *Harvard Business Review*, June 21, 2017, https://hbr.org/2017/06/uber-cant -be-fixed-its-time-for-regulators-to-shut-it-down.

9. Thomas Philippon, "Has the US Finance Industry Become Less Efficient? On the Theory and Measurement of Financial Intermediation," *American Economic Review* 105, no. 4 (2015): 1408–1438.

10. David Yermack, "Blockchains and Corporate Finance: 'In a Blockchain Market, Shareholder Activists Might Play Much Less of a Role,'" *Promarket,* June 14, 2017, https://promarket.org/blockchains-corporate-finance-blockchain-market-shareholder -activists-might-play-much-less-role.

11. Symbiont's Caitlin Long, who spent over two decades on Wall Street before joining the blockchain start-up, emphasizes that "Blockchain is the first technology to come along (ever?) that may justify wholesale replacement of legacy [financial industry information technology] systems, because it enables sufficient cost savings to cover transition costs by a multiple." Interview with author (June 30, 2017).

12. Nick Szabo, "Money, Blockchains, and Social Scalability," *Unenumerated,* February 9, 2017, https://unenumerated.blogspot.com/2017/02/money-blockchains-and -social-scalability.html.

13. Slacknation, "If Your Exchange Is Related to 0x027BEEFcBaD782faF69FAD-12DeE97Ed894c68549, Withdraw Immediately, They Screwed up a Few Days Ago and Lost 60,000 Ether," Reddit, June 2017, https://www.reddit.com/r/ethereum /comments/6eruqb/if_your_exchange_is_related_to.

14. QuadrigaCX apparently made its customers whole, thus reducing its profits by about $14 million. Stan Higgins, "Ethereum Client Update Issue Costs Cryptocurrency Exchange $14 Million," *CoinDesk,* June 2, 2017, https://www.coindesk.com /ethereum-client-exchange-14-million.

15. Vlad Zamfir, "About My Tweet from Yesterday ...," *Medium,* March 5, 2017, https://medium.com/@Vlad_Zamfir/about-my-tweet-from-yesterday-dcc61915b572. Similarly, in September 2017, Vitalik Buterin stated on Twitter, "I think bitcoin and ethereum are both deeply flawed in their current forms. And I say this in some way in most presentations I make ..." Vitalik Buterin (@vitalikbuterin), Twitter, September 14, 2017, 5:57 a.m., https://twitter.com/VitalikButerin/status/908268522890985472.

16. Vlad Zamfir (@VladZamfir), Twitter, December 14, 2017, 3:16 a.m., https://twitter.com/VladZamfir/status/941220330294644736.

17. Amy Castor, "MIT and BU Researchers Uncover Critical Security Flaw in $2B Cryptocurrency IOTA," *Forbes*, September 7, 2017, https://www.forbes.com/sites/amycastor/2017/09/07/mit-and-bu-researchers-uncover-critical-security-flaw-in-2b-cryptocurrency-iota.

18. While the 51-percent attack is the most widely discussed scenario, security researchers have identified several other potential attack vectors against Bitcoin. Joseph Bonneau, Andrew Miller, Jeremy Clark, Arvind Narayanan, Joshua A. Kroll, and Edward W. Felten, "Research Perspectives and Challenges for Bitcoin and Cryptocurrencies," *Proceedings of the 36th IEEE Symposium on Security and Privacy*, 3, July 20, 2015, http://www.jbonneau.com/doc/BMCNKF15-IEEESP-bitcoin.pdf, 7–9.

19. Jon Matonis, "The Bitcoin Mining Arms Race: GHash.io and the 51% Issue," *CoinDesk*, July 17, 2014, https://www.coindesk.com/bitcoin-mining-detente-ghash-io-51-issue.

20. More generally, public blockchains must maintain sufficient scale and network effects to remain viable. Joshua Fairfield, "BitProperty," *Southern California Law Review* 88 (2014): 823–824.

21. Frederick Reese, "As Bitcoin Halving Approaches, 51% Attack Question Resurfaces," *CoinDesk*, July 6, 2016, https://www.coindesk.com/ahead-bitcoin-halving-51-attack-risks-reappear. Other blockchains do not necessarily use the halving mechanism, but all those employing proof of work face the concern about incentives when the price of the cryptocurrency falls.

22. Bonneau et al, "Research Perspectives and Challenges for Bitcoin and Cryptocurrencies, 1.

23. Olga Kharif, "1,000 People Own 40% of the Bitcoin Market," *Bloomberg Businessweek*, December 8, 2017, https://www.bloomberg.com/news/articles/2017-12-08/the-bitcoin-whales-1-000-people-who-own-40-percent-of-the-market.

24. Jon Russell, "Former Mozilla CEO Raises $35M in Under 30 Seconds for His Browser Startup Brave," *TechCrunch*, June 1, 2017, http://techcrunch.com/2017/06/01/brave-ico-35-million-30-seconds-brendan-eich/.

25. As of fall 2017, just four mining groups were collectively responsible for half of Bitcoin hashing power. The seven largest groups represented three-quarters of the total hashing power. Blockchain.info, October 18, 2017, https://blockchain.info/pools?timespan=4days.

26. Ethereum mining was even more concentrated than Bitcoin in fall 2017, with just two mining pools collectively controlling half the hashing power, and the five largest controlling four-fifths. "Ethereum Top 25 Miners by BLOCKS," Etherscan, October 18, 2017, https://etherscan.io/stat/miner?range=7&blocktype=blocks.

27. Fred Ehrsam, "Funding the Evolution of Blockchains," *Medium,* August 24, 2017, https://medium.com/@FEhrsam/funding-the-evolution-of-blockchains-87d160988481.

28. Brett M. Frischmann, *Infrastructure: The Social Value of Shared Resources* (Oxford: Oxford University Press, 2013).

29. Arvind Narayanan, "Analyzing the 2013 Bitcoin Fork: Centralized Decision-Making Saved the Day," *Freedom to Tinker,* July 28, 2015, https://freedom-to-tinker .com/2015/07/28/analyzing-the-2013-bitcoin-fork-centralized-decision-making -saved-the-day/.

30. Saheli Roy Choudhury, "Chinese ICOs: China Bans Fundraising through Initial Coin Offerings, Report Says," CNBC, September 4, 2017, https://www.cnbc.com /2017/09/04/chinese-icos-china-bans-fundraising-through-initial-coin-offerings -report-says.html. The Chinese decision may well be temporary and a stepping stone to a comprehensive regulatory regime for cryptocurrencies.

31. Josiah Wilmoth, "PBoC Digital Currency Chief Calls for State Cryptocurrency," CryptoCoinsNews, October 15, 2017, https://www.cryptocoinsnews.com/pboc-digital -currency-chief-calls-for-government-cryptocurrency.

32. Daniel Oberhaus, "Putin Will Require Cryptocurrency Miners to Register with the Government in 2018," *Motherboard,* October 24, 2017, https://motherboard.vice.com /en_us/article/7x4vad/putin-cryptocurrency-russia-mining-regulations-ico-bitcoin -ethereum.

33. Ari Juels, Ahmed E. Kosba, and Elaine Shi, "The Ring of Gyges: Investigating the Future of Criminal Smart Contracts," 2016 ACM SIGSAC Conference on Computer and Communications Security, Vienna: 283–295, http://www.arijuels.com/wp -content/uploads/2013/09/Gyges.pdf.

34. Zikai Alex Wen and Andrew Miller, "Scanning Live Ethereum Contracts for the 'Unchecked-Send' Bug," *Hacking, Distributed,* June 16, 2016, http://hackingdistri buted.com/2016/06/16/scanning-live-ethereum-contracts-for-bugs.

35. Interview with author, September 22, 2017.

36. "An Open Letter," Pastebin, June 18, 2016, https://pastebin.com/CcGUBgDG.

37. Vitalik Buterin, "Thinking about Smart Contract Security," *Ethereum Blog,* June 19, 2016, https://blog.ethereum.org/2016/06/19/thinking-smart-contract-security.

38. Ian Bogost, "Cryptocurrency Might Be a Path to Authoritarianism," *The Atlantic,* May 30, 2017, https://www.theatlantic.com/technology/archive/2017/05/blockchain -of-command/528543. Adam Greenfield makes a similar point. Adam Greenfield, *Radical Technologies: The Design of Everyday Life* (London and New York: Verso, 2017).

39. Kevin Werbach and Nicolas Cornell, "Contracts ex Machina," *Duke Law Journal* 67 (2017): 101–170.

40. David Weinberger, "Copy Protection Is a Crime," *Wired*, June 1, 2003, https://www.wired.com/2003/06/copy-protection-is-a-crime.

41. Izabella Kaminska, "Building Blockchain Banks with ICOs," FT Alphaville, June 7, 2017, https://ftalphaville.ft.com/2017/06/07/2189826/building-blockchain-banks-with-icos.

42. The earlier mining business was criticized bitterly and accused of being a scam. IconFirm, *Bitcointalk Bitcoin Forum* (June 26, 2017, 5:43:39 p.m.), https://bitcointalk.org/index.php?topic=1970796.msg19786878; *Bitcointalk Bitcoin Forum*, thread, https://bitcointalk.org/index.php?topic=1848751.1700.

43. Estonian Financial Supervision Agency, "Notice Regarding the Activities of Polybius Foundation OÜ," June 6, 2017, http://www.fi.ee/public/hoiatusteated/20170606_Hoiatusteade_Polybius.pdf.

44. "Swiss EY Team Joins Polybius Cryptobank as Advisors, ICO to Follow," *The Business Journals*, press release, May 13, 2017, 5:45 p.m. EDT, https://www.bizjournals.com/prnewswire/press_releases/2017/05/13/NY89961.

45. Polybius, home page, https://polybius.io/team.

46. Kaminska, "Building Blockchain Banks with ICOs."

47. Nick Szabo (@nickszabo4), Twitter, June 17, 2017, 9:05 p.m., https://twitter.com/NickSzabo4/status/876244539211735041.

48. "The Rise of Cybercrime on Ethereum," *Chainalysis Blog*, August 7, 2017, https://blog.chainalysis.com/the-rise-of-cybercrime-on-ethereum/. Overall, counting thefts, broken smart contracts, and lost cryptographic keys, estimates are that over 20 percent of all bitcoin, worth billions of dollars, is already lost. Jeff John Roberts and Nicolas Rapp, "Exclusive: Nearly 4 Million Bitcoins Lost Forever, New Study Says," *Fortune*, November 25, 2017, http://fortune.com/2017/11/25/lost-bitcoins/.

49. Amir Mizroch, "Large Bitcoin Exchange Halts Trading after Hack," *Wall Street Journal*, January 6, 2015, "Digits" section, https://blogs.wsj.com/digits/2015/01/06/large-bitcoin-exchange-halts-trading-after-hack; Robert McMillan, "The Inside Story of Mt. Gox, Bitcoin's $460 Million Disaster," *Wired*, March 3, 2014, https://www.wired.com/2014/03/bitcoin-exchange.

50. "Security Alert," Parity Technologies, November 8, 2017, http://paritytech.io/blog/security-alert-2; Ryan Browne, "'Accidental' Bug Froze $280 Million Worth of Ether in Parity Wallet," CNBC, November 8, 2017, https://www.cnbc.com/2017/11/08/accidental-bug-may-have-frozen-280-worth-of-ether-on-parity-wallet.html. Parity is proposing several mechanisms, generally requiring limited hard forks, to unlock the stored currency. Frederic Lardinois, "Parity CEO Is Confident That $150M in Frozen Ethereum Isn't Lost Forever," *TechCrunch*, December 5, 2017, http://techcrunch.com/2017/12/05/parity-ceo-says-shes-confident-that-its-280m-in-frozen-ethereum-isnt-lost-forever.

51. An Uber autonomous vehicle killed a pedestrian during testing in Arizona in March 2018. Troy Griggs and Daisuke Wakabayashi, "How a Self-Driving Uber Killed a Pedestrian in Arizona," *New York Times*, March 21, 2018, https://www.nytimes.com/interactive/2018/03/20/us/self-driving-uber-pedestrian-killed.html.

Chapter 7

1. Joshua Davis, "The Crypto-Currency," *The New Yorker*, October 3, 2011, https://www.newyorker.com/magazine/2011/10/10/the-crypto-currency.

2. Vili Lehdonvirta, "The Blockchain Paradox: Why Distributed Ledger Technologies May Do Little to Transform the Economy," Oxford Internet Institute, November 21, 2016, https://www.oii.ox.ac.uk/blog/the-blockchain-paradox-why-distributed-ledger-technologies-may-do-little-to-transform-the-economy.

3. Izabella Kaminska, "Blockchain's Governance Paradox," *FT Alphaville*, June 14, 2017), https://ftalphaville.ft.com/2017/06/14/2190149/blockchains-governance-paradox.

4. Adam Ludwin (@adamludwin), Twitter, July 26, 2017, 4:55pm, https://twitter.com/adamludwin/status/890314573760184320. Some cryptocurrency experts accept this point, but others do not. Nick Szabo, for example, states that "blockchains also need a human governance layer that is vulnerable to fork politics." Nick Szabo, "Money, Blockchains, and Social Scalability," *Unenumerated*, February 9, 2017, https://unenumerated.blogspot.com/2017/02/money-blockchains-and-social-scalability.html. On the other hand, Bitcoin Core developer Adam Back argues, "Governance is a dirty word, it implies anything is changeable if governor's [sic] agree. Bitcoin is not for changing, social contract must stand." Adam Back (@Adam3US), Twitter, June 12, 2017, 3:07 a.m., https://twitter.com/adam3us/status/874161328826535936.

5. Permissioned distributed ledgers can apply the conventional governance mechanisms of consortia or membership-based standards organizations because they can identify participants and their responsibilities. Even though no one actor has control, a relatively small group can work together to agree upon rules. Public blockchains, however, allow open entry and decentralize authority more extensively.

6. Vili Lehdonvirta, "Governance and Regulation," in Mark Walport, *Distributed Ledger Technology: Beyond Block Chain* (UK Government Office for Science, 2016), https://www.gov.uk/government/uploads/system/uploads/attachment_data/file/492972/gs-16-1-distributed-ledger-technology.pdf.

7. I am indebted to Julie Cohen for clarifying my thinking on this point.

8. Elinor Ostrom, "Beyond Markets and States: Polycentric Governance of Complex Economic Systems," in *Les Prix Nobel*, edited by Karl Grandin (Stockholm: Nobel Foundation, 2010), 408.

9. For an effort to map Ostrom's principles for common-pool resource management to the blockchain world, see Scott Shackelford and Steve Myers, "Block-by-Block: Leveraging the Power of Blockchain Technology to Build Trust and Promote Cyber Peace," *Yale Journal of Law and Technology* 19 (2017): 334.

10. Cf. Vlad Zamfir, "Against On-Chain Governance," *Medium*, December 1, 2017, https://medium.com/@Vlad_Zamfir/against-on-chain-governance-a4ceacd040ca (rejecting the claim that blockchain governance is an idealized design problem that can be implemented completely through automated rules).

11. Tom R. Tyler, *Why People Obey the Law* (Princeton, NJ: Princeton University Press, 2006).

12. Edward Shils, "The Concept of Consensus," in *International Encyclopedia of the Social Sciences* (Editor D.L. Sills, New York: Macmillan, 1968): 260–266, https://www.encyclopedia.com/science-and-technology/computers-and-electrical-engineering/computers-and-computing/consensus.

13. Geraint Parry, "Trust, Distrust, and Consensus," *British Journal of Political Science* 6, no. 2 (1976): 129–142, https://journals.cambridge.org/article_S0007123400000594.

14. Andrew L. Russell, "'Rough Consensus and Running Code' and the Internet-OSI Standards War," *IEEE Annals of the History of Computing* 28, no. 3 (July 2006): 48–61, https://doi.org/10.1109/MAHC.2006.42.

15. Philipp Güring and Ian Grigg, "Bitcoin & Gresham's Law—the Economic Inevitability of Collapse," IANG.org, 2011, http://iang.org/papers/BitcoinBreachesGreshamsLaw.pdf.

16. Vitalik Buterin, "Notes on Blockchain Governance," Vitalik Buterin's Website, December 17, 2017, https://vitalik.ca/general/2017/12/17/voting.html. Buterin cleverly uses Byzantine armies as his example, harkening back to the cryptographic roots of Nakamoto Consensus.

17. Ostrom, "Beyond Markets and States," 432.

18. These terms were popularized by economist Richard Thaler and law professor Cass Sunstein. Richard H. Thaler and Cass R. Sunstein, *Nudge: Improving Decisions about Health, Wealth, and Happiness* (New Haven, CT: Yale University Press, 2008).

19. Avner Greif, *Institutions and the Path to the Modern Economy: Lessons from Medieval Trade*, Political Economy of Institutions and Decisions series (Cambridge: Cambridge University Press, 2006).

20. Oliver E. Williamson, "Transaction-Cost Economics: The Governance of Contractual Relations," *Journal of Law and Economics* 22, no. 2 (October 1, 1979): 233–261.

21. Avner Greif, "Commitment, Coercion, and Markets: The Nature and Dynamics of Institutions Supporting Exchange," *Handbook of New Institutional Economics*, 2005, 727.

22. Interview with author (October 23, 2017).

23. Jonathan Ore, "How a $64M Hack Changed the Fate of Ethereum, Bitcoin's Closest Competitor," CBC News, August 28, 2016, http://www.cbc.ca/news/technology/ethereum-hack-blockchain-fork-bitcoin-1.3719009.

24. Vitalik Buterin (@VitalikButerin), Twitter, August 3, 2017, 9:48 a.m., https://twitter.com/VitalikButerin/status/893106415446876160.

25. Stephan Tual, "On DAO Contractors and Curators," Slock.it, April 9, 2016, https://blog.slock.it/on-contractors-and-curators-2fb9238b2553.8wneaxn30.

26. "Explanation of Terms and Disclaimer," The DAO, https://daohub.org/explainer .html. Cf. "DAOs, Hacks, and the Law," *Medium,* June 17, 2016, https://medium.com/@Swarm/daos-hacks-and-the-law-eb6a33808e3e.vy0qr1pgf (explaining the significance of this provision).

27. Interview with author (October 23, 2017).

28. Vlad Zamfir, "Dear Ethereum Community," *Medium,* July 7, 2016, https://medium.com/@Vlad_Zamfir/dear-ethereum-community-acfa99a037c4.m7f6k44ap.

29. *The Federalist* No. 10, at 77 (James Madison) (edited by Clinton Rossiter, 1961) (describing factions as "mortal diseases under which popular governments have everywhere perished. …").

30. There may be overlap among these groups. On a proof-of-stake network, for example, the largest token holders may also be the most significant validators.

31. Paul Vigna and Michael J. Casey, *The Age of Cryptocurrency: How Bitcoin and Digital Money Are Challenging the Global Economic Order* (New York: St. Martin's Press, 2015), chapter 2. Both sides claim Satoshi Nakamoto's legacy.

32. Pete Rizzo, "Xapo Moves to Switzerland Citing Customer Privacy Concerns," *CoinDesk,* May 15, 2015, https://www.coindesk.com/xapo-switzerland-privacy-concerns. Financial analyst Chris Burniske estimated the following year that 60 percent of assets on Coinbase, the largest Bitcoin exchange, were purchased strictly to hold for the long term as a store of value, not for trading. Christopher Burniske, "Bitcoin: A Significantly Investable Asset," NASDAQ.com, August 24, 2016, https://www.iris.xyz/market-strategist /bitcoin-significantly-investable-asset.

33. Lily Katz, "Bitcoin Acceptance among Retailers Is Low and Getting Lower," Bloomberg.com, July 12, 2017, https://www.bloomberg.com/news/articles/2017-07 -12/bitcoin-acceptance-among-retailers-is-low-and-getting-lower.

34. One response to the volatility of cryptocurrencies is the creation of "stablecoins" that are pegged to fiat currencies or baskets of asset prices. Even if these projects succeed, which is an open question, they simply push the necessary trust from the original cryptocurrency to the stablecoin arrangements.

35. Shannon Liao, "Steam No Longer Accepting Bitcoin Due to 'High Fees and Volatility,'" *The Verge*, December 6, 2017, https://www.theverge.com/2017/12/6/16743220/valve-steam-bitcoin-game-store-payment-method-crypto-volatility.

36. Andrew Marshall, "Bitcoin Scaling Problem, Explained," *CoinTelegraph*, March 2, 2017, https://cointelegraph.com/explained/bitcoin-scaling-problem-explained.

37. On-chain governance technologies on some blockchain networks under development could implement governance changes automatically, without any action by miners. The benefits and limitations of this approach are discussed in chapter 10.

38. Nathaniel Popper, "Some Bitcoin Backers Are Defecting to Create a Rival Currency," *The New York Times*, July 25, 2017, "DealBook" section, https://www.nytimes.com/2017/07/25/business/dealbook/bitcoin-cash-split.html.

39. Laura Shin, "Bitcoin Hard Fork Called Off, Averting Major Disruptions and Turbulence in Cryptocurrency," *Forbes*, November 8, 2017, https://www.forbes.com/sites/laurashin/2017/11/08/bitcoin-hard-fork-called-off-averting-major-disruptions-and-turbulence-in-cryptocurrency/.

40. Zamfir, "Dear Ethereum Community."

41. Vlad Zamfir (@VladZamfir), Twitter, August 3, 2017, 10:20 a.m., https://twitter.com/VladZamfir/status/893114355562274816.

42. Nathaniel Popper, "Move Over, Bitcoin. Ether Is the Digital Currency of the Moment," *New York Times*, June 19, 2017, "DealBook," https://www.nytimes.com/2017/06/19/business/dealbook/ethereum-bitcoin-digital-currency.html.

Chapter 8

1. Vlad Zamfir (@VladZamfir), Twitter, June 13, 2017, 7:50 a.m., https://twitter.com/VladZamfir/status/874594731124281344.

2. John Rawls, *The Law of Peoples* (Cambridge, MA: Harvard University Press, 2001); Thomas Donaldson and Thomas W. Dunfee, *Ties That Bind: A Social Contracts Approach to Business Ethics* (Cambridge, MA: Harvard Business School Press, 1999).

3. Kenneth J. Arrow, Robert Forsythe, Michael Gorham, Robert Hahn, Robin Hanson, John O. Ledyard, et al., "The Promise of Prediction Markets," *Science* 320 (2008): 877.

4. Like a stock exchange, the prediction market can make money on a spread between buy and sell prices, or through listing fees.

5. James Surowiecki, *The Wisdom of Crowds* (New York: Anchor Books, 2005).

6. Bo Cowgill, Justin Wolfers, and Eric Zitzewitz, "Using Prediction Markets to Track Information Flows: Evidence from Google," First International Conference on Auctions, Market Mechanisms and Their Applications, Boston, MA, May 8, 2009 Lecture

Notes of the Institute for Computer Sciences, Social Informatics and Telecommunications Engineering 14 (Berlin: Springer, 2009).

7. Andrew Rice, "The Fall of Intrade and the Business of Betting on Real Life," BuzzFeed, February 20, 2014, https://www.buzzfeed.com/andrewrice/the-fall-of-intrade-and-the-business-of-betting-on-real-life.

8. CFTC rules prohibit the listing of "[a]n agreement, contract, transaction, or swap based upon an excluded commodity, as defined in Section 1a(19)(iv) of the Act, that involves, relates to, or references terrorism, assassination, war, gaming, or an activity that is unlawful under any State or Federal law." 17 CFR 40.11(a)(1).

9. This discussion focuses on Augur, but there are other blockchain-based prediction market platforms under development, including Gnosis.

10. Don Tapscott and Alex Tapscott, *Blockchain Revolution* (New York: Penguin Random House, 2016), 84.

11. "Trust Is Risk: A Decentralized Trust System," *OpenBazaar Blog*, August 1, 2017, https://www.openbazaar.org/blog/trust-is-risk-a-decentralized-trust-system.

12. For example, see Timothy B. Lee, "Reddit Conducts Wide-Ranging Purge of Offensive Subreddits," *Ars Technica*, October 26, 2017, https://arstechnica.com/tech-policy/2017/10/reddit-conducts-wide-ranging-purge-of-offensive-subreddits (noting that even though Reddit is the most permissive social media site, even it finds it necessary to delete offensive content sometimes).

13. Joseph Cox, "US, Europol, and the Netherlands Announce Shutdowns of Two Massive Dark Web Markets," Motherboard, July 20, 2017, https://motherboard.vice.com/en_us/article/evd7xw/us-europol-and-netherlands-announce-shutdowns-of-two-massive-dark-web-markets.

14. Clay Shirky, "A Group Is Its Own Worst Enemy," *Clay Shirky's Writings About the Internet*, July 1, 2003, http://www.shirky.com/writings/herecomeseverybody/group_enemy.html.

15. Lawrence Lessig, "The New Chicago School," *Journal of Legal Studies* 27, no. S2 (June 1, 1998): 661–691.

16. Lawrence Lessig, *Code and Other Laws of Cyberspace* (New York: Basic Books, 1999).

17. Kevin Werbach, "The Architecture of Internet 2.0," *Release 1.0*, February 1999, http://downloads.oreilly.com/radar/r1/02-99.pdf; Kevin D. Werbach, "A Layered Model for Internet Policy," *Journal on Telecommunications and High-Tech Law* 1 (2002): 37-67.

18. For example, see Josh Stark, "Making Sense of Cryptoeconomics," *CoinDesk*, August 19, 2017, https://www.coindesk.com/making-sense-cryptoeconomics.

19. David R. Johnson and David G. Post, "Law and Borders—the Rise of Law in Cyberspace," *Stanford Law Review* 48 (1997): 1367.

20. John Perry Barlow, "A Declaration of the Independence of Cyberspace," Electronic Frontier Foundation, February 8, 1996, https://www.eff.org/cyberspace-independence.

21. Post and Johnson, "Law and Borders."

22. Jack L. Goldsmith and Tim Wu, *Who Controls the Internet? Illusions of a Borderless World* (New York: Oxford University Press, 2006).

23. Aaron Wright and Primavera De Filippi, "Decentralized Blockchain Technology and the Rise of Lex Cryptographia," Social Science Research Network (SSRN), March 10, 2015, https://ssrn.com/abstract=2580664, 44–47; Primavera De Fillipi and Aaron Wright, *Blockchain and the Law: The Rule of Code* (Cambridge, MA: Harvard University Press, 2018); Joel Reidenberg, "Lex Informatica: The Formulation of Information Policy Rules Through Technology," *Texas Law Review* 76 (1998): 553-593.

24. Wright and De Filippi, "Decentralized Blockchain Technology and the Rise of Lex Cryptographia," 40.

25. "BITNATION Pangea: The World's First Virtual Nation—a Blockchain Jurisdiction," Global Challenges Foundation, https://globalchallenges.org/en/our-work/quarterly-reports/remodelling-global-cooperation/bitnation-pangea.

26. Kevin D. Werbach, "The Song Remains the Same: What Cyberlaw Might Teach the Next Internet Economy," *Florida Law Review* 69 (2017): 887-957; Goldsmith and Wu, *Who Controls the Internet?*

27. There are similar problems with Josh Fairfield's appealing argument that smart contracts could be used to negotiate terms of service with online sites, returning power to users. Joshua Fairfield, "Smart Contracts, Bitcoin Bots, and Consumer Protection," *Washington and Lee Law Review Online* 71 (2014): 36, https://scholarlycommons.law.wlu.edu/wlulr-online/vol71/iss2/3. It is unclear why service providers would budge.

28. Adam Greenfield, *Radical Technologies: The Design of Everyday Life* (London and New York: Verso, 2017), 161.

29. David Weinberger, "Copy Protection Is a Crime," *Wired*, June 1, 2003, https://www.wired.com/2003/06/copy-protection-is-a-crime.

30. Satoshi Nakamoto, "Re: Bitcoin P2P E-cash Paper," Cryptography mailing list, November 17, 2008, 9:04:47 a.m., https://www.mail-archive.com/cryptography@metzdowd.com/msg10006.html.

31. For example, see Tapscott and Tapscott, *Blockchain Revolution*, 109; Andrew Keys, "Memo from Davos: We Have a Trust Problem. Personal Responsibility and Ethereum Are the Solutions," *Consensys Blog*, January 19, 2017, https://media.consensys

.net/memo-from-davos-we-have-a-trust-problem-personal-responsibility-and
-ethereum-are-the-solutions-19d1104946d8.c46zvkcks.

32. Harry Surden, "Computable Contracts," *U.C. Davis Law Review* 46 (2012): 629.

33. "Explanation of Terms and Disclaimer," The DAO, https://archive.fo/0trrl.

34. Oliver D. Hart, "Incomplete Contracts and the Theory of the Firm," *Journal of Law, Economics, and Organization* 4 (1998): 119, 123.

35. Ian R. Macneil, "Contracts: Adjustment of Long-Term Economic Relations Under Classical, Neoclassical, and Relational Contract Law," *Northwestern University Law Review* 72 (1978): 854.

36. Both the common law and the statutory regime of the Uniform Commercial Code (UCC) offer a variety of such gap-filling rules.

37. Sinclair Davidson, Primavera De Filippi, and Jason Potts, "Economics of Blockchain," 2016 Public Choice Conference, https://papers.ssrn.com/sol3/papers.cfm?abstract_id=27447. In economic terms, blockchain-based systems assume that contracts are complete, meaning that they specify outcomes for every possible state of the world. This is quite often not the case in reality.

38. Anna Irrera, "U.S. Blockchain Startups R3 and Ripple in Legal Battle," Reuters, September 8, 2017, https://www.reuters.com/article/us-r3-ripple-lawsuit/blockchain-startup-r3-sues-competitor-ripple-idUSKCN1BJ27I.

39. Frank B. Cross, "Law and Trust," *Georgetown Law Journal* 93 (2005): 1457-1545; Tamar Frankel and Wendy J. Gordon, eds., "Symposium: Trust Relationships," *Boston University Law Review* 81 (2001): 321-478; Tom R. Tyler, *Why People Obey the Law* (Princeton, NJ: Princeton University Press, 2006); Sim B. Sitkin and Robert J. Bies, "The Legalistic Organization: Definitions, Dimensions, and Dilemmas," *Organization Science* 4, no. 3 (1993): 345–351.

40. Mary Ann Glendon, *Rights Talk: The Impoverishment of Political Discourse* (New York: Free Press, 1994); Philip K. Howard, *The Death of Common Sense: How Law Is Suffocating America* (New York: Random House, 2011); Robert A. Kagan, *Adversarial Legalism: The American Way of Law* (Cambridge, MA: Harvard University Press, 2009).

41. Deepak Malhotra and J. Keith Murnighan, "The Effects of Contracts on Interpersonal Trust," *Administrative Science Quarterly* 47, no. 3 (2002): 534–559; Laetitia Mulder, Eric van Dijk, David De Cremer, and Henk A. M. Wilke, "Undermining Trust and Cooperation: The Paradox of Sanctioning Systems in Social Dilemmas," *Journal of Experimental Social Psychology* 42 (March 1, 2006): 147–162.

42. David Charny, "Nonlegal Sanctions in Commercial Relationships," *Harvard Law Review* 104 (1990): 428.

43. Oliver E. Williamson, "Calculativeness, Trust, and Economic Organization," *Journal of Law & Economics* 36, no. 1 (1993): 463 ("[I]t ... can be misleading to use the term 'trust' to describe commercial exchange for which cost-effective safeguards have been devised in support of more efficient exchange. ...").

44. Fernando L. Flores and Robert C. Solomon, "Rethinking Trust," *Business & Professional Ethics Journal* 16, no. 1/3 (1997): 47–76.

45. R. K. Woolthuis, "Trust, Contract, and Relationship Development," *Organization Studies* 26, no. 6 (June 1, 2005): 813–40.

46. I give credit to Ifeoma Ajunwa for helping me clarify this formulation.

47. See chapter 1. The DTCC operates in the United States. There are similar central securities depositories in all other major financial markets.

48. Steven Davidoff Solomon, "Dole Case Illustrates Problems in Shareholder System," *The New York Times*, March 21, 2017, "DealBook" section, https://www.nytimes.com/2017/03/21/business/dealbook/dole-case-illustrates-problems-in-shareholder-system.html.

49. Matt Levine, "Dole Food Had Too Many Shares," Bloomberg.com, February 17, 2017, https://www.bloomberg.com/view/articles/2017-02-17/dole-food-had-too-many-shares.

50. Kyle Torpey, "Chicago's Cook County to Test Bitcoin Blockchain-Based Property Title Transfer," *Bitcoin Magazine*, October 6, 2016, https://bitcoinmagazine.com/articles/chicago-s-cook-county-to-test-bitcoin-blockchain-based-public-records-1475768860.

51. James Schneider, Alexander Blostein, Brian Lee, Steven Kent, Ingrid Groer, and Eric Beardsley, *Profiles in Innovation: Blockchain—Putting Theory into Practice* (Goldman Sachs, May 24, 2016), https://www.finyear.com/attachment/690548.

52. Karl Baker, "Delaware Eases Off Early Blockchain Zeal After Concerns Over Disruption to Business," Delaware Online, February 1, 2018, https://www.delawareonline.com/story/news/2018/02/02/delaware-eases-off-early-blockchain-zeal-after-concerns-over-disruption-business/1082536001/.

53. Jerry Brito and Bridget C. E. Dooling, "An Orphan Works Affirmative Defense to Copyright Infringement Actions," *Michigan Telecommunications and Technology Law Review* 12 (2005): 75.

54. U.S. Copyright Office, "In re Orphan Works," No. 537, Comment of the Carnegie Mellon University Libraries, March 22, 2005, https://www.copyright.gov/orphan/comments/OW0537-CarnegieMellon.pdf.

55. Patrick Murck, "Waste Content: Rebalancing Copyright Law to Enable Markets of Abundance," *Albany Law Journal of Science and Technology* 16 (2006): 383-422.

56. Jake Goldenfein and Dan Hunter, "Blockchains, Orphan Works, and the Public Domain," *Columbia Journal of Law and the Arts* 41 (2017): 1–43. A registry for the works themselves would be more desirable. However, no mandatory copyright registry is permitted, thanks to the prohibition on formalities in international copyright agreements.

57. Similarly, the blockchain could be used to create unique digital assets that allow for a digital version of copyright's longstanding first sale doctrine. Patrick Murck, "The True Value of Bitcoin," *CATO Unbound,* July 31, 2013, https://www.cato-unbound .org/2013/07/31/patrick-murck/true-value-bitcoin.

58. Kevin Gallagher, "Ad Fraud Estimates Double," *Business Insider,* March 16, 2017, http://www.businessinsider.com/ad-fraud-estimates-doubled-2017-3.

59. "MetaX and DMA Join Forces to Launch AdChain: A Blockchain Solution to Digital Advertising Fraud," TheDMA.org, June 12, 2017, https://thedma.org/news /metax-dma-adchain-blockchain-solution-ethereum-advertising-fraud/.

60. Joel Valenzuela, "Uber Switches to Bitcoin in Argentina after Govt Blocks Uber Credit Cards," *CoinTelegraph,* July 6, 2016, https://cointelegraph.com/news/uber -switches-to-bitcoin-in-argentina-after-govt-blocks-uber-credit-cards.

61. The Buenos Aires government could not block Uber riders from using the distributed Bitcoin network. However, it could probably issue an order against the Swiss firm, Xapo, that provided the debit cards that translate between bitcoin and the local currency.

62. Hernando de Soto, *The Mystery of Capital: Why Capitalism Triumphs in the West and Fails Everywhere Else* (New York: Basic Books, 2000).

63. Laura Shin, "Republic of Georgia to Pilot Land Titling on Blockchain with Economist Hernando De Soto, BitFury," *Forbes,* April 21, 2016, https://www.forbes.com /sites/laurashin/2016/04/21/republic-of-georgia-to-pilot-land-titling-on-blockchain -with-economist-hernando-de-soto-bitfury/#bb3668f44da3; Roger Aitken, "Bitland's African Blockchain Initiative Putting Land on the Ledger," *Forbes,* April 5, 2016, https://www.forbes.com/sites/rogeraitken/2016/04/05/bitlands-african-blockchain -initiative-putting-land-on-the-ledger/59ee9ab11029.

64. Pete Rizzo, "Blockchain Land Title Project 'Stalls' in Honduras," *CoinDesk,* December 26, 2015, https://www.coindesk.com/debate-factom-land-title-honduras.

65. Kevin Mwanz and Henry Wilkins, African Startups Bet on Blockchain to Tackle Land Fraud, Reuters, February 16, 2018, https://www.reuters.com/article/us-africa -landrights-blockchain/african-startups-bet-on-blockchain-to-tackle-land-fraud -idUSKCN1G00YK

66. Tapscott and Tapscott, *Blockchain Revolution,* 188–192.

67. Michael del Castillo, "United Nations Sends Aid to 10,000 Syrian Refugees Using Ethereum Blockchain," *CoinDesk,* June 13, 2017, https://www.coindesk.com/united -nations-sends-aid-to-10000-syrian-refugees-using-ethereum-blockchain.

Chapter 9

1. N.Y. Comp. Codes R. & Regs. tit. 23, § 200 et seq. (2016).

2. New York Department of Financial Services, "NYDFS Announces Final BitLicense Framework for Regulating Digital Currency Firms," June 3, 2015, https://web.archive .org/web/20150604023248/http://www.dfs.ny.gov/about/speeches/sp1506031.htm.

3. "Comments Regarding the Proposed Virtual Currency Regulatory Framework," New York Department of Financial Services, http://www.dfs.ny.gov/legal/vcrf_com ments.htm.

4. Daniel Roberts, "Behind the 'Exodus' of Bitcoin Startups from New York," *Fortune,* August 14, 2015, http://fortune.com/2015/08/14/bitcoin-startups-leave-new -york-bitlicense.

5. Michael del Castillo, "The 'Great Bitcoin Exodus' Has Totally Changed New York's Bitcoin Ecosystem," *New York Business Journal,* August 12, 2015, https://www .bizjournals.com/newyork/news/2015/08/12/the-great-bitcoin-exodus-has-totally -changed-new.html.

6. N.Y. Comp. Codes R. & Regs. tit. 23, § 200.2(q)(2)–(5) (2016).

7. Yessi Bello Perez, "The Real Cost of Applying for a New York BitLicense," *CoinDesk,* August 13, 2015, https://www.coindesk.com/real-cost-applying-new-york-bitlicense.

8. Michael del Castillo, "Bitcoin Exchange Coinbase Receives New York BitLicense," *CoinDesk,* January 17, 2017, https://www.coindesk.com/bitcoin-exchange-coinbase -receives-bitlicense.

9. Provision of Interstate & Int'l Interexchange Telecomms. Serv. via the "Internet" by Non-Tariffed, Uncertified Entities, Petition for Declaratory Ruling, Special Relief, & Institution of Rulemaking, Rulemaking No. 8775, March 4, 1995, https://transition .fcc.gov/Bureaus/Common_Carrier/Comments/actapet.html.

10. Kevin Werbach, "Off the Hook," *Cornell Law Review* 95 (2010): 535, 564–565.

11. "Federal Communications Commission, Voice Telephone Services: Status as of June 30, 2016," https://apps.fcc.gov/edocs_public/attachmatch/DOC-344500A1.pdf.

12. Ironically, a class-action lawsuit led by Christopher Strunk, arguing that unfair competition from Bitcoin-based operators undermined his efforts to start a private banking business, reads almost exactly like the 1995 ACTA petition against VOIP. Tabish Faraz, "Bitcoin Fraud & Unfair Competition Class Action Lawsuit Filed,"

CoinReport, October 1, 2017, https://coinreport.net/bitcoin-fraud-unfair-competition -class-action-lawsuit-filed/. The plaintiff attempted to sue Satoshi Nakamoto for promoting fraudulent activity through Bitcoin, which will make an interesting hearing if the suit gets into court.

13. Stephen Palley, "Blockchain Jurisdiction," LinkedIn, May 11, 2016, https://www .linkedin.com/pulse/blockchain-jurisdiction-stephen-palley.

14. *United States v. Budovsky,* 2015 U.S. Dist. LEXIS 127717 (D. S.D.N.Y. 2015).

15. Selena Larson, "WannaCry: Someone Has Emptied Ransom Accounts Tied to the Cyberattack," CNNMoney, August 3, 2017, http://money.cnn.com/2017/08/03 /technology/wannacry-bitcoin-ransom-moved/index.html.

16. Jeff John Roberts, "Companies Can Put Shareholders on a Blockchain Starting Today," *Fortune,* August 1, 2017, http://fortune.com/2017/08/01/blockchain -shareholders-law.

17. Stan Higgins, "Arizona Governor Signs Blockchain Bill into Law," *CoinDesk,* March 31, 2017, https://www.coindesk.com/arizona-governor-signs-blockchain-bill-law.

18. Vermont Statutes Online, https://legislature.vermont.gov/statutes/section/12 /081/01913.

19. Delaware Senate Bill 69 (2017), https://legiscan.com/DE/text/SB69/2017.

20. 15 U.S. Code § 7001(a)(1).

21. Securities Act of 1933, Pub. L. 73–22, 48 Stat. 74, codified at 15 U.S.C. § 77a et seq.; Securities Exchange Act of 1934, Pub.L. 73–291, 48 Stat. 881, codified at 15 U.S.C. § 78a et seq.

22. *SEC v. W.J. Howey Co.,* 328 U.S. 293 (1946).

23. Jonathan Rohr and Aaron Wright, "Blockchain-Based Token Sales, Initial Coin Offerings, and the Democratization of Public Capital Markets," Social Science Research Network (SSRN), October 5, 2017, https://papers.ssrn.com/sol3/papers.cfm ?abstract_id=3048104. Even if ICOs are not regulated securities or investment contracts, their issuers may face legal obligations. As Valerie Szczepanik, the head of the SEC's distributed-ledger task force, has stated, "Whether or not you are regulated by the SEC, you still have fiduciary duties to your investor. If you want this industry to flourish, protection of investors should be at the forefront." "U.S. SEC Official Urges Companies Issuing Tokens to Protect Investors," Reuters, May 26, 2017, https: //www.reuters.com/article/us-sec-blockchain/sec-official-urges-companies-issuing -tokens-to-protect-investors-idUSKBN18K05Q.

24. Securities and Exchange Commission (SEC), "Report of Investigation Pursuant to Section 21(a) of the Securities Exchange Act of 1934: The DAO," Release No. 81207, July 25, 2017, https://www.sec.gov/litigation/investreport/34-81207.pdf.

25. Wolfie Zhao, "Bitfinex to Bar US Customers from Exchange Trading," *CoinDesk*, August 11, 2017, https://www.coindesk.com/bitfinex-suspends-sale-select-ico-tokens -citing-sec-concerns/.

26. Emily, "ShapeShift and Tokens as Securities," *ShapeShift*, August 17, 2017, https: //info.shapeshift.io/blog/2017/08/17/shapeshift-and-tokens-securities.

27. Laura Shin, "After Contact by SEC, Protostarr Token Shuts Down Post-ICO, Will Refund Investors," *Forbes*, September 1, 2017, https://www.forbes.com/sites/laura shin/2017/09/01/after-contact-by-sec-protostarr-token-shuts-down-post-ico-will -refund-investors.

28. A Polybius executive acknowledged on a message board that its tokens would be considered securities under U.S. law, giving this as a reason why they are not listed on U.S.-based exchanges. Bears, "Re: [ANN][ICO] Polybius—Regulated Bank for the Blockchain Generation," *BitcoinTalk Bitcoin Forum*, July 25, 2017, 1:44:06 p.m., https: //bitcointalk.org/index.php?topic=1848751.4180.

29. "FAQ," Polybius, https://polybius.io/en/faq.

30. Jon Russell, "First China, Now South Korea Has Banned ICOs," *TechCrunch*, September 28, 2017, http://techcrunch.com/2017/09/28/south-korea-has-banned-icos.

31. Tokens subject to airdrops can still be classified as securities, but the issuers are in a stronger position in claiming that utility rather than investment profit was their primary purpose.

32. In the Matter of Munchee, Inc., Securities and Exchange Commission, Order Instituting Cease-and-Desist Proceedings Pursuant to Section 8a of the Securities Act of 1933, Making Findings, and Imposing a Cease-and-Desist Order, Release No. 10445, December 11, 2017, https://www.sec.gov/litigation/admin/2017/33-10445 .pdf.

33. Jonathan Rohr and Aaron Wright, "Blockchain-Based Token Sales, Initial Coin Offerings, and the Democratization of Public Capital Markets," Social Science Research Network (SSRN), October 4, 2017, https://ssrn.com/abstract=3048104.

34. Olga Kharif, "Only One in 10 Tokens Is in Use Following Initial Coin Offerings," Bloomberg.com, October 23, 2017, https://www.bloomberg.com/news/articles/2017 -10-23/only-one-in-10-tokens-is-in-use-following-initial-coin-offerings.

35. Paul Vigna, "Tezos Raised $232 Million in a Hot Coin Offering, Then a Fight Broke Out," *Wall Street Journal*, October 18, 2017, "Markets" section, https://www .wsj.com/articles/tezos-raised-232-million-in-a-hot-coin-offering-then-a-fight-broke -out-1508354704; "Special Report: Backroom Battle Imperils $230 Million Crypto-currency Venture," Reuters, October 19, 2017, https://www.reuters.com/article/us -bitcoin-funding-tezos-specialreport/special-report-backroom-battle-imperils-230 -million-cryptocurrency-venture-idUSKBN1CN35K.

36. Jen Wieczner, "Tezos Finally Plans to Launch ICO Coin After Ousting Swiss Foundation Head," *Fortune*, February 22, 2018, http://fortune.com/2018/02/22/tezos -coin-ico-launch-foundation.

37. Microsoft's chief technology officer, Nathan Myhrvold, called this a "vig," a gambling term for a bookmaker's fee. Ken Auletta, "The Microsoft Provocateur," *The New Yorker*, May 5, 1997, https://www.newyorker.com/magazine/1997/05/12/the -microsoft-provocateur.

38. Camila Russo, "Ethereum Co-Founder Says the Crypto Coin Market Is a Ticking Time-Bomb," Bloomberg.com, July 18, 2017, https://www.bloomberg.com/news /articles/2017-07-18/ethereum-co-founder-says-crypto-coin-market-is-ticking-time -bomb (quoting Ripple CEO Brad Garlinghouse, who said, "ICOs operating in the Wild West of finance is [sic] not sustainable," and "If it talks like a duck and walks like a duck, the SEC will say it is a duck.").

39. Richard Kastelein, "Global Blockchain Innovation: U.S. Lags, Europe and China Lead," *VentureBeat*, April 16, 2017, https://venturebeat.com/2017/04/16/global -blockchain-innovation-u-s-lags-europe-and-china-lead.

40. "MAS Clarifies Regulatory Position on the Offer of Digital Tokens in Singapore," Monetary Authority of Singapore (MAS), August 1, 2017, http://www.mas.gov.sg /News-and-Publications/Media-Releases/2017/MAS-clarifies-regulatory-position-on -the-offer-of-digital-tokens-in-Singapore.aspx.

41. Peter Van Valkenburgh, "The ULC's Model Act for Digital Currency Businesses Has Passed. Here's Why It's Good for Bitcoin," Coin Center, July 19, 2017, https:// coincenter.org/entry/the-ulc-s-model-act-for-digital-currency-businesses-has-passed -here-s-why-it-s-good-for-bitcoin.

42. Lucinda Shen, "Bitcoin Traders Are Relieved at CFTC and SEC Cryptocurrency Senate Hearing Testimony," *Fortune*, February 7, 2018, http://fortune.com/2018/02 /06/bitcoin-price-cftc-sec-cryptocurrency-hearing.

43. Robert P. Merges, "A New Dynamism in the Public Domain," *University of Chicago Law Review* 71 (2004): 183.

44. *MGM Studios, Inc. v. Grokster, Ltd.*, 545 U.S. 913 (2005).

45. There will be times when "legitimate" purposes are contested. The suggested approach would start with the easier cases, in which there is consensus about the basic objectives and legitimacy of the legal rules.

46. Andy Greenberg, "The Fed-Proof Online Market OpenBazaar Is Going Anonymous," *Wired*, March 6, 2017, https://www.wired.com/2017/03/fed-proof-online -market-openbazaar-going-anonymous.

47. The analogue in the file-sharing world is BitTorrent, a widely used protocol for sharing video files. Illicit services widely use BitTorrent's open-source technology.

However, regulators have not gone after BitTorrent, Inc. or its founder, Bram Cohen, because they are not bad actors. They operate services that exclude unauthorized content, and they offer them based on the performance improvements or cost savings of the technology. Eric Bangeman, "BitTorrent Creator, MPAA Strike Deal," Ars Technica, November 23, 2005, https://arstechnica.com/uncategorized/2005/11/5615-2.

48. "Frequently Asked Questions," OpenBazaar Docs, https://docs.openbazaar.org /09.-Frequently-Asked-Questions.

49. "Overstock.com Announces Historic Blockchain Public Offering," Overstock.com, March 16, 2016, http://investors.overstock.com/mobile.view?c=131091&v=203&d=1 &id=2230245.

50. "LedgerX Gets U.S. Approval for Derivatives on Digital Currencies," Reuters, July 24, 2017, https://www.reuters.com/article/us-usa-cftc-digitalcurrency/cftc-approves -ledgerx-license-to-clear-settle-digital-currency-derivative-contracts-idUSKBN1A92FZ.

51. Nathaniel Popper, "S.E.C. Rejects Winklevoss Brothers' Bid to Create Bitcoin E.T.F.," *New York Times*, March 10, 2017, "DealBook" section, https://www.nytimes .com/2017/03/10/business/dealbook/winkelvoss-brothers-bid-to-create-a-bitcoin-etf -is-rejected.html.

52. Interview with author, October 18, 2017.

53. Lily Katz and Benjamin Bain, "Winklevoss Twins Have a Plan to Police Cryptocurrency Trading," Bloomberg Markets, March 13, 2018, https://www.bloomberg.com /news/articles/2018-03-13/winklevoss-twins-have-a-plan-to-police-cryptocurrency -trading.

54. Jay Clayton, "Statement on Cryptocurrencies and Initial Coin Offerings," SEC .gov, December 11, 2017, https://www.sec.gov/news/public-statement/statement -clayton-2017-12-11.

55. "SEC Announces Enforcement Initiatives to Combat Cyber-Based Threats and Protect Retail Investors," SEC.gov, September 25, 2017, https://www.sec.gov/news /press-release/2017-176.

56. Federal Communications Commission (FCC), "Petition for Declaratory Ruling that Pulver.com's Free World Dialup Is Neither Telecommunications nor a Telecommunications Service," *FCC Record* 19 (2004): 3307, 3312–3324.

57. "Petition for Declaratory Ruling that AT&T's Phone-to-Phone IP Telephony Services Are Exempt from Access Charges," *FCC Record* 19 (2004), 7457, 7465–7468.

Chapter 10

1. Nathaniel Popper, "Decoding the Enigma of Satoshi Nakamoto and the Birth of Bitcoin," *New York Times*, May 15, 2015, "Business Day" section, https://www.nytimes .com/2015/05/17/business/decoding-the-enigma-of-satoshi-nakamoto-and-the-birth

-of-bitcoin.html. A linguistic analysis pointed to Szabo as the creator of Bitcoin. Kim Lachance Shandrow, "Who the Heck Is Nick Szabo and Is He the Real Father of Bitcoin?" *Entrepreneur*, April 16, 2014, https://www.entrepreneur.com/article/233143.

2. Amusingly, reports about Szabo often falsely describe him as a law or economics professor.

3. Tim Ferriss, "The Quiet Master of Cryptocurrency—Nick Szabo," *Tim Ferriss Show*, June 4, 2017, https://tim.blog/2017/06/04/nick-szabo.

4. Bruce A. Ackerman, *We the People. 1: Foundations* (Cambridge, MA: Harvard University Press, 1993).

5. Communications Decency Act of 1996, Pub. L. No. 104–104, § 502, 110 Stat. 133, 134–35 (codified as amended at 47 U.S.C. § 223 (2012)); Pub. L. No. 105–304, § 202, 112 Stat. 2860, 2877–78 (codified as amended at 17 U.S.C. § 512 (2012)).

6. Peter Van Valkenburgh, "Congress Should Create a Blockchain Technology Safe Harbor. Luckily They Already Figured It Out in the '90s," Coin Center, April 6, 2017, https://coincenter.org/entry/congress-should-create-a-blockchain-technology-safe -harbor-luckily-they-already-figured-it-out-in-the-90s.

7. "Financial Conduct Authority Provides Update on Regulatory Sandbox," Financial Conduct Authority, June 15, 2017, https://www.fca.org.uk/news/press-releases /financial-conduct-authority-provides-update-regulatory-sandbox.

8. Financial Conduct Authority, *Regulatory Sandbox Lessons Learned Report*, October 2017, https://www.fca.org.uk/publication/research-and-data/regulatory-sandbox -lessons-learned-report.pdf.

9. "CFTC Launches LabCFTC as Major FinTech Initiative," Commodity Futures Trading Commission, May 17, 2017, http://www.cftc.gov/PressRoom/PressReleases /pr7558-17.

10. Christopher D. Clack, Vikram A. Bakshi, and Lee Braine, "Smart Contract Templates: Foundations, Design Landscape, and Research Directions," arXiv Preprint 1608.00771 (2016), https://arxiv.org/pdf/1608.00771.pdf. (This document defines "operational aspect" as "the parts of the contract that we wish to automate, which typically derive from consideration of precise actions to be taken by the parties and therefore are concerned with performing the contract.").

11. Or perhaps it would create a new niche for legal hackers. Following the attack on The DAO, security expert Robert Graham suggested that "in the past, people hired lawyers to review complicated contracts. In the future, they'll need to hire hackers. After a contract is signed, I am now motivated to hire a very good hacker that will keep reading the code until they can find some hack to my advantage." Robert Graham, "Ethereum/TheDAO Attack Simplified," Errata Security, June 18, 2016, https://blog.erratasec.com/2016/06/etheriumdao-hack-similfied.html.

12. There are already technical auditing firms that review smart-contract code for bugs or security vulnerabilities. Alyssa Hertig, "Blockchain Veterans Unveil Secure Smart Contracts Framework," *CoinDesk,* September 15, 2016, https://www.coindesk.com /blockchain-veterans-unveil-secure-smart-contracts-framework. Traditional auditing firms are also considering how they might participate in this new world. As PWC blockchain strategist Grainne McNamara stated at a financial services conference, "We're looking at how to audit the technology using the technology." American Banker Blockchains + Digital Currencies Conference, New York, NY (June 13, 2017) (transcribed by author), http://conference.americanbanker.com/conferences/blockchains.

13. "Introducing OpenLaw," Consensys, July 25, 2017, https://media.consensys.net /introducing-openlaw-7a2ea410138b.

14. "Clause.io Sets out Strategy with Its Smart Contract Engine," Artificial Lawyer, July 6, 2017, https://www.artificiallawyer.com/2017/07/06/clause-io-sets-out-strategy -with-its-smart-contract-engine; "Agrello Becomes 1st LegalTech Co. to Launch Its Own Digital Currency," Artificial Lawyer, July 17, 2017, https://www.artificiallawyer .com/2017/07/17/agrello-becomes-1st-legaltech-co-to-launch-its-own-digital -currency/.

15. Clack et al., "Smart Contract Templates."

16. Tim Hazard and Thomas Hardjono, "CommonAccord: Towards a Foundation for Smart Contracts in Future Blockchains,"W3C Position Paper, June 9,2016, https:// www.w3.org/2016/04/blockchain-workshop/interest/hazard-hardjono.html; Judith Balea,"Singapore Startup's Audacious Goal to Create a Programming Language for the Legal Industry," TechInAsia, January 9,2017, https://www.techinasia.com/singapore -legalese-audacious-goal-to-create-a-programming-language-for-the-legal-industry.

17. Juan Batiz-Benet, Jesse Clayburgh, and Marco Santori, "The SAFT Project: Toward a Compliant Token Sale Framework," October 2, 2017, https://saftproject.com/static /SAFT-Project-Whitepaper.pdf.

18. Stan Higgins, "$200 Million in 60 Minutes: Filecoin ICO Rockets to Record amid Tech Issues," *CoinDesk,* August 10, 2017, https://www.coindesk.com/200-million-60 -minutes-filecoin-ico-rockets-record-amid-tech-issues.

19. The SAFT transaction is acknowledged to be a regulated investment contract because there is no operational network in which buyers might participate.

20. "Cryptocurrency Exchanges Are Increasingly Roiled with These Problems," Reuters, September 29, 2017, http://fortune.com/2017/09/29/cryptocurrency-exchanges -hackings-chaos.

21. Stan Higgins, "Ethereum Traders File Class Action Lawsuit over Kraken Flash Crash," *CoinDesk,* July 5, 2017, https://www.coindesk.com/ethereum-class-action -lawsuit-filed-against-digital-currency-exchange-kraken.

22. Corrado Rizzi, "Five File Class Action against Kraken over May 7 Ether Cryptocurrency 'Flash' Crash," ClassAction.org, July 5, 2017, https://www.classaction.org/news/five-file-class-action-against-kraken-over-may-7-ether-cryptocurrency-flash-crash.

23. Securities and Exchange Commission (SEC), "Report of Investigation Pursuant to Section 21(a) of the Securities Exchange Act of 1934: The DAO."

24. All eleven of The DAO's curators were either employees of the Ethereum Foundation or key members of its development team. Stephan Tual, "Vitalik Buterin, Gavin Wood, Alex van De Sande, Vlad Zamfir Announced amongst Exceptional DAO Curators," *Slockit Blog*, April 25, 2016, https://blog.slock.it/vitalik-buterin-gavin-wood-alex-van-de-sande-vlad-zamfir-announced-amongst-stellar-dao-curators-44be4d12dd6e.

25. Jack Balkin, "Information Fiduciaries in the Digital Age," Balkinization, March 5, 2014, https://balkin.blogspot.com/2014/03/information-fiduciaries-in-digital-age.html; Jonathan Zittrain, "Facebook Could Decide an Election without Anyone Ever Finding Out," *New Republic*, June 1, 2014, https://www.newrepublic.com/article/117878/information-fiduciary-solution-facebook-digital-gerrymandering.

26. Angela Walch, "Call Blockchain Developers What They Are: Fiduciaries," *American Banker*, August 9, 2016, https://www.americanbanker.com/opinion/call-blockchain-developers-what-they-are-fiduciaries.

27. This is true only once the network is operating and tokens are trading. ICO groups raising funds for preoperational blockchain systems could, in theory, take the money and run.

28. Kevin Werbach and Nicolas Cornell, "Contracts ex Machina," *Duke Law Journal* 67 (2017): 101–170.

29. Ian Grigg, "The Ricardian Contract," First IEEE Workshop on Electronic Contracting, San Diego, CA (2004), https://www.researchgate.net/publication/4085229_The_Ricardian_contract.

30. The Ricardo platform that Grigg was building never took off.

31. Bailey Reutzel, "BNP Paribas Works with Blockchain Startup to Open Source Law," *CoinDesk*, May 5, 2016, https://www.coindesk.com/commonaccord-legal-smart-contracts-prove-beneficial-one-bank-veritcal/; Ian Allison, "Barclays' Smart Contract Templates Stars in First Ever Public Demo of R3's Corda Platform," *International Business Times*, April 18, 2016, http://www.ibtimes.co.uk/barclays-smart-contract-templates-heralds-first-ever-public-demo-r3s-corda-platform-1555329.

32. "Putting the Contracts in Smart Contracts," Eris:Legal, http://archive.fo/BRe4n.

33. "Introducing OpenLaw."

34. In the wake of the attack on The DAO, researchers have proposed technical mechanisms tantamount to the recission of smart contracts, without necessarily

involving judicial actors. For example, Ittay Eyal and Emin Gün Sirer, "A Decentralized Escape Hatch for DAOs," Hacking, Distributed, July 11, 2016, hackingdistributed.com/2016/07/11/decentralized-escape-hatches-for-smart-contracts/; Bill Marino and Ari Juels, "Setting Standards for Altering and Undoing Smart Contracts," International Symposium on Rules and Rule Markup Languages for the Semantic Web, New York, NY (2016).

35. Stefan Thomas and Evan Schwartz, "Smart Oracles: A Simple, Powerful Approach to Smart Contracts," GitHub, July 17, 2014, https://github.com/codius/codius/wiki /Smart-Oracles:-A-Simple,-Powerful-Approach-to-Smart-Contracts.

36. Maria Terekhova, "Thomson Reuters Is Making a Blockchain Push," *Business Insider,* June 15, 2017, http://www.businessinsider.com/thomson-reuters-is-making -a-blockchain-push-2017-6; "Thomson Reuters Makes Its Market Data Blockchain-Friendly," Reuters, June 14, 2017, http://www.businessinsider.com/r-thomson-reuters -makes-its-market-data-blockchain-friendly-2017-6.

37. Oraclize. Home page, http://www.oraclize.it.

38. Aaron Wright and Primavera De Filippi, "Decentralized Blockchain Technology and the Rise of Lex Cryptographia," Social Science Research Network (SSRN), March 10, 2015, https://ssrn.com/abstract=2580664, 50.

39. Balaji S. Srinivasan, "Thoughts on Tokens," News.21.co, May 27, 2017, https:// medium.com/@balajis/thoughts-on-tokens-436109aabcbe.

40. Ethereum creator Vitalik Buterin has speculated about a regime of "decentralized courts" to resolve disputes. Vitalik Buterin, "Decentralized Court," Reddit /r/etherium, April 26, 2016, https://www.reddit.com/r/ethereum/comments/4gigyd/decentralized _court/; Izabella Kaminska, "Decentralised Courts and Blockchains," FT Alphaville, April 29, 2016, https://ftalphaville.ft.com/2016/04/29/2160502/decentralised-courts -and-blockchains/.

41. Luke A. Walker, "ICANN's Uniform Domain Name Dispute Resolution Policy," *Berkeley Technology Law Journal* 15 (2000): 289.

42. Michael Abramowicz, "Cryptocurrency-based Law," *Arizona Law Review* 58 (2016), 405.

43. Michael del Castillo, "Lawyers Be DAMNed: Andreas Antonopoulos Takes Aim at Arbitration with DAO Proposal," *CoinDesk,* May 26, 2016, https://www.coindesk .com/damned-dao-andreas-antonopoulos-third-key/. The proposal was based on the New York Convention, under which sixty-five countries agreed that their courts would enforce decisions of recognized arbitrators.

44. "Mattereum Draft for Public Comment," Google Docs, https://docs.google.com /document/d/1H18vvIurp8s1lSZnZx4zkDzTCnz5gxC0W0a7nGKXECA.

45. James Grimmelmann and Arvind Narayanan, "The Blockchain Gang," Slate .com, "Future Tense" section, February 16, 2017, http://www.slate.com/articles /technology/future_tense/2016/02/bitcoin_s_blockchain_technology_won_t _change_everything.html.

46. Pete Rizzo, "Augur Bets on Bright Future for Blockchain Prediction Markets," *CoinDesk*, March 1, 2015, https://www.coindesk.com/augur-future-blockchain-pre diction-market/.

47. Tony Sakich, Jeremy Gardner, and Joey Krug, "What Is Reputation?" http:// augur.strikingly.com/blog/what-is-reputation.

48. Augur, "Augur Master Plan," June 9, 2017, https://medium.com/@AugurProject /augur-master-plan-42dda65a3e3d.

49. Augur's vision is interesting to compare to the system that Facebook CEO Mark Zuckerberg outlined in his February 2017 manifesto, "Building a Global Community," https://www.facebook.com/notes/mark-zuckerberg/building-global-community /10154544292806634/. Facebook faces the same kind of challenge that Augur does in policing activity on its service. What is considered ethical (or even legal) by one group of users may not be seen as such by another group. Facebook, however, hopes to use artificial intelligence (AI) to identify distinct communities and allow them leeway to define their own standards. Augur hopes to achieve something similar through a bottom-up cryptoeconomic mechanism.

50. Interview with author (October 18, 2017). Intriguingly, this perspective mirrors that of business ethics scholars suggesting that a limited set of common international "hypernorms" may be able to govern business conduct across cultures. Thomas Donaldson and Thomas W. Dunfee, *Ties That Bind: A Social Contracts Approach to Business Ethics* (Cambridge, MA: Harvard Business School Press, 1999): 27.

51. Tatu Kärki, "Aragon Network Jurisdiction Part 1: Decentralized Court," Aragon, July 18, 2017, https://blog.aragon.one/aragon-network-jurisdiction-part-1-decentralized -court-c8ab2a675e82.

52. Federal Arbitration Act, 9 U.S.C. §§ 1–16 (2012).

53. BIP stands for "Bitcoin Improvement Proposal." It is a mechanism to propose technical changes to Bitcoin for community review, based on the IETF's Request for Proposal process.

54. This process was technically referred to as BIP 91.

55. Sergio Demian Lerner, "Rootstock Platform: Bitcoin Powered Smart Contracts," November 19, 2015, https://uploads.strikinglycdn.com/files/90847694-70f0-4668 -ba7f-dd0c6b0b00a1/RootstockWhitePaperv9-Overview.pdf.

56. Christine Chiang, "Decred Launches Decentralized Voting Process for Blockchain Protocol Changes," Brave New Coin, June 17, 2017, https://bravenewcoin.com/news

/decred-launches-decentralized-voting-process-for-blockchain-protocol-changes/; Fred Ehrsam, "Blockchain Governance: Programming Our Future," *Medium*, November 27, 2017, https://medium.com/@FEhrsam/blockchain-governance-programming -our-future-c3bfe30f2d74; Nathana Sharma, "Building the Blockchain to End All Blockchains," Singularity Hub, October 8, 2017, https://singularityhub.com/2017/10 /08/building-the-blockchain-to-end-all-blockchains.

57. Vlad Zamfir, "Against On-Chain Governance," *Medium,* December 1, 2017, https://medium.com/@Vlad_Zamfir/against-on-chain-governance-a4ceacd040ca.

58. I label law as "subjective" in this procedural sense of representing the choices made by human communities. Jurisprudential theories such as natural law or law and economics argue that those choices converge to objective principles. The governance process involved is still ineluctably subjective. I do not mean to take a position on whether law is an expression of the power of dominant groups, as some would argue.

59. Adam Greenfield, *Radical Technologies: The Design of Everyday Life* (London: Verso, 2017), 168–170.

60. Douglass C. North, *Institutions, Institutional Change, and Economic Performance* (Cambridge: Cambridge University Press, 1990).

61. Tom R. Tyler, *Why People Obey the Law* (Princeton, NJ: Princeton University Press, 2006).

62. Andrew L. Russell, "'Rough Consensus and Running Code' and the Internet-OSI Standards War," *IEEE Annals of the History of Computing* 28, no. 3 (July 2006): 48–61, https://doi.org/10.1109/MAHC.2006.42.

63. Theymos, Reddit r/Bitcoin, November 3, 2015, https://www.reddit.com/r/Bitcoin /comments/3rejl9/coinbase_ceo_brian_armstrong_bip_101_is_the_best/cwoc8n5/.

64. Josh Fairfield, *Delta: The Law of Technological Change* (Cambridge University Press, forthcoming).

65. Oliver E. Williamson, "Calculativeness, Trust, and Economic Organization," *Journal of Law & Economics* 36, no. 1 (1993): 453–486.

Chapter 11

1. *The Unpredictable Certainty: Information Infrastructure Through 2000* (National Research Council, 1996), https://www.nap.edu/read/5130.

2. Ibid., at 7.

3. Ibid., at 4.

4. Ibid., at 12.

5. "May 26, 1995: Gates, Microsoft Jump on 'Internet Tidal Wave,'" *Wired*, May 26, 2010, https://www.wired.com/2010/05/0526bill-gates-internet-memo.

6. Farhad Manjoo, "Jurassic Web," *Slate*, February 24, 2009, http://www.slate.com /articles/technology/technology/2009/02/jurassic_web.html.

7. Roxanne Bauer, "Media (R)evolutions: Time Spent Online Continues to Rise," *People, Spaces, Deliberation*, February 10, 2016, http://blogs.worldbank.org/public-sphere/media-revolutions-time-spent-online-continues-rise.

8. Clifford Stoll, "Why the Web Won't Be Nirvana," *Newsweek*, February 26, 1995, http://www.newsweek.com/clifford-stoll-why-web-wont-be-nirvana-185306.

9. Joi Ito, "How Blockchain Is Like or Not Like the Internet," YouTube, January 18, 2015, https://www.youtube.com/watch?v=1E49s5D6-1A.

10. Marc Andreessen, "Why Bitcoin Matters," *New York Times*, January 21, 2014, "DealBook" section, https://dealbook.nytimes.com/2014/01/21/why-bitcoin-matters.

11. John Kennedy, "The Digital Revolution Needs a Trust Revolution, Tech Leaders Tell Davos," Silicon Republic, January 22, 2015, https://www.siliconrepublic.com /companies/the-digital-revolution-needs-a-trust-revolution-tech-leaders-tell-davos.

12. Internet Society, "Internet Facing Unprecedented Challenges; Time to Act Is Now Says Internet Society," news release, December 7, 2016, https://www.internetsociety.org /news/internet-facing-unprecedented-challenges-time-act-now-says-internet-society.

13. Francis Fukuyama, *Trust: The Social Virtues and the Creation of Prosperity* (New York: Free Press, 1995).

14. The original version of TLS was called secure sockets layer (SSL). Rolf Opplinger, *SSL and TLS: Theory and Practice* (Norwood, MA: Artech House, 2009), 67–69.

15. Chelsea Barabas, Neha Narula, and Ethan Zuckerman, "Defending Internet Freedom through Decentralization: Back to the Future?" MIT Media Lab, August 2017, 10.

16. Rachel Botsman, "We've Stopped Trusting Institutions and Started Trusting Strangers," TED Talk, June 2016, https://www.ted.com/talks/rachel_botsman_we_ve _stopped_trusting_institutions_and_started_trusting_strangers/transcript?language=en.

17. As Botsman observes, malicious actors can game these reputation systems. Rachel Botsman, *Who Can You Trust? How Technology Brought Us Together and Why It Might Drive Us Apart* (New York: PublicAffairs, 2017): 146–149.

18. Gus Hurwitz, "Trust and Online Interaction," *University of Pennsylvania Law Review* 161 (2013), 1588–1597 (arguing that the commercialization and growth of the Internet actually represented a loss of trust in online interactions).

19. Lina M. Khan, "Amazon's Antitrust Paradox," *Yale Law Journal* 126 (2017): 710, https://www.yalelawjournal.org/note/amazons-antitrust-paradox.

20. Jonathan T. Taplin, *Move Fast and Break Things: How Facebook, Google, and Amazon Cornered Culture and Undermined Democracy* (New York: Little, Brown and Company, 2017).

21. Franklin Foer, *World without Mind: The Existential Threat of Big Tech* (New York: Penguin Press, 2017); Siva Vaidhyanathan, *The Googlization of Everything: And Why We Should Worry* (Berkeley: University of California Press, 2011).

22. Alice Marwick and Rebecca Lewis, "Media Manipulation and Disinformation Online," *Data & Society*, May 15, 2017, https://datasociety.net/output/media-manipulation-and-disinfo-online.

23. Emin Gün Sirer (@el33th4xor), Twitter, October 23, 2017, 10:25 a.m., https://twitter.com/el33th4xor/status/922469133211578368.

24. Kate Conger, "Cloudflare CEO on Terminating Service to Neo-Nazi Site: 'The Daily Stormer Are Assholes,'" *Gizmodo*, October 4, 2017, https://gizmodo.com/cloudflare-ceo-on-terminating-service-to-neo-nazi-site-1797915295.

25. Vaidhyanathan, *The Googlization of Everything*.

26. Yochai Benkler, "Degrees of Freedom, Dimensions of Power," *Daedalus* 145, no. 1 (2016): 18–32, https://www.mitpressjournals.org/doi/abs/10.1162/DAED_a_00362.

27. Andreessen, "Why Bitcoin Matters"; Morgen E. Peck, "The Future of the Web Looks a Lot Like Bitcoin," *IEEE Spectrum*, July 1, 2015, https://spectrum.ieee.org/computing/networks/the-future-of-the-web-looks-a-lot-like-bitcoin.

28. Alec Liu, "What Happened to the Facebook Killer? It Is Complicated," Motherboard, October 2, 2012, https://motherboard.vice.com/blog/what-happened-to-the-facebook-killer-it-s-complicated.

29. Andy Oram, ed., *Peer-to-Peer: Harnessing the Benefits of a Disruptive Technology* (Cambridge, MA: O'Reilly, 2001).

30. Yochai Benkler, *The Wealth of Networks: How Social Production Transforms Markets and Freedom* (New Haven, CT: Yale University Press, 2006), 418–21.

31. Nicholas G. Carr, *The Big Switch: Rewiring the World, from Edison to Google* (New York: W.W. Norton, 2013).

32. Remarkably, Paul Baran and others of his time anticipated this development. Kevin Werbach, "The Network Utility," *Duke Law Journal* 60 (2010): 1761.

33. "Reweaving the Web," *The Economist*, June 18, 2016, https://www.economist.com/news/business/21700642-slew-startups-trying-decentralise-online-world-reweaving-web; Dan Gillmor and Kevin Marks, "How to Break Open the Web," *Fast Company*, June 29, 2016, https://www.fastcompany.com/3061357/the-web-decentralized-distributed-open; Joshua Kopstein, "The Mission to Decentralize the Internet,"

The New Yorker, December 12, 2013, https://www.newyorker.com/tech/elements/the
-mission-to-decentralize-the-internet.

34. Liat Clark, "Tim Berners-Lee: We Need to Re-Decentralize the Web," *Wired UK,*
February 6, 2014, http://www.wired.co.uk/article/tim-berners-lee-reclaim-the-web.

35. Quentin Hardy, "The Web's Creator Looks to Reinvent It," *New York Times,* June
7, 2016, https://www.nytimes.com/2016/06/08/technology/the-webs-creator-looks
-to-reinvent-it.html.

36. Kevin Werbach, *Digital Tornado: The Internet and Telecommunications Policy* (Federal Communications Commission Office of Plans and Policy, Working Paper No. 29,
1997), 10 n.12, https://www.fcc.gov/Bureaus/OPP/working_papers/oppwp29pdf.html;
Kevin Werbach, "Only Connect," *Berkeley Technology Law Journal* 22 (2008): 1233.

37. David D. Clark, "Interoperation, Open Interfaces, and Protocol Architectures," in
The Unpredictable Certainty: White Papers 133–135 (National Academies Press, 1998);
David D. Clark, "The Design Philosophy of the DARPA Internet Protocols," *Computer
Communications Review* 18 (1988): 106, http://ccr.sigcomm.org/archive/1995/jan95
/ccr-9501-clark.pdf.

38. Conceptually, this arrangement in which everyone commits to a fundamental
obligation in order to free themselves to act in other ways parallels Thomas Hobbes's
imagined story of the Leviathan.

39. Jerome Saltzer, David Reed, and David Clark, "End-to-End Arguments in System
Design," *ACM Transactions Computer System* 2, no. 4 (November 1984): 277–288,
https://doi.org/10.1145/357401.357402.

40. Mark A. Lemley and Lawrence Lessig, "The End of End-to-End: Preserving the
Architecture of the Internet in the Broadband Era," *UCLA Law Review* 48 (2001):
925–972.

41. Don Tapscott and Alex Tapscott, *Blockchain Revolution* (New York: Penguin
Random House, 2016), 12–14 (explaining enthusiasm for the blockchain as the "return
of the internet").

42. Lawrence Lessig, "Deja Vú All Over Again: Thinking Through Law & Code,
Again," Vimeo, December 11, 2015, https://vimeo.com/148665401.

43. Interview with author (October 24, 2017).

44. William Mougayar, *The Business Blockchain: Promise, Practice, and Application of
the Next Internet Technology* (Hoboken, NJ: John Wiley & Sons, 2016).

45. Mark Scott, "Google Fined Record $2.7 Billion in E.U. Antitrust Ruling," *The
New York Times,* June 27, 2017, "Technology" section, https://www.nytimes.com
/2017/06/27/technology/eu-google-fine.html.

46. Chris Dixon, "Crypto Tokens: A Breakthrough in Open Network Design," *Medium*, June 1, 2017, https://medium.com/@cdixon/crypto-tokens-a-breakthrough -in-open-network-design-e600975be2ef; Balaji Srinavasan, "Thoughts on Tokens," News.21.Co, May 27, 2017, https://news.21.co/thoughts-on-tokens-436109aabcbe; Joel Monegro, "Fat Protocols," *Union Square Ventures Blog*, August 8, 2016, http://www .usv.com/blog/fat-protocols.

47. Ethernet Name Service, https://ens.domains/; "Blockstack DNS vs. Traditional DNS," *BlockStack Blog*, https://blockstack.org/docs/blockstack-vs-dns.

48. "Blockstack and the Power of Choice," *BlockStack Blog*, July 24, 2017, https:// blockstack.org/blog/blockstack-and-the-power-of-choice/.

49. Christopher Allen, "The Path to Self-Sovereign Identity," *CoinDesk*, April 27, 2016, https://www.coindesk.com/path-self-sovereign-identity.

50. Decentralized Identity Foundation, "The Rising Tide of Decentralized Identity," *Medium*, October 11, 2017, https://medium.com/decentralized-identity/the-rising -tide-of-decentralized-identity-2e163e4ec663.

51. Interview with author (January 3, 2018).

52. Theo Douglas, "Illinois Announces Key Partnership in Birth Registry Blockchain Pilot," GovTech, September 8, 2017, http://www.govtech.com/data/Illinois-Announces -Key-Partnership-in-Birth-Registry-Blockchain-Pilot.html.

53. Stephan Tual, "Web 3.0 Revisited—Part Two: 'Introduction to Polkadot: What It Is, What It Ain't,'" StephanTual.com, July 9, 2017, https://blog.stephantual.com/web-three -revisited-part-two-introduction-to-polkadot-what-it-is-what-it-aint-657782051d34.

Chapter 12

1. "Mike Hearn: Autonomous Agents, Self Driving Cars and Bitcoin," YouTube, uploaded March 26, 2017, https://www.youtube.com/watch?v=MVyv4t0OKe4.

2. Paul Vigna and Michael J. Casey, *The Age of Cryptocurrency: How Bitcoin and Digital Money Are Challenging the Global Economic Order* (New York: St. Martin's Press, 2015).

3. Mike Hearn, "The Resolution of the Bitcoin Experiment," *Mike's Blog*, January 14, 2016, https://blog.plan99.net/the-resolution-of-the-bitcoin-experiment-dabb30201f7.

4. Daniel Cawrey, "Gregory Maxwell: How I Went from Bitcoin Skeptic to Core Developer," *CoinDesk*, December 29, 2014, https://www.coindesk.com/gregory-max well-went-bitcoin-skeptic-core-developer.

5. In the blog post, Hearn argues that Satoshi was on his side, based on their email exchanges.

6. Mark Bagnoli and Barton L. Lipman, "Provision of Public Goods: Fully Implementing the Core through Private Contributions," *Review of Economic Studies* 56, no. 4 (October 1, 1989): 583–601.

7. Nathaniel Popper, "A Bitcoin Believer's Crisis of Faith," *New York Times*, January 14, 2016, "DealBook" section, https://www.nytimes.com/2016/01/17/business/dealbook/the-bitcoin-believer-who-gave-up.html.

8. Joseph Young, "How Mike Hearn Sold All His Bitcoins in 2016 and Market Proved Him Wrong," *Cointelegraph*, February 25, 2017, https://cointelegraph.com/news/how-mike-hearn-sold-all-his-bitcoins-in-2016-and-market-proved-him-wrong.

Index